RIDDLE, MYSTERY, AND ENIGMA

Riddle, Mystery, and Enigma

Two Hundred Years of British–Russian Relations

DAVID OWEN

First published in 2021 by
Haus Publishing Ltd
4 Cinnamon Row
London SW11 3TW

This paperback edition published in 2022

Cartography produced by Rhys Davies

Maps contain Ordnance Survey data © Crown copyright and database right 2020

Map of the Arctic Circle reproduced with permission from *Prisoners of Geography*
by Tim Marshall (Elliott & Thompson, 2015), created by JP Map Graphics Ltd.

Contains public sector information licensed under the Open
Government Licence v3.0 (quotations from Hansard up to 1988)

Contains Parliamentary information licensed under the Open
Parliament Licence v3.0 (quotations from Hansard from 1989)

For quotes reproduced from the speeches, works and writings of Winston S. Churchill:
Reproduced with permission of Curtis Brown, London on behalf of
The Estate of Winston S. Churchill
© The Estate of Winston S. Churchill

For the quotation from *In Pursuit of British Interests: Reflections on
Foreign Policy Under Margaret Thatcher and John Major*:
Reproduced with permission of Curtis Brown Ltd, London, on behalf of
the Estate of Sir Percy Cradock. Copyright 1997 © Percy Cradock

With thanks to Esther Gilbert and the Sir Martin Gilbert estate
(*www.martingilbert.com*) for permission to reproduce quotations
from his many insightful publications on Winston Churchill

A CIP catalogue for this book is available from the British Library

ISBN 978-1-913368-67-8
eISBN 978-1-913368-40-1

Typeset in Garamond by MacGuru Ltd
Printed in the UK by Clays

www.hauspublishing.com
@HausPublishing

To
David Ludlow

A Russian speaker, whose wise counsel I have greatly appreciated when working together in the Balkans from 1992 to 1995 and over the years since, including while writing *British Foreign Policy After Brexit* (2017) together.

Contents

The Russian Empire
at its height c.1914

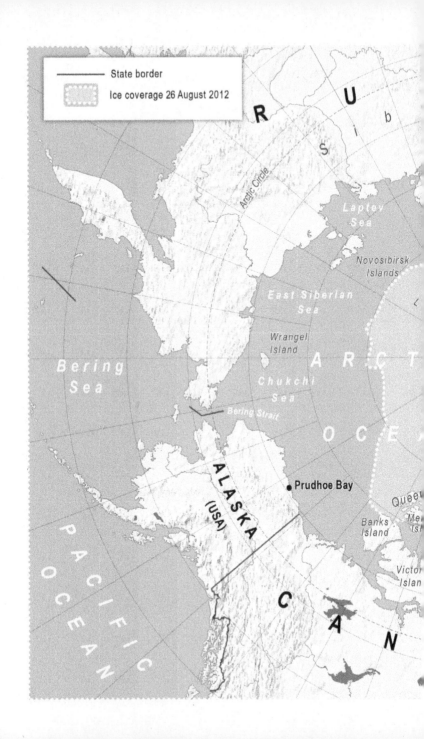

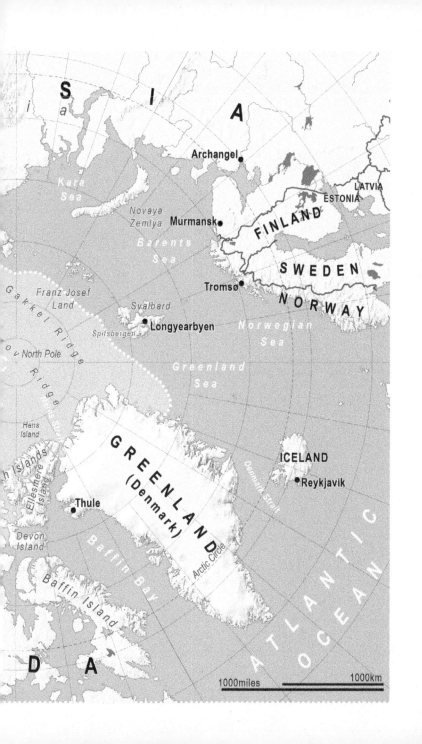

Introduction

'A riddle wrapped in a mystery inside an enigma.'[1] To many, this phrase still encapsulates the challenge posed by dealing with Russia over the last 200 years (or the Soviet Union, as it was known between 1922 and 1991, and since then the Russian Federation). It is still physically the largest country in the world, covering 6.6 million square miles and crossing eleven time zones. Its population is approximately 145 million people, home to well over one hundred ethnic groups, although by far the largest being Russians. The idea persists, particularly among those with little direct experience of the country or its people, that it is difficult, if not impossible, for outsiders to understand; that it is a strange place with such a different outlook and customs that we cannot deal with it in the way we do other countries. There is no doubt that Russia can take time and effort to understand, much like any country, and particularly one so large and with such a rich history and cultural mix.

Churchill, who retained a fascination with Russia for his whole life, clearly crafted his phrase for rhetorical effect, and it is important to put it in context. What he actually said was: 'I cannot forecast to you the action of Russia. It is a riddle wrapped in a mystery inside an enigma; but perhaps there is a key. That key is Russian national interest.' Seeking to understand the UK's relationship with Russia, in both the past and the future, is something that has fascinated me throughout my life – as a medical physician, a politician, a businessman, and, more broadly, as an internationalist.

According to his biographer, Churchill changed his stance towards the USSR frequently, and his explanation 'was not so much a lack of consistency, as is often alleged, but a consideration of what was in the "historic life-interests" of the British Empire at each stage'.[2] Under tsarist Russia in 1915, Churchill had detailed discussions about the Dardanelles and Constantinople before any military action took place. But once the Bolsheviks were established in Russia by 1917, he became unremittingly hostile to them and supported the Whites against the Reds in their civil war. Then, in 1938, before the Second World War was inevitable, he supported a deal with Stalin's Russia but only up until the Molotov–Ribbentrop Pact. When Russia was attacked by Hitler, Churchill moved fast to make Stalin a full partner – only to denounce Stalin's 'Iron Curtain' in 1946. However, as prime minister from 1951, he strove to start direct talks with Russia on nuclear weapons.[3]

The national interests of Britain and Russia have been intertwined for centuries, though some might argue that our periods of allegiance have been for pragmatic reasons rather than any deeper affinity. An early example is Peter the Great visiting London – not for leisure or pleasure but to study shipbuilding. The royal families of the two countries over a few generations were also intertwined.

In my own lifetime, the relationship has gone from wartime allies to cyber adversaries with periods of deep mutual fear. We were arch-enemies early in the Cold War but full of exuberant optimism and hope in the years following the collapse of the Soviet Union. My first recollection as a four-year-old in 1942 when refusing some food was to be told, 'think of the poor starving children in Russia'. Yet by the time I was a student at Cambridge, a university that had earlier produced some of the Soviet Union's most successful spies, I joined the protests against the Soviet invasion of Hungary in 1956 and listened to the radio as the Hungarian broadcaster calling for help was suddenly cut off by the Soviet censors.

Yet NATO did not intervene, as it was a defence alliance and Hungary was part of the Warsaw Pact. Countries can disagree with each other profoundly, but that does not of itself entitle them to go to war. To declare war, one must have a reason for going to war – a *casus belli* aligned with a just cause, as I discuss at some length in Chapter 1. NATO is committed to go to war if an attack is made on one of the signatories to that treaty, in which case the war applies to all members of the alliance. This was not the case when the USSR attacked Hungary. Nor, as discussed later, when the Russian Federation attacked Ukraine.

Before the Berlin Wall began to be built in 1961, I crossed through Checkpoint Charlie in Berlin and drove to Communist Prague in January. In late 1962, shortly after I qualified as a doctor, I watched the Cuban Missile Crisis unfold on TV with Khrushchev versus Kennedy. I then worked as a neurologist for the psychiatrist Dr William Sargant, whose book *Battle for the Mind* drew on work by the eminent Russian scientist Ivan Pavlov on the breakdown of his experimental dogs following a severe trauma. I saw from Pavlov's work the depths of Soviet science. A few years later, in 1968, as an MP and under-secretary for the navy, I was duty politician on the night of the Soviet invasion of Czechoslovakia, and yet again NATO did not intervene militarily. There were critics of NATO's stance who wanted military action. The proof of the wisdom of NATO's

policy of containment came when Hungary and Czechoslovakia, which split by democratic decision into two states, all
became NATO members after the fall of the Berlin Wall.

I first visited Russia when I was minister of health from
1974 to 1976. High on the agenda was cooperation over the
pharmaceutical industry, as I was the sponsoring minister,
but in my own mind the big issue was the way psychiatry was
used in the incarceration of political dissidents in psychiatric
hospitals under the term 'philosophical intoxication', a loath-
some practice.[4] As foreign secretary in 1977, I met with Soviet
leaders Andrei Gromyko and Leonid Brezhnev in Moscow,
with whom I discussed human rights and signed a treaty on
nuclear weapons. The most controversial issue at the time was
our different interpretations of the 1975 Helsinki Final Act and
my refusal to accept that Estonia, Latvia, and Lithuania, as part
of the Final Act, were now part of the Soviet Union. That unresolved dispute goes a long way to explain why British soldiers,
as part of a NATO deployment, are stationed in Estonia today
and why the Baltic states are angry and fearful about Putin's
two invasions of Ukraine in 2014 and 2022.

My focus on a minimum nuclear deterrent for the UK has
remained constant during my political career, from the point
of my meeting with the last rulers of the Soviet Empire as
foreign secretary in 1977 through to my involvement and later
leadership of the Social Democratic Party in the 1980s, and my
meeting with Mikhail Gorbachev in 1984. In the early 1980s,
outside government, I also met a wide range of Soviet officials
and academics by virtue of my role as treasurer of the Independent Commission on Disarmament and Security Issues, chaired
by Olof Palme. The Commission membership included
Russian figures such as the political scientist Georgi Arbatov,

who was adviser to five general secretaries of the Communist Party, and General Mikhail Milstein, previously chief intelligence officer to Marshal Zhukov. Other members included my long-time friend and former US secretary of state Cyrus Vance, and the three-time prime minister of Norway Gro Harlem Brundtland. The Commission's report, *Common Security: A Programme for Disarmament*, was published in 1982. Its main impact was fortuitous in providing new thinking on defence for Gorbachev coming into power. It was not until 1987 that President Reagan and General Secretary Gorbachev signed the Intermediate-Range Nuclear Forces (INF) Agreement, before which I had supported Reagan's response to the deployment of Soviet SS-20 missiles with what was in European politics a controversial deployment of Pershing and Cruise missiles to Europe, including in West Germany and Britain. It sparked off the Greenham Common women's protest on the periphery of the former US airbase near Newbury.

Following the fall of the Berlin Wall in 1989, and as Russia emerged from the wreckage of its Soviet Empire in the early 1990s, Yeltsin started to carve out a new international role for Russia. I worked closely with Russian foreign minister Andrei Kozyrev during the early stages in my role from 1992 to 1995 as EU co-chair of the International Conference on the Former Yugoslavia working alongside the UN co-chair, first Cyrus Vance and then his successor Thorvald Stoltenberg (whose son, Jens, is the current secretary-general of NATO). I was also a member of the Carnegie Commission on Preventing Deadly Conflict from 1994 to 1999, with fellow Russian member Roald Sagdeev, Gorbachev's former scientific adviser.

I have visited Ukraine only once, with Thorvald Stoltenberg in May 1993 in our efforts to implement the Vance–Owen Peace

Plan (VOPP) for Bosnia-Herzegovina. At that time the Russian government, through its excellent foreign secretary Andrei Kozyrev, was committed to 'progressive implementation' of the VOPP. In Kyiv we found the president engaged and ready to contribute Ukrainian forces to the United Nations Protection Force to help implement the hard edges that NATO had identified so well within the VOPP. We also visited Belarus, where we found a similar readiness. At that time there was no doubt whatever that we were dealing with two sovereign countries in a broadly friendly relationship with Russia.

Beyond the political arena, and my bringing the experience I had gained as a board member of two large international companies, Coats Viyella and Abbott Laboratories, I chaired the board of two small British companies with Russian interests: Middlesex Holdings (later named GNE) and Europe Steel, from 1995–2015. From 2003–2006 I was chairman of Yukos International. The parent company Yukos, a major Russian oil company, wanted to build up its assets held outside Russia with a view to going on the New York stock exchange. This varied experience showed me not only the technical strengths of the Russian steel and oil industries but also its employees' skills, and the benefits that well-run commercial companies were starting to bring to Russian people, particularly in Stary Oskol, a steel city 600 km from Moscow, and in the oilfields of Siberia. I was a businessman, not a politician, though operating in, where major businesses were concerned, a highly politicised environment – a place where business law, as generally understood, did not hold sway, where corruption was rife, and authoritarian government intervention was the norm.

Russia has therefore featured in my professional life to varying degrees, and I set out to write this book from the perspective that we need to understand what Russia regards as its national interest, and what has shaped that national interest, if we are to build a relationship on firm foundations. This does not mean we have to accept everything we find, but we should be prepared for the likely reaction to any criticisms we make or opposition we present.

When thinking about how Russia has acted, or is likely to act, we must understand how the country's collective experiences have influenced and continue to influence its leaders' thought processes. Their analysis of any given situation may differ from ours, but that does not mean it is necessarily invalid or not genuinely held. There are many points of similarity and intersection in British and Russian history. Yet the reality of shared experiences and circumstances has often been very different. Both have been key actors in Europe and have controlled major empires, but Britain's withdrawal from empire and recalibration of its influence was slower and more measured. Both have fought two world wars, but only Russia suffered invasion and occupation (including, let us not forget, in the First World War by British forces), and an almost unimaginable death toll in the Second World War. While Britain's democracy has developed over many centuries and remains imperfect, Russia's experience with democracy barely spans a decade. In highlighting these differences (and there are naturally many more), I am not apologising for President Putin's Russia; I am simply pointing out that Russia's path to attacking its neighbours, where we find ourselves today, has been in some areas very different from ours. But in other areas, Russia's rich European culture – ballet, music, poetry, literature – is comparable to ours and presents an opportunity to establish some common ground while facing up to areas of dispute.

This book considers recent and not-so-recent history to explore the ups and downs of the relationship between Britain and Russia. In doing so, it demonstrates that this relationship need not be one of ever-increasing antagonism; rather, it can again grow in some areas into one of mutual benefit. As a starting point to this book, I have taken an event of personal and long-standing interest as an example of cooperation between Britain and Russia. Since travelling to Greece as a medical student, I have held a great affection for the country and its people, and, twenty-two years ago, on the Peloponnese, I built a house there, now sold by my children. I still have a small house near Pylos, where in 1827 one of Britain's great naval victories took place. A combined fleet of British, Russian, and French ships destroyed a major Ottoman naval force sheltering in the Bay of Navarino. It was the last major battle under sail in British naval history and a key battle in the Greeks' struggle to throw off the Ottoman yoke. Every year, except 2020 because of the pandemic, the battle is celebrated first in the church in Pylos and then in the town square. The Greek Navy always sends a ship, as often does the Russian Navy. More rarely, the British and French send ships. The four countries' wreaths are presented at the memorial to the sound of each national anthem. So many times I have asked myself over these twenty years: why can we not produce today the same harmony between our nations in the world outside Navarino Bay?

The victorious Russian, French, and British allies were under the command of Admiral Codrington, who was to become the Member of Parliament for the constituency of Plymouth Devonport for a short time purely to legislate for bounty to be paid to the widows and wounded from the battle, which had been outrageously refused by the Admiralty. Parts of the constituency that voted him in I represented for twenty-six years in parliament from 1966–1992.

This book examines some of the key questions facing the two countries since our highly successful cooperation at Navarino nearly 200 years ago. What caused Britain and Russia to oppose each other in the Crimean War of 1853–6? Did Britain's obsession with thwarting a Russian threat to India, which gave rise to the so-called Great Game, distort its approach to Russia? Could the British, French, and US governments have done more to immediately sustain the short-lived internationally recognised government in Petrograd from March to November 1917? Could the Second World War have been avoided if Britain, France, and Russia had come together in 1938? What can we learn from the way Britain dealt with the Soviet Union during the Cold War?

These are, of course, mere flashbacks; I make no attempt to document the whole history of British–Russian/Soviet relations. There are many others much better qualified than me to do that. Rather, this book captures a series of personal views on a relationship that has been deteriorating in recent years. There have been missed opportunities, and the relationship is now in a dangerously fragile situation. No one, surely, can believe it is safe for two nuclear-weapon states to confront each other without striving for a more ordered relationship. The history of Russia and the US already shows that, by accident, nuclear weapons have come very close to being used – far too close for comfort.

With this in mind, the key question I want to address is how Britain, through NATO, can set about building a relationship with Russia that could help to better maintain a rules-based international system, one where nuclear-weapon states work together to address today's security problems. We could just aim to keep Russia at arm's length, as many seem ready to contemplate. But a post-Brexit UK, rethinking its foreign policy priorities, has, I think, a responsibility to engage with Russia in a more committed way. Mostly Britain's approach to Russia will be similar to that of France, with whom we work closely on the UN Security Council. With Germany, we share the view that it is essential to keep the US committed with troops in Europe as part of NATO. But there will be times when an Anglo-Russian relationship of itself could be beneficial and valued by friendly allies; indeed, such a time exists now with the British relationship with Ukraine.

It has never been a British tradition to opt out of dealing with major countries with whom we do not see eye to eye. We are used to taking a measured approach where necessary, not just with Russia but in all our key relationships with the US, France, Canada, India, and China. Though I acknowledge, from personal experience, that this is much easier said than done. The Callaghan government in 1977–9 put human rights in Russia and the then Warsaw Pact countries at the heart of the British government's foreign policy, yet it was greatly helped in many areas of the world, not least Russia, by being in sync with President Carter's human rights policies worldwide, particularly in Africa. I warned at the time that the price of advocating human rights was bound to be inconsistency in its application. The hard reality is that many ethical decisions conflict with economic and security policies. There have to be painful compromises. To govern is to choose.

Over the past few decades, Britain's foreign policy has become increasingly subject to major swings, where a more nuanced initial approach would have been more appropriate.

With China, the UK threw itself head first into developing fast a commercial relationship with little regard to how the new President Xi Jinping's leadership was also intent on building up its military strength at home and internationally. By 2022, China's treatment of the Uighurs, its abandonment of the treaty signed by Margaret Thatcher and Deng Xiaoping in Hong Kong, and its continued military expansionism worldwide was forcing a major reappraisal both in Washington and London.

After the ill-judged US–UK invasion of Iraq ended in 2008, NATO took the decision to expand its membership to Ukraine and Georgia under the leadership of George W. Bush and Prime Minister Gordon Brown. Britain, still then in the EU, foolishly under Prime Minister Cameron disengaged from top-level policymaking before, during, and after the first Russia–Ukraine war of 2014 in which Crimea was annexed. With the second Russian invasion of Ukraine in 2022, Britain had already been engaged in helping to train Ukraine's armed forces, and under Prime Minister Boris Johnson and Secretary of State for Defence Ben Wallace, the UK became, with the US, a key supporter of Ukraine and supplier of defensive military weapons. The UK was an important political influence on the very difficult task within NATO of defining a role as a defensive organisation while helping Ukraine to resist aggression. It is a sign of how effectively NATO has conducted itself so far that following Russia's second invasion both Finland and Sweden have applied for NATO membership.

It is obvious NATO will be most effective, as the Russia–Ukraine struggle deepens, if the US and the UK work closely with Germany and France. We need to recognise above all the gravity of letting Putin's Russia succeed in occupying large areas of Ukraine. If Putin were to succeed his expansionist policies are most likely to continue, following in the steps of his hero, Peter the Great. We should not forget the scale of the second invasion of Ukraine, which initially involved a massive use of force to take control of Ukraine's capital, Kyiv, in what Putin called a 'special military operation'. The first of many shocks for Putin came when, during an emergency UN Security Council debate, China and India chose to abstain while Russia, of course, used its veto. Putin also discovered that his armed forces were far more ineffective than he could ever have believed. Ukrainian forces were able to push back the Russian forces, decimating many of their tanks, and thereafter the Russian military tactics shifted to focus on capturing the Donbas region.

No one can be sure how this war will end, for Russia, for Ukraine, or for NATO. Fortunately, President Biden reasserted NATO's status as a defensive organisation. This means reacting to events rather than pre-empting them. Biden was adamant that NATO would not provoke World War III. At times pundits have advised NATO governments to ignore all restraints to ensure the defeat of Russia. Putin, at times, has hinted at the tactical use of nuclear weapons. In every nerve and fibre of my body I believe such a world war must be avoided, since it would very likely involve nuclear weapons on a scale impossible to predict. President Biden and Secretary of State Blinken have told Putin bluntly and truthfully that using nuclear weapons will unleash American power in unspecified ways. But as the war progresses and the Russians increase their firepower, NATO countries, in my judgement, should feel able to increase the supply and sophistication of their weaponry for Ukraine's use with the justification that they are responding to the greater number of Russian military personnel being put into Ukraine, as well as the deployment of more Russian weapons.

We can anticipate in Ukraine a military stalemate across many of the battlefronts, particularly given deteriorating weather conditions during the winter months. For NATO, the situation calls for a leap in the imagination similar to that which culminated in the Berlin airlift of 1948. The closure of all road and rail routes to and from West Berlin by Stalin could have been a body blow to Europe. Yet the loophole of an air supply corridor to Berlin was ripe for bringing in food, fuel, and everyday supplies. From 1949 onwards, NATO set out to contain the Soviet Union. A similar challenge faces the West today, to contain Putin's Russia. France rejoined NATO's integrated military command structure in 2009. Germany, in the aftermath of the Russian invasion in 2022 and in a fundamental shift of policy, has vastly increased its defence budget and is now playing a much more committed security role. It is these two countries, along with the US and UK, who need to provide the core grouping necessary to outplay Russia in Ukraine. The days of President Macron's direct discussions with Putin, across embarrassingly long tables, are now over. NATO must constantly re-evaluate its own defensive decisions in collaboration with other NATO frontline countries, such as Poland, who have behaved magnificently towards helping Ukraine. NATO must be ready to publicly state that Odesa, for example, is a port that will not be allowed to fall to the Russians for the simple reason that Ukraine cannot survive as a sovereign nation without an exporting port into the Black Sea from which its agricultural products can go out into the world. The world's food supplies cannot be guaranteed without Ukraine's agricultural products.

There are many reasons, in my view, as to why there has been no war between NATO nations and Russia since 1948, as readers of this book will discover. First and foremost this is because NATO is a defensive alliance and only becomes an offensive alliance if one of the signatories to its treaty is attacked. Also, its members operate in many ways unconnected to military defence, not least championing the merits of democracy, the existence of human rights, and the necessity of respecting the UN Charter and international treaties.

When President Putin stationed Russian military forces around the borders of Ukraine in 2022 he constantly told the world that he had no intention of invading Ukraine. Not only was that a lie, but by attacking Ukraine he broke the UN Charter and the specific 1994 Budapest Memorandum commitment signed by Russia and Ukraine which respected the internationally agreed borders. Then – and only then – once Putin's forces had crossed the border in February 2022, were economic sanctions applied to Russia by individual NATO countries and other countries operating in the many different economic frameworks that those countries were involved in. It was only on 3 August 2022 that a study by Yale University School of Management was published that gave an authoritative overview of the effect of those economic sanctions on the Russian Federation to a world that was getting used to unsubstantiated claims and counterclaims as to their impact.

Measuring economic activity over the five-month period since the invasion, the report said that the Russian economy was heading for 'economic oblivion'. The findings of their 'comprehensive economic analysis of Russia are powerful and indisputable: Not only have sanctions and the business retreat worked, they have thoroughly crippled the Russian economy at every level. Russian domestic production has come to a complete standstill with no capacity to replace lost businesses, products and talent.' The study claimed that even crucial imports from China, who had shown support to Russia, had fallen by more than half. Industrial production in June had contracted by 4.5% in manufacturing compared with the previous month, while other sectors saw an even greater slump, with car production down by 89% year-on-year.[5]

I am very conscious that as I write with the war in progress, its outcome is difficult to predict.

George Canning and the Path to Navarino

Three titans strode the British political stage in the early part of the nineteenth century: William Pitt the Younger, Robert Stewart (Lord Castlereagh), and George Canning. In this chapter, I focus on the latter, who played a critical role both in steering Britain's relationship with Russia and in delivering Greek independence. While Canning is perhaps more generally known for his support of independence movements in Latin America, his name lives on in Greece; indeed a central square in Athens is named after him: Plateía Kánningos. In London, he is commemorated by a statue in Parliament Square. What attracts me to Canning is his overall strategic view and how, once he had chosen his course, he prepared the path ahead by sacking or moving those diplomats whom he considered obstacles, by building alliances with powerful countries, and by negotiating peace but with a readiness to enforce settlements.

Canning was born on 11 April 1770. His father, the eldest son of an Irish landowner, was disinherited for his marriage to a beautiful but poor girl who became an actress to make ends meet. Fortunately, Canning's education was paid for by his uncle, Stratford Canning, a wealthy London merchant whose own son would also play important diplomatic roles. Thanks to his uncle's generosity, Canning went to Eton, then in 1787 to Christ Church, Oxford, where he gained a reputation for both his scholarship and his debating, and where he took to writing poetry. In his second year, Canning won the Chancellor's Medal for a poem describing a pilgrimage to Mecca. While there, he was an identifiable Whig (what would later be known as a Liberal), and he abandoned his initial membership of the Eton Club on the advice of his tutor, who viewed it as too political for someone who, on leaving Oxford, would have to earn a living as a professional man, as Canning initially did; he became a lawyer in 1791.

He entered parliament in 1793 as a protégé of William Pitt the Younger who, in 1783 at the age of twenty-four, had become the youngest prime minister of Great Britain. Like Pitt, Canning firmly identified with Catholic Emancipation, the removal of all discrimination against Catholics. He also shared Pitt's support for William Wilberforce's campaign against the slave trade, and more generally attempted to benefit the people by enacting wide-reaching reforms.

Another issue on Pitt's agenda was Russian expansion in Crimea at the expense of the Ottoman Empire. In peace talks following the Russo-Turkish War of 1787–92, the Russians refused to hand over the strategic Ochakov fortress, as demanded by Pitt, who had taken over negotiation from his foreign secretary. The Russian ambassador in London at the time, Semyon Vorontsov, went as far as organising a public opinion campaign to garner favour for Russia's position. Pitt had difficulty in convincing his parliamentary colleagues that this should be of importance for Britain, and despite winning a vote in the House of Commons he gave up on Ochakov.

Pitt appointed the up-and-coming backbencher Canning

to the position of under-secretary of state for foreign affairs in 1795, and *The Times* wrote on 5 February 1799 that 'No man transfuses his character more naturally with his speeches ... a just mixture of wit and argument and a happy compound of information, modesty and good humour.' By then, Britain was at war with revolutionary France. Once the news reached London of Nelson's Battle of the Nile, when Nelson defeated the French at Aboukir Bay on 1–3 August 1798, Canning wrote, 'Never, no never in the history of the world, was there a victory at once so brilliant in itself and so important in its consequence.'[1] Wendy Hinde, a biographer of Canning, perceptively draws attention to these early comments, writing,

> He was understandably, if exaggeratedly, elated. Nelson's victory effectively scotched Bonaparte's plans for Eastern conquests to which he had turned when he realised that the invasion of England was for the moment impractical; it re-established the Royal Navy in the Mediterranean, and it encouraged the indecisive Tsar, Paul I, to take up arms in support of the Austrians who in 1798 had again been attacked by France.[2]

This was an early sign that Canning was interested in the navy and its capacity to project British influence.

Despite sharing a common enemy in France, Britain's relationship with Russia was not easy. In 1800, when Britain established a protectorate in Malta after the capitulation of the occupying French forces, the then Russian emperor, Paul I, took great offence; he was the Grand Master of the Knights Hospitaller in Malta. Paul I ordered a secret plan for a Russo-French expeditionary force to take possession of British assets in India, later referred to as the Indian March of Paul. Though it came to nothing, it may well have been the progenitor of the alarms around the Great Game involving India.

The situation improved somewhat as Pitt worked to put together a new coalition against France, with Russia and Britain joining the alliance in 1805. Henry Kissinger writes that, in bringing about this alliance,

> Pitt now found himself in much the same position vis-à-vis Alexander as Churchill would find himself vis-à-vis Stalin nearly 150 years later. He desperately needed Russian support against Napoleon ... On the other hand, Pitt had no more interest than Churchill would later have in replacing one dominant country with another, or in endorsing Russia as the arbiter of Europe.[3]

The alliance, though outlasting Pitt, who died in 1806, was to be short-lived.

Following defeat by France at the Battle of Friedland, Russia signed the Treaty of Tilsit in July 1807, which obliged it to cease maritime trade with Britain – part of Napoleon's plans to isolate the latter through his so-called Continental Blockade. By then, Canning was foreign secretary, having been appointed by Prime Minister Lord Portland in March 1807. Though Canning had not served in the armed forces, he had some relevant experience, having been both paymaster of the forces (1800–1) and treasurer of the navy (1804–6). As foreign secretary, he was astute about the significance of the use of military power. Early in that first term, he asked the king to write a personal letter of flattery to the tsar, and in September 1807 he authorised the seizure of the Danish Navy, thereby helping sidestep the intentions of Napoleon, who wanted Denmark to pledge its fleet to France – such was Canning's answer to more timid British politicians. Britain needed to keep open the sea lanes in the North and Baltic Seas. This incident did, however, spur Tsar Alexander I to declare war on Britain. Yet war was never actively prosecuted, and both sides limited their response, resulting primarily in some minor naval engagements in the Baltic and Barents Seas. By 1810, as Russia's relationship with France had become strained, trade between Britain and Russia began to pick up again.

A key, concurrent theme in Canning's career was to be his rivalry with Castlereagh, then secretary of state for war and the man responsible for the advancement of the Duke of Wellington's (Lord Arthur Wellesley's) military career, a man who would also become an opponent of Canning's. On the surface, it appeared that personal relations were not too bad. In April 1809, Canning spoke in Castlereagh's defence when he faced a charge of corruption in the House of Commons and again on a different charge when even Wilberforce voted against Castlereagh. Canning, however, was manoeuvring behind the scenes and putting blame for setbacks in the war in the Peninsula and in Holland on Castlereagh. Canning then made a deal with Prime Minister Portland, who was not in good health, that he would remove Castlereagh from office. When he heard of this, Castlereagh resigned. The rivalry between the two men culminated in a duel at dawn on 21 September 1809. Both survived, but it would temporarily finish both their political careers. Indeed, Castlereagh's impetuous demand for a duel was an early sign of his later instability and suicide.[4] Canning, who had never fired a shot in his life, had no alternative but to accept the challenge. Both missed with their first shot; one assumes neither wished to kill the other, since most duels were about honour, not death. But on the second attempt, Canning was shot in the thigh. Still, Castlereagh walked Canning to a neighbouring house on Putney Heath for treatment. Wellington's role in Canning's dubious dealings with Portland is obscure, but Wellington wrote to Castlereagh describing Canning's behaviour as one of 'Indignation, Ambition, Want of Judgement, Vanity'.[5] Wellington later opposed many of Canning's policies as foreign secretary and prime minister.

On Portland's death, it was Spencer Perceval – not Canning – who became prime minister, and Canning refused to serve despite efforts to bring him back into government. Castlereagh even offered to step down to allow Canning to return as foreign secretary, suggesting he himself could become chancellor of the exchequer. In 1812, Perceval was assassinated by a lone aggrieved merchant and Lord Liverpool became prime minister. Russia and Britain were again allies against Napoleon, and they cooperated during the Congress of Vienna in 1814–15, where Castlereagh as foreign secretary firmly established his reputation as one of history's great statesmen, negotiating with two other towering figures of diplomatic history, Bourbon France's Charles-Maurice de Talleyrand-Périgord and Austria's Prince Klemens von Metternich-Winneburg, to reorganise Europe after the Napoleonic Wars.

The Vienna negotiations set the scene for the 'Great Powers' – the Quadruple Alliance of victors, Britain, Prussia, Russia, and Austria, importantly, and wisely, joined later by post-Napoleonic France – to dominate developments on the continent for the coming century. As with the treaties marking the ends of other major periods of European conflict, Westphalia (1648) and Utrecht (1713), the congress set out to prevent any one power emerging to dominate Europe. It saw a redrawing of Europe's borders, stripped France of its conquests, and created new territorial units that were designed to be large enough to deter aggression though not to provide a challenge to the Great Powers. These units included the creation of a German Confederation and the establishment of the United Kingdom of the Netherlands. It also set up a system to resolve future disputes through the holding of congresses to resolve disputes and agree action. The legacy of Vienna has been long debated. Some see it as inherently conservative, designed to stifle change, particularly of the type seen in the French and American revolutions, and suppress legitimate nationalist movements. Others view it, at least in concept, as a precursor of the United Nations.

These are not questions to be addressed here. However, early on, there was a clear divergence between Britain and its fellow victors, creating a fault line that was to have a particular bearing on how and when the Great Powers were to intervene in disputes. Separately to the Quadruple Alliance, Tsar Alexander brought Russia, Prussia, and Austria together in what was known as the Holy Alliance. While significant for bringing together these three powers, which were generally regarded as conservative, the alliance was seen as largely meaningless in terms of substance, including by Castlereagh, who described it as 'this piece of sublime mysticism and nonsense',[6] and Britain was to remain aloof from it. Britain and France, with their more liberal viewpoints, were frequently to find themselves holding differing views to the trio, particularly when it came to the independence of small states and the rights of minorities. We do not need to look beyond the border of Europe to see that such issues continue to trouble politicians and diplomats today, a subject I shall return to later.

Castlereagh's lasting reputation stemmed from his handling of Europe as foreign secretary from 1812 to 1822 and his seminal State Paper of 5 May 1820, which was circulated to the principal governments in Europe. In this paper (which was subsequently endorsed by Canning in 1823, when he himself was foreign secretary), Castlereagh wrote: 'The principle of one State interfering by force in the internal affairs of another, in order to enforce obedience to the governing authority, is always a question of the greatest possible moral as well as political delicacy.'[7] We have seen this recently in the case of President George W. Bush and Prime Minister Blair's flawed intervention in Iraq in 2003 (see pages 18–19) when President Saddam Hussein was found not to have resumed the production of nuclear, biological, and chemical weapons. This action followed President George H. W. Bush's well-designed intervention with a multilateral force to counter Hussein's invasion of Kuwait in 1990. Following Iraq's defeat in 1991, the UN located and destroyed Iraq's chemical stockpile, and its biological and nuclear weapons programme was halted as required by the UN Security Council. Intervention in foreign affairs was a subject for debate as the nineteenth century progressed when Lord Palmerston, as we shall see later in this book, attracted criticism for his interventionist policies. I believe it is worth pausing to address the differing viewpoints on military intervention, given their overall relevance both to many of the historical events which follow and to a number of the challenges faced in our relationship with Russia today.

A book written in 1866 by Canning's private secretary, Augustus Granville Stapleton, entitled *Intervention and Non-Intervention; or, the Foreign Policy of Great Britain from 1790–1865*, went beyond a personal critique of Palmerston's foreign policy to build on Canning's position. Given the height of

Palmerston's reputation at the time, Stapleton said he found it 'no pleasant task' to find fault with his approach, as he recognised he would find few sympathisers and run counter to public opinion. His case was that:

> Of all the principles in the code of international law, the most important – the one on which the independent existence of all weaker States must depend – is this: no State has a right FORCIBLY to interfere in the internal concerns of another State, unless there exists a *casus belli* against it. For if every powerful State has a right at its pleasure forcibly to interfere with the internal affairs of its weaker neighbours, it is obvious no weak state can be really independent. The constant and general violation of this law would be, in fact, to establish the law of the strongest.
>
> This principle as here laid down is the true principle of 'non intervention'. But by leaving out the word *forcible*, and by then applying it, without limitation or explanation, much confusion respecting it has arisen.[8]

Palmerston had set out his own thinking on the difference between the theory and practice of non-intervention in the House of Commons on 20 May 1864 in response to a question about the situation in China.

> My hon. Friend started with a general theory; but nothing is so liable to mislead as a general theory. My hon. Friend said that the principle upon which the British Government ought to act is that of non-intervention in the affairs of other States; a very plausible principle, and one which in many cases ought to be strictly adhered to; but my hon.

Friend forgets that there are cases in which we have treaty rights – that there are cases in which we have national interests – and if his doctrine were to be applied rigidly and in every case, our treaty rights would be abandoned and our national interests would be sacrificed. It is not true that non-intervention is the principle invariably acted on by the British Government. We have interfered with great success in the affairs of other countries, and with great benefit to the countries concerned. We so interfered, for instance, in the affairs of Greece, and we established the independence of that State ... We interfered in the Crimean war, and I do not think any man in this House will say that in that struggle we were unsuccessful. We have interfered in the affairs of China. Why? Because our treaty rights were endangered and our national interests were at stake.[9]

In the quote from Stapleton above, he refers to the need for an appropriate *casus belli*, or reason for going to war. This issue has kept philosophers occupied over the centuries, and I shall not go into detail here other than to say that, for many, and I would number myself among them, the *casus belli* must be aligned with a just cause, *jus ad bellum*, a war underpinned by lawful authority and good intent to right a serious wrong. To others, there is an additional criterion – the conduct of any such a war has to be *jus in bello*, sparing non-combatants and not making things worse.[10] In the context of intervention, Castlereagh's long analysis endorsed by Canning set a standard. The idea of conducting certain tests before declaring war was emphasised by Stapleton, and those views became part of our history, reflected after 1945 in the negotiations over the founding of the UN and its Charter, which was hugely influenced by the events of the First and Second World Wars and the experience of the League of Nations.

I carried a small copy of the Charter in my hip pocket most days for the two and a half years I served as the EU's peace negotiator in the Balkans, and I was left with profound respect for its every word. It remains my 'bible' on the issues. Lawyers are always trying to extend the boundaries of existing laws, but in truth the key to the UN Charter is that it is founded on realpolitik. National governments represented on the UN Security Council interpret the Charter. The secretary-general can have views and declare a council decision illegal, but it carries no more strength than the reputation of the individual who pronounces. The decision taken in the Security Council has the force of international law. Despite what some lawyers claim, there is no court of final appeal. The Security Council's veto structure for its five permanent members – the US, China, the UK, France, and Russia – frustrates politicians and lawyers, but again there is no appeal against the veto and no other 'court of law' that can override it.

Throughout the Iraq War in 2003, many criticised and denounced the US and UK's invasion, but there was no serious attempt in the Security Council to override their interpretation of the UN Charter, which relied on much earlier resolutions on Iraq. In 2017, speaking at Aberystwyth University, Sir Lawrence Freedman, emeritus professor of war studies at King's College, London, delivered a speech on the criteria for intervention and retrospectively analysed Blair's speech in Chicago before the April 1999 intervention by NATO in Kosovo to which Freedman had made a major contribution by providing the first extensive draft.[11] The Chicago speech is often seen as foreshadowing Blair's support for the invasion of Iraq and was considered by the Chilcot Inquiry, of which Sir Lawrence was a member and had already declared his interest. His draft of the speech and the very few additions made by Blair are part of the Chilcot documentation.

The Chicago speech, both in its draft and delivery, defined,

The most pressing foreign policy problem of the 1990s [as being] to identify the circumstances in which we should get actively involved in other people's conflicts ... no state should feel it has the right to change the political system of another or ferment subversion or seize pieces of territory to which it feels it should have some claim ... Acts of genocide can never be a purely internal matter. When opposition produces massive flows of refugees which unsettle neighbouring countries, they can properly be described as 'threats to international peace and security.' ... Around the world there are many regimes that are undemocratic and engage in barbarous acts. If we wanted to right every wrong that we see in the modern world then we would be doing little else but interventions constantly in the affairs of other countries. We soon would not be able to cope.

While Freedman used the word 'tests', Blair's final version instead used the term 'considerations', which as Freedman points out is a far less demanding term. It is a telling difference and a foretaste of what we were to see over the invasion of Iraq in 2003.

Freedman writes that this was his first test.

Are we sure of our case? Many conflicts are confused in their origins. We must not rush in on the basis of media reports of terrible events that lack any context. We must acknowledge that war, as we have seen, is an imperfect instrument for easing humanitarian distress. In the process of doing good innocents can easily get hurt. But war is sometimes the only means of dealing with the political forces ready to inflict such distress, and to ensure that they enjoy no lasting gain.

The final version of the speech, as delivered by Blair, simply said: 'First, are we sure of our case? War is an imperfect instrument for righting humanitarian distress; but armed force is sometimes the only means of dealing with dictators.'

The effect, as Freedman adds, was to change his meaning, because his version retained the link with humanitarian motives, whereas the final version broke this link to a degree, and in fact made a case, no doubt with Milošević in mind at the time, about the need to deal forcefully with dictators when they caused humanitarian distress. The analysis of his words foreshadows the mistakes to come over the Iraq invasion. Had Saddam Hussein been developing nuclear and biological weapons in 2003 as he had previously been doing in the early 1990s, the 2003 invasion could have been justified. But he was not. Despite an extensive search on the ground by UN specialists, no evidence of a nuclear or chemical weapons programme was found during 2003 or subsequently.

It is very rare to have this insight into how speeches, even one initially drafted from outside with no input from the Foreign Office, are prepared and delivered by prime ministers and, what's more, how the text is changed either by close staff or the prime minister themselves. It is also hugely revealing of Blair's underlying views. Kosovo gave him the certainty to act over Iraq as he did and, sadly, to the 'disingenuous' way in which he treated the evidence given to him by officials on weapons of mass destruction. In a speech in the House of Lords in 2007, Lord Butler, a former cabinet secretary for Blair, who had earlier chaired the Review of Intelligence on Weapons of Mass Destruction, speaking in a personal capacity, said:

> Here was the rub: neither the United Kingdom nor the United States had the intelligence that proved conclusively that Iraq had those weapons. The Prime Minister was disingenuous about that. The United Kingdom intelligence community told him on 23 August 2002 that we 'know little about Iraq's chemical and biological weapons work since late 1988'. The Prime Minister did not tell us that. Indeed, he told Parliament only just over a month later that the picture painted by our intelligence services was 'extensive, detailed and authoritative'. Those words could simply not have been justified by the material that the intelligence community provided to him.[12]

Using the word 'disingenuous' in a speech in the House of Lords comes very close to the word that is not allowed to be used in parliament: 'lying'.

President Putin never ceases to remind the world that his military interventions in Syria and Ukraine have far greater legitimacy in terms of international law than NATO's intervention in Kosovo in 1999 and the US and UK's intervention in Iraq in 2003.

Dealing with the issues posed by interventions – threatened and real – was to be a key element in the work of Castlereagh and his Austrian counterpart, Metternich, as they still needed to deal with their partner at Vienna, Tsar Alexander.

They were well aware that Russia could now, as it had so often since Peter the Great, seek to expand its territory and its influence at the expense of the Ottoman Empire. Addressing this 'Eastern Question' was to be a thread running through the politics of Europe in the coming decades and has been described as the Achilles heel of the congress system by historian Edward Ingram.[13]

The Greek Revolution, which sought – and gained – independence from the Ottoman Empire, had its roots in the French Revolution, though many individual Greeks prospered in various parts of the empire and the dissatisfaction mainly stemmed from within Greece itself. The secret Philikí Etaireía organisation in Odesa, supported by the Russians, was also aimed at establishing an independent Greek state. Its leader was Alexander Ypsilantis, whose family had fled to Russia during the Russo-Turkish War in 1805. In 1817, aged twenty-five, he became a major general in the Russian Army, having served as aide-de-camp to Tsar Alexander I. In February 1821, with the Ottomans distracted by war with Persia and the Great Powers focused on revolutions in Italy, Spain, and Portugal, the Greeks saw a window of opportunity. Ypsilantis led a force across the River Prut and entered Moldavia, calling on all Greeks and Christians to rebel against the Ottomans. Ypsilantis had hoped his action would lead to a Russian intervention on his behalf, but by June he was ignominiously defeated by the Ottoman Army and had been both dismissed by the Russian Army and excommunicated from the Orthodox Church. Ypsilantis's actions in the Danube Principalities, as Moldavia and Wallachia (now Moldova and Romania) were called, spurred the Greeks in Morea – the Peloponnese – to call for independence and expel the Turks. What was known by the Greeks as the 'Agonas' or 'Struggle' had thus begun. The uprisings in the Peloponnese were followed by revolts in central Greece, with the Greeks seeing a number of initial successes.

The Turkish reaction in 1821 within the Ottoman Empire was, as might have been expected, very harsh. One famous incident took place on Easter Sunday when the Greek Patriarch of Constantinople, who occupied a special place in the administration of the empire, was hanged and his body left for three days suspended from the gate of the Patriarchate.[14] Other prominent Greeks in Constantinople were killed, and there was a pogrom in Smyrna. Tsar Alexander was incensed; the Greek Orthodox Church, his co-religionist, was being challenged. It was also a test for the post-Vienna settlement. The Great Powers were already engaged in a follow-up congress in Laibach (Ljubljana) when the Greek revolt broke out. They were primarily focused on the revolts in Italy, Spain, and Portugal and maintaining the new order established under the Concert. To the dismay of the Greeks, they merely denounced the action.

As realpolitik clashed with idealism, the Greek revolt experienced a feature that was to become increasingly prominent in decision-making, particularly in Britain and France: public opinion at variance with foreign policy. In its most extreme form, this would see individuals taking up arms for foreign causes. In this case, some of the philhellenes who rallied to the cause of Greece joined the 'Byron Brigade' alongside the British poet. Byron embarked for Greece in July 1823 to devote his energies, his money, and his life to the Greeks' fight for independence. In 2021, as Greece celebrated 200 years since its war of independence, the Greek state archives unearthed a bank note showing that Lord Byron loaned £4,000 to the Greeks, the equivalent of £332,000 today.[15] Later, in much the same way, volunteers from Britain and elsewhere would take part in the Spanish Civil War while their governments held back from intervening, and many from the Arab world joined the mujahideen in Afghanistan in their fight against Soviet occupation in the 1980s.

The tsar thought the inspiration for the Greek revolt came from Paris. Metternich considered the Ottomans and the Greeks 'beyond the pale of civilisation', and Sultan Mahmud II believed Russia was responsible, a view he was to hold for a long time and that would be confirmed to him in 1827 at Navarino. Castlereagh (who had not attended the Laibach Congress as he did not see a British interest in the issues being discussed) had been neutral on the uprising, though he went on to denounce the Sublime Porte (the central government of the Ottoman Empire) for 'ferocious and hateful barbarism'. This left Russian Tsar Alexander in a difficult position, torn between his desire to assist his co-religionists and his fear of encouraging revolution at home, as well as the broader wish to uphold the new order. He assured Metternich on 11 July that he would only respond with his allies. Castlereagh was also in contact with Alexander, writing on 16 July on his own initiative. He did not mince his words, saying the Turkish atrocities 'made humanity shudder', but he appealed for the tsar to effectively stay his hand, referring to the fundamental obligations of the Alliance and the European congress system which 'will long continue to subsist for the safety and the repose of Europe'.[16]

Nevertheless, when the Russian ambassador in Constantinople sailed for Odesa in August, war looked imminent. Alexander, however, drew back from conflict. Metternich and Castlereagh met for the last time in October 1821, and Metternich talked to George IV. They discussed how to prevent a war between Russia and the Ottoman Empire, with both sides wanting to retain allied solidarity. Recognising that war between Russia and the Ottoman Empire would get neither what they wanted, Castlereagh and Metternich were to continue their efforts, though they faced intransigence from the Turks, who were concerned that the Russians were colluding with the Greeks. In their dealings with the tsar, Metternich and Castlereagh pointed out similarities between the revolutions that were being put down elsewhere in Europe – Spain, Portugal, Italy – and what was happening in Greece. Castlereagh had even suggested, in instructions to the British ambassador in St Petersburg, that Russia should consider intervening against the Greeks, though the ambassador diplomatically declined to raise this. Castlereagh had indeed recognised that this might be problematic, given the religious aspect, and rightly so. The tsar was torn between a desire to support his co-religionists and his fear of the spread of revolutions along with a wish to preserve the Great Power alliance. While Metternich continued his diplomacy with the Russians, the Turks unexpectedly pulled back from the Principalities in May 1822, facing pressure from a war with Persia that had broken out in September of the previous year. Thus, as is so often the case in world events, a combination of active diplomacy and fortunate timing – in this case the diversion of Ottoman attention to the Persian war in particular – meant a Russo-Turkish war was averted. Still, the congress system had been put under great stress.[17]

When Castlereagh had his last interview with the king in August 1822 he said, 'Sir, it is necessary to say goodbye to Europe; you and I alone know it and have saved it; no one after me understands the affairs of the Continent.'[18] Four days later, Castlereagh cut his own throat, having been in an overwrought state for some days. Nobody better summed up the significance of Castlereagh's death than the French minister of foreign affairs, François-René de Chateaubriand, who said:

> I believe that Europe will gain by the death of the first minister of Great Britain. I have often spoken to you of his anti-Continental policy. Lord Londonderry [Castlereagh] would have done much harm ... His connections with Metternich were obscure and disquieting; Austria, deprived of a dangerous support, will be forced to come near to us.[19]

But whatever the significance, the king now needed to find a successor to Castlereagh; with great reluctance, he turned to Canning.

Canning had returned to government in 1816 as president of the Board of Control overseeing the British East India Company, but he tendered his resignation from that position in 1820. The reason was a deep-seated clash with the then prince regent (later George IV) over the way he was treating his wife, Caroline, for whom Canning had a long-held respect and affection.[20] Following this incident, Canning believed he would never return to government, as the king had not forgiven him for speaking in the House of Commons in defence of Queen Caroline. But his popularity with the public was such that when Castlereagh committed suicide, the king, himself very unpopular, felt he had no alternative but to ask Canning back – not just for a second term as foreign secretary, but also as leader of the House of Commons.

Canning had been due to leave Britain to take up the governor-generalship of India. His ship was waiting on the Thames, and indeed he seemed to have little interest in a further political role in Britain. Canning said nothing for a fortnight after Castlereagh's suicide. He wrote to a friend, 'There is nothing in domestic politicks to tempt me, and as to foreign politicks what is there remaining but the husk without the kernel? Ten years have taken away all that was desirable, and ten such years have taken away almost the desire itself.'[21] However, since Wellington had supported the king in the clash with the public over the queen, there was no one else who could be appointed foreign secretary without further public anger. Canning knew this and so, despite his bitterness, did the king.

In the meantime, the Greek revolt had continued, though in a fragmented and sporadic fashion, and it continued to inflame passions among the European public, particularly in France and Britain. In April 1822, the Ottoman Army devastated the island of Chios to quell an uprising, during which 25,000 Greeks were killed and 45,000 were taken as slaves. The tragedy was depicted in the famous painting by Delacroix in 1824, *Scène des massacres de Scio*, and denounced throughout Europe. It was not all one-sided, however. Greeks were also responsible for massacres of Turks, for example at Tripolis in October 1821 where between 8,000 and 15,000 were killed. Still, this raised little public ire in Europe; nor did others that occurred in Corinth and Athens. This was in marked contrast to the public anger and frustration felt from 1992 to 1996 over the siege of Sarajevo, not just in Europe but in the Muslim world and the United States of America, helped by being played out worldwide on TV screens in people's homes.[22]

The Eastern Question was one issue Castlereagh had been expected to address next with his colleagues in the series of post-Vienna congresses in Verona in October 1822. Interestingly, Castlereagh's 1822 instructions, now given to the British representative, the Duke of Wellington, were not altered by Canning, though he observed that 'the Turks now seem to have the upper hand', and he went on to indicate that it was inadvisable for Britain 'to interfere between Russia and the Porte or between the Porte and the Greeks'.[23] In his essay 'The Philhellenes, Canning and Greek Independence',[24] Allan Cunningham goes out of his way to challenge the image of Canning as the 'generous liberal, who subverted the ultra-conservative Congress system', let alone the 'liberator' of South America as well as Greece. He sees Canning's image historically as owing a lot to the writings of Stapleton, his loyal private secretary, as well as Canning's 'flair for devising popular justifications for his diplomatic decisions' and draws attention to P. J. V. Rolo's assessment that there is very little evidence to support the idea that Canning was ever disposed to sentimentality in diplomacy.[25] I agree with that depiction and, indeed, Canning was fond of saying of Greece that nothing could be done 'for the sake of Epaminondas' (a reference to Bryon's poem *Childe Harold's Pilgrimage*).[26]

Still, it was Canning who in 1823 recognised the status of the revolting Greeks as belligerents,[27] though Castlereagh had been moving towards doing so. Canning also showed his support in the spring of 1823 by attending the lunch given for the Greek leaders Ioannis Orlandos and Andreas Louriotis to mark the first loan raised by Greece in the London markets; the amount disbursed was only £472,000 – 59 per cent of its nominal value of £800,000 – largely because of the risk of lending before Greece became a sovereign state. A second loan was raised in 1825,[28] though this was followed by Greece's first bankruptcy in 1827, when it failed to make interest payments on the loans.

In January 1824, Russia proposed that there should be three

autonomous Greek principalities. This was discussed at two conferences at St Petersburg in June 1824 and March 1825. The Greeks, of course, rejected the proposal in a letter to Canning, who replied in December 1824. Here, he interestingly revealed that while neutral Britain might mediate in the future, it would not be a party to an agreement unacceptable to the Greeks.[29]

Also in January 1824, Lord Byron had arrived at Messolonghi dressed in military uniform and was received with a twenty-one-gun salute. According to Gary Bass in his book *Freedom's Battle*, 'The Ottomans had repeatedly asked Canning to stop Byron [arriving in Greece] but the foreign secretary refused.' Rather, Canning turned a 'blind eye to Byron's mission'.[30] Bass cites John Cam Hobhouse, writing to Bowring on 30 November 1823: 'the English civil & military authorities ... seem very well inclined to further the objects of his visit to Greece'.[31] Byron died of a fever on 19 April 1824 at the age of thirty-six. Although his Byron Brigade fought no battles, he was in today's terms an international megastar and, as a result of his popularity, was influential in supporting Greece in European countries. The first two cantos of *Childe Harold* also raised money for Greece and brought his own special form of poetic glamour to the Greek cause. It was his friend and fellow philhellene, Percy Shelley, in his poem *The Mask of Anarchy*, who wrote of the Greeks:

> Rise like Lions after slumber
> In unvanquishable number –
> Shake your chains to earth like dew
> Which in sleep have fallen on you.

Many years later during the Second World War, when referring to the Greek resistance to the Italian and later German invasions, Winston Churchill is purported to have drawn on that sentiment: 'We will not say hereafter that the "Greeks fight like heroes but heroes fight like Greeks".'[32]

There are many excellent histories of the Greek struggle for independence and in this book, as I mentioned in the introduction, I have focused on one key event: the Battle of Navarino. It must not be forgotten, however, that had the Greeks themselves not fought valiantly on land and on sea, it would never have been necessary for the sultan to take the 'bold but desperate step'[33] of seeking the help of Muhammad Ali Pasha, the governor of Egypt, to send naval forces. While Muhammad Ali did not have to agree to this request, it would have been very difficult for him to refuse to uphold the authority and standing of the Ottoman Empire. And so he sent his son, Ibrahim Pasha, at the head of an Egyptian navy and an army. The army landed in the Peloponnese on 24 February 1825 and laid siege to Messolonghi. Since Byron had made this small place well known in Europe, it had political significance, and its fall in 1826 attracted public sympathy to the Greek cause.

Many strategists in France wanted closer links to Egypt at that time, particularly in the military, a view shared by some in Britain who wanted to split Egypt from the Ottoman Empire if Britain could not control it. Even at this time, a common way of referring to the Ottoman Empire was to merely refer to the 'Turks'. Egypt's intervention therefore split opinion. Chateaubriand wrote to the French king and other monarchs in the congress to counter this strategic view in a note entitled '*en Grèce*': 'Will our Century watch hordes of savages extinguish civilisations at its rebirth on the tomb of a people who civilised the world? Will Christendom calmly allow Turks to strangle Christians?'[34]

In the preface to his poem *Hellas*, Shelley captured this sentiment: 'We are all Greeks, our laws, our literature, our religion.'
Canning, himself a writer of poetry as already mentioned, was
certainly aware of the poetic influence of both Shelley and
Byron. Indeed, his closeness to Byron was noted by his biographer H. W. V. Temperley, who wrote he 'had known Byron
well; he was the only statesman whom the poet admired'.[35] But
Canning never allowed his love of poetry to sway his political
judgement on this or any other issue. He was an emotional man
but hard-headed and always calculating risk.

It was not just in Britain that the Greek revolt had captured
the attention of poets and wider society. In Russia, the great
Romantic poet Alexander Pushkin also enthusiastically hailed
Ypsilantis's undertaking:

> In the mountains and on the banks of Danube
> Our one-armed Prince [Ypsilantis] is rising in revolt.[36]

Pushkin wrote many other poems, letters, and stories dedicated
to the Greek struggle, inspired 'by his compassion and love for
the anguish of a people who fought to throw off the yoke of
foreign tyranny'.[37]

Canning, probably more so than Castlereagh, had recognised
the importance of working closely with the Russians in dealing
with the Ottoman Empire and deliberately started a diplomatic
process to bring the two powers closer. The sequence of Canning's detailed preparation for negotiations are very clear. All
through 1824, he was less keen on Britain's involvement in the
congress machinery and its method of working. He also moved
those he judged as having no stomach for a fight, if one became
necessary, from key diplomatic positions. He transferred

Ambassador Charles Bagot from Russia to Holland when he discovered, much to his anger, that Bagot had attended two congress conferences on Greece on 17 June and 2 July 1824. In doing so, Canning disconnected himself from this process. In Bagot's place, Canning appointed Ambassador Viscount Strangford, a diplomat who had been plainspoken in his dealings with Turkey, but he did not trust Strangford as much as his cousin, Stratford Canning, who was sent as ambassador to the Ottoman Empire in Constantinople.

Metternich wanted a conference to stay the hand of Tsar Alexander who, for his part, wanted a congress to give him support for war against Turkey. Canning privately derided both in the words of a popular song: Metternich was 'cruel Polly Hopkins' and Alexander 'silly Mr Tomkins'. He was clearly separating himself from the neo 'Holy Alliance' over Greece.

Prime Minister Canning's instructions to Stratford Canning were deliberately kept from Strangford, whom he still regarded as a congress supporter and so he fobbed Strangford off with, 'The Instructions which I have now to give your Excellency are comprised in a few short words – to be quiet'.[38] The task was, as Canning already knew, to maintain the process of wooing the Russians into becoming a negotiating partner. He had asked the Russians to keep their long-standing ambassador, Prince Christoph Heinrich von Lieven, in London. In June 1825, the ambassador's wife, Dorothea Lieven, went to St Petersburg. Both she and her husband had been told privately by Canning 'that England would be ready at the right time to resume discussion'.[39] But if Canning was an intriguer, so was Dorothea. She had, in fact, spoken to King George about how to get rid of Canning, and she was now ready to use her not inconsiderable feminine skills to get to Tsar Alexander who, hermit-like, was living apart from his wife and had become ever more religious, suspicious, and almost mystical. He received her more than once but was vague as to his intentions. On the night of her departure for England on 30 August, she received an urgent message from the tsar's foreign minister, Count Nesselrode, that he must see her the next morning to receive an urgent communication on behalf of his majesty the emperor.[40] When they met, Nesselrode said he would speak as minister to minister, relaying word for word what the tsar said. Their conversations were only published much later.[41]

Alexander held Dorothea Lieven in high regard and, recognising her influential connections in London, he saw her as a conduit for an offer to re-engage in negotiations with the Russians in St Petersburg. The message he wanted passed was as follows.

The Turkish power is crumbling; the agony is more or less long, but it is stricken with death. I am still here, armed with all my power, but strong in my known principles of moderation and disinterestedness. How will it not profit me, with my aversion from any project of conquest to reach a solution of the question which is incessantly disturbing Europe? So long as I follow them [my principles], they [Metternich] try to profit by it. I cannot remain in this position for long.

Affairs become daily more complicated. I am pushed, urged on, by all my entourage. My people demand war; my armies are full of ardour to make it, perhaps I could not long resist them. My Allies have abandoned me. Compare my conduct to theirs. Everybody has intrigued in Greece, I alone have remained pure. I have pushed scruples so far as not to have a single wretched agent in Greece, not an intelligence agent even, and I have to be content with the scraps that fall from the table of my Allies. Let England think of that. If they grasp hands [with us] we are sure of controlling events and of establishing in the East an order of things conformable to the interest of Europe and to the laws of religion and humanity.[42]

The flattered lady described herself as amused and disturbed, noting that it was a novel approach to entrust such a mission to a woman. She observed that all the British ministers were pro-Turk and had a horror of Greek revolutionaries: 'the King sharing all these prejudices, the public very cold'. But on the other hand, Canning was 'one who easily took up an idea that was great and new'. The challenge in her mind was that Russia 'had shut our mouths in England', to which Nesselrode replied that a woman 'knows how to make people speak, and that is precisely why the Emperor considers you have a unique opportunity'. Lieven was shocked that the emperor planned to break with his allies and enter into a separate engagement with England to drive the Turks from Europe. Nesselrode conceded that 'it is possible that that is what he dreams of'. Given the significance of what was being asked of her, Lieven demanded instructions in writing, but the prudent Nesselrode confined himself to writing: 'Believe all the bearer tells you.' She was to be 'a living dispatch' to inform Canning that Alexander was ready to break with the Holy Alliance and to work separately with England over Greece.[43] She was to hint that his dignity forbade him to make an overture himself, but that, if England initiated proposals in the sense indicated, they would not be rejected. On 13 September 1825, Alexander left for Crimea. By 1 December, he was dead.

Meanwhile, on 25 October 1825, the Lievens met Canning at Seaford, where he was staying. They came there to convince Canning of what is sometimes labelled the 'barbarisation project'. Dorothea Lieven claimed to have been told about it in St Petersburg.

> The Court of Russia had positive information that before Ibrahim Pasha's army was put in motion, an agreement was entered into by the Porte with the Pasha of Egypt, that whatever part of Greece Ibrahim Pasha might conquer should be at his disposal; and that his plan of disposing of his conquest is (and was stated to the Porte to be and has been approved by the Porte) to remove the whole Greek population, carrying them off into slavery in Egypt or elsewhere, and to re-people the country with Egyptians and others of the Mohammedan religion.[44]

Temperley writes of this Russian propaganda story as 'a masterstroke' but then two paragraphs later questions his own words by writing, 'Canning excelled in divining the hidden meaning of an opponent's words ... Doubtless also, if he disregarded the communication about the depopulating of Morea, Lieven would see the British public heard of it.'[45] As I will come back to later, my own view is that Canning was not influenced by this Russian propaganda.

The democratic control by foreign ministers and the head of government of foreign policy is an absolute necessity; yet many diplomats over the centuries seem to have believed their skills were without need of democratic endorsement, a tradition that can still be found in 2022. Just before Alexander had died, a serious problem had surfaced in Russia for Canning.

Ambassador Strangford in St Petersburg had gone off on his own initiative. Lieven told Canning on 17 December 1825 how Strangford had tried to bring Austria into the negotiation and, even worse, suggested that Russia, under some circumstances, would have the right to go to war. Canning was furious. He told Strangford to tell all involved in his personal initiative in Russia and elsewhere that he had been disavowed by the foreign secretary. Not only was he told to be quiet, but he had been put under what was later referred to as a 'padlock' and was from then on in effect voiceless on all diplomatic matters. Canning thus deservedly humiliated Strangford and retained the negotiation in his hands. But this was yet another sign that, on top of Wellington's opposition to his support for engagement in Greece, Canning had enemies in the Foreign Office and in government. It was thus another portent of what was to come in October 1827.

As Tsar Alexander died without a legitimate heir, his brother Constantine was the heir apparent, but he renounced the throne. His younger brother, Nicholas, stepped in to take power, but by that time a number of military officers had already sworn allegiance to Constantine. In this confused period, a revolutionary group who wanted constitutional government attempted a coup. They were the first in the history of modern Russia to unite in a campaign against the absolute power of the tsars in favour of a constitutional monarchy. They also sought to abolish serfdom. Their revolt started on 14 December 1825 in St Petersburg, hence the 'Decembrist Revolt' and their later name 'the Decembrists'. They were labelled gentlemen revolutionaries who saw serfdom as a national disgrace. Their uprising, however, failed to garner widespread support and was quashed by January 1826. The leaders were executed or sent into exile. The fascinating story of the charismatic Princess

Maria Volkonsky who went to Siberia to be with her husband is told in *The Princess of Siberia*.[46] The pair were not amnestied until 1856 on the accession of Tsar Alexander II, having left a legacy in Siberia that some believe can still be identified today. Tsar Nicholas I, who was to reign until 1855, believed political liberalisation was not favoured by the Russian people, who preferred instead to embrace orthodoxy, autocracy, and nationality under the guidance of a stern father figure. President Putin has been compared to him 'with respect to their use of nationalism to justify statist policies and political authoritarianism'.[47]

Canning's task was to divert Russia from the straightforward but powerful wish to attack the Ottoman Empire. Strangford reported to London from St Petersburg: 'the young Emperor Nick does not care a straw for the virtuous and suffering Greeks. He considers armed intervention or indeed any intervention at all as little better than an invitation to his own subjects to rebel'.[48] A plan for how to deal with Russia was developed when King George invited the Lievens and Canning to stay at Windsor Castle between 31 January and 2 February 1826. Dorothea Lieven claims she brought the king and Canning together, and this is evidenced by a letter from the king to Nicholas dated 7 February, the essence of which was to disclaim any territorial ambition on the part of Britain or jealousy of Russia: 'In the union of the two Powers the best chance of success was to be found'.[49] Temperley sums up how Nicholas's bluff was called over his stated lack of interest in Greece, and this, combined with Wellington's neglect of Greece, gave way to Canning's policy: 'Cooperation with Russia, with the possibility of force being used against Ibrahim, but nowhere else.'[50]

After she and her husband visited St Petersburg in April, Dorothea explained:

He [Canning] relied on us and the vanity of the Duke of Wellington to get the Greek question pushed on at St Petersburg, but always within prudent limits ... we desired a regular state of things, a hierarchical discipline, all of which sounded well in the ears of the Duke of Wellington. He entered under full sail into this order of ideas.

Nicholas's readiness to agree had been boosted by his success in resolving a dispute with the Turks through the threat of military action. On 4 April, the St Petersburg Protocol on the emancipation of Greece to settle the Greek War of Independence was signed by Wellington and Nesselrode.

It was a step in the right direction, but there was still a long way to go. While the Greeks would choose their own government, the sultan would play 'une certaine part' in selecting their leaders and Greece would need to pay an annual tribute to the Sublime Porte. The new borders would be agreed at a later date through talks involving British and Russian diplomats as well as the Greeks and Turks.

It associated Russia with most of Canning's policies in Portugal, Spain, and America as well as, to a greater extent than Canning had dreamt of, in Greece. When Canning sent troops to Portugal in December, he gave a famous speech. Though predominantly about Portugal, he also spoke about his wider philosophy, spelling out his overall policy approach with clarity and candour. His speaking style, use of words, and the compelling nature of his presentation are seen in the following extract from his address on the king's message in the House of Commons debate on 12 December 1826.

I dread [war] from an apprehension of the tremendous

consequences which might arise from any hostilities in which we might now be engaged. Some years ago ... [I] stated that the position of this country in the present state of the world was one of neutrality, not only between contending nations, but between conflicting principles; and that it was by neutrality alone that we could maintain that balance, the preservation of which I believed to be essential to the welfare of mankind. I then said that I feared that the next war which should be kindled in Europe would be a war not so much of armies, as of opinions. Not four years have elapsed, and behold my apprehension realized! [51]

The limited agreement of two of the Great Powers – Britain and Russia – on a plan to impose mediation under threat of force and grant the Greeks a limited independence cut right across the principles of the congress system. Metternich rejected it out of hand. Prussia followed Austria's lead. France, however, was caught between two competing motivations: its traditional support for the Ottomans, and the pro-Greek sentiment of its population.

Unusually, Canning spent a month in Paris in October 1826 with his friend the ambassador, during which the foundations were laid for French involvement over Portugal but also – most crucially – paved the way for French participation with Russia in the Battle of Navarino. He was invited to dine with the French king, Charles X, a distinction only given before to two other individuals unconnected with the families of reigning European potentates (the others being Wellington and Metternich). Canning was the only untitled person to whom this honour was ever accorded. He was also building a personal relationship with his key French interlocutor, Joseph de Villèle. All this diplomacy and socialising sought to convince Nicholas I that a partnership with France was possible and that the memories of the 1812 Patriotic War could be put behind them. Under Alexander I, the Russians had defeated Napoleon in what was the greatest and bloodiest of the Napoleonic campaigns; Napoleon had marched on Moscow with the largest army ever known only to find Moscow abandoned and then subsequently to suffer from the onset of the Russian winter and lack of food.

On 16 October from Paris, Canning penned an unusually frank letter to Liverpool marked 'Most Secret' in which he wrote:

> The D of W [Duke of Wellington] is very angry at my coming here. Two years ago he interfered with the King to prevent my doing so. But I suppose he felt that after he had himself been here in the interval, and after Westmoreland had been preaching here for two months his ultra and philo-Turkish principles, I was not likely to be again so easily turned from my purpose. I am right glad that I came.[52]

There is no doubt that Canning left Paris with the French readier than ever before to combine diplomatically and, if necessary, militarily with Russia to ensure Greek independence.

In January 1827, a significant change took place in the Ottoman forces. Ibrahim was given control over the sea as well as the land forces, taking over from the Turkish naval commander-in-chief, Khosrow Muhammad, who had initially been his superior. This was because the Greeks' performance at sea had been better than expected, and one of their key bases – the island of Hydra – had not been taken by the Turks. Under Ibrahim, the Egyptian Navy soon overpowered the Greek Navy

and captured Navarino in May, which allowed Ibrahim to effectively coordinate the actions of his navy in support of his well-
trained, 11,000-strong army. The Ottoman Empire was now
working with one purpose: to smash Greek resistance with an
efficiency and ruthlessness that would have made the outcome
over the next few years certain. Nevertheless, in the face of this
onslaught, the Greeks did reconquer the Peloponnese.

In February 1827, there was a similar change on the British
side with Sir Edward Codrington succeeding Sir Harry Burrard
Neale as commander-in-chief of the Mediterranean station.
A link might be suggested between this move and a question
Canning had posed to the British Admiralty in the second
week of November 1825, when he asked if the naval force in the
Mediterranean was 'sufficient to enforce an armistice between
the belligerent parties (Greece and Turkey) and if not, whether
it could be speedily and adequately reinforced'.[53] This was not a
query from a man unable to contemplate force, but rather from
a man planning to be ready to enforce an armistice.

It was very soon apparent that Codrington shared French
Admiral Henri de Rigny's sympathetic view of the Greeks.
Codrington had already 'written to the Duke of Clarence,
before taking up his command, on the possibility of entering
the Bay of Navarino and forcing Ibrahim to break camp'.[54] The
duke was then the Lord High Admiral, becoming King William
IV in 1830 and earning the sobriquet of the 'Sailor King'. He
privately supported Codrington over the Battle of Navarino in
October 1827 but could not do so in public.

By the start of 1827, the so-called barbarisation or deportation threat was seen to be absurd. Russia had negotiated a
better relationship with Turkey through the October Akkerman Convention, which required Ottoman forces to withdraw

from certain parts of the Balkans, but this treaty did not cover Greece. A further treaty would thus be required, and this was important to the French. Ultimately it would bring the French together with Britain and Russia by building on the St Petersburg Protocol.

Negotiations on the Treaty of London, as it was to become, started with France submitting the first draft on 10 January 1827, though this did not include the means of enforcement; I have learnt from my own experience in the Balkans between 1992–5 how critical this is in such negotiations. In March, Russia put forward a draft that envisaged a naval blockade. Unfortunately, on 17 February, Canning's firmest supporter, Prime Minister Liverpool, had had a stroke, and settling who should become prime minister was proving fractious. The relationship between the king and Canning had, however, improved. Eventually, nothing in London could stand in the way of Canning becoming prime minister and he took office on 12 April 1827, though his cabinet was not fully formed until the end of the month.

In the end, it wasn't until May that the Russian draft could be addressed, and Canning demanded that it should be made clear in the preamble that it was the Greeks who had asked for mediation by the British. Lieven and Canning then agreed to a secret article agreeing the use of force if necessary. Meanwhile, the Greek Assembly gave Russia and Britain a sense of unity by electing the British-trained naval commander Thomas Cochrane and General Sir Richard Church to be their commanders-in-chief of sea and land. Meanwhile, Count Kapodistrias, who had served in the Russian diplomatic service, was made Greek president for a seven-year term.

The Treaty of London was signed on 6 July 1827 by representatives of Britain, Russia, and France. In essence, its basis was the Anglo-Russian Protocol of 1826 though others – particularly the French – were not reminded of this in the text. One week later, the whole earlier secret text appeared in the London *Times* according to Woodhouse, in effect saying that, 'if the Porte would not accept mediation within one month, the three allies would send Consuls to Greece ... and that if either the Greeks or the Turks rejected the proposed armistice, the three countries would interpose themselves'.[55] The Protocols of Conferences held in London were presented to parliament by command of His Majesty in May 1830, as 'Papers Relative to the Affairs of Greece'. As many of the provisions of the treaty have never received much attention, I have chosen to quote them in full in order to archive a measure of finality as to what was set out rather than what people think was set out.

The instructions to the three admirals – Codrington for Britain, de Rigny for France, and Lodewijk van Heiden for Russia[56] – were set out in Annexes D and E of the treaty. Understanding these instructions is key both to understanding the battle itself and to assessing the treaty's legitimacy as a tool for enforcing an armistice prior to a negotiation. Under the terms of the treaty, Britain, France, and Russia agreed 'to offer their mediation' to the Turks and the Greeks and 'to demand at the same time of the contending parties an immediate armistice between them, as the preliminary condition indispensably to be fulfilled previously to the opening of any negotiation'.[57]

The naval commanders of the three powers were ordered to approach the Commission of the Provisional Government of Greece, and it was made clear they were 'to act only in concert and in such a manner that none of them may seem to have the pre-eminence over the other'.[58] The need for urgency was impressed upon the commanders, as was the expectation that they would act with 'zeal, prudence and ability'. In obtaining a response, they were encouraged to try to obviate the need for the Greek Commission to consult the Greek Assembly, which was then in session at Troezen. Once answers had been obtained, they were to be reported to London and the ambassador in Constantinople as soon as possible. If there was a positive Greek response, the commanders were to:

> consider, in concert with your colleagues, of the measures which may be most proper and most expeditious for putting a period to hostilities and to the effusion of blood. The moment that the war shall be suspended ... you will suggest to the Commission of the Greek Government the propriety of appointing Plenipotentiaries charged with the principal negotiation between them and the Porte.

They would be informed of the outcome in Constantinople and, if it was favourable, they were to 'urge the meeting of the respective Plenipotentiaries'.[59]

The second instruction was based on the same supposition as the second declaration supplied to the ambassadors for use in Constantinople, namely that the Porte might refuse or ignore the first proposition, but it also took account of the possibility, much less likely though it was, that the Greeks might refuse.[60] The commanders were informed that there was a secret article of the treaty which stated that, if the Turks had not accepted the offer of mediation and agreed to an armistice within a month of the message being delivered by the ambassadors, the three powers:

would exert themselves by all means which circumstances might suggest to their prudence, to obtain the immediate effects of the armistice ... The measures to be adopted ... will consist in an immediate communication with the Greeks, and the union of the squadrons of the high Powers for the purpose of preventing all Turkish or Egyptian succours of men, arms, vessels, and warlike stores, from arriving in Greece or in the islands of the Archipelago.

In that event, the commanders were to 'treat the Greeks as friends, without, however, taking part in the hostilities betwixt the contending parties'. The commanders were told that they would be informed of the outcome of the negotiations in Constantinople directly by their ambassadors, and that they should act together in implementing any instructions they received. According to the treaty, they were to 'intercept every supply sent by sea of men, arms, etc., destined against Greece and coming either from Turkey or Africa in general' and, working in close coordination and offering mutual assistance if required, they were to 'defend the approach to the Greek continent or islands'.

However, the orders were caveated; the commanders were

to be most particularly careful that the measures which you may adopt against the Ottoman navy do not degenerate into hostilities. The formal intention of the Powers is to interpose as conciliators, and to establish, in fact, on sea, the armistice which the Porte would not conclude as a right. Every hostile proceeding would be at variance with the pacific ground which they have chosen to take, and the display of the forces which they have assembled is destined to cause that wish to be respected; but they must not be put into use unless the Turks persist in forcing the passages which they have intercepted.

If the Greeks were to reject the armistice, or subsequently break it, the commanders were to 'endeavour to maintain the armistice without taking part in hostilities between the two contending parties' and were to 'judge of the best means to attain this object'.

The treaty's instructions recognised that, in an age without rapid communications and where not all possible outcomes could be legislated for in advance, the field commanders had to be given 'a certain latitude' to act – so long as they had 'a perfect knowledge of the object proposed by the Powers, and of the means on which they reckon to effect it'. Still, they were warned that 'the slightest deviation on the essential points would impede the progress of the negotiations and remove indefinitely the object wished to be obtained'.

Codrington received the detailed instructions on 7 August, even though *The Times* had published the whole treaty on 13 July. Canning wrote to his foreign secretary, John Ward, the first Earl of Dudley, about his suspicion that the French had leaked the terms of the treaty, perceptively ending: 'If the Pasha's fleet has not sailed before Cradock reaches him, I flatter myself it will remain in port...' He continued, 'Greece thus disposed of – we shall come next to the Peninsula, But I must take a few days rest between for I am quite knocked up. I go to Chiswick for that purpose tomorrow.'[61]

There are those today who believe the decision by Canning to use force against Ibrahim's forces was the first humanitarian intervention in world history. I do not believe this to be the case in the sense that it has come to be used in the United

Nations. In the context of genocides in Rwanda and Srebrenica, UN members agreed in their 2005 Declaration on the Responsibility to Protect (known as 'R2P') that:

> The international community, through the United Nations, also has the responsibility to use appropriate diplomatic, humanitarian and other peaceful means ... to help protect populations from genocide, war crimes, ethnic cleansing and crimes against humanity. In this context, we are prepared to take collective action, in a timely and decisive manner, through the Security Council ... on a case-by-case basis and in cooperation with relevant regional organisations as appropriate, should peaceful means be inadequate and national authorities manifestly fail to protect their populations from genocide, war crimes, ethnic cleansing and crimes against humanity.[62]

While, as mentioned, the Greek War of Independence undoubtedly involved massacres of civilians which would fall under the humanitarian criteria outlined above and might today be used to justify the allied action, there are dangers in attributing contemporary standards and motivations to an intervention that was made primarily for political reasons. The origins of the view that Navarino represented a humanitarian intervention stem, at least in part, from Stapleton's *Intervention and Non-Intervention*, written almost forty years after the battle, which claims that 'national independence in another country ought to be respected', and that Canning 'never ceased to maintain and put forward this principle'. Stapleton goes on to refer to Canning being 'solicited by one of the belligerents [Russia]' and that 'it was evident that the Pacha was carrying on a war of extermination wherever there was the slightest resistance'. Furthermore, he wrote that the Turks were 'labouring to blot out of existence a whole Christian people and establish a new Barbary State on the shores of the Mediterranean in the very midst of Europe. Mr Canning held this to be a *casus belli* giving all nations a right to interfere by force.'[63]

This, however, was referring to the – non-existent – 'barbarisation project' mentioned above. Rather, the facts suggest that Canning was not influenced by this Russian propaganda and that Stapleton's later memory was playing tricks on him. Canning always foresaw that force might well be needed against the Ottoman Empire, but negotiations were his clear preference; he understood, unlike too many politicians, that negotiations succeed best when your opponents realise that force *will* be used if faced by intransigence over starting or completing negotiations.

I was to witness this first-hand in the context of the Vance–Owen Peace Plan (VOPP) negotiations during the Bosnian War. On 27 April 1993, US Secretary of State Warren Christopher, giving testimony before a Senate appropriations committee, laid out four strict tests for the use of force: the goal must be stated clearly; there must be a strong likelihood of success; there must be 'an exit strategy'; and the action must win substantial public support. It was clear that none of these conditions was likely to be met in the early stages of implementation. I began to understand that Christopher's insistence in an earlier statement of 10 February on not imposing a settlement, which I had thought was to protect himself against having to impose a settlement on a particular group, the Bosnian Muslims, was in truth applicable to all sides. He was not ready to impose a settlement even when, as was then the case, we had reached a position where it was the Serbs who were holding out against the agreement and demanding more land. By sticking strictly to the line of no imposition, Christopher had made it very unlikely that there would be any US involvement with any implementation. So, by adding these four additional factors at his Senate testimony, he was making it virtually impossible. It seemed an odd preparation for his proposed trip to Europe to discuss a new US policy initiative.[64] It took a Serb genocide of Bosnian Muslims under General Mladić in July 1995 for Richard Holbrooke to convince President Clinton that only NATO airstrikes could impose a negotiated settlement, which was eventually achieved with the Dayton Accords.

The retrospective humanitarian justifications of the Battle of Navarino reached their modern apotheosis in *Freedom's Battle: The Origins of Humanitarian Intervention* by Gary Bass. Bass argues that 'Canning's diplomacy had taken the future out of the Austrian diplomat's hands', an assessment with which I agree, but he then adds, 'and into the hands of a British navy man sailing a warship off the Greek coast', a statement with which I totally disagree.[65] Bass, to my mind, compounds this mistaken judgement by quoting extensively from sentimental words Codrington and the French and Russian admirals committed to paper before and after the battle, which led him to conclude that the Battle of Navarino was 'the first modern humanitarian intervention'.[66] By contrast, in the chapter entitled 'Navarino', Bass describes how Codrington is given a very clear instruction that he fulfils to the letter; in other words, whatever the admirals' feelings, they were the instruments of British, Russian, and French politicians whose objective was to achieve an armistice between the Ottoman Empire and Greece. Military force was an integral part of their diplomatic strategy to achieve this.

What's more, as someone who has produced an anthology of poetry,[67] I would love to share Bass's belief that Byron was so influential on Canning. However, as mentioned earlier, I see no grounds for believing Byron's poetic virtuosity had any influence on Canning's policies and strategic vision. Quite the contrary. Canning, as usual, would have wanted popular opinion on his side, but he was well aware of how fickle the public can be when it comes to war. Canning was ready to take the risk and put the force of arms behind the British strategy of negotiation. He knew the people *love* a victory but also *hate* defeat. But despite my differences with Bass on these aspects, I should add that his book is a *tour de force* and essential reading for those interested in learning more about the subject. Five chapters in part two of *Freedom's Battle* dealing with the Greeks – 'Lord Byron's War', 'Canning', 'The Holy Alliance', 'A Rumour of Slaughter', and 'Navarino' – provide a brilliant and moving account that catches the flavour of the moment in Byron's own words as quoted by Bass:

> For Freedom's battle once begun
> Bequeath'd by bleeding sire to son
> Though baffled oft is ever won.[68]

In his chapter in the book *Humanitarian Intervention: A History*, John Bew argues that the battle 'was much easier to defend when it had a moral justification'.[69] Bew also flags an assessment in W. A. Phillips's *Great Britain and the Continental Alliance* that Canning 'liked to shape public opinion rather than being driven by it'.[70] Certainly, Canning had already shaped public opinion to expect war. As a Plymothian I am perhaps more aware than most of the significance of Canning's speech in 1824, which is quoted by Bew, when he pointed to the warships moored in Plymouth and compared them to England herself: 'Apparently passive and motionless, she silently concentrates the power to put forth on an adequate occasion'.[71] Navarino was just such an occasion.

Too many historians have made the judgement that Navarino was primarily a humanitarian intervention. As Bew rightly claims, 'international humanitarian ends were served' in 1827 in the aftermath of the Battle of Navarino. He also says that, 'notably, however, the humanitarian rationale loomed increasingly large in retrospective justification of the action'.[72] But in my view, the Battle of Navarino was the result of a political decision to challenge the right of the Ottoman Empire to block an independent Greece. Interestingly, Bew also cites Lord Salisbury's bemoaning of the Battle of Navarino as an unfortunate consequence of the practice of foreign intervention in domestic squabbles 'and another example from the history of the last seventy years strewn with the wrecks of national prosperity which those well-meant interventions have caused'.[73] This is a sentiment that many would share when reflecting on the interventions of the more recent past, like the invasion of Iraq in 2003.

The reality is that Canning had designed his initiative with deliberation and care. It was built not on sentiment but calculation. The Ottoman leaders had a choice throughout: negotiate a settlement or face a battle. Once Codrington's force was fired on, he had little freedom of choice; his and his colleagues' flexibility was in the phases leading up to that point. He entered battle with fewer ships and won a stunning victory against the odds because of the Ottoman commanders' intransigence. It was the latter who fired first, and repeatedly. It was certainly not 'accidental', a word that appeared in *The Times* on 21 November 1827 in the shadow of an outrageous British government statement that had already labelled the battle 'an Untoward Event' in a change of tack. Canning never lived to see how his planning played out. On 8 August 1827 he died. He had long suffered from severe gout, and his physician, in describing his patient's last few days, said that he had seen nothing so agonising. In contrast, his legacy was to be long-lasting.

John Marriott, in *George Canning and His Times*, wrote: 'In a sense, larger, perhaps, than he understood, Canning called a new world into existence to redress the balance of the old. His rivals and contemporaries among the statesmen of Europe belonged to the old era; he himself belonged to the new.' He continued, 'It was his conspicuous merit to have perceived and realised that the settlement laboriously evolved at Vienna could not last; that the diplomatic edifice was built upon a shifting sand ... Nationality, in fact, has proved to be, in the main, a unifying and consolidating principle in the nineteenth century. This truth Canning intuitively grasped.'[74] In my view, Canning was a great political leader and it is apt that this is recognised by a statue of him in Parliament Square.

It is fitting to end this chapter with the description of Canning's funeral written by his private secretary, Stapleton.

At the early hour of his death, crowds (which subsequently amounted to between three and four thousand persons) had congregated outside the lodge at Chiswick. Sorrow, deep and universal, fell upon them when the fatal termination became known. On the day of the funeral, the whole way from Downing Street to the Abbey was lined with spectators, and the large space in front of the great western door was densely covered with people. The short duration of his illness had prevented men's minds being prepared for the worst. He had just attained the highest object of a subject's ambition, and great results were expected; but it pleased God to bring his days suddenly to an end. The hopes of millions were buried in his grave: many and bitter were the tears of those numerous friends and admirers who had come from all parts to witness the sad ceremony. The funeral was a private one; there was no choral service; the solemn silence was more impressive than the organ's peal.

The plain and decent homage best defined
The simple tenor of his mighty mind.[75]

2

The Untoward Event

As indicated in the previous chapter, Canning's policies reached their apotheosis on 20 October 1827 at the Battle of Navarino. Had he still been alive and prime minister instead of the ineffective Viscount Goderich, world history would have taken a very different course. The victory met with an unqualified welcome on the streets of London, St Petersburg, and Paris and prompted a shared pride in the contribution of the British, Russian, and French Navies. I believe Canning, as prime minister, would have fully shared British public opinion's delight in victory. He would have brushed aside Wellington's criticism of any battle against the Ottoman Empire, and he would have continued to have the support of his former adversary, the king. But the London elite, led by the Duke of Wellington, as if ashamed of the victory, talked only of an 'untoward event'.

The British admiral Codrington and the French admiral de Rigny were determined to follow their instructions. They were no cavalier sailors, keen to exploit ambiguous orders. They wanted clear instructions, and so on 12 August Codrington wrote to Ambassador Stratford Canning in Constantinople saying that neither he nor the French admiral could make out how they were 'by force to prevent the Turks, if obstinate, from pursuing any line of conduct' which they were 'instructed to oppose, without committing hostility. Surely it must be like a blockade,' he wrote, 'if an attempt be made to force it, then by force only can that attempt be resisted'.[1] The ambassador replied in a letter dated 1 September, writing that he had consulted with his colleagues and making clear that, 'although it is clearly the intention of the Allied Governments to avoid, if possible, anything that may bring on war, yet the prevention of supplies, as stated in your instructions, is ultimately to be enforced, if necessary, and when all other means are exhausted, by cannon-shot'.[2] This was an unequivocal message, and its substance was embodied by Codrington in a general order to the British squadron, which he dated 8 September, the day on which he received it.[3] From that date onwards, Codrington was under clear instructions, in effect with explicit rules of engagement. No longer was he under any opaqueness, doubt, or equivocation.

The sultan had met in secret with his ministers on 27 August, and they had decided to resist any intervention from the allies. They had never even fully subscribed to the existence of an armistice. On 30 August, the *Reis-Effendi* (the Ottoman equivalent of a foreign minister) conveyed to the allies their 'positive, definitive, invariable, eternal' decision that the Porte would accept no proposition whatsoever concerning the Greeks.[4] The next day, the *Reis-Effendi* told the allies, 'If it is a declaration of war that you have to make, say so.'[5]

The Turko-Egyptian fleet that set out from Alexandria in early August to join Ibrahim was commanded by his brother-in-law, Moharram Bey. The combined fleet was made up of three squadrons, and they joined Ibrahim's forces in the Bay of Navarino on 8 September – the very day that Codrington had received clarification of his instructions. At every stage of the battle, the fleet facing Codrington far outnumbered the allied fleet that was assembling outside the bay. He himself arrived outside the Bay of Navarino during the night of 11–12 September. Just as Ibrahim started to move out of the bay on 21 September, and as Codrington was preparing his under-sized fleet for battle, de Rigny brought his seven French vessels up from the south to the entrance of the bay and met with Codrington on his flagship, the *Asia*, late that evening. The following day, de Rigny wrote a letter to Ibrahim, signed by himself and Codrington, offering a meeting.

The crucial meeting between the three admirals took place on 25 September inside the bay. The most colourful account comes from Codrington's son, who was serving as a midshipman and wrote of it in a letter to his sister.[6] He described the Ottoman commander's green tent, where he received Codrington sat on his sofa with its 'embroidered velvet cushions' and 'mattress with gold fringes', surrounded by "is [sic] officers, pachas, beys, etc., and attendants'. He was none too complimentary about the pasha himself, whom he depicted as 'about 40 years old, not at all good-looking, but with heavy features, very much marked with the smallpox, and fat as a porpoise', though he noted, 'his manners were very good indeed'. He continued: 'The conversation first began about the weather and such commonplace things, for ... he does not talk of business till after coffee'. Fortified by sweetened coffee, which the young Codrington understood to be a 'great favour' and drawing on their *chibouques* – Turkish pipes 'studded with diamonds and other precious stones' – they got down to business in front of the assembled entourage so that 'his officers might also understand the whole'.

According to his son, Admiral Codrington did the bulk of the talking at the meeting and, in effect, he bought the allies some time by agreeing that Ibrahim send two dispatch vessels carrying a courier to Constantinople for instruction. The bulk of the British and French ships temporarily sailed away to patrol the wider coastline, leaving a smaller allied force to guard the entrance to the bay. On 3 October, Turko-Egyptian forces assembled outside the bay. Codrington assumed they were heading for Patras, where fighting was continued while the Greeks awaited the Ottoman response to the Treaty of London. Though outnumbered and outgunned, he positioned his forces to stop them reaching their destination. No battle materialised, and the ships went back into the Bay of Navarino.

On 6 and 7 October, Codrington sailed again to prevent Ibrahim's forces progressing north to Patras. This coastline from Patras to Methoni has no decent sheltered ports, apart from the Bay of Navarino, and enforcing a naval blockade of the bay in winter was never going to be easy given the poor sailing conditions. (I can attest to this myself, having kept a twenty-five-foot Fisher motor sailing boat for nearly twenty years inside the bay at the town of Pylos.) Eventually, the three allied admirals, Codrington, de Rigny, and the Russian Heiden, met on 13 October outside the bay – though this would only be for a short time, since Admiral de Rigny would not stay on board the *Asia* while the Russian admiral, Heiden, was present. Relations between Codrington and Heiden, by contrast, were excellent. Heiden had told Codrington about the speech by Nicholas I to his fleet at Kronstadt, which was one of full-hearted support, and implied that 'no criticism would fall on a Russian admiral who joined battle on the slightest provocation'.[7]

As noted in Chapter 1, the French had maintained close

relations with Egypt. On 15 October, de Rigny returned to his ship off Navarino, having only the day before supposedly removed the French officers who were advising the Turko-Egyptian ships within the bay on preparing a strong defensive line, demonstrating how close the two navies were. Codrington, with a mixture of indignation and anger, called them the 'renegadoes' and had been pushing for their removal.[8]

Two days later, on 17 October, a letter to Ibrahim signed by all three allied admirals again accused him of violating the armistice by his actions against the Greeks. Ibrahim and his army, however, were still not at Navarino but at Methoni.[9] Inside the bay, the Turko-Egyptian fleet were moored, Codrington's spies informed him, in the form of a crescent 'with springs [ropes to secure ships at anchor] on their cables, the larger ones presenting their broadsides towards the centre'.[10] Codrington knew the history of the bay and the critical part it had played at the time of the Peloponnesian war between Sparta and Athens. Back then, in 425 BC, the Spartans were forced to surrender in a humiliating defeat on the island of Sphacteria, which forms the north side of the bay. Over two millenia later, the island was about to bear witness to another crushing defeat of a powerful empire.

On 18 October, sensing that battle was soon to commence, the allied commanders drafted their protocol justifying their action in implementing the decisions of the Treaty of London, though they only completed it after the battle was won two days later. Not unreasonably, it appealed to the emotions of the allied sailors about to risk their lives and to people in Greece and beyond who wanted to see the Ottomans defeated. They accused Ibrahim of violating the provisional suspension of hostilities and in particular of 'carrying on a species of warfare more destructive and exterminating than before, putting women and children to the sword, burning habitations, and tearing up trees by the roots, in order to complete the devastation of the country'.[11] In order to put 'a stop to atrocities which exceed all that has hitherto taken place', the admirals outlined three possible courses of action in a protocol dated 18 October.

> 1st. The continuing throughout the whole of the winter a blockade, difficult, expensive, and perhaps useless, since a storm may disperse the squadrons and afford to Ibrahim the facility of conveying his destroying army to different points of the Morea and the islands;
>
> 2ndly. The uniting of the allied squadrons in Navarin itself, and securing by this permanent presence the inaction of the Ottoman fleets; but which mode alone leads to no termination, since the Porte persists in not changing its system;
>
> 3rdly. The proceeding to take a position with the squadrons in Navarin, in order to renew to Ibrahim propositions which, entering into the spirit of the Treaty, were evidently to the advantage of the Porte itself.

They unanimously chose to pursue the third on the grounds that it might, 'without effusion of blood and without hostilities, but simply by the imposing presence of the squadrons, produce a determination leading to the desired object'.

On the following day, 19 October, Codrington gathered his colleagues and senior captains aboard the *Asia* and outlined his operational orders. These were summarised in a brief written order, the key elements of which are outlined below. Codrington began by setting out how the allies were to deploy their ships.

It appears that the Egyptian ships in which the French officers are embarked, are those most to the south-east ... de
Rigny should place his squadron abreast of them. As the
next in succession appears to be a ship of the line with a flag
at the main, I propose placing the *Asia* abreast of her, with
the *Genoa* and *Albion* next to the *Asia*; and ... Heiden will
... place his squadron next in succession to the British ships
of the line. The Russian frigates in this case can occupy the
Turkish ships next in succession to the Russian ships of the
line; the English frigates forming alongside such Turkish
vessels as may be on the western side of the harbor abreast of
the British ships of the lines; and the French frigates forming
in the same manner, so as to occupy the Turkish frigates, etc.
abreast of the French ships of the line.[12]

Codrington clearly did not necessarily anticipate an immediate hostile reaction from the Turks, as the order goes on to
state that, 'if time permits, before any hostility is committed
by the Turkish fleet, the ships are to moor with springs on the
ring of each anchor'. He also ordered that, 'no gun is to be fired
from the combined fleet without a signal being made for that
purpose, unless shot be fired from any of the Turkish ships; in
which case the ships so firing are to be destroyed immediately'.
Anticipating that there would inevitably be confusion once
battle commenced, he told his officers that 'in the words of
Lord Nelson, "No captain can do very wrong who places his
ship alongside that of an enemy"'.

It is also noteworthy that, on the eve of battle, Codrington chose to call out the equivocal nature of de Rigny's position by drawing attention to the Egyptian ships on which the
French officers were embarked. He thereby demonstrated that

he did not believe de Rigny's claim that he had been able to remove them all. Nor, in closing, did Codrington shrink from highlighting Nelson's tactics at the Battle of Trafalgar, where his captains brought their British vessels alongside the French, allowing their gun-carrying sailors to jump onto the French ships. It was a tough statement, but a justified demonstration of his overall authority. During all Canning's diplomatic efforts to align France and Russia with Britain, the French had been the most difficult to corral. But on 20 October, the day of the battle, the allied admirals were united, and they set sail into the Bay of Navarino, with cannons loaded and with considerable extra ammunition at hand.

By midday, the *Asia* set off through the entrance to the harbour ahead of the *Albion*, *Dartmouth*, and *Genoa*. The French squadron followed, with the *Sirene* in front, and behind them the Russian vessel *Azov*. In total, there were twelve British ships carrying 456 guns, seven French ships with 352, and eight Russian ships with 490. A total of 17,500 men and twenty-seven ships were now facing the much larger Turko-Egyptian fleet of sixty-five ships with 2,000 guns and 22,000 men.

At 2 p.m., the *Asia* passed through the entrance and under the Turkish guns at the harbour entrance. These guns only fired one blank shot. A small boat from the flagship of Moharrem Bey then came alongside the *Asia* and asked Codrington not to proceed. Codrington's reply was that he was coming to give orders, not to receive them. At 2:10 p.m., the *Asia* anchored close to Moharrem Bey's flagship, with the *Albion* and *Genoa* following to its north, together with the *Dartmouth*, which was keeping watch for fireships in the south-east corner of the bay.

A small boat was sent from the *Dartmouth* to a Turkish boat to convey the message that no harm was intended, but the

British coxswain was shot dead. The British lieutenant, Fitzroy, repeated that no violence was intended, but the crew of the Turkish fireship opened fire again, killing and wounding other members of the crew. When a cutter was sent to tow the boat clear, Fitzroy was killed by musket shots from the crew of the burning fireship. Two shots were then fired by an Egyptian corvette, one of which struck the *Sirene*, and this was followed by fire from the shore batteries.

Woodhouse's account was that 'neither the Turkish nor the Egyptian commander-in-chief, Tahir Pasha and Moharrem Bey, intended the fatal incident' involving Lieutenant Fitzroy, but that 'the folly of the Turkish ship firing on Fitzroy's boat started the battle at 2:25 p.m.'[13] He does, however, entertain the idea they were in any case planning to attack at nightfall with fireships. In all the controversy, no credible assertion has ever been made that anyone from the British, French, or Russian forces fired first. At some stage, the Ottoman forces were definitely intent on aggressive action.

Following an all-out battle, when night fell, the allied forces had not lost a single ship, though 174 allied seamen had been killed and 475 wounded. The Turko-Egyptian forces had for their part lost sixty ships and, according to Codrington's own estimates, 6,000 men had been killed and 4,000 wounded.[14] Regardless of whether these figures are exaggerated – and indeed other estimates of Ottoman casualties are much lower – the fact was that the Ottoman fleet had been annihilated and the Greek people knew that the fledgling Greek state was saved. As the guns fell silent at dusk in Navarino Bay, news of the outcome spread over the Peloponnese and to the rest of Greece. Church bells started a continuous peal into the night. People rushed into village squares to be greeted by the news that the Ottoman sultan and his hated vassal Ibrahim Pasha no longer possessed a Mediterranean fleet. The rejoicing lasted for several days. Huge bonfires were lit on the mountaintops of the Peloponnese and Mount Parnassus in central Greece.[15] Following the battle, Codrington and his Russian allies set sail for Malta to repair and refit their ships, where they were warmly received as victors.

After the victory, unbelievable though it may appear, the British ambassador in Constantinople, acting on instructions from London, expressed regrets to the Porte on 2 November. In response, on 9 November the Porte presented a statement to the three ambassadors demanding that they should admit their countries were in error and agree to pay compensation. A war of words followed, but it was a shameful way of proceeding after a great and legitimate naval victory. Stratford Canning's biographer records from the ambassador's memoirs:

> The Ambassadors could allege in defence of the admirals that they had not entered the harbour with any hostile intentions, that they had transgressed no law or treaty by taking that step for the convenience and eventual safety of their ships, that 'they had not opened fire till after they had been fired upon, and that if the Turkish fleet had suffered a heavy loss, the responsibility rested with those who had ordered the attack. There was much plausibility, not to say reason and truth, in this explanation.' ... 'Whatever justification the admirals might derive from local circumstances, neither the letter nor the spirit of their instructions could be cited to warrant their hazardous but effective decision. (The recommendation of cannon-shot applied only to the stoppage of warlike supplies.)'[16]

In contrast, the victory was warmly welcomed by the allies. In November, the tsar wrote from St Petersburg to congratulate Codrington enthusiastically and to offer him a ship until the *Asia* was repaired. As a gesture of gratitude and to demonstrate the esteem that he had inspired in Russia, he was also awarded the Military Order of St George. The tsar had spoken of the 'Three Great Powers' zeal for the cause whose noble character is all the more emphasised by their disinterestedness'.[17] Like the Greeks, the Russians also rejoiced on the streets. Likewise, there was delight at the news in Paris – and, in both, an emphasis that the Turks had fired the first shot. The French government awarded the three admirals the Grand Cross of the Order of St Louis.

In London, however, while the public celebrated a great victory, the official reaction was cool and muted. Such a crushing defeat of the Turks was seen as upsetting the delicate balance in the region and threatening to allow the Russians, albeit Britain's allies in the battle, to make further unwelcome advances. Sir John Gore, a friend of Codrington's, wrote to the admiral saying that the ministers were utterly astonished at the news. The foreign secretary, Dudley, also wrote to Codrington with a 'List of Queries' about his conduct at Navarino. Codrington read these in December, but he had already written to Dudley on 8 November and Stratford Canning on 12 November expecting approval for his actions. Indeed, on 13 November, the Duke of Clarence, Lord High Admiral, had awarded Codrington the Grand Cross of the Order of the Bath – though admittedly he had done so without consulting his political masters. Codrington had followed up on 15 November with a letter to the Admiralty claiming the routine payment of compensation for the personal losses of his officers and men, though he received no immediate response to this.

Faced with this split in public and official opinion, the prime minister, Viscount Goderich, offered to resign. In fairness, Goderich had had to take note of King George IV's feelings, who had summed up his attitude to the award to Codrington: 'I have sent him a riband [ribbon] and it should have been a halter.'[18] Goderich again offered his resignation on 14 December, but it was again refused by the king, who was becoming aware of public sentiment in favour of Codrington. By then the *London Gazette* had published its 'Extraordinary Edition' of 10 November, which carried the dispatch received that day from Vice Admiral Sir Edward Codrington. Alongside it was 'A New Song' which told of 'a glorious Victory' and a 'great and gallant Action' won by the 'brave Codrington'. The song went so far as to point out that 'to spare the loss of blood was bold Codrington's design'. In closing, the song expressed the hope that 'the sufferings of the Greeks now very soon will cease' and called for a toast to 'the gallant tars who gained this Victory'. It could not have been clearer where this influential publication's support lay. However, in the end, and despite all this public support for Codrington, the king replaced Goderich as prime minister with Codrington's long-time opponent, the Duke of Wellington, on 22 January 1828.

The political campaign against Codrington was publicly ignited at the opening of the parliamentary session on 29 January when the king, on the advice of Wellington, spoke of 'this untoward event' and deeply lamented the conflict with 'an ancient ally'.[19] Wellington was left floundering in the House of Lords, trying to justify the phrase to Codrington's many supporters, who recognised the battle as an important step in furthering the Greek struggle for independence. Lord Morpeth, speaking two days later in the debate on the king's speech, said, 'the expression in the Speech [untoward] was unjustifiable ... Why use such an ungracious expression, unless it was intended to condemn that which all the good and great hailed with delight? Could the English language apply no other epithet to one of the most brilliant achievements in the naval history of this country?'[20]

The campaign against Codrington was maintained with echoes of the earlier allegations around the 'Barbarisation Project', discussed above, and Codrington was accused of not having prevented a number of Greeks being taken to Egypt as slaves when the Pasha's fleet left Navarino. He himself had reported their transportation but had noted that he had no instructions to stop and search the Egyptian ships.[21] William Huskisson, who retained his post as secretary of the colonies in the cabinet, put it in a letter to the new prime minister in April 1828.

> I have adverted to the Greek slaves in a manner which I hope will meet your approbation. You will see that I assume that a dispatch has already been written by Dudley to our Consul at Alexandria to try to get them back by a strong appeal to the Pacha of Egypt.[22]

In August 1828, Codrington was relieved of his command, though not before he had secured another major success – negotiating the return home of Egyptian troops still stationed in Greece.

After a humiliatingly long wait, Codrington's request for compensation for those of his sailors who had lost their lives was disgracefully rejected by the Admiralty with no explanation. In defiance, Codrington – who did not need to resign his commission – put himself up for election in 1832 as Member of Parliament for Devonport. He told his potential constituents that, if elected, he would put forward the case for compensation and bounty for his men and, if it passed through parliament, he would resign his seat and return to being a naval officer. This is exactly what happened. In the House of Commons on 17 June 1834, his motion was opposed by the government on the dubious grounds 'that it was a general rule not to grant head-money or gratuities for actions unless they were preceded by a declaration of war'.[23] Yet every speaker supported Codrington, and the government had to withdraw their opposition. The House of Commons then presented an address to His Majesty. The government, facing certain defeat, arranged for the Admiralty to find £60,000. Codrington was thus totally vindicated by the people and parliament. He promptly resigned as MP, and the government had no choice but to accept his promotion to Admiral of the Red[24] in 1837. He subsequently became commander-in-chief at Portsmouth from 1839 to 1842.

Codrington died on 28 April 1851, and the Greek Chamber of Deputies unanimously passed a motion of official gratitude from Greece, an honour also given to Byron. De Rigney went on to serve as foreign minister of France, while Heiden finished his career in 1850 as military governor of Reval (now Tallinn). To their credit, Heiden and de Rigney always fully supported Codrington, as did the British people and his constituents in Devonport. He was not the easiest of men, but he was an admiral of whom Nelson, under whom he had served at Trafalgar, would have been justly proud. Today, a plaque indicating a house in which he lived in Brighton has been removed because of his connections to the transatlantic slave trade.

This is the moment to pause and reflect on how Canning

would have reacted if he had still been prime minister following the battle. Every sign would suggest that the man whose
career had been marked by a respect for public opinion, whose
careful designs had delivered a mortal blow to any hope the
Porte had that they could stop Greek independence, would
have ridden this wave of public opinion and been the first to
welcome Codrington as a hero. But I believe he would have
gone further; he would have played up the role of Russia,
publicly lavished praise on Tsar Nicholas I and used that as a
powerful lever to halt Russian plans to go to war with Turkey.
Canning would not have considered for one moment making
a scapegoat of Codrington; instead, he would have portrayed
him as a hero.

In his book *Navarino*, which was commissioned in 1877 by
Tsar Alexander II to mark the fiftieth anniversary of the battle,
E. V. Bogdanovich wrote in Russian that:

> Russia felt that, following centuries-long struggle with the
> fierce oppressor of their brothers in faith, an era of true lib-
> eration was finally coming, and, in a rapture of joy, it also
> extended its brotherly feelings towards England which did
> not spare its blood to help Russia heroically accomplish its
> holy feat.[25]

He then drew attention to 'a sad change in views, principles
and courses of action, which has regretfully occurred since
then in Western Cabinets' politics and which slowed down the
great cause they were beginning together with Russia'. This, he
alleged, had led to Western Europe 'disputing Russia's natural
influence on the Christian East', which had resulted in England
and France sacrificing 'the innocent blood of thousands of their

fearless sons'. Clearly looking back on events from a Russian perspective, he went on to ask: 'Is it not obvious that the same purpose would have been obtained in a much easier, much simpler and much nobler way if England and France continued to follow the path of the ingenious politics onto which Canning put them under the influence of the Russian Czar's charming energy?'[26]

Bogdanovich goes on to claim that Canning, 'having decided to go hand in hand with Russia in the cause of Greece's liberation, was almost sure of a peaceful outcome of the matter'. He laid blame for the eventual hostilities firmly at the door of the Turks, and he criticised the British and French for not capitalising on the victory at Navarino as 'the first step toward the liberation of all Christians on the Balkan Peninsula'.[27] He saw Wellington and his camp as following 'a political programme diametrically opposing that pursued by Canning', and he interpreted the 'untoward event' comment as signalling 'the note of withdrawal; [which] gave distrust to Russia, umbrage to France, and a courage of opposition to Turkey'.[28] Alexis Heraclides and Ada Dialla, in their comprehensive presentation of humanitarian intervention in the nineteenth century, also noted the impact of Canning's death on the British position: 'If one absence was deeply felt in the Greek camp it was that of Canning, especially from the moment Wellington took over.'[29]

I share the view that Canning would have worked with Tsar Nicholas I and that, very likely, there would have been no Russo-Turkish War in 1828–9. The three allies – Britain, France, and Russia – would have continued working together, with Britain and France tempering the ambitions and actions of both the Russians and the Turks. As it was, with Wellington unwilling to step in to influence either party, conflict was virtually inevitable.

Bogdanovich saw England and France as 'doing all they could to evade their obligation under the Treaty of London to force the Porte to accept its terms, and ... the Porte itself, inspired by the confidence that it had nothing to fear from the two Western powers, was doing its best to provoke a war with Russia'.[30]

Ultimately, war broke out following Turkish repudiation of the 1826 Akkerman Convention. This had covered Russia's rights in the Danubian Principalities, allowing elections every seven years by the Divans (legislative assemblies) of Moldavia and Wallachia, as well as its freedom of navigation in the Black Sea and Russia-bound ships through the Bosporus. Sultan Mahmud II closed the Dardanelles to Russian ships, a deeply inflammatory action that was partly taken in retaliation for Russian involvement in the Battle of Navarino. Russia was bound to respond, and war was declared on Turkey in April 1828. It was a war that was longer and harder-fought than anticipated – perhaps showing that fears of Russian power were exaggerated and/or the collapse of the Ottomans not so imminent. An eventual Russian victory was marked by the Treaty of Adrianople in September 1829 and, among its provisions, the treaty gave Russia territory, including most of the eastern shore of the Black Sea and the Danube delta, as well as sovereignty over north-western parts of what is today Armenia and Georgia. The sultan was also finally forced to accept the Treaty of London and, with it, Greek autonomy. Greece's independence was thus finally guaranteed by Britain, France, and Russia jointly in the London Protocols of 1829 and 1830. According to the historian Roderick Beaton, writing on 16 January 2021 in the Greek newspaper *Ekathimerini*, the key event on the key date was:

February 3, 1830. It happened not on the battlefield or even in Greece at all, but in a dry conclave of dignitaries held at the British Foreign Office in Whitehall. On that day the foreign ministers of Great Britain, France and Russia signed a document known as the 'London protocol.' It declared, for the first time: 'Greece will form an independent State, and will enjoy all those rights – political, administrative, and commercial – attached to complete independence.' Greece (or 'Hellas'/Ellada in Greek) was born that moment and took its place on the political map of Europe. The revolution wasn't yet over – because it would take another two years for all the details to be worked out, including frontiers and the system of government. But that date in February 1830 marks the turning point.

The final details of Greek independence were settled at the London Conference of 1832 (by which time Wellington's government had fallen and Palmerston, a supporter of Greece, was foreign secretary). For the time being, Russia had achieved its goals. Tsar Nicholas I was advised that the Ottoman Empire would continue to decline without further intervention – which would, in any case, risk the re-engagement of other powers.

It is hard to resist the conclusion that Russia's unilateral action was a logical step after first the British – in the main, thanks to Wellington – and then the French retreated from the Canning strategy. Indeed, J. A. R. Marriott writing in *George Canning and His Times* states that '[Canning's] death left the path open to Russia, and the Treaty of Adrianople was the result'.[31] Marriott also wrote that:

Canning was no more friendly to the advance of Russia than the Duke of Wellington; but he clearly saw that the sooner the contest was ended between Greece and the Porte, the less opportunity would there be for Russia to attain her ends. He held, further, that the legitimate interests of Great Britain in the Eastern Question could be most effectually maintained by a frank understanding with Russia.[32]

Britain and Russia were not to be allies in battle again until the First World War. Even so, it took until August 1941 for their two navies to once again join forces, when they sought to protect the Arctic Convoys during the Second World War. Instead, in their next encounter on the battlefield in 1854, they were to be on opposite sides of the Crimean War, Britain's only European land war between Waterloo and the outbreak of the First World War. And this conflict, like Navarino, had its roots in the Eastern Question and the ongoing shifts in the balance of power both in Europe and further afield.

3

British and Russian Relations with the Ottoman Empire, 1825–1914

From the high-water mark of cooperation at Navarino, Britain's relationship with Russia was to deteriorate – and dramatically so – in the decades that followed. While, as I explained in the introduction, I have not set out to provide a comprehensive history of relations between Britain and Russia, particularly prior to the onset of the twentieth century, I nevertheless think it is useful to have a general picture of developments in this period between the Battle of Navarino and the First World War. Readers who seek more detail are encouraged to explore the many sources referenced.

The seeds of deterioration were sown in the difficult relationship between Prime Minister Canning and the war hero-turned-reluctant politician the Duke of Wellington. In 1818, the prime minister, Lord Liverpool, invited the latter to be Master General of Ordnance, the only military position in the cabinet. Extremely reluctant, Wellington was finally persuaded by Castlereagh. But, as we have seen, when Wellington became prime minister his approach to debate was rigid and uncompromising, and he refused to consider economic or parliamentary reforms. He fell out with the leading Canningites

– Huskisson, Dudley, and Palmerston – and lacked parliamentary skills. Finally losing control of the parliamentary legislature, he resigned on 22 November 1830.

After the Battle of Navarino, British policy – and, as far as possible, French policy, as mentioned in Chapter 2 – should have been able to prevent war between Russia and the Ottoman Empire and to challenge the shape and policies of the Ottoman Empire from 1827. Instead, Britain was left to deal with the fallout from the Russo-Turkish War and to try to play a balancing role in Europe and protect India.

The focus should have been on moving to separate Egypt from the Ottoman Empire as the first of many steps over the next few decades – in effect, doing *before* the First World War what was done in Paris in 1919 but over a longer period: reducing the Ottoman Empire to Turkey itself. As for Russia, nothing was inevitable about continuing good relations with Britain. As Kissinger put it: 'For most of its history, Russia has been a cause looking for an opportunity.'[1] In the decades after Navarino, Russia's search for an opportunity would contribute to instability in Europe.

A key part of the challenge in managing its relationship with the Russian and Ottoman Empires and effectively choosing sides was that, considering itself a self-professed champion of democracy and liberalism, Britain faced a choice between what it saw as two often-hard-to-distinguish evils; both were autocratic, repressive regimes that paid scant regard to the rights of their own people. This issue was to intensify as the period went on, with the British public, fired up by the press and political speeches, increasingly focused on foreign policy issues, and with the dividing line between domestic and foreign policy blurred.

Palmerston – who was to dominate British foreign policy up

until 1865, first as foreign secretary, then as home secretary and ultimately prime minister – made clear his position on which states Britain should align with in a speech on Germany in August 1832.

> I am prepared to admit, that the independence of constitutional States, whether they are powerful, like France or the United States, or of less relative political importance, such as the minor States of Germany, never can be a matter of indifference to the British Parliament, or, I should hope, to the British public. Constitutional States I consider to be the natural Allies of this country.[2]

He was, however, also a consummate pragmatist and, particularly early in his period in office, he saw Russia as a potential balance to a resurgent France. As such, Tsar Nicholas I's crushing of the November Uprising in Poland in 1830 and its subsequent absorption into the Russian Empire went unchallenged by Palmerston. When questioned much later, in 1848, as to why he had not supported Poland's struggle, Palmerston spoke of the practical challenges of intervention.

> When we are asked why the British Government have [sic] not enforced treaty rights in every case, my answer is, that the only method of enforcing them would have been by methods of hostility; and that I do not think those questions were questions of sufficient magnitude in their bearing on the interests of England, to justify any Government in calling on the people of this country to encounter the burdens and hazards of war for the purpose of maintaining those opinions.[3]

He then went on to set out his much-examined position on interventionism:

> I hold that the real policy of England—apart from questions which involve her own particular interests, political or commercial—is to be the champion of justice and right; pursuing that course with moderation and prudence, not becoming the Quixote of the world, but giving the weight of her moral sanction and support wherever she thinks that justice is, and wherever she thinks that wrong has been done.[4]

In ending his speech, Palmerston set out further general principles of his foreign policy approach, including the famous passage on interests.

> It is a narrow policy to suppose that this country or that is to be marked out as the eternal ally or the perpetual enemy of England. We have no eternal allies, and we have no perpetual enemies. Our interests are eternal and perpetual, and those interests it is our duty to follow.

Obviously our friends, he pointed out, follow much the same course and pursue the same objectives, and these alliances have staying power. Yet Palmerston was also clear that:

> It is our duty to make allowance for the different manner in which they may follow out the same objects. It is our duty not to pass too harsh a judgment upon others, because they do not exactly see things in the same light as we see; and it is our duty not lightly to engage this country in the frightful responsibilities of war, because from time to time we

may find this or that Power disinclined to concur with us in matters where their opinion and ours may fairly differ.[5]

The reign of Nicholas I has been summarised as built on orthodoxy, autocracy, and nationalism. It brutally crushed revolts in Romania and Hungary in 1848–9 without provoking intervention from Britain. This reaction to the popular uprisings of 1848 was seen in Western Europe as further evidence of the threat Russia posed to their societies and resulted in increased Russophobia.

It was not just illiberal political systems that marked out Russia and Turkey as different from the other leading powers in Europe. Their contiguous land empires were on a different scale, reaching far out into Asia and encompassing a disparate range of peoples. They embodied different religious traditions, though their subjects were of a mix of faiths, which was to be another issue of friction.

In terms of understanding the Ottoman Empire, an interesting old book is H. A. Gibbons's *Foundation of the Ottoman Empire*, which explains that history has in fact seen several Turkic empires, the 'Empires of the Steppe'.[6] Gibbons writes how the Turks had taken over the imperial machinery of Byzantium, and indeed many writers have noted the similarities between the Ottoman and Byzantine Empires, leading to the saying, 'Better the sultan's turban than the cardinal's hat'. In addition, Gibbons wrote, 'the subjects of the Byzantine Empire present a dead uniformity of abject vices, which are neither softened by the weakness of humanity nor animated by the vigour of memorable crimes'.

Russia, on the other hand, had its own peculiarities. Kissinger describes it as a 'latecomer' on the European scene, one that also encompassed elements of the Asian and Muslim world.

Russia contained populations of each, and hence was never a national state in the European sense. Constantly changing shape as its rulers annexed contiguous territories, Russia was an empire out of scale in comparison with any of the European countries. Moreover, with every new conquest, the character of the state changed as it incorporated another brand-new, restive, non-Russian ethnic group.[7]

Maintaining that empire required the numerically impressive (though qualitatively less so) military forces that, combined with its seemingly continual territorial expansion, contributed to the perception of the threat it posed.

How to prevent Russia from upsetting the balance of power in Europe (potentially leading to another continent-wide war) and, in Britain's case, threatening India by taking advantage of a declining Ottoman Empire were the two central elements of what was to be known as the Eastern Question. These concerns were to play a critical part in British and wider European politics over the course of the century and ultimately contributed to the outbreak of the First World War. For Britain, as a maritime power, the key issue (at least initially) was control of Constantinople, given its strategic position on the lines of communication to India as well as controlling access to the Black Sea (with the ability to threaten Russia directly from the sea). Austria, meanwhile, had a multinational empire in central and eastern Europe and saw Russia as its key competitor for Turkish-controlled territories to the south. For its part, Germany saw Russia as the only real challenger as a land-based military power in Europe.

I believe that Britain's concerns over Russian activity in India and Asia, which were to spark the 'Great Game', immortalised by Rudyard Kipling in *Kim*, were exaggerated. In his book *Britain and the Eastern Question*, the historian G. D. Clayton goes as far as saying: 'It is apparent now that the lasting hostility between Britain and Russia was based on a quite unreal fear in each of the other's supposed aggressive intentions.'[8] Britain's capacity to conduct land campaigns was limited, and Russia's military capabilities were not as effective in practice as expected. This was demonstrated in Crimea and in campaigns against the Turks, particularly when supply lines were stretched. Russia did address its supply difficulties to some degree by extending its railway networks in the later part of the nineteenth century. Indeed, railways were to change the face of warfare more widely, and to some extent undermine Britain's naval dominance. But regardless of whether either Britain or Russia had a conscious objective of encroaching on the other's territory, Russia's general strategy was of expansion around its borders – a strategy also followed by others at the time, such as the United States. For Britain, especially after the Indian Rebellion of 1857, proximity of any foreign power that could potentially offer support to rebels in India was enough to constitute a threat, almost regardless of how realistic that threat might be. I agree with David Fromkin, who draws a comparison with later history.

For ourselves it might well provide a useful reminder of how often Russian strength has been exaggerated and Russian intentions misunderstood; and of how much of the time Russia acts out of mistaken fear of our intentions rather than out of aggressive intentions of her own that are directed against us.[9]

Some twenty years before the Russo-Turkish War of 1829, the British were already keen to address Russia's presence in Central Asia and wanted to establish good relations with Persia. This process had started under Wellington's elder brother, Lord Wellesley, resulting in the Preliminary Anglo-Iranian Treaty (1809). This agreement, he believed, had to be followed by establishing an island fortress in the Persian Gulf but one that was not threatening to Russia. In 1812, Wellesley was replaced in the Foreign Office by Castlereagh, who criticised Wellesley's Persian policy. Ingram alleges that this was following Canning's policy of 1807, whereby 'mediating' between Russia and Persia meant persuading the Persians to do as the Russians asked.[10] Canning said in October 1826 that transferring the Persian mission from England to India sought not to strengthen but 'to relax the bonds of a most inconvenient compact', namely the Anglo-Iranian Treaty.[11] In these years, Canning was trying to embrace Russia and to concentrate on the balance of power in Europe and in particular vis-à-vis France; Wellington, however, argued that Canning should try to hold back both Persia and Russia. Ultimately, Britain did not get involved in the Russo-Persian War that broke out in 1826 and concluded in 1828 with the Treaty of Turkmenchay. This resulted in Persia ceding several areas, including Erivan and Nakhchivan, to Russian control as well as control of the passes from the Caucasus to Azerbaijan. In losing the Persian connection, the direction of British policy in the Near East evolved into the Great Game in Asia.[12]

In his book *The Designs of Russia* published in London in 1828, Sir George de Lacy Evans asserted that if Russia wanted to invade India, its troops would not march from Azerbaijan across Persia to Herat but would come from the east coast of the

Caspian to Khiva, sail up the Oxus (now the Amu Darya) and cross the Hindu Kush to the Khyber Pass. The general level of paranoia about Russia's intentions towards India was reflected in government. The Earl of Ellenborough, for example, who was also an unofficial adviser on foreign policy to Wellington, sought information about Russian invasion routes in 1830. He went on to be four times in charge of the Board of Control and, from 1842 to 1844, general governor of India, thereby crystallising this suspicion at the heart of British government. And so the seeds were sown for a long period of distrust and diplomatic and military manoeuvrings as Britain and Russia played out the game. The Wellesley brothers' narrow Anglo-Indian conception of Britain's vital interests bedevilled the future relationship with the Indian people. It was a tragedy that more was not done to plan for the inevitable, namely India's independence. Instead Britain chose to side with the Ottoman Empire from 1828 in an 'India-first' strategy. In his book *The Beginning of the Great Game in Asia 1828–1834*, Ingram judges every foreign secretary in the first half of the nineteenth century by how well they cooperated over India with colleagues on the Board of Control.[13] Ingram sees the Great Game as 'Britain's response after 1829 to the treaties of Turkmanchay and Adrianople, a watershed in Anglo-Russian relations, because they forced the British to ask how they could defend India from Russia'.[14] To achieve this, Ingram says, 'the balance of power in Europe and the stability of British India both depended upon the existence of Turkey as a buffer state'.[15] At times that policy seemed as if it had to be sustained at any cost. Canning, by contrast, had seen engagement with Russia not only in the context of Europe but in the context of the Middle East – and as just as important as India.

Palmerston, who had supported Canning in the run-up to the Battle of Navarino, by 1833, as foreign secretary, pleaded in vain with the cabinet to provide support for the Ottoman Empire, which was then on the brink of collapse, faced with an attack from the armies of their supposed vassal in Egypt, Mehmed Ali. The French, to whom the Ottomans also turned for help, were friendly to Mehmed yet also declined to intervene. Palmerston felt that, in refusing help, the cabinet had created an opening for Russia, who signed the Treaty of Unkiar Skelessi on 8 July and thereby established a defensive alliance between Russia and the Ottomans. Palmerston saw this as a critical development that, left unaddressed, would significantly strengthen the Russian position. Thereafter, he became far too supportive of Turkey.

Palmerston did focus on the question of neutralising any potential Russian threat to India by creating a gigantic buffer zone in Central Asia, and he saw Afghanistan as a key part of that strategy. In 1838, he supported the British occupation of Afghanistan. Against the advice of their own envoy in Kabul, and using the pretext of reinstating the previous, ousted ruler Emir Shah Shuja Durrani, Britain sought to remove Dost Mohammad Khan who, feeling his overtures to the governor general of India had been rebuffed, had turned to the Russians. This move led to the Anglo-Afghan War of 1839–42. Yet as resentment against British behaviour grew and opposition against Shah Shuja rose, Dost Mohammad's son led a rebellion that ended with the surrender of the 4,500-strong garrison of British and Indian troops in Kabul. The troops' subsequent withdrawal, along with some 12,000 camp followers, led to one of the worst disasters for the British Army in the nineteenth century, severely undermining its prestige. Promised a safe passage by the Afghans but without the expected escort, a bedraggled column was forced to undertake an arduous journey across the harsh, mountainous terrain. Under constant attack, the column was cut to pieces. Only one Briton made it back to India, as captured in the famous painting by Lady Butler, *Remnants of an Army*, though others who had been taken hostage were later freed when a relief force recaptured Kabul in 1842. Britain decided it would be too costly to retain a presence in Afghanistan and, Shah Shuja having been murdered, Dost Mohammed returned to the throne. Despite these setbacks in Afghanistan, Britain kept up its diplomatic efforts, securing Persia's withdrawal from the strategic town of Herat (captured in 1837). Britain also signed a commercial treaty with Afghanistan in 1841. Yet for all this, one British Prime Minister Harold Macmillan learnt from this experience, and talked of the first rule of British politics apparently being: 'don't invade Afghanistan'.[16] In this instance, however, Palmerston managed to deflect blame onto others, benefiting from a controversial victory in the so-called first Opium War with China (1839–42).

During this time, the Russians made efforts to improve relations with Britain, hoping to lure it away from France, but Palmerston was not interested in formalising any such arrangement. Nicholas I personally returned to the charge in Palmerston's period out of government following elections in 1841, visiting Britain in 1844 and meeting his successor as foreign secretary, Lord Aberdeen, in whom he found a sympathetic ear. They discussed cooperation in the event of an Ottoman collapse, with the Russian objective being to keep France out of the Middle East. Britain was having its own issues with France at the time, and it appears Nicholas I left with the belief that 'Britain would no longer oppose Russia and that she would not take independent action to defend Turkey'.[17] Despite Russian attempts to pin Aberdeen down, he remained non-committal, and misunderstandings would become ever more significant in the years to come.

When Palmerston returned to the Foreign Office in 1846, he re-engaged on the Eastern Question. Following the Hungarian Revolution of 1848–9, which had been quashed by Austria and Russia, a number of refugees, including one of the revolution's key figures, Lajos Kossuth, fled to Constantinople. The sultan refused to accede to Austrian and Russian demands to hand anyone over. He was supported by the British ambassador, Stratford Canning. Palmerston, with the backing of the cabinet, stood behind the Ottoman Empire and dispatched a fleet to the Dardanelles, which fortunately had the desired effect. Yet this move was potentially very provocative given the tightening of rules concerning military access to the Black Sea through the Dardanelles and Bosporus in the London Straits Convention of 1841.

When Aberdeen became prime minister in 1852, Tsar Nicholas I continued making overtures to Britain with further proposals on how to manage the collapse of the Ottoman Empire. The British did not wish to pursue these, though Nicholas I still seemed to believe that they at least shared an understanding.

Constantinople was not the only city to see an influx of political refugees in the years after the 1848 revolutions. London was to become a centre for, among others, opponents of the Russian tsars, ranging from liberal intellectuals to political revolutionaries and anarchists. All were generally tolerated so long as they did not cause trouble in Britain itself. Alexander Gertsen (or Herzen), who arrived in Britain in 1852, set up the Free Russian Press in 1853. He was later joined by the poet and political activist Nikolai Ogaryov, with whom Gertsen published a range of uncensored books and periodicals featuring a wide range of content, including banned poems by Pushkin. Radicals would continue to seek refuge in Britain over the following decades. The leading anarchist thinker Pyotr Kropotkin would spend time in England following his escape from Russia in 1876 and eventually settled there in 1886 to set up an anarchist newspaper with British supporters. After the assassination of Alexander II in 1881, another wave of radicals arrived, including Felix Volkhovsky and Sergius Stepniak who established the journal *Free Russia* and drew support from the Society of Friends of Russian Freedom, established in 1890. Two of the most influential figures of the Bolshevik revolution also spent time in London. Lenin stayed several times between 1902 and 1911, and Lev Davidovich Bronstein, exiled to Siberia for revolutionary activity, escaped to England in 1902 with the name Trotsky on his forged passport. Stalin too (although then a more minor figure) visited London during this time. It is, therefore, not a new feature for Russian dissidents to find London an attractive place in which to live and work. Successive British governments have adopted much the same policy as their predecessors of accepting both opponents and supporters of any Russian government.

The mid-nineteenth century was also to see the start of changes in the Ottoman Empire – the Tanzimat, or reorganisation – which lasted from 1839 to 1876. Some would argue that this was not entirely coincidental, and that Ottoman efforts at reform tended to come when they most needed outside support. Certainly these changes were, at least initially, well received in Britain, particularly at a time when anti-Russian sentiment was growing, with elements of the press focusing on

Russia's expansion towards India. The Ottoman Empire, meanwhile, was at times exceptional in granting religious autonomy to its non-Muslim subjects. Under the 1839 Edict of Gülhane, the Ottomans introduced a new Western-inspired concept of law and justice, moving away from the *millet* system, which focused on autonomous religious- (rather than geographic-) based communities (including Armenian, Catholic, Jewish, and Orthodox). Ottoman citizenry was adopted as the basis for the relationship between the state and its subjects and, for some communities, privileges related to the *millet* system were abolished. Over time, the changes would lead to the proclamation of the Imperial Reform Edict of 1856, which promised to remove the legal and *de facto* inequality between Muslims and non-Muslims. The poll tax (*jizya*) that was collected from non-Muslims was abolished. The ban on employment in the public sector and on military service of non-Muslims was lifted, and the prohibition of acting as witnesses against Muslims in a court of law stopped. Under the terms of the reform edict, members of minority groups were accorded the right to be represented in local and regional parliaments as well as in important state institutions such as the council of state, which covered legislative matters.

But instead of improving integration and communication between Muslims and non-Muslims, the introduction of European laws and institutions during the Tanzimat period and the gradual adoption of Western human rights doctrine by the state unexpectedly resulted in a sharp increase of complaints by both Muslims and non-Muslims. A considerable percentage of non-Muslim subjects, particularly the Greek Orthodox community, opposed Tanzimat reforms. Greek Orthodox subjects ranked second only to the Muslims in the hierarchy of *millets*, and they did not want to accept an equality of status with other non-Muslim communities.

What the Ottomans regarded as rebellion and lawlessness, the European powers considered the honourable struggle of oppressed people for independence. Military expeditions into the Ottoman territories were justified as 'protecting Christian minorities'. Deprived of its traditional foundations, the empire began to lose cohesion, its inner strength, the basic rationale of its laws, and, consequently, its powerful sense of identity. The Tanzimat period ended with the destruction of Ottoman society.

That notion of protecting Christian minorities was to be at the heart of the events leading to the outbreak of the Crimean War. For those wanting to study the causes and consequences of this war – which actually saw fighting in many more areas, including far to the north in the Baltic and White Seas, than its name suggests – *Crimea* by Orlando Figes is an excellent read. In his book, Figes describes how Britain wandered into the Crimean War (1853–6) under Prime Minister Lord Aberdeen, and Palmerston took us out. In Figes's view, this was predominantly a French and Ottoman war against Russia's pressure on Turkey.

Then, as now, access to the holy sites of Jerusalem and its surroundings was a contentious issue. With Napoleon III looking to strengthen France's position in the Middle East (an issue of concern for Britain), he was vying with Tsar Nicholas I to be seen as the protector of the Ottoman Christians, both jockeying for position with the sultan. For the traditionalist Nicholas I, the champion of orthodoxy, this was an unacceptable challenge. Figes goes as far as saying that, 'throughout his reign [Nicholas I] was governed by an absolute conviction in his divine mission to save Orthodox Europe from the Western heresies of liberalism, rationalism and revolution'.[18] It was a potent mix of religious tensions and imperial rivalries that was to unleash a truly modern war, whose horrors were covered by an international press corps and accompanying war photographers.

Seeing the French making progress with the sultan, Tsar Nicholas I took a hard-line stance, demanding that Russia have rights of protection of Orthodox Christians throughout the Ottoman Empire – a major escalation of the original issue around the Holy Land and a clear infringement of Turkish sovereignty. At this stage, it appears Nicholas I still expected the British to side with him. The Turks, for their part, sought the assistance of Britain and France. The cabinet, still concerned about French intentions, was divided and played for time. The Russians broke off relations with the Turks and, to step up the pressure, Nicholas I ordered the occupation of the Danube Principalities, planning to use them as a bargaining chip.

The British remained divided. The prime minister, Aberdeen, saw some justification in the Russian move and continued to seek a peaceful solution; Palmerston, backed by a vociferous British press, wanted action against the Russians. Again, a fleet set sail for the Dardanelles to demonstrate intent. The situation in the principalities deteriorated, with fears growing that the tsar intended more than a temporary occupation. Despite a flurry of diplomatic activity to defuse the situation, Russia ultimately refused to accept modifications requested by Turkey to a (deliberately) vaguely drafted proposal on Russian rights to protect the Orthodox subjects of the sultan. The sultan, faced with popular pressure to launch a holy war on Russia, declared war. Initial actions were on the Danube and in the Caucasus. When the Turkish fleet, acting in support of action in the

Caucasus, was destroyed by the Russians at the Battle of Sinope, the battle was portrayed as a massacre in Britain. Public opinion in Britain swung behind demands for war, supported by Palmerston, who had earlier resigned from the government. Faced with French government proposals to act alone in support of Turkey, Aberdeen reluctantly dispatched the British fleet to the Black Sea in December 1853 as an indication of military support but without involving the army. Further attempts to prevent a descent into a wider conflict were rebuffed by Tsar Nicholas I, and France and Britain issued an ultimatum requiring Russia's withdrawal from the principalities. Nicholas I held firm. From their initial mission to help defend the Turks, British and French war aims became much more focused on limiting Russia's power. Russia finally withdrew from the principalities in July 1854, thereby essentially removing the initial cause of the war. Despite this, the British Army became involved with an assault on the Crimean Peninsula, with the objective of capturing the Russian naval base at Sevastopol. It would have been wiser for Britain to leave the large French Army to fight on the ground and keep to only using the navy in the Black Sea.

The ensuing campaign is chiefly remembered in Britain for the tragic failure of the Charge of the Light Brigade, immortalised in Alfred, Lord Tennyson's poem, and developments in nursing spearheaded by Mary Seacole and Florence Nightingale, after whom the emergency hospitals constructed during the coronavirus pandemic were named. In reality, the fighting turned into trench warfare, a precursor of what was to come in the First World War, during an eleven-month siege of Sevastopol. The slow progress of the campaign was to lead to the collapse of Aberdeen's government in January 1855 and the seventy-year-old Palmerston becoming prime minister. Sevastopol did not fall until September 1855 and, while Palmerston had unwisely attempted to widen the war to further weaken Russia, the French were ready for peace; faced with the threat of Austrian intervention, the new Russian tsar, Alexander II, was also ready for peace. Negotiations began in Paris in 1856. France had provided around three times the number of troops as Britain and were, therefore, the key power. The British cabinet would have been wiser, given its doubts, to have limited any involvement to its navy.

The Crimean War was to have profound consequences, both immediate and in the longer term, though ultimately the Eastern Question remained unresolved. While there were relatively few territorial changes, Russia had to accept the demilitarisation of the Black Sea, with no naval vessels permitted in its waters; their fortifications were also to be demolished. This represented a humiliating defeat for Russia, and it contributed to a national sense of betrayal by the West and growing nationalism and pan-Slavic sentiment. While a general war in Europe had been avoided and a balance of power restored, there had been significant shifts – not least, the close relationship between the conservative powers of Russia and Austria had weakened and, following the peace, France and Russia became increasingly aligned.

The shortcomings the war had revealed in Russian society, both civil and military, prompted Tsar Alexander II to embark on a programme of reform, including, in 1861, the Emancipation of the Serfs. However, the reforms brought underlying tensions to the fore, pitting Westernisers against traditionalists. Equality of all before the law ran counter to a historic reliance on strong central authority. Emancipating the serfs did not provide them with immediate access to good-quality land, and it also upset the big landowners who had depended on their labour. It did set in motion a broadening of the small middle class, which in turn created a pool of potential revolutionaries. The reforms failed to achieve Alexander's ambitions, and the reaction against them led to a return to old ways. Tragically, he was assassinated before he could put in place further steps to address the problems, and his successor, Alexander III, would usher in a new wave of repression.

It was not long before both Britain and Russia were once again involved in military action in Asia, paving the way for the next phase of the Great Game. Britain, victorious in the Anglo-Persian War of 1856–7, again evicted the Persians from Herat. Russia made advances in the Caucasus and Central Asia, and by the end of the 1860s had taken control of Tashkent and Samarkand, ever closer to Afghanistan, prompting a 'forward' policy of defence from Britain, as advocated in Sir Henry Rawlinson's 1875 book, *England and Russia in the East*.

Back in Europe, the Eastern Question was to creep up the agenda again, though the pieces had been moving on the political chessboard in the interim. Britain had stepped back from continental Europe to focus on its empire, while a united Germany had emerged in 1871 following the Franco-Prussian War. The German chancellor, Otto von Bismarck, the driving force behind unification, had started crafting a new network of alliances. To prevent France reasserting itself by linking up with its rivals, Bismarck allied Germany to Russia and Austro-Hungary in what was known as the *Dreikaiserbund* or League of the Three Emperors in 1873. For its part, Britain, disappointed at the lack of progress in reform, was becoming less and less attached to Turkey. This time, William Gladstone was to be a leader in the public debate, facing off against his bitter rival

Benjamin Disraeli. As anti-Turkey as Palmerston had been anti-Russia, Gladstone had denounced the 'glare of glory' and the false glamour and romantic excitement of war.[19] He had never had a good word to say about Palmerston, and he believed England was responsible for the power Turkey had and abused. Notably, Gladstone was in power when Russia refused to abide by the key terms of the Paris Treaty any longer, namely the neutrality of the Black Sea, the key British gain from the Crimean War. An international conference was held in London in 1871, which criticised the Russian action and set out the principle that international agreements could not be amended or ended unilaterally. Nevertheless, the treaty subsequently approved changes to the Paris Treaty and restored Russian access to the Black Sea with a compensatory clause to allow the sultan of the Ottoman Empire latitude to close the straits in times of war. Further detail on this period can be found in Richard Shannon's book *Gladstone and the Bulgarian Agitation 1876*, which raises many humanitarian questions, and M. S. Anderson's *The Eastern Question 1774–1923*, which deals with the Ottoman Empire.[20]

Gladstone resigned as leader of the Liberal Party in 1875, but he returned to public prominence in the wake of public revulsion at the massacre of reportedly 15,000 Bulgarians by Turkey following nationalist insurrection throughout the Balkan region against Ottoman rule. Disraeli, when questioned about the Bulgarian massacres in the summer of 1876, dismissed them. As more reliable reports became available, Gladstone published a pamphlet – *The Bulgarian Horrors and the Question of the East* – on 6 September, which sold almost 200,000 copies. In it, he demanded that the Turks be cleared 'out of Europe as the anti-specimen of humanity with bag and baggage'.[21] On 9

September, Gladstone spoke at Blackheath and, after denouncing Turkey, declared it to be the duty of England to act with Russia to secure the independence of the Christian provinces of the Ottoman Empire. Disraeli, now Lord Beaconsfield, continued to see Constantinople as critical to the protection of India, and he said by way of reply that England should resist Russia, hinting that he was prepared for war. Gladstone retorted at a national conference of Liberals on 8 December that the English people should be content with nothing less than the strict fulfilment of those duties to the Christian subjects of the Ottomans which resulted from the Crimean War.

Early in 1877, Gladstone engaged in an active campaign against the Disraeli government's inclination to support Turkey. In the House of Commons on 16 February, he drew attention to a dispatch from the foreign secretary, Lord Derby, condemning the Bulgarian massacres. Then, on 24 April 1877, Russia declared war on the Ottoman Empire. Gladstone, now in opposition to the government, gave notice that on 7 May he would move resolutions in the Commons. These resolutions were too strong to garner the support of the whole Liberal Party, and the only one he moved – which censured the Turks – was rejected. At the conclusion of the debate on 14 May, he declared himself in favour of coercing the Porte by a united Europe.

The Russian threat to Constantinople continued to cause concern, and British antipathy to Russia was reflected in a popular music hall song of the era, 'MacDermott's War Song' by G. W. Hunt, whose chorus gave rise to the term 'jingoism', often used as a term of abuse as was done falsely (in my view) at the time of the 1982 Falklands War.

We don't want to fight but by jingo if we do...
We've got the ships, we've got the men, and got the money too!
We've fought the Bear before... and while we're Britons true!
The Russians shall not have Constantinople...

During the Queen's Speech on 17 January 1878, it was announced that the Turkish authorities had requested the assistance of Great Britain. The Mediterranean Fleet was ordered to Constantinople, ostensibly to protect British subjects. On 4 February, Gladstone denounced the government for seeking 'prestige' in its foreign policy. However, on 3 March, without any need for the British to engage with the Russians, the war concluded with the Treaty of San Stefano. The treaty called for the rearrangement of the Balkans, whereby a large Bulgaria would be created under the protection of Russia. However, the Russian gains in the treaty alarmed the Western powers and sparked a major diplomatic initiative on the part of the British, which paved the way for the treaty's revision at the Congress of Berlin in 1878. This produced a new Balkan arrangement; a much smaller Bulgaria was created, and a series of compensations arranged for some of the powers. The Balkan provinces of Bosnia and Herzegovina were put under Austrian occupation and administration, and Cyprus was temporarily ceded to the British. Despite it being a short war, therefore, it sowed the seeds for 1914, the origins of which I have written about in *The Hidden Perspective: The Military Conversations 1906–1914*.[22]

Meanwhile, in Greece, Charilaos Trikoupis became prime minister after the fall of the Koumoundouros government in 1880. Trikoupis was the most important Greek reformer of the nineteenth century, but he was defeated in 1885 by the populist Theodoros Deliyannis. The alternation of power continued until 1896. Trikoupis gave priority, by and large, to domestic politics while Deliyannis favoured territorial gains. In 1897, the Greco-Turkish War was a disaster for the Greeks, who would have been wiser to have stuck with the moderation of Trikoupis.[23] Disraeli and Salisbury had returned from the Berlin Congress claiming peace and honour. However, the historian Richard Shannon suggests that nothing substantial was achieved by the British delegates except gestures to please the public. Salisbury was later to regret the efforts he had made on the part of Greece. 'When I first came to the Foreign Office in 1878 I believed strongly in the Greeks', he claimed, adding that the pro-Greek changes in the Treaty of Berlin were 'largely, if not entirely due to my urgent pressure'.[24] But by 1889, he was saying, 'Now that I know Greece better – I regret what I did ... She is the blackmailer of Europe.'[25]

Gladstone was to return to his attack on Disraeli's approach during the Midlothian campaigns of 1879 and 1880 in which he accused the Tories of operating a foreign policy designed to stifle liberty and progress and, for his own part, insisted on a libertarian foreign policy derived from Canning.

In analysing Gladstone's position, views differ. Shannon suggests that Gladstone's pursuit of the Eastern Question forged a moral compact with the electorate. Martin Swartz, on the other hand, argues that Gladstone's political mission had more to do with the reconstruction of a divided Liberal Party and that he used the Bulgarian agitation as a means to this end.[26] I believe his position was both principled and correct.

Gladstone became prime minister for the second time in 1880, and he was to be responsible for a significant military success (never, however, called a war) which was to mark a major strategic step in securing the supply lines to India and further afield in Asia. In Egypt, a revolt broke out in 1881, led by a Colonel Arabi, who was calling for 'Egypt for the Egyptians'. Initially France and Britain planned a joint response, but France dropped out and Britain proceeded alone. In the words of Roy Jenkins:

> Unlike nearly every other British military enterprise between Waterloo and 1914, the Wolseley expedition was a neat, quick and resounding success. He met the Arabi army at Tel-el-Kebir, fifty or so miles to the north-east of Cairo, on 13 September and gained a complete victory with few casualties. Arabi was captured and exiled to Ceylon, and Tewfik was maintained as khedive [viceroy], but as a client of the British agent general.[27]

Thus, a lid was put on Egyptian nationalism until the emergence of Colonel Nasser in the 1950s, and Britain was now sitting astride the recently opened Suez Canal. Further east, the Great Game continued to play out, with the Russians pushing closer to Afghanistan (since the Second Afghan War of 1878–80, a British protectorate) through what is now Turkmenistan, and they were building a railway to support their advances. While talks about the Afghan border continued, Russian and Afghan forces clashed around Panjdeh in 1885. Outright conflict between Britain and Russia was averted through diplomatic channels, and work on delineating the border culminated in signing a protocol in 1887. The Great Game was, however, to continue in the ever more inhospitable mountain areas of the Pamirs, Himalayas, and Tibet.

In 1892–4, Gladstone – far too old – formed his last government. He continued Britain's period of splendid isolation, refusing any association with Germany and Austria. Russian–Austrian relations had deteriorated over tensions in the Balkans, which led to the collapse of the *Dreikaiserbund*, but Russia had remained allied to Germany through Bismarck's secret Reinsurance Treaty of 1887. With Bismarck forced to resign in 1890 by the new Kaiser, Wilhelm II, Russia found Germany unwilling to renew the treaty; in response, it signed an agreement with France in 1891 that included a clause obliging France to give Russia diplomatic support in any colonial conflict with Great Britain. Gladstone threatened to resign once too often during a cabinet meeting on 9 January 1894. Queen Victoria, when told by Gladstone of his wish to resign, never wavered. She told him she did not require his advice on his successor, appointing Lord Rosebery, under whose administration the future foreign secretary Edward Grey was to be a rising star as a junior minister in the Foreign Office. The Liberals were then heavily defeated by Lord Salisbury's Conservatives in the general election of July 1895.

Lord Salisbury was the most sceptical interventionist of any British foreign secretary in the last 250 years, and he was famous for his caustic journalism. Dealing with the Eastern Question would be an important element in his premiership. Prior to the general election, there was a growing consensus – of which Grey was a part, alongside Disraeli and Salisbury – about the central strategic role of the Russian Empire in Britain's international relations.[28] Britain's relationship with Turkey had by then also deteriorated further, and both Germany and Austro-Hungary had been making major inroads in developing political and economic ties – worrying the British, French, and Russians. Meanwhile, Turkey's repression of its Armenian population, which led to widespread massacres between 1894 and 1896, caused public outrage in Britain and elsewhere. In a speech in Liverpool, the eighty-seven-year-old Gladstone called for British intervention. Salisbury was unable to garner support for united action among the European powers; nor could he secure cabinet support for unilateral action, since the Royal Navy was concerned that a naval expedition against the Turks would provoke a Russo-French reaction.

This setback led to a significant shift in British policy. When he met Tsar Nicholas II during his visit to Britain in 1896, Salisbury indicated flexibility in his position on Constantinople, and that it was no longer valid to argue about its importance to India; Egypt was much more important. However, there was still no British enthusiasm for accelerating the collapse of the Ottoman Empire. Following a rebellion in Crete in 1897, the Europeans had forced the Turks to grant Crete local autonomy, but the Greeks, sensing potential Turkish weakness, launched a wider war in which they were defeated. The subsequent settlement saw the Turks evicted from Crete, though no other strong action was taken against them. While Salisbury had appeared to be making progress in relations with Russia, Russian expansion in the Far East – which posed a threat to British interests in China – eventually led to Britain's alliance with Japan in 1902. This continuation of Russo-British tension suited the Germans but worried the French, who saw it potentially drawing them into a war with Britain on the side of Russia. It provided impetus for them to settle colonial disputes with Britain in 1904's Entente Cordiale, which, it should be noted, did not constitute a formal alliance.

Despite having an alliance with Japan, Britain stayed out of the Russo-Japanese War which broke out in February 1904 when Japan launched a surprise attack on Russia (possibly because of its increased confidence following the alliance with Britain). However, Britain almost found itself accidently at war with Russia as a result of a bizarre incident in the North Sea in October of that year. The Russian Baltic Fleet, en route to the Far East to bolster its forces against Japan, mistook a British trawler fleet working the Dogger Bank area for Japanese torpedo boats, which were rumoured to be operating off Denmark. In their confusion, the Russians opened fire, with tragic consequences. Two British trawlermen died and six more were injured, with one trawler sunk and others damaged, including one Russian cruiser, hit by friendly fire. The incident caused a serious diplomatic conflict and public outcry in Britain, but war was averted with an agreement to go to international arbitration. Russia, much to its humiliation, was to go on to lose the war with Japan. This costly defeat, and the 1905 revolution, would fuel French concerns over the real benefits of their alliance.

In 1904, Halford John Mackinder wrote an article for the Royal Geographical Society in which he developed his concept of the pivotal area, extending his heartland theories and placing them at the centre of what he called the World-Island compromising Europe, Asia, and Africa (Afro-Asia).[29] The heartland stretched from the Volga River to the Yangtze River, from the Himalayas to the Arctic, at the time ruled by Russia. In his book *Democratic Ideas and Reality*, published in 1919, he argued:

Who rules East Europe commands the Heartland;
who rules the Heartland command the World-Island;
who rules the World-Island commands the world.

Edward Grey became foreign secretary after the Liberal victory in the December 1905 elections. He had had concerns about both Germany and Russia and had welcomed the 1904 Entente Cordiale with France. With the Germans working to bring a now weakened Russia into their orbit, Grey recognised the importance of maintaining the balance of power. Following the model of its agreement with France, Britain agreed an entente with Russia in August 1907, which settled outstanding issues in Afghanistan, Persia, and Tibet, and this brought about the Triple Entente of France, Russia, and Britain. It did not, however, prevent further periods of stress, both over Russia's aspirations in the Balkans and over Persia in a serious incident in 1911.

Although specifically denied by the Germans at the time, a feeling of encirclement grew in the nation after the Triple Entente. As might have been expected, in his autobiography, Grey explains away, rather unconvincingly, the theory of the encircling policy as having been encouraged by the Germans to hold their public to high levels of defence expenditure. Grey touches on the dilemma within the Triple Entente, and particularly in relation to Persia, in volume I of his books.[30] For Russia, the policy would have been a success if it promoted a grand design in Europe in which Russia would play an integral part. This did not happen. For Britain it would have been a success if it did no more than stabilise Anglo-Russian rivalries in Central Asia and Persia. Yet the Triple Entente drifted while domestic political pressures in Russia did nothing to help its wavering commitment to any Franco-British-Russian alliance. Even the term Triple Entente, much favoured by the French, was rarely used by Russia and Britain, and some continued to confuse it with the Triple Alliance of 1882 between Germany, Austro-Hungary, and Italy. In retrospect, a Triple Entente could and should have been given a much higher priority for

Britain and France from 1827 until 1907. For Kissinger, the Triple Entente marked 'the beginning of the end for the operation of the balance of power';[31] with Britain joining France and Russia, there was no longer a balancing power in Europe, and the options for diplomacy were fast disappearing.

As Grey had feared, the Balkans remained an area of tension in Europe. With the Young Turk Revolution of 1908, which forced the sultan of the Ottoman Empire to make constitutional reforms, Austro-Hungary and Russia sensed an opportunity to exploit Turkish weakness. Austria announced that it would annex Bosnia-Herzegovina, with Russia expecting changes to the arrangements on the Straits as a trade-off for acceptance. Bulgaria also declared independence. Some considered these moves to be breaches of the Treaty of Berlin and precipitated a major crisis, ultimately defused in a flurry of diplomatic activity, which made changes to the treaty. Britain and France, however, would not agree changes to the arrangements on the Straits, an embarrassing setback for Russia. Germany and Austro-Hungary were now more closely aligned in the Balkans, and this caused a strain on Russo-German relations. France and Britain's desire to keep out of the Balkans also became more evident.

Turkey still controlled a significant amount of territory in Europe, which was eyed by Austro-Hungary, Bulgaria, and others. These ambitions for acquiring more territory were festering, and they erupted in the Balkan Wars of 1912–13. The result was a major defeat for the Ottoman Empire. Fearing an escalation into a wider European war, Grey organised an international conference in London, the consequences of which saw the Turks cede control over the bulk of their European territories to the Balkan League of Bulgaria, Greece, Montenegro, and Serbia.

In Bosnia-Herzegovina, Turkish rule, which ended in 1878, had left as its legacy 'deep social cleavages along ethno-religious lines, as well as a society steeped in military traditions and values. The ethnic communities in Bosnia, even in the early 1990s, approached the national question from the "outside in"'. So argues a book by Steven L. Burg and Paul S. Shoup.[32] It is an objective account, very hard to achieve, of the wars of 1992–5 in Bosnia-Herzegovina. It reveals why a pawn in the Eastern Question that preoccupied Europe for most of the nineteenth century was destined to be at the centre of another violent catastrophe as Yugoslavia broke apart in the 1990s.

The 1913 Treaty of London did not define the split of territory between the victors, and disagreements led to the outbreak of a second war. This conflict ended in the defeat of Bulgaria, which had taken on the other league members as well as Romania and Turkey, but the wars had ultimately failed to resolve all the underlying territorial issues, and the scene was set for the diplomatic crisis that triggered the First World War.

4

Winston Churchill and the Russian Revolution

There was, in addition to Canning, another British statesman who had a critical role in guiding and setting Britain's relationship with Russia in the twentieth century: Winston Churchill. At the start of the First World War, Churchill was in the Liberal Party and on the threshold of his fourth year as first lord of the Admiralty, having been appointed by the Liberal prime minister, Herbert Asquith, in October 1911. He had previously served as both president of the Board of Trade and secretary of state for the Home Department. Churchill had been as busy as ever during that pre-war period, and he could and did claim important achievements.

Churchill had already earned a reputation for taking decisive – if at times controversial – action. By the start of the war in 1914, the Royal Navy's fleet had been transformed from a traditional coal-burning fleet into an oil-burning fleet (which heightened the importance of the Persian oil fields). He had done so with, by and large, the support of an even more controversial figure, Admiral Lord Jacky Fisher. Another of Churchill's proud boasts was that, on the day the war started, he had already mobilised the fleet and sent it up north to Scapa Flow, where it was best positioned to deal with any surprise attacks from the German Navy. What was surprising is that doing so, and having told the prime minister he had used his own executive powers and not war powers, was arguably an illegal act. Nevertheless, he won much praise with the general public.

In the summer of 1914, Churchill again acted decisively and without regard for the legal niceties in seizing two battleships that were being built in British shipyards for the Ottoman Navy. Although Churchill had been pro-Turk before the war, and indeed one of the most pro-Turk members of the Asquith cabinet, he had no compunction in making this move to strengthen the Royal Navy in the face of the German threat. In fact, he was soon to be pushing hard for military action against Turkey.

By this stage, Turkey was already moving closer to the German camp. On 24 July 1914, the kaiser had personally overturned the earlier decision of the German ambassador in Constantinople not to have Turkey as an ally, instead instructing his representatives to explore the offer made by Turkey's war minister, Enver Pasha, to form part of an alliance. Secret talks took place in Constantinople between German officials and the grand vizier, Prince Said Halim, as well as the foreign minister and war minister. At the same time, Austria's ultimatum to Serbia – that Austrian officials should take part in the investigation of the assassination, which ultimately led to the outbreak of war – had been delivered. On 28 July, the Ottoman leaders forwarded a draft alliance document to Berlin. The German chancellor remained unenthusiastic about Germany getting involved with the Ottoman Empire, but he sent a cable to his ambassador in Constantinople instructing him not to sign the alliance document unless he was sure that Turkey either could or would take action against Russia.

In reality, the Turks hoped they would not be embroiled in a war, and there was a provision in their agreement with Germany that the arrangements in which they were involved should remain secret. The Germans had also guaranteed the Turks that they would not allow the Ottoman Empire to be partitioned, whereas the Turks felt that, regardless of any assurances, an allied victory would see it broken up, given Russia's continued efforts in that regard. Publicly, to mask their true intentions, some Turkish spokesmen even went as far as to suggest that Turkey might join the British and French allies. Meanwhile, the German chief of staff, hitherto against linking with Turkey as he did not believe they would be an asset, began to press for Turkish assistance against both Britain and Russia. Each side was spreading confusion.

As a consequence, it was not until September that British advisers to the Turkish Navy were withdrawn (to be replaced by Germans), following Britain's pursuit of the German warships, the *Goeben* and the *Breslau*, across the Mediterranean.[1] Breaking the rules governing passage through the Bosporus, those two ships reached Constantinople and were to provide support to the Turks following the seizure of Ottoman ships by the British. In a further breach of their international obligations, the Turks also mined the entrance to the Dardanelles, cutting the shipping route to Russia, after one of their own boats had been turned back by the Royal Navy – acting under the authorisation of Churchill – for carrying German sailors on board.

The Germans, working through Enver, an Ottoman military officer who formed one third of the dictatorial triumvirate known as the 'Three Pashas', continued to press the Turks to enter the war. The Ottoman senior leadership, however, remained divided; their fear was that by joining a war against

Russia, they could open themselves to an attack from Bulgaria. As part of his efforts to swing the debate, it was Enver who had ordered the *Goeben* and *Breslau* into the Black Sea, with the intention of staging an action that he would claim had been started by the Russians. In the event, the ships disobeyed orders and bombarded the Russian coast, which led to a crisis in Constantinople and an apology being issued to the Russians. Enver, however, had intentionally included in the apology an allegation that the attack had been provoked by Russian action. Unsurprisingly, the Russians rejected this, declaring war on 2 November. Following the original incident, Churchill had ordered the Royal Navy to take action against Turkey on 31 October, though none materialised until 3 November, when the forts guarding the Dardanelles were shelled, and it was not until 5 November that Britain formally declared war.

The extent of the intrigue between Germany and Turkey in the run-up to and in the early stages of the First World War is often overlooked, but it reveals how alliances were shifting prior to its outbreak. David Fromkin's detailed account of these events is but a small part of his exceptional book on the Middle East and how Iraq, Israel, Jordan, Syria, and Lebanon came about following the break-up of the Ottoman Empire.[2] Sean McMeekin, in his *The Berlin–Baghdad Express*, explores how Germany saw an alliance with Turkey as a way to gain influence in the Islamic world and to portray Germany as a champion for Muslims suffering under British and French colonial rule. Compared to Germany's other allies, McMeekin writes:

The Ottoman Empire, by contrast, could threaten Russia's vulnerable Caucasian underbelly, along with Egypt and the Suez Canal, the strategic linchpin of the entire British Empire. It could only do this, however, if the Sultan's largely phantom authority over the distant provinces of his empire was buttressed by a great trunk railway to the Near East.[3]

Railways did have a strategic significance but so did waterways, and for Turkey nothing was more strategically important than retaining control of the waterways between the Black Sea and the Sea of Marmara opening onto the Aegean Sea.

On 27 December 1914, Churchill wrote to Prime Minister Asquith suggesting two possible ways of breaking the impasse in Europe and creating a second front. One of these was to force a passage through the Dardanelles, either with or without the army occupying the Gallipoli Peninsula, and put a fleet of warships into the Sea of Marmara, threaten Constantinople, and make the Turks sue for peace. Although operationally challenging, strong strategic rationales supported this approach. Furthermore, in January, the Russians had called for a diversionary attack against Turkey to help relieve pressure on them in the Caucasus (though by the time of the operation, they had already gained the upper hand against the Turks).[4]

Controversy over the Dardanelles operation still resonates in the twenty-first century, but one fact should not be forgotten: on 13 and 28 January 1915, Churchill argued for a solely naval attack. However, with his attention focused on the navy mounting the attack, Churchill had never fully engaged with Field Marshal Kitchener on his second-front strategy at Gallipoli and securing the forces that would be required to conduct a successful operation. It was only in the middle of February 1915 that the decision was taken to send in the army as well, just six days before the naval bombardment was originally due to start, though, in the event, the bombardment was postponed by eight days to 19 February.

In its initial stages, the Gallipoli campaign went well. The naval bombardment, which ran until the middle of March, silenced the Turkish guns overlooking the Dardanelles. The navy higher command, however, was then not ready to sail immediately through the Dardanelles to lay siege to Constantinople. Instead, the admirals vowed to take up Kitchener's belated offer to assist with troops. The fatal flaw in this new plan was that the armed military forces only landed on the Gallipoli peninsula towards the end of April. By then, they were facing a very determined and well-prepared adversary, and the battle descended into the very trench warfare that had led to the stalemate on the Western Front. After suffering heavy losses, a decision to evacuate was finally taken in December.

Overarching the failed operation were the personality clashes between the first lord of the Admiralty, Churchill, and the first sea lord, Fisher, an egotist whom Churchill had unwisely brought back into the Admiralty. Fisher had appeared to be in favour of the operation because he had not raised any opposition in the War Council – until the council of 14 May, that is, when he announced that he had been against the Dardanelles expedition from the beginning and that Asquith and Kitchener were well aware of this. It is worth recalling here Asquith's extraordinary decision to bring Kitchener into his government on 5 August as secretary of state for war, who then 'promptly expressed his profound contempt for the strategy, policy and role assigned to the British Army by the Anglo-French plan'.[5] Kitchener regarded the purpose of the Expeditionary Force with deep misgivings and was no admirer of the commander-in-chief designate, Sir John French.

When Fisher resigned, Churchill saw Asquith and offered to resign but, according to Roy Jenkins's account, Asquith 'did not wish it'.[6] Churchill seemed blissfully unaware that an impending political upheaval was already underway when he arrived to see Asquith with his recommendations for new Admiralty Board names, without Fisher, only to be told, 'No, this will not do. I have decided to form a national government.'[7] Asquith asked Churchill if he would take office in the new government, or if he would prefer a command in France. Churchill had never considered the latter before, but it was what he ended up doing after an unsatisfactory short period in a sinecure position as chancellor of the Duchy of Lancaster. Even that offer owed much to Clementine Churchill's letter to Asquith campaigning for his retention within the cabinet.

> Winston may in your eyes & in those with whom he has to work have faults but he has the supreme quality which I venture to say very few of your present or future Cabinet possess, the power, the imagination, the deadliness to fight Germany.[8]

Thus, Churchill returned to the front and served with his old regiment, though he still yearned to be able to justify his position over Gallipoli. He saw the opportunity when the Dardanelles Commission of Enquiry convened in August 1916, and he pushed for full disclosure of the decision-making process leading up to the operation. However, when he read the draft report in February 1917, he was surprised to discover that the evidence on which it was based was not going to be published. He immediately prepared notes for the commission on those parts that, in his view, needed to be amended, stressing that the events had to be considered in context of the wider war.

The report did make clear that Asquith had wanted to attack and defeat Turkey. It also pointed out that Kitchener had not given colleagues sufficient detail of the military plans for the campaign. In the debate on the report in the House of Commons on 20 March 1917, while also emphasising the points he had made to the commission, Churchill acknowledged the report was 'at any rate, an instalment of fair play' and that 'the burden that I have hitherto borne alone is now shared with the most eminent men which this country has produced within the lifetime of a whole generation in Parliament, in the Army, or the Fleet'.[9]

It became an important political fact twenty-five years later that the man who was to become Churchill's deputy leader in the 1940 coalition government – the Labour leader Clement Attlee – had fought at Gallipoli as a major in the army. Indeed, he was the last man off the beaches, accompanying the commanding general, when the final withdrawal took place. Attlee always believed that Churchill was correct in opening up a new Gallipoli front and that, in practice, he was a profound strategic thinker on military matters. Most importantly, Attlee continued to believe this through the ups and downs of 1940–5.

In entering a war against Turkey, as Churchill had ultimately pushed for, Britain faced a dilemma in its relationship with Russia. While it needed Russian engagement on the Eastern Front to counter the might of Germany, Russia's long-term strategic goals would be served by the defeat of the Turks. It is interesting that, even in November 1914, George V had told the Russian ambassador, Benckendorff, 'As far as Constantinople is concerned, it is clear that the City should be yours'.[10] This recognition was a key element during negotiations between the allies in March and April 1915 as the Gallipoli campaign got underway. When Churchill was in government, the British had conceded that, if the assault was successful and British forces reached the Bosporus, the Russians would be handed control of the territory from Gallipoli to Constantinople, and indeed the territory opposite Constantinople on the eastern shore. On 23 January 1915, the British foreign secretary, Edward Grey, had instructed the British minister in Athens, Sir Francis Elliot, to offer '"most important territorial compensations for Greece on the coast of Asia Minor" in return for Greek participation in the war on the side of the Entente'.[11] However, given Greece's own aspirations in relation to Constantinople, its participation in the Dardanelles campaign was blocked by Russia, and Greece remained neutral, not joining the allies until 1917. Not unreasonably, the British extracted from Russia, in the negotiations prior to Gallipoli, 'possession of the neutral zone in Persia (where most of the oil-fields lay)'.[12] Oil was essential for the movement of forces when the Royal Navy abandoned coal and relied on oil-fired engines in their new ships.

France was, in effect, bought off later with the secret Sykes–Picot Agreement of January 1916, which gave it control of south-eastern Turkey (Cilicia) and Syria; Britain gained control of Mesopotamia and the area south of the French-controlled region linking it to Egypt, the principal British base in the Middle East (which it had declared a British protectorate in December 1914). Following subsequent talks, Russia was promised Armenia and Kurdistan in May. The agreements with the Russians set the objective of the Great Game to one side; as Clayton points out, 'the buffer between British and Russian territory had in practice gone'.[13]

All these issues were to return to the negotiating table in Paris in 1919 in various forms, though they were somewhat simplified by Lenin renouncing Soviet claims over Turkish territory. The Treaty of Sèvres (August 1920) proclaimed the partitioning of the Ottoman Empire and, among a number of territorial changes, led to the British mandate in Palestine and the French mandate over Syria and Lebanon. But it was overtaken by events and never ratified. Mustafa Kemal, who had commanded a division in Gallipoli, split with the sultan's government. Kemal, by then commonly called Atatürk, led his nationalists to victory in the Turkish War of Independence and was the creator of the new Republic of Turkey. Armenians resisted and, in a notable early diplomatic success, the Soviet Union absorbed what remained of the Armenian state following the signature of the Treaty of Kars, which established the boundary between Turkey and the now Soviet republics of Armenia, Azerbaijan, and Georgia. The Turks also forced French troops back in the south. To the west, the Greco-Turkish War raged until 1922. By its end, the Turks had destroyed the Greek Army, pushing them out of the Smyrna region. The city of Smyrna (Izmir) itself was set on fire, destroying Greek and Armenian homes and businesses. Thousands of refugees crammed the waterfront to escape the fires, some rescued by allied ships, many deported by the Turks to Anatolia. The Turks had already systematically killed and deported Armenians from Turkey in 1915. Winston Churchill, when he came to write the history of the period, did not equivocate on this issue. 'In 1915 the Turkish government began and ruthlessly carried out the infamous general massacre and deportation of Armenians in Asia Minor ... there is no reasonable doubt that this crime was planned and executed for political reasons.'[14] It would take over a century for the US president to formally describe the 1915 massacres as genocide, which President Biden did in 2021.

Since Mustafa Kemal did not recognise the Treaty of Sèvres, the Conference of Lausanne in 1922–3 sought to negotiate a new settlement with Turkey. The Treaty of Lausanne, as well as agreeing controversial population exchanges, reached an agreement on the Straits issue. Under the auspices of the League of Nations Straits Convention, the eastern and western shores of both the Dardanelles and the Bosporus were demilitarised in 1923. Freedom of passage for all merchant ships was guaranteed, and warships up to 10,000 tonnes were allowed to pass through. In the Black Sea, the total number of ships from Britain, France, or Italy could not exceed that of Russia. For Britain, this was the first time the Royal Navy had a clear right to sail into the Black Sea with or without the approval of Turkey. Much later, in 1936, the terms of the Montreux Convention gave Turkey control of the Bosporus and the Dardanelles, again guaranteeing free passage of civilian vessels but restricting the passage of naval ships not belonging to Black Sea states.

Although Russia had been an ally during the first few years of the war, and became significantly weaker following the revolution, there were still those in Britain who were – unjustifiably, in my view – obsessed by the threat it posed to British interests in India, just as in the heyday of the Great Game. I believe that India's future as an independent state should have been considered at the Imperial War Conference called by David Lloyd George, who had taken over as prime minister from Asquith in December 1916. On 16 March 1917, when Britain's debt to the contribution of forces from South Africa, Canada, Australia, New Zealand, and India was apparent to everyone, a resolution was passed allowing the first four countries to become independent after the end of the war – but there was no mention of India. All that resolution needed to contain was a reference to Indian independence being openly examined once the war was over. The failure to do so was a missed opportunity for far-sighted statesmanship by Lloyd George. Although Churchill's opposition can be assumed, he was not then in the coalition government. Senior Conservatives might have been opposed, but the extent of that opposition was never tested. Once the war was over and the extraordinary debt Britain owed to Indian troops was clear, a slow, grudging process of formally discussing India's long-term future began. But the real opportunity was lost until Attlee became prime minister in 1945 and advanced the right to independence.

Overall, in the First World War, Russia never lived up militarily to the hopes vested in it, especially by France. Although it took heavy casualties – an estimated 1.8 million Russians were killed in its share of the fighting from the onset of war – by 1917, the cracks in Russian society had widened even more deeply. Much blame for the military setbacks had been laid at the feet of Tsar Nicholas II, who had taken upon himself the role of commander-in-chief. In March 1917, following widespread protests against food shortages, strikes, and rioting, troops in Petrograd mutinied (the February Revolution, according to the old Russian calendar), and by 15 March the tsar had abdicated, leaving two contenders to vie for power in Petrograd. A provisional government was established by members of the State Duma (the lower house of the federal assembly) and recognised by the allies, who wanted Russia to remain in the war. Alongside it, however, was the Petrograd Soviet of Workers' and Soldiers' Deputies. Russia was now heading towards the next phase of revolution. In April, the Germans, seeking to hasten Russia's exit from the war, arranged Lenin's free passage to Petrograd. Once there, he called for the overthrow of the provisional government and the ending of the war. At this critical juncture, Churchill was to return to centre stage.

On 16 July 1917, despite six weeks of speculation and to the fury of many prominent Conservatives, Lloyd George brought Churchill back into the cabinet in his chosen position as minister of munitions, a post Lloyd George himself had held previously. Conservative protests continued, though Andrew Bonar Law, the chancellor of the exchequer, who had not been formally consulted, nevertheless acquiesced. On 11 December 1917, Churchill made a public speech in Bedford which few other politicians could or would have made, for its underlying sympathy for Russia was self-evident.

> Russia has been thoroughly beaten by the Germans. Her great heart has been broken, not only by German might, but by German intrigue; not only by German steel, but by German gold. It is this melancholy event which has prolonged the war that has robbed the French, the British and the Italian armies of the prize that was perhaps almost within their reach this summer; it is this event alone, that has exposed us to perils and sorrows and sufferings which we have not deserved, which we cannot avoid but under which we shall not bend.[15]

It is important to remember that Germany devastated Russia during the First World War. It was not Lenin; that came later. Russia was always the country Germany feared and hated most, and Bolshevism and Communism were used by the Germans to destabilise Russia and weaken its ability to project power. Churchill was right to highlight 'intrigue' and 'gold'.

Following their seizure of power in the October Revolution,

the Bolsheviks set about reaching an armistice with the Germans. They needed a respite and hoped that their example would lead to revolutions breaking out in the West. An armistice was agreed with the Central Powers in December 1917, and peace negotiations opened in Brest-Litovsk. In Britain, attention was turning to how to deal with post-revolutionary Russia. On 14 December 1917 Britain's War Cabinet decided to provide funds to anti-Bolshevik Russians, 'for the purpose of maintaining alive in south-east Russia the resistance to Central Powers'.[16] Twelve days later, on 26 December, Churchill was invited to attend the War Cabinet, where the question about the formation of an anti-Bolshevik force of Russians again arose. The minutes record that, 'Mr Churchill said he understood that a number of Russian officers were most anxious to be kept together, either in France or England, as a Russian unit to form a rallying point to those Russians who remained loyal to the *Entente*. In his opinion such a nucleus would be a valuable political asset.'[17] On the same day, after pressure from the French prime minister, Clemenceau, the War Cabinet agreed that the French should direct all activity against the Bolsheviks in Ukraine, while the British were allotted the Armenian, Cossack, and Caucasian regions as their sphere of anti-Bolshevik activity. This agreement was dubbed the Convention of December 1917.

In the peace talks, the Bolsheviks had split into three factions. The largest, led by Bukharin, favoured a revolutionary war against Germany, with the goal of igniting a broader war in the West. Trotsky's faction came up with the slogan 'Neither war nor peace'. Lenin headed up the smallest faction, which called for a separate peace – and the sooner the better: 'The bourgeois has to be throttled and for that we need both hands free.' Lenin had backing from Stalin and Zinoviev for the internal battle to be the priority, but he needed Trotsky to outvote Bukharin. The German generals, Ludendorff and von Hindenburg, pushed for a tough, expansionist settlement, and they were encouraged by Ukraine, which had declared independence, agreeing a separate treaty on 8/9 February. This move helped revive Ukrainian national identity – an identity that, as I shall return to later, is still contested by President Putin today. On 9 February, the Germans issued an ultimatum to reach agreement or restart the fight. The following day, Trotsky told the conference Russia was 'leaving the war' but it would not sign the German peace treaty.

In response, on 16 February, the Germans announced that hostilities would recommence in two days, and indeed they did. Faced with this renewed German advance, and after much debate, Trotsky switched his backing to Lenin and the Central Committee voted 116 to 85 for Lenin to cable Berlin accepting unconditionally. Lenin was decried by some as a traitor, but the Treaty of Brest-Litovsk was nevertheless signed on 3 March 1918. Under its terms, the Soviet Republic lost 34 per cent of its population, some 55 million people; 32 per cent of its agricultural land; 54 per cent of its industrial enterprises; and 89 per cent of its coalmines.[18] Fulfilling the German ambition of pushing its territory eastwards, the treaty caused the Russian Empire to lose Ukraine, Finland, Estonia, Lithuania, Poland, and what was called Courland, a part of western Latvia. These were all granted independence under German protection. All Russian forces were also to withdraw from Ukraine, with German and Austrian occupying troops moving in immediately. However, Germany's harsh requisition policy left the Ukrainian peasants in open revolt, and guerrilla warfare led to the destruction of bridges and railway lines, leaving Germany with no solid base in Ukraine.

For Lenin, accepting the loss of so much land was the prerequisite for winning control of the west of the country. He recognised that exporting Communism was by this stage mere talk, as Orlando Figes explains: 'To all intents and purposes the "permanent revolution" had come to an end and from this point on, in Lenin's famous phrase, the aim of the regime would be limited to the consolidation of Socialism in one country.'[19] Moscow was to be the new capital, and Lenin and Trotsky moved into the Kremlin.

Meanwhile, in March 1918, Lloyd George decided to send British troops into the northern ports of Murmansk and Archangel to protect the vast stock of British military supplies that had been sent to Russia in 1916 and 1917.[20] Relations between Britain and France and the Bolshevik government were helped by an agreement to allow 60,000 Czech prisoners of war captured by the Russians on the Austrian front in 1915 to leave Russia along the Trans-Siberian Railway to Vladivostok. But things went downhill after 10,000 Czechs reached their destination on 26 May only to find that Bolshevik troops had attacked a Czech unit at Irkutsk. The remaining 50,000 Czechs then took control of all railway stations on the 800-mile stretch between Omsk and Krasnoyarsk, putting them in control of an important strategic asset and giving them the opportunity to influence the fighting between the White Russians and the Red Bolsheviks.

Churchill wrote to Lloyd George on 17 June 1918 arguing against shipping the Czechs from Vladivostok by sea to Europe and, in a cabinet memorandum on 22 June, he dealt with the issue in dramatic (though perhaps rather overstated, given the continuing arrival of American forces on the Western Front) terms.

We must not take 'No' for an answer either from America or from Japan. We must compel events instead of acquiescing in their drift. Surely now when Czech divisions are in possession of large sections of the Siberian railway and in danger of being done to death by the treacherous Bolsheviks, some effort to rescue them can be made? Every man should ask himself each day whether he is not too readily accepting negative solutions?[21]

Lloyd George and Clemenceau appealed to President Wilson for military support for the Czech forces in Siberia, and, very reluctantly, in July, the Americans agreed to send troops to Russia in a mission to guard allied supplies and support the Czechs. This involvement is a relatively overlooked aspect of American military history, to the extent that two US presidents have made speeches aimed at Russian audiences claiming that America has never been at war with Russia. In 1984, President Reagan said on TV beamed into Russia, 'Our sons and daughters have never fought each other in war.' President Obama conveyed similar sentiments in 2009 when attempting to 'reset' relations with Russia. Yet there were 4,500 American troops in the multinational force of 20,000 that fought the Reds around the port of Archangel according to a new book, *The Lenin Plot*.[22]

Every allied government had now agreed to strengthen its forces operating in Russia. Though most were British, some American, French, Italian, and even Japanese forces landed at Murmansk and Archangel. Major General Alfred Knox, chief of the British military mission in Siberia, was ordered to go to Vladivostok. Lord Robert Cecil explained to the War Cabinet 'that friendly elements among the Russian troops should be collected and formed into an army'.[23] British troops were also present in Baku on the Caspian Sea and Batumi on the Black Sea, guarding the southern flank against possible threats to the Middle East and India.

The advance of the Czech troops may well have precipitated the killing of the tsar. The royal family were being held in Yekaterinburg in western Siberia, which had originally been far from any military activity. However, the Czechs' rapid progress brought them close to the town, where they might potentially free the royal captives. On 17 July, the tsar and his family were all shot in cold blood. Fears of the Czechs taking the town were not unfounded, and just a week after the murders it did indeed fall to them. History might have been very different if this had happened before the tsar was killed. As it was, when the deaths were announced, the main mood in Russia was described as indifference.[24]

In Britain, views were divided over the question of intervention, particularly as the situation deteriorated into civil war in Russia. At War Cabinet meetings on 17 and 22 July, Lloyd George seemed less keen on military involvement. He argued that, for the sake of liberty, the Russian nation should have the right to set up any government they chose: 'If they chose a Republican government or a Bolshevist government or a Monarchical government it was no concern of ours.'[25] Nevertheless, cabinet policy did not change. The Czech troops increased their control of the Trans-Siberian Railway with the help of the allied forces. As the civil war gathered momentum, the allied troops increasingly came into conflict with Bolshevik forces.

Unlike Lloyd George, Churchill was a key figure in the pro-interventionist camp, though as he was not formally a full member, he only attended War Cabinet meetings occasionally. Following the shooting of a personal acquaintance, the British naval attaché Captain Cromie, during a Bolshevik raid on the embassy in Petrograd on 31 August, Churchill wrote a hard-line paper for the War Cabinet. In it he outlined a strategy that Britain was never in a position to implement but whose central essence has recently come back into international human rights policy, for example, in the poisoning of Russian opposition leader Alexei Navalny (see Chapter 10).

> The only policy which is likely to be effective, either for the past or the future, is to mark down the personalities of the Bolshevik government as the objects upon whom justice will be executed, however long it takes, and to make them feel that their punishment will become an important object of British policy to be held steadily in view through all phases of the war and of the settlement. The exertions which a nation is prepared to make to protect its individual representatives or citizens from outrage is one of the truest measures of its greatness as an organised State.[26]

The War Cabinet consequently sent a telegram to the Soviet government threatening reprisals. More broadly, Churchill pushed for the intervention to continue, saying in the War Cabinet of 6 September that Britain should not give up the Allied control of the Trans-Siberian Railway in any circumstances.

But Churchill appears not to have been present on 18 October when the question of continuing British intervention in Russia was discussed and differences of opinion were aired. Foreign Secretary Balfour argued that the main justification for British involvement in the war had been 'to prevent German aggression and absorption of that country'. The South African General Smuts spoke of Bolshevism as 'a danger to the whole world'. Lord Cecil said that he 'hated the idea of abandoning to Bolshevik fury all those who had helped us', but he could not see how Bolshevism could be destroyed by 'military interference'.[27] Churchill was, however, invited to a subsequent session on 10 November 1918, the day before the Armistice. There, Churchill is recorded as saying, 'We might have to build up the Germany Army as it was important to get Germany on her legs again for fear of the spread of Bolshevism' – speaking, it would seem, as a realist, as distinct from a romanticist.[28]

On 13 November, Balfour chaired an emergency meeting in the Foreign Office with two other members of the War Cabinet, Milner and Cecil, to discuss the situation in Russia. Balfour set out two principles for discussion, which are recorded in the minutes.

> 1. The British Government cannot embark on an anti-Bolshevik crusade in Russia. It was natural that our advisers on the spot should take a contrary line, as they were obsessed with the external and visible violence of Bolshevism. On the other hand, the people of this country would not consent to such a crusade.
>
> 2. It is necessary that support should be afforded to the border States of Western Russia from the Baltic to the Black Sea. These States should be recognised, and support should follow on recognition.[29]

Ultimately, their decisions were in favour of continued British intervention, including: continued occupation of Murmansk and Archangel; recognition for the anti-Bolshevik forces at

Omsk; maintenance of British troops in Siberia; provision of military supplies for the anti-Bolshevik commander General Denikin; occupation of the Baku–Batumi railway in the Caucasus; provision of military supplies to Latvia, Lithuania, and Estonia.

At the War Cabinet meeting the next day, Balfour noted that 'a military crusade against Bolshevism was impossible, and would involve us in military operations of unknown magnitude'. Cecil added that 'it would be fatal to let it be thought that we were committed to an anti-Bolshevik crusade'. As, according to Balfour, it 'was useless to attempt anything in Great Russia', the focus should be in Siberia and south-east Russia. He went on to say that, in relation to the western border states of Russia, he 'took the view that we could not allow them to be overwhelmed by Central Russia and incorporated into Central Russia, as these States contained populations of different race, language, and religion, and were, on the whole, more civilised and cultivated than the Great Russians'.[30] Lloyd George supported Balfour. The minutes run as follows: 'The Prime Minister stated that he was in entire agreement with the Foreign Secretary as to the general line of policy to be pursued.'[31]

The minutes of that meeting also point to domestic concerns, recording that:

The Prime Minister said that it was important that the public in England should realise more fully what Bolshevism meant in practice. France was more secure against Bolshevism, owing to the existence of a large population of peasant proprietors. Here we had a great, inflammable, industrial population, and it was very desirable that our industrial population should know how industrial workers had suffered equally with the rest of the population of Russia at the hands of the Bolsheviks.[32]

In this regard, the Foreign Office was tasked with collecting as much material as possible on the behaviour of the Bolshevik government with a view to its quick publication. Churchill was to play his part too. A fortnight later, in a speech in his Dundee constituency, he said:

Russia is being rapidly reduced by the Bolsheviks to an animal form of barbarism. The cost of living has multiplied 37 times. The paper money will not buy food or necessaries. Civil war is proceeding in all directions. The Bolsheviks maintain themselves by bloody and wholesale butcheries and murders carried out to a large extent by Chinese executioners and armoured cars. Work of all kinds is at a standstill. The peasants are hoarding their grain. The town and cities only keep themselves alive by pillaging the surrounding country. We must expect that enormous numbers (probably more than we have lost in the whole war) will die of starvation during the winter. Civilisation is being completely extinguished over gigantic areas, while Bolsheviks hop and caper like troops of ferocious baboons amid the ruins of cities and the corpses of their victims.[33]

Following the general election in December 1918, which secured a massive victory for the governing coalition under Lloyd George, with the Conservatives winning 379 seats and the Coalition Liberals 127 seats, Churchill was appointed secretary of state for war and air. His work was to be dominated by Russia and on reducing the size of the post-war army. Not unreasonably, the public wanted early demobilisation; certainly, there are few more popular slogans for politicians than to promise to 'bring the boys home'. The cabinet therefore faced a huge dilemma in terms of how it dealt with Russia now the war was formally over. By the end of 1918, Martin Gilbert states, more than 180,000 non-Russian troops were deployed within the frontiers of the former Russian Empire: British, American, Japanese, French, Czech, Serb, Greek, and Italian. These troops were being increasingly drawn into the civil war between the Bolsheviks and their opponents. By this time, the anti-Bolshevik White Russian forces amounted to over 300,000 men, and they were looking for military, financial, and moral support from the allies as they started driving the Bolsheviks back towards Moscow.[34]

Against this backdrop, Churchill wrote in a memorandum:

Most people wish to get free from Russia and to leave her to work out her own salvation or stew in her own juice assisted by any good advice we may have to spare. Nobody wants to intervene in Russian affairs. Russia is a very large country, a very old country, a very disagreeable country inhabited by immense numbers of ignorant people largely possessed of lethal weapons and in a state of extreme disorder. Also Russia is a long way off ... We wish now to bring home our soldiers, reduce our taxes and enjoy our victory. On these points there is general agreement here. Unhappily, events are driving in a different direction and nowadays events are very powerful things. There never was a time when events were so much stronger than human beings. We may abandon Russia: but Russia will not abandon us. We shall retire and she will follow. The bear is padding on bloody paws across the snow to the Peace Conference.[35]

This was a very thoughtful analysis of the democratic dilemma that often faces politicians in the aftermath of war. Churchill tended to lose sight of these democratic constraints in his passionate wish to get rid of Lenin and his policies in what was always a long shot. Lloyd George, far more sensitive to public opinion and less ready to rely on military solutions to political problems, was prepared to use his authority to constrain Churchill. This was not achieved through indecision or prime ministerial command but predominately through democratic debate within the coalition government. Lloyd George was patient but ultimately firm with Churchill.

A meeting of the Imperial War Cabinet[36] was convened on 31 December 1918 to address the policy towards the Bolsheviks. Lloyd George said the existing position was 'highly unsatisfactory' since the allies 'were neither interfering effectively in Russia nor evacuating it'.[37] Rather than proposing a British, or imperial, solution, he suggested that the essential thing was to arrive at 'a definite Allied policy towards Russia', and this should be the first 'essential task' at the Paris Peace Conference. Summarising the difficulties in deciding what course to take, Lloyd George noted that:

He himself had found himself frequently leaning first in one direction, and then in another, owing to the absolute contradiction between the information supplied from Russia by men of equally good authority. We were, in fact, never dealing with ascertained, or, perhaps, even ascertainable, facts. Russia was a jungle in which no one could say what was within a few yards of him. In any case nothing could be worse than having no policy, and it was better to proceed resolutely on a wrong hypothesis than to go on hesitating as the Allies had been doing.[38]

I have considerable sympathy with Lloyd George's views on hesitation and indecision, that 'nothing could be worse than having no policy, and it was better to proceed resolutely'. I saw the perils of indecision in Iran when the shah could not make up his mind during the autumn of 1978. It was obvious that support for the shah inside Iran was weakening, and his own hesitation and indecision was the problem.[39] He could not decide whether to clamp down militarily, leave the country, or admit his own cancer and appoint a regent with the toughness to clamp down militarily. With the rulers in the Gulf States in late 1978 watching Britain's every move and fearing weakness, it was decided Britain would remain a friend, stay on course, and not cancel the queen's visit to Iran, as predictably the shah did this himself, nor to hedge one's bets by opening discussions with Ayatollah Khomeini's people outside Paris, as the Americans eventually did. I saw it, too, in the Balkans from January 1993 when Warren Christopher became secretary of state and President Clinton's incoming administration was indecisive and divided. Clinton only agreed to use force to implement a settlement after the genocide of Bosnian Muslim men and boys in and around Srebrenica in July 1995 (see pages 226–8).[40]

In Lloyd George's cabinet in 1919, Churchill argued that the more the Allies, the US, and France attempted to move away from this problem the more entangled they would become. He favoured joint action. While he was all for negotiations, the minutes record that he considered there to be:

no chance of securing such a settlement unless it was known that we had the power and the will to enforce our views. What we should say to the Russians was that if they were ready to come together, we would help them: and if they refused, we would use force to restore the situation and set up a democratic government. In his view, Bolshevism in Russia represented a mere fraction of the population and would be exposed and swept away by a General Election held under Allied auspices.[41]

Subsequent events were to demonstrate that this last thought of Churchill's was far too optimistic a view of the revolutionary struggle in Russia. A scene in the film of Boris Pasternak's wonderful novel *Doctor Zhivago* shows the beautiful scenery of the fictitious Yuriatin in the Ural Mountains set alongside the Trans-Siberian Railway. It gave, and continues to give, viewers a hopelessly romantic image of the civil war, in part because of the beauty of the landscape and the isolation of the two lovers, Lara and Yuri, waiting for the fighting to resolve itself. In reality, there was never any ethereal quality to this bitter, brutal struggle.

A number of developments made for a longer and more difficult struggle for the anti-Bolshevik Whites as 1919 approached. The sizeable contingent of Czech soldiers marooned in Russia had lost the will to fight on in Russia since the declaration of Czech independence on 28 October 1918. In November, Admiral Kolchak had become Supreme Ruler of the Whites. As Orlando Figes explains,

For the next fourteen months Kolchak was the paramount leader of the counter revolution, along with [Deputy

Supreme Ruler General] Denikin. It is somewhat fitting that an Admiral without a fleet should have been the leader of a government based 4,000 miles from the nearest port, for Kolchak was one of history's misfits.[42]

Neither Kolchak nor Denikin had sufficient knowledge of politics, and, while they had some military successes, they were too firmly rooted in the old Russia and not attuned to the aspirations of the people, including a broad spectrum of national minorities who did not want to return to the former structures. Denikin's propaganda unit saw their main aim as convincing the allies, rather than his own compatriots, of the merits of the Whites' cause. The factory workers and villagers, meanwhile, were left to soak up Lenin's messages about the new revolution, promising improvements in their deplorably low standard of living.

By the time Paris Peace Conference convened in January 1919, seven British generals were already operating in Russia, commanding 14,000 British troops sent there during 1918 while Milner had been secretary of state for war.[43] However, the British Army officers advising the Whites had huge problems in understanding – let alone influencing – Denikin's strategy and tactics. The battles fought between the Whites and Reds in south Russia were very different from the war they had left on the Western Front, where many of the British officers had served. By the end of the First World War, they had become used to fighting in operations that effectively combined the firepower of infantry, artillery, and, eventually, tanks, supported from the air and backed up by an efficient logistics chain. The Russian Army had been much less successful in adjusting its own military doctrine. While Denikin's forces had made rapid advances in the late spring and summer of 1919, they were to be held back by logistical problems. They began to rely increasingly on the railways, positioning cavalry units on the flanks while the armoured trains advanced and engaged the enemy. The infantry followed in light peasant carts, *droshkies*, which also carried machine guns.[44] Those tactics worked as long as they controlled the railway lines, but the Reds soon focused their activity on disrupting the rail links.

Ahead of the peace conference, the Imperial War Cabinet gave Lloyd George all the authority he needed from the countries like Australia, Canada, New Zealand, and others to guide him in Paris. The minutes summed up Lloyd George's preferred policy and, while Churchill had been allowed to make his case for more intervention, Churchill had lost his argument. Sir Henry Wilson, chief of the imperial general staff, met Lloyd George for lunch when he arrived in Paris on 12 January, recording in his diary: 'LG is opposed to knocking out Bolshevism. He does not like any proposal to arm Russian prisoners now in Germany even if they express a wish to go and fight ag[st] [against] the Bolshevists.'[45] Writing the following day, after a meeting of the Imperial War Cabinet chaired by Lloyd George, Wilson noted: 'It was quite clear that the meeting favoured *no* troops being sent to fight Bolshevism but on the other hand to help those States which we considered were Independent States by giving them arms etc.'[46]

Churchill arrived in Paris ten days later, only to find that Lloyd George and Wilson had agreed to invite the Bolsheviks to talks on the island of Prinkipo, near Constantinople. This was a major decision by any standard, as it gave some form of recognition to the Bolsheviks, who had been excluded from the main conference. On the morning of 24 January, an angry

Churchill had met the head of the military mission in Paris, General Spears, whose wife's diary entry mentions that her husband 'had a long talk with Winston who said he had a row with LG, while the latter was shaving, about Russia. It seems it was LG's idea to invite Bolsheviks to Prinkipo & Wilson rushed in and took it all on himself. Angrily, Winston told LG "one might as well legalise sodomy as recognise the Bolsheviks".'[47]

Russia proved to be a crucial moment in Churchill's political career. He owed his reinstatement after Gallipoli to Lloyd George, at some considerable cost in personal relationships with Conservative ministers in his government. Furthermore, Lloyd George had extended every political courtesy, enabling him to argue his case in both the War Cabinet and the Imperial War Cabinet. Now Churchill was not only opposing his own Liberal Party prime minister, known as 'the man who won the war', but he was also challenging the president of the United States. Time would reveal it to be a foolish choice.

It was clear that both Lloyd George and Wilson saw the Paris Peace Conference as a place for international negotiations, but Churchill could not or would not recognise the political realities within which these two heads of government operated. Both Lloyd George and Wilson had elements of populism as part of their political appeal. More importantly, both recognised the military limitations they faced in Russia. If ambition was Churchill's driving force, as many believed, it would have been wiser to roll with the punch and accept the Prinkipo talks. If he tried to do so, it was not obvious, and he was not the only one rightly sceptical of Lenin and Trotsky ever being ready to sit round the negotiating table. The reality should have been very clear to Churchill. Lloyd George was not ready to embark on another war. Churchill must have hoped Lloyd George was the same man who, in the face of the events of 1914, had been stiffened by Churchill to accept war.[48] In reality, Lloyd George was a man programmed in his own mind for peace. Churchill never seriously contemplated resignation. He would stay in Lloyd George's government until it was voted down by Conservative MPs in 1922.

On 27 January 1920, Churchill wrote a comprehensive letter to Lloyd George setting out his views on the way forward in Russia. It shows that Churchill was not as intransigent as might have been suggested by earlier correspondence.

> From the mere War Office standpoint, I object very much indeed to keeping soldiers in the field who are denied the transport, the technical services, the doctors, the hospital staffs and even the mules that they require according to their numbers. But that is what we are doing. These poor men are writing cheques on our account and in our name which we have neither the intention nor the means to honour. They have written a good many already.
>
> (1)...
>
> I consider, in view of what you have told me, that the anti-Bolshevik Russians should be told that they have got to shift for themselves, that we wish them well, but that all we can do is to give them moral support by the presence of such volunteers – officers and men – who are ready to serve in these theatres, and material in money, arms and supplies.[49]

On 5 February, Lloyd George responded to Churchill's letter, saying any reinforcements needed 'to secure the health, comfort and nourishment of troops should be sent without delay'.[50]

On 4 February, the Bolsheviks agreed to come to Prinkipo,

but they had flagged a number of issues of concern to them, including repayment of debts and territorial compensation. At the request of Balfour, the British foreign secretary, Clemenceau called a meeting in Paris on 14 February of the so-called Council of Ten to discuss the response to the Bolsheviks, as President Wilson was shortly due to return home.

As well as the British delegation, which included Balfour and Churchill, there were representatives from France (Clemenceau, Marshal Foch, and Pichon, the foreign minister), Italy (Baron Sonnino, the foreign minister), and the United States (President Wilson and General Bliss). At Balfour's request, Churchill laid out the British cabinet's position and highlighted the need for a decision to end the uncertainty around the military intervention. He ended by saying that if the Prinkipo meeting did not result in an end to hostilities in Russia, 'this unsatisfactory condition might last an indefinite time'.[51]

The allies held differing opinions. Prime Minister Clemenceau argued that a short and unexpected meeting was not the place to settle such an important issue. President Wilson contended that the allies should withdraw their troops from all parts of Russian territory, as they were not doing any good and as there was no clarity on what they were trying to achieve, or indeed who they were fighting for. Often the allies found themselves supporting groups, such as the Cossacks, who were focused on their own regional issues rather than an overall solution. President Wilson saw the Prinkipo meeting as an opportunity to find out more about what the Russians were thinking and planning, and, to that end, he was ready to send an American representative to meet the Bolsheviks.

Churchill agreed on the need to establish a clear policy, and he noted that a complete withdrawal was at least logical and clear. He feared, however, that this would lead to the collapse of the resistance efforts and the defeat of the anti-Bolshevik forces. Wilson acknowledged that it was a challenging dilemma, but, in his view, it was not possible to provide further troops. In any case, the allies would ultimately have to withdraw, and so in reality they were only deferring the problem. When asked by Churchill if the council would approve of arming the anti-Bolshevik forces if the Prinkipo talks failed, Woodrow Wilson replied 'that he hesitated to express any definite opinion', but that whatever the council decided, he would 'cast in his lot with the rest'.[52]

In reporting on the outcome of the meeting to Lloyd George, Churchill added a personal recommendation that, in the event of the Prinkipo talks failing, the allies should undertake a high-level military review of the situation and consider the likelihood of successful action against the Bolsheviks. They could then make an informed decision on whether to engage or withdraw completely. Churchill also proposed a wireless message to the Bolsheviks, repeating the Prinkipo invitation, on the condition that there was a ceasefire and that within days, by 25 February, the Bolsheviks would have withdrawn at least five miles from the anti-Bolshevik frontline.

Lloyd George replied to Churchill on 16 February, though he was not to receive it until the following day, by which time Churchill had sent a second message. This expanded on his initial proposal, calling for the immediate establishment of a military commission that would prepare a plan for war against the Bolsheviks, along with recommendations on its chances of success. The second message fuelled Lloyd George's concerns that Churchill was advocating war against the Bolsheviks. In his initial reply on 16 February, sent via his secretary Philip

Kerr, Lloyd George approved the approach Churchill had laid out in his original message, but he made clear that, if the Bolsheviks did not accept the conditions, Churchill should not commit Britain to any major contribution of men or money. In his view:

> The main idea ought to be to enable Russia to save herself if she desires to do so, and if she does not take advantage of the opportunity then it means either that she does not wish to be saved from the Bolsheviks or that she is beyond saving. There is only one justification for interfering in Russia, that Russia wants it. If she does then Kolchak, Krasnoff and Denikin ought to be able to raise a much larger force than the Bolsheviks. This force we could equip and a well-equipped force of willing men would soon overthrow the Bolshevik army of unwilling conscripts especially if the whole population is against them.
>
> If on the other hand Russia is not behind Krasnoff and his coadjutors it is an outrage of every British principle of freedom that we should use foreign armies to force upon Russia a Government which is repugnant to its people.[53]

Lloyd George followed up with a second telegram making clear that the cabinet had not considered doing anything other than provide equipment to forces in anti-Bolshevik areas, and only in the event that there was no chance of reaching a peaceful solution. If the Russian population was indeed anti-Bolshevik, that support should suffice. If, in fact, the Russian people were not anti-Bolshevik, then Britain had no business in intervening in their affairs. Indeed, there was a risk that the course Churchill was proposing would only serve to drive anti-Bolsheviks into the arms of the Bolsheviks. In any case, Britain could not afford another war. And furthermore, Lloyd George noted that any proposal to go to war against the Bolsheviks could stir up opposition to the continuing war among British workers at home.

The Council of Ten reconvened in the afternoon of 17 February. They were divided on Churchill's proposal that their military representatives should examine a possible intervention. The French and Italians supported him, but Wilson's adviser, Colonel House, strongly protested and, much to Churchill's annoyance, Balfour supported House. Following the session, Churchill again wrote to Lloyd George. He informed him that, given US opposition to establishing a formal military commission, Balfour had proposed informal talks between the military representatives of both sides, who would report back to their own respective delegations on the outcome. This approach was agreed by the allies, though Clemenceau had noted that this informal route was a strange one for the allies to be taking on such an important issue. Churchill concluded by telling Lloyd George: 'You are therefore committed at some date in the near future to receiving an informal document embodying certain military opinions bearing upon Russia. You are committed to nothing else.'[54]

A few days later, Churchill spoke at a lunch at the Mansion House, having earlier met with Lloyd George. It appeared that their positions were finally converging. In his speech, he said:

> If Russia is to be saved, as I pray she may be saved, she must be saved by Russians. It must be by Russian manhood and Russian courage and Russian virtue that the rescue and regeneration of this once mighty nation and famous branch of the European family can alone be achieved. ... Russia must

be saved by Russian exertions, and it must be from the heart of the Russian people and with their strong arm that the conflict against Bolshevism in Russia must be mainly waged.[55]

Still, differences remained, particularly over the detail of what support for the anti-Bolsheviks would entail in practice. Churchill remained deeply frustrated and concerned that no clear policy on Russia was emerging, and that this would lead to problems in the future for Britain and the allies. In a letter to Lloyd George, which he drafted but never sent, he wrote in frustration: 'When we have abandoned Russia, she will be restored by Germany and Japan, and these three Powers together will constitute a menace for Britain, France and the United States very similar to that which existed before the present war.'[56] This was a prescient warning for what lay ahead in the short-term Ribbentrop/Molotov reconciliation (see page 127).

Returning to France, Churchill breakfasted with Lloyd George on 9 March, and he followed up in writing on the conclusions of their discussion on Russia. Murmansk and Archangel were to be evacuated once weather conditions allowed, and volunteers could be sent to facilitate the withdrawal, but there would be no ongoing occupation. British forces would also be withdrawn from the Caucasus; however, given the geographic extent of the deployment, Churchill noted that it could take three to four months to conduct this in an orderly fashion. As for General Denikin's anti-Bolshevik forces, they would be provided with military supplies and equipment, and assisted by a military mission, up to 2,000 strong, providing technical assistance and training. These men would be volunteers, signed up specifically for this duty; there was no question of ordering troops to undertake these roles. This support would be subject to Denikin undertaking not to attack Georgia and other areas in the south. Similarly, a volunteer military mission would replace the British troops deployed in support of the Whites at Omsk. This was certainly not the substantial British support package that the anti-Bolsheviks had been hoping for. Church-ill, meanwhile, was apparently accepting the defeat of his poli-cies towards Russia gracefully.

Before long, however, Churchill was recoiling from this position, as seen in an extraordinary outburst on 14 March, when he wrote bitterly and emotionally to Lloyd George about the allies' decision to pull back from Russia. While acknowl-edging that Wilson and Lloyd George had taken their decision on how to deal with Russia, he nevertheless wrote as if for the history books:

> It is my duty, however, to warn you of the profound mis-givings with which I watch the steady degeneration of so many resources and powers which, vigorously used, might entirely have altered the course of events ... when their armies are menacing Persia and Afghanistan and their mis-sionaries are at the gates of India, when one after another the Border States in the West have been undermined by want and propaganda or overborne by criminal violence, not only the League of Nations but the British Empire, with which we are particularly concerned, will wake up to the fact that Russia is not a negligible factor in world politics.[57]

On receiving this, Lloyd George must have wondered whether Churchill had lost all sense of proportion. Worse, his judge-ment was showing signs of lacking the maturity appropriate for a minister in command of the armed services. In a further blow,

Lloyd George was told that the French would withdraw from Odesa, as they did not believe Denikin's anti-Bolshevik forces would prevail. The next day, Churchill contacted Marshal Foch directly, stating, 'The facts at our disposal do not confirm the adverse views you have formed.'[58] He later followed up with a letter to Clemenceau, asking for French assistance in extricating the allied forces.

The War Cabinet also remained divided. At its 31 March meeting, which Churchill only arrived at when the discussion on Russia was concluding, Lord Curzon argued against an early evacuation of Archangel and Murmansk. When the chancellor of the exchequer, Austen Chamberlain, proposed reaching an arrangement with the Bolshevik government to facilitate the withdrawal of the troops, Curzon challenged him: 'Any recognition of, or negotiations with, even a provisional Bolshevik government would give considerable impetus to Bolshevik prestige throughout Russia.'[59]

The French went ahead with the withdrawal of their forces from Odesa on 5 April, without informing Denikin in advance; indeed, they destroyed a lot of equipment that his forces could have used. On 8 April, the minister of education, H. A. L. Fisher, recorded a private conversation with Churchill in his diary, writing that: 'Winston says he will seriously consider resignation before submitting to ignominious withdrawal from Russia ... After conquering all the huns – tigers of the world – I will not submit to be beaten by the baboons!'[60]

Churchill continued to express fears that the Bolshevik Revolution would spread in the same way as the French Revolution had spread, and, in the first instance, its spread to a defeated Germany had to be prevented. In a letter of 9 April to Lloyd George, Churchill summed up his policy as 'Feed Germany;

fight Bolshevism; make Germany fight Bolshevism', though he added that 'it may well be that it is too late for this'.[61] Violet Bonham Carter, Asquith's daughter, later recalled Churchill as saying his policy was 'Kill the Bolshie, kiss the Hun.'[62] The fundamental problem for Churchill was that Germany, having lost the war, had not the slightest interest in getting into another. What's more, no one in the cabinet shared his enthusiasm for either Admiral Kolchak or General Denikin; they simply wanted the war to end.

Concerns about the way the anti-Bolshevik forces were conducting the war were also on the rise. In the House of Commons on 29 May 1919, Colonel Josiah Wedgwood, a friend of Churchill's and member of the Labour Party, spoke of the 'White Terror', including outrages committed by Denikin: 'At Jekaterinoslav Denikin ordered every Red Russian found in possession of Red literature to be shot forthwith. At Batarsk, in the Don district, every man with a son in the Red Guard was killed. In one place every tenth workman was shot as an example to the rest.'[63] Churchill said he was 'astounded' by the allegations against Denikin, which he was not aware of, and which he believed would surely have been reported by the British officers with Denikin. Nevertheless, Churchill said he would investigate. Churchill went on to speak of Denikin's successes, 'aided by rebellions which have broken out among the people'. He added that with supplies of British munitions now increasing, he had been 'advised that we may look forward with a very reasonable measure of confidence to the immediate future prospects of General Denikin's Army', though he acknowledged that 'a considerable setback has occurred on the southern sector of Admiral Koltchak's front'. The next day, the *Daily Herald*, a Labour-supporting newspaper, had a leading article criticising

Churchill: 'The gambler of Gallipoli ... expounded the policy of the "second throw" ... The gambler's first throw was Gallipoli ... His second throw is the new war in Russia, to back reaction in the persons of Kolchak and Denikin'.[64]

In reality, the anti-Bolshevik forces were suffering serious problems. In June, Kolchak's forces were beaten back on all fronts, in particular suffering a serious setback in Siberia, where they were beaten by a heavily outnumbered Bolshevik force. Nevertheless, Churchill continued his outspoken opposition to the Bolsheviks, and this, combined with his support of Denikin, caused public concern. On 27 June 1919, the Labour Party Conference at Southport voted unanimously to condemn intervention in Russia. At the War Cabinet on the same day, the permanent secretary at the Ministry of Labour warned that labour circles had very strong feelings over intervention in Russia. According to the minutes, 'He himself had been surprised at the extent to which men of all classes were now coming round to supporting the Labour view that the Soviet Government ought to be given a fair chance.'[65]

Denikin's forces made good progress over the summer, and, continuing to fight the general's corner, Churchill prepared a 5,000-word memorandum entitled 'Russian Policy', which was circulated to the cabinet on 22 September 1919. In it, he explained that Denikin remained in a strong position and that he controlled a region with a population of some thirty million. Deserting him would 'make certain that whatever else may be the outcome, we have a hostile Russia to face'.[66]

Lloyd George was angered by Churchill's memorandum, and he wrote exasperated to him that same day to make 'one last effort to induce you to throw off this obsession which, if you forgive me for saying so, is upsetting your balance'.[67] This is an exact description of what was happening to Churchill under the admitted strains and stresses of the crisis. Perhaps recognising the futility of his request, Lloyd George had added, 'I again ask you to let Russia be, at any rate for a few days.'[68] He was bluntly accusing Churchill of being 'so obsessed by Russia' that he was neglecting the core task with which he had been entrusted, namely reducing the military expenditure of the War Office and Air Department across all spheres of operation. He explained that the cabinet, at considerable cost, had lived up to all the commitments they had made in supporting Churchill's previous efforts in Russia, but, while they would stick by the agreed policy, they were not prepared to go any further. Lloyd George also added that the French, despite their anti-Bolshevik talk, were also not prepared to do any more. Both he and France considered the German situation to be the priority.

Churchill replied to Lloyd George's letter also on 22 September 1919 with a mixture of hurt pride, contrition, and a little defiance. After first pointing out the challenges of meeting his mandate to demobilise an immense army and reduce expenditure given ongoing commitments to a range of operational theatres, including Ireland, Palestine, Egypt, and Mesopotamia, Churchill turned his attention to Russia. He expressed his frustration about what British policy towards Russia really entailed: 'I have publicly asked to be told what commitment in Russia is due to me. No one has been able to reply.' Churchill also pointed out that the decisions on deploying troops in Russia and providing arms and munitions to the Whites had been taken before he became the minister responsible. He was trying to 'wind up these commitments if possible without dishonour'. Ultimately, he said, his goal in writing to Lloyd George, 'chief & oldest political friend', had been to 'try to impress upon you the realisation I have of the intense & horrible situation in Russia & of its profound influence upon all our affairs. I may get rid of my "obsession" or you may get rid of me: but you will not get rid of Russia: nor of the consequences of a policy wh[ich] for nearly a year it has been impossible to define.'[69]

Lloyd George was to hold fast to the withdrawal plan, despite Churchill's protestations. Gilbert describes an informal meeting between Lloyd George, H. A. L. Fisher, and others on 23 September. 'We discuss the unpopularity of the Russian policy,' Fisher recorded in his diary. 'LG thinks Winston is a greater source of weakness than of strength to the Gov.' Lloyd George went on to describe Churchill as like the counsel employed by a solicitor, not because he is the best man, but because 'he would be dangerous on the other side'.[70] Lloyd George must have wondered, too, whether he had been right to rescue Churchill from his linkage to Gallipoli and defy his Conservative critics within the cabinet.

Was Churchill obsessed by Russia? Could the Bolsheviks have been defeated? Churchill's behaviour suggests he was obsessed, at least by the situation in Russia, and Lloyd George certainly thought he was. Indeed, such an obsession is understandable in the light of the threat he believed Russian Communism posed, and to which history bears witness, and his desire to tackle it before it had the opportunity to root. But with Britain and its allies exhausted by war, Churchill was championing a lost cause. The Bolsheviks, by any standard, needed to be defeated. Perhaps there was a moment in 1917, not 1918, when Churchill came back into government, that the anti-Bolshevik forces might have been able to beat the Reds, helped only by money from America, Britain, and France. But in terms of serious fighting, it was always going to have to be done by the Russians. There was no scope to divert troops to Russia that year while the war against Germany, not yet won, was bound to have first call on men and munitions. Nor did the allied politicians have the time to form a proper assessment of, let alone transform, internal Russian politics.

Two figures were crucial to the Provisional Russian Government's struggle and success in 1917, and they needed to work together. One was General Alexey Brusilov, one of the best professional soldiers in the Imperial Army, who became commander-in-chief of the Russian Army in May 1917 (and later served as a senior adviser to the Red Army). The other was Alexander Kerensky, 'the ideal figure to bring the coalition back together: as a member of both the Soviet and Duma circles which had formed the Provisional Government he made a human bridge between the socialist and liberal camps'.[71] Yet Kerensky's fatal mistake as minister of war, just before he became prime minister, was to rashly dismiss Brusilov, following the failure of the 'Kerensky offensive' in July 1917, the last Russian offensive of the war. He replaced him with his former deputy, General Kornilov, who was to become a rival and eventually launch a coup attempt, which severely weakened Kerensky's position. By the time of the October Revolution, Kerensky's earlier popular appeal had gone to his head, and he had become hubristic and vainglorious. He took over Alexander III's luxurious suite and slept in the tsar's huge bed. Confident of victory, Kerensky declared war on the Bolsheviks, only to find that the Military Revolutionary Committee, masterminded by Lenin, was, in the words of Orlando Figes, 'able to supersede the authority of the Provisional Government inside the Petrograd garrison and become the leading organisational force of the Bolshevik insurrection'.[72]

In retrospect, it is difficult to make a convincing case that by January 1919 there was anything that the allied victors, starting to assemble in Paris, could have done to rescue Russia from Bolshevism. Such a cause would, at the very least, have required a significantly different policy approach by the British cabinet. It also would have needed a far greater readiness to understand the depth of feeling and legitimate grievances of the many Russian people supporting the Reds. Under the tsars, the Russians had not seen anything like the progress towards government by the people that those living in Europe's other monarchies had witnessed both prior to, and as a result of, the war.

As for Churchill, he was completely right to warn Lloyd George that 'you will not get rid of Russia'. In his book on Churchill, Roy Jenkins writes that what he calls Churchill's 'Russian adventurism' not only pitched him on the right of the Conversative Party for the first time but also distanced him further from Labour and trade union opinion than Liberal politicians and even many Conservatives.[73]

He also highlights confrontation between Churchill and Ernest Bevin, then the leader of the newly amalgamated Transport and General Workers' Union, over whether the ship the *Jolly George* should sail with arms to Poland for use against the Red Army in May 1920. Poland had launched a major offensive against the Bolsheviks in April 1920, to Lloyd George's great alarm. Churchill was also faced with growing public opposition to anti-Bolshevik intervention among the British population, with the 'Hands Off Russia!' movement gaining momentum. Bevin won; the arms were not loaded, and Britain avoided further intervention.

Despite these differences with Lloyd George, Churchill stayed on as secretary of state for war, mainly dealing with

Ireland and Turkey before succeeding Lord Milner as colonial secretary on 14 February 1921. While still obsessed by the Bolshevik crisis, Churchill also took issue with Lloyd George's Middle East policies and was critical of the Greeks; he believed that without a balanced peace treaty with Turkey, it would be impossible to resolve the issues of the Middle East. Lord Riddell's diary entry on 26 June 1920 records Lloyd George's views on the issue.

> The Turks nearly brought about our defeat in the war. It was a near thing. You cannot trust them and they are a decadent race. The Greeks on the other hand, are our friends, and they are a rising people. We want to be on good terms with the Greeks and the Italians. We must secure Constantinople and the Dardanelles. You cannot do that effectively without crushing the Turkish power.[74]

Lloyd George's views were to prevail, and Britain sided with Greece in the Greco-Turkish War, which lasted until 1922. However, as mentioned above, this could not prevent a Greek defeat by Mustafa Kemal, who would become President Atatürk.

Later in 1920, with a nod to the days of the Great Game, Churchill wrote a memorandum for the cabinet dated 23 November.

> We ought to come to terms with Mustapha Kemal and arrive at a good peace with Turkey which will secure our interests at Constantinople and ease our position in Egypt, Mesopotamia, Persia and India. We should thus recreate that Turkish barrier to Russian ambitions which has always been of the utmost importance to us.[75]

But the Bolsheviks were a step ahead of Churchill. Norman Stone writes, 'The Bolsheviks of 1920 had an extraordinary understanding as to how central Asia, the Turkic world of "Great Turan" should be handled. They played a very weird chess...'[76] To counter Enver Pasha, Stone claims that,

> the Bolsheviks used the Ankara nationalists, and did a bargain: Turkey would renounce the Caucasus and central Asia. 1,000 kg of gold, and 1,000s of rifles reached Ankara, and that defeated the French in Cilicia. Then the French came to terms; and in 1921 the nationalists were strong enough to defeat the Anglo-Greek attack on the River Sakarya in September.[77]

At the end of February 1921, successful Soviet diplomacy saw Russia sign a Treaty of Friendship with Persia, where Britain had significant interests, and then establish relations with Mustafa Kemal's Turkey with the signature of the Treaty of Moscow in March – an agreement between two governments that had yet to achieve international recognition.

Meanwhile, Lloyd George had proposed a conference to deal with major economic, financial, and political issues arising from the war; this was scheduled for April 1922 in the Italian city of Genoa. The question of recognising the Russian government was on the agenda. An important step towards granting recognition, certainly in the eyes of the Bolshevik leadership, had been the British signature in March 1921 of an Anglo-Soviet trade agreement, following Bolshevik victory in the civil war. Churchill had, unsurprisingly, opposed this, but as often happens trade can precede full recognition. Yet Churchill was adamantly opposed to Lloyd George's move towards recognising the Bolshevik government even in spite of its humanitarian need, with over ten million people having died of hunger in 1921. The US did not attend the Genoa Conference but had already decided not to recognise Russia. Writing to Lloyd George, Austen Chamberlain urged a cabinet discussion: 'putting aside any feelings of our own, you will readily perceive that our position would be impossible if Winston retired because he was more Tory than the Tory Ministers'.[78] He urged Lloyd George to have a personal talk with Churchill before the cabinet meeting and, on recognition, questioned perceptively whether it would be wise for Britain to grant it 'isolated recognition'.[79]

When Lloyd George spoke in the House of Commons on 3 April in advance of the Genoa Conference, he described the deeper questions about peace with Russia – 'perhaps the most controversial part' of the agenda – as:

> a subject where perhaps legitimate prejudices cloud reason. The doctrine, the demeanour, and the actions of the Bolshevists have undoubtedly been of a character which has excited wrath and just anger, and made it exceedingly difficult for us to exercise judgment when we come to deal with the problem of our relations with that country.

Lloyd George then went on to compare the present situation to that faced by Pitt after the French Revolution and spelt out, not unreasonably, the conditions that had to be met for recognising Russia.

> In substance they mean that Russia must recognise all the conditions imposed and accepted by civilised communities

as the test of fitness for entering into the comity of nations. She must recognise her national obligations. A country that repudiates her obligations because she changes her Government is a country you cannot deal with.

There are long-standing conventions and traditions for maintaining a measure of continuity even when dealing with new governments, and Lloyd George was right to make them explicit for Lenin and his compatriots to understand what recognition entailed.

There was no question of Britain merely recognising regardless, and the conference achieved very little apart from agreeing to reconvene at The Hague (recognition was only to come in 1924 under Britain's first Labour prime minister, Ramsay MacDonald). Lloyd George had judged the mood of the country rightly as cautious over the issue, and no one resigned. Despite the great numbers that welcomed him back at Victoria Station, he did not risk offending anyone.

The coalition was limping along and Ireland had become another divisive issue. On this, Churchill was becoming more attuned to the Tories. Lloyd George's many appointments to the House of Lords had become a sordid dispute, bringing in some cronies for money for his party rather than for what they would contribute. Not much has changed in 2021. In this day and age, a chamber with legislative powers, as in the House of Lords, should at the very least be democratically elected.

Lloyd George's policy towards Turkey, which since 1919 had been embroiled in war against Greece, was, however, a truly major issue and gave rise to serious concerns among the Tories, who feared Britain would be sucked into further military interventions. The retired Conservative Party leader Andrew Bonar

Law published a letter in *The Times* and *Daily Express* on 9 October 1922, ostensibly in support of the strong stand the Lloyd George government had taken against Turkey in an incident at Chanak. He wrote: 'We cannot alone act as the policeman of the world. The financial and social conditions of this country make that impossible.' Bonar Law had made a rare public stand. It was isolationist in tone and reiterated the true Conservative Party position: pro-Turk and deeply alienated by Lloyd George's pro-Greek crusade.[80] The following month, the Conservatives were to contest – and win – the general election as a Conservative Party rather than in coalition with Lloyd George, who was never to hold office again. Churchill also lost his seat.

Lloyd George's final years in office, including his handling of the Russia question, had damaged his legacy. Lord Beaverbrook, the owner of the *Daily Express*, was not the most dispassionate of men, but he knew much about the wielding of power and, in 1922, was a frequent correspondent with Lloyd George. By the time he published his thoughts on Lloyd George in 1963, he had served under Prime Minister Churchill as minister for air production, minister of supply, and lord privy seal. In contrast to his lavish praise of Lloyd George's wartime years, he was a bitter critic of his post-war premiership and felt that hubris was at the root of his problems.[81]

> The Greeks told us of a man in high position, self-confident, so successful as to be overpowering to all others. Then his virtues turned to failings. He committed the crime of arrogance … He struggled against fate, but he was doomed. So it was with Lloyd George in the year 1921 and into 1922. Then all was over. His plans good and bad came to nothing. He fell and never rose again.

The brilliant schemes and stratagems which he resorted to in war ... to save Britain, he now applied with daring and skill to save himself from defeat by the Members of the House of Commons ... To keep the seat of power, the place of patronage, he was prepared to stand out as the leader of Empire-minded men – or appear as the Liberal Apostle of Free Trade: as the Man of Peace in Europe – or the Man of War against Turkey and France: as the hammer of the Russian Bolsheviks – or their noble conciliator ... He took up each position in turn during those tragic years of 1921 and 1922 ... Sometimes and simultaneously he took up contradictory standings. His daring was wonderful to look upon. But to those who never forgot his greatness in his great days, the spectacle wore thin and ere long became pathetic.[82]

As for Churchill, long after the opportunity for 'calming down', as Jenkins noted, he was still writing about Russia using 'the most extravagant language'.[83] In *The Aftermath* (1929), the last volume of Churchill's series on the First World War, he wrote of:

not a wounded Russia only, but a poisoned Russia, an infected Russia, a plague-bearing Russia; a Russia of armed hordes smiting not only with bayonet and with cannon, but accompanied and preceded by typhus-bearing vermin which slew the bodies of men, and political doctrines which destroyed the health and even the soul of nations.[84]

Britain had formally recognised the USSR in February 1924, only to see diplomatic relations broken off by the Baldwin government in 1927 following allegations of espionage. The relationship was finally restored in 1929 under Ramsay Mac-Donald's second Labour government.

Another ten years were to pass before Churchill would shift from his frequent and vehement denunciations of Bolshevist Russia, but there would be a very significant shift coming on the eve of the Second World War.

5

Churchill and Stalin: World War to Cold War

On 18 March 1939, three days after Hitler's troops occupied
Czechoslovakia, Maxim Litvinov, the Soviet commissar for
foreign affairs, proposed an immediate conference in Bucharest, inviting Britain, France, Poland, Romania, and Turkey
to join Russia in forming a 'peace front' against expansionist Germany. Litvinov also proposed a Soviet alliance with
Britain and France, hoping to expand the alliance to countries
under threat in the East. The French did not respond. The next
day, a Sunday, the Soviet ambassador, Ivan Maisky, called on
the foreign secretary, Lord Halifax, to ask why Britain had
responded that such a proposal was 'not acceptable'. Maisky
wrote in his diary:

> He had already exchanged opinions with the PM earlier in
> the morning ... Halifax finds the proposal 'premature'. If the
> conference is not prepared properly in advance it could cul-
> minate in failure ... suggests the prompt issuing of a 'declara-
> tion of the four' (Britain, France, USSR and Poland) ... It
> is clear that Chamberlain does not want a genuine struggle
> against aggression. He is still working for appeasement.[1]

The contents of the diaries need more than a normal scepticism given the constraints on Soviet diplomats operating abroad, but Maisky certainly had amazing contacts among senior British politicians. By early 1939, USSR foreign policy gave the impression that it had shifted fundamentally. Russia had joined the League of Nations in 1934; formed a defence alliance with France in 1935; supported sanctions against Italy from 1935–6; and offered to join in sanctions against Germany following the reoccupation of the Rhineland in 1936.[2]

On 23 March 1939, with the Russian proposal in mind, Prime Minister Chamberlain said the government took a dim view of establishing 'opposing blocs'. Then, at the Foreign Policy Committee on 27 March, Halifax – feeling that Britain had to choose between Poland and Russia, and swayed by Poland's sizeable military force of fifty divisions – chose Poland: 'we were faced with a dilemma of doing nothing or entering into a devastating war. If we did nothing this in itself would mean a great accession to Germany's strength'.[3]

On 31 March, Chamberlain told parliament that, in the event of an attack on Poland, 'His Majesty's government would feel themselves bound at once to lend the Polish government all support in their power.'[4] This was designed to act as an assurance against forcible aggression and, if successful in its intention, there would be no need to carry out the guarantee at all.[5] Britain should have offered no guarantee to Poland unless Poland and Romania entered into the association offered by Russia, in which case the guarantee might have been enforceable.

Two days later, Chamberlain asked Lloyd George to come and see him. According to Maisky's diary, presumably based on a briefing from Lloyd George, Chamberlain had said Hitler would never risk a war on two fronts, prompting Lloyd George to ask, 'Where is your second front?' Chamberlain answered, 'Poland'. Lloyd George mocked this response. 'There cannot be a second front without the USSR.' Chamberlain had no answer.[6]

In the House of Commons on 3 April 1939, Churchill noted that Labour had proposed that 'the attitude of His Majesty's Government towards Russia' be summed up in the phrase 'the maximum cooperation possible'.[7] Churchill thought that this was 'a very accurate and convenient phrase'. He went on to ask,

> Why should we expect Soviet Russia to be willing to work with us? ... No one can say that there is not a solid identity of interest between the Western democracies and Soviet Russia, and we must do nothing to obstruct the natural play of that identity of interest.[8]

This was a remarkable shift of opinion by Churchill, still a back-bencher; in essence, he was saying that Stalin was an acceptable partner against Hitler. The Labour Party shared Churchill's view, as did Churchill's allies in the Conservative Party. This was potentially a major new direction for British foreign policy, representing a new geographically based realignment that made sense in terms of realpolitik.

This was a window of opportunity, and Maisky had come into the gallery of the Commons to hear Churchill speak. Interestingly, there is no Maisky diary entry published for this day. Maisky saw Halifax on 6 April and again on the 11th, telling him the only way 'to form a "peace bloc" was around "the big Troika", Britain, France and the USSR'.[9]

On 13 April, Churchill argued again in the House of Commons for an approach to the Kremlin based on:

the deep interest that Russia [has] against further Eastward expansion of the Nazi power. It is upon that deep, natural, legitimate interest that we must rely, and I am sure we shall hear from the Government that the steps they are taking are those which will enable us to receive the fullest possible co-operation from Russia, and that no prejudices on the part of England or France will be allowed to interfere with the closest cooperation between the two countries.[10]

On 15 April 1939, the Soviet government received formal proposals from Britain and France. Britain asked Russia to follow the British example and affirm the independence of Poland and Romania. France, meanwhile, proposed that Britain, France, and the Soviet Union should come to one another's aid should Germany wage war on any one of them. Chamberlain and Halifax, however, were not prepared to spell this out in such clear terms.

Two days later, on 17 April, Stalin authorised Litvinov to present a draft agreement to Britain and France. Russia would not only provide mutual assistance if either country were attacked by Hitler; 'the treaty would also be backed by a specific commitment defining the strength and objectives of their armies, navies, and air forces'.[11] Poland was at liberty to join if it chose. The signatories would 'render mutually all manner of assistance, including that of a military nature, in case of aggression in Europe' against any member of the alliance or against 'Eastern European States situated between the Baltic and Black Seas and bordering on the USSR'. Signatories would neither negotiate nor make peace 'with aggressors separately from one another and without common consent of the three Powers'.[12]

Sean McMeekin accuses Stalin of 'bad faith', noting that on

17 April he had also authorised his ambassador in Berlin, A. F. Merekelov, to visit the German Foreign Ministry in order to reassure the German state secretary, Ernst von Weizsäcker, that Stalin's foreign policy was in no way anti-German.[13] Chamberlain had already written to his sister on 26 March noting that Soviet Russia was 'both hated and respected by many of the smaller states, notably by Poland, Romania and Finland'.[14] Meanwhile, on 22 April, the French had without much enthusiasm agreed Litvinov's proposals were a basis for negotiation. Whitehall delayed.

The permanent under-secretary at the Foreign Office, Alexander Cadogan, hurriedly drafted a response to the Russian draft agreement explaining:

> We have to balance the advantage of a paper commitment by Russia to join in a war on one side against the disadvantage of associating ourselves openly with Russia. The advantage is, to say the least, problematical ... if we are attacked by Germany, Poland under our mutual guarantee will come to our assistance, i.e. make war on Germany. If the Soviets are bound to do the same, how can they fulfil that obligation without sending troops through or aircraft over Polish territory, this is exactly what frightens the Poles.[15]

Litvinov knew that Stalin would be very suspicious of any delay. He stipulated that military conversations between the three powers should begin immediately. Harold Macmillan, then a backbench Conservative MP, felt that 'This was Litvinov's last chance. It was also ours.'[16] William Manchester wrote: 'On April 19 the cabinet's Foreign Policy Committee considered the Litvinov initiative. The Foreign Office was startled by its airtight language; by contrast – and by design – Britain's Polish Guarantee was a sieve of loopholes.'[17]

Cadogan cleared his message on what he called the 'mischievous' Soviet proposals in advance with Halifax, who was not present at the meeting.[18] Hurriedly drafted, it accepted the prevailing opinion that Russian military assistance would be of doubtful value outside its own frontiers and described the Russian plan as 'extremely inconvenient', suggesting that Soviet military strength was trivial, and declared that 'from the practical point of view there is every argument against accepting the Russian proposal'. Yet he recognised that 'there is great difficulty in rejecting the Soviet offer ... The Left in this country may be counted on' to exploit a refusal. There was also a 'very remote' possibility that the Russians might join hands with the Germans. Nevertheless, Cadogan ended, 'on balance', Litvinov's offer should be turned down.[19]

On the night of 3 May 1939, the Soviet Foreign Ministry in Moscow was surrounded by NKVD troops in a blunt coup that saw Litvinov and his top appointees physically removed from the premises, along with virtually all its Jewish employees. Stalin had embarked on his courtship of Hitler.[20] He appointed Molotov as Litvinov's successor. Assurances were given that Russian policy would remain unchanged, but change it did.

On 8 May, three weeks after the Soviet Union had announced its initiative, London replied to the Russian proposal. However, the terms of the reply strengthened suspicions in Moscow that Chamberlain was not willing to make a military pact with Russia to prevent Hitler seizing Poland. Another opponent of appeasement, the former foreign secretary, Anthony Eden (who had resigned in protest at Chamberlain's policy towards Mussolini), had now joined Lloyd George and Churchill; all agreed on the necessity of an immediate arrangement with Russia of the most far-reaching kind.

That Eden took this view following a meeting with Polish Foreign Minister Józef Beck, and had spoken to Chamberlain about seeking some form of understanding with Russia, was significant. It meant that, as *The New York Times* reported on 9 May 1939, 'ideological Conservative Party objections to any alliance with the Soviets, without which guarantees to Poland would be worthless, had largely dissipated. The main reservation was now over Russian military capability.'

Churchill spoke in the House of Commons again on 19 May.

If His Majesty's Government, having neglected our defences for a long time, having thrown away Czechoslovakia with all that Czechoslovakia meant in military power, having committed us without examination of the technical aspects to the defence of Poland and Rumania, now reject and cast away the indispensable aid of Russia, and so lead us in the worst of all ways into the worst of all wars, they will have ill-deserved the confidence and, I will add, the generosity with which they have been treated by their fellow-countrymen.[21]

A storm of criticism faced Chamberlain in parliament, and he grudgingly agreed to negotiate with the Soviets on the basis of a British–French–Soviet alliance.

A split between Chamberlain and his foreign secretary, Halifax, was also becoming ever more apparent. Halifax wanted a coalition government. He mixed socially with Churchill, and it was becoming clear that the two should have combined over Russia to make the Polish guarantee credible. Between 19 and 24 May, Halifax's position turned from distaste at Soviet 'blackmail and bluff' to commending a Russian alliance to cabinet.[22] Cadogan was also now in favour, but it was all too late.

If there was ever to have been an agreement, it could have only come from Litvinov. London did not understand Stalin's new position, which had been missed by Maisky, Litvinov's man. Stalin saw that war between Germany, Britain, and France was looking increasingly inevitable, and he was considering how to capitalise on that inevitability. The significance of the change to Molotov was picked up on 5 May by Hitler's propaganda chief, Joseph Goebbels, who issued instructions to Nazi journalists that they should suspend their attacks on the Soviet Union until they received new orders.

Talks continued between Britain and Russia in June and July 1939, but the Russians were also talking to Germany, and Stalin soon calculated that those talks with Germany could deliver more of what Russia lost at Versailles: Estonia, Latvia, Lithuania, Poland, Romania, and the Balkans. The Russian–German talks were also influenced by a little-known and surprising military collaboration which had run from 1922 to 1933 when General Hans von Seeckt, head of the Reichswehr (the German army) from 1920 to 1926, had been eager to work with Soviet Russia to circumvent the bans on German military activity under the terms of the Versailles Treaty.[23] Trotsky considered joining with Germany against Poland to be crucial to Soviet strategy.[24]

In 1923, the Reichswehr and the Red Army had a series of secret meetings during which they established a framework for military cooperation. German firms took over Russian shipyards, aircraft, arms and munitions factories, chemical weapons plants, and other critical facilities. While German businesses expected to profit from these ventures, the German government saw them as a way to test and produce equipment banned under the Versailles Treaty and which could eventually supply a future German army. The Soviets, for their part, hoped to enhance and increase their arms industry using German technology. Problems in Russia meant many ventures failed, including the Junkers aircraft production facility outside Moscow. In 1926, the owner leaked details about the German programme in Russia to members of the German parliament and, on 3 December, *The Manchester Guardian* carried the headline, 'Cargoes of Munitions from Russia to Germany! Secret Plan between Reichswehr Officers and Soviet[s], STARTLING DISCLOSURES'. More might have been done by the Britain and France diplomatically, but the German government, largely ignorant of Reichswehr efforts in the Soviet Union, collapsed after losing a vote of no confidence.

Even after the disclosures of 1926, undaunted German and Soviet officers continued to study and train together. Teams of engineers and scientists worked on new weapons systems and reverse-engineered US, British, and French military equipment. Two bases were devoted to chemical weapons production (thankfully later viewed as incompatible with the mobile, combined arms warfare doctrine under development), another to aviation training, and one more to armoured warfare. All this helped to modernise and enhance the capabilities of both the German and Soviet forces (though the latter were subsequently to be severely weakened by Stalin's purges of the officer class). This collaboration continued until 1933, when Hitler, having concealed his antipathy for the Soviet Union at least to some extent, no longer felt any need to hide German rearmament. Although the cooperation had lasted less than a decade, it helped pave the way for negotiations on the Molotov–Ribbentrop Pact, the notorious Soviet–German non-aggression agreement signed in Moscow on 23 August 1939.

The fundamental duplicity of Russian–German relations lay in the hearts and minds of only two men: Stalin and Hitler. Both played their cards very close to their chests, and there was no way in which diplomats in European capitals representing either man could always be counted on to anticipate their political agenda, let alone this one.

In his book *Stalin's War*, Sean McMeekin records another hint about Stalin's revisionist foreign policy aims in April 1938 and that, unbeknownst to Litvinov, he sent Boris Yartsev to Helsinki as a special envoy to demand permission to build Soviet military bases on Finnish territory. Yartsev's demands were refused, so Stalin sent an NKVD officer to request a thirty-year lease on the island of Gogland (Suursaari) and four smaller islets in the Gulf of Finland.[25]

Even if Britain and France had reached an arrangement with Russia, Hitler would no doubt have attacked Russia at some stage, but it would have delayed the start of the Second World War. We know that Hitler's readiness to launch an attack on Poland (originally scheduled for dawn on 26 August) was based on his confidence that Britain and France would not intervene following the signing of the pact. 'I have met the umbrella men, Chamberlain and [French Prime Minister] Daladier, at Munich and got to know them', he told his generals when they expressed doubts. 'They can never stop me solving the Polish question. The coffee sippers in London and Paris will stay still this time too.'[26] However, on 25 August, when he saw the British press coverage of Chamberlain's defiant speech in support of Poland and a mutual assistance treaty, he told the British ambassador in Berlin, Nevile Henderson, that he would make a final effort towards an understanding with England. The proposal came too late, but it was a sign that Hitler was wrong in his initial assessment.

Germany invaded Poland on the morning of 1 September 1939. Chamberlain delivered his ultimatum at 9 a.m. on Sunday, 3 September, one hour before the French delivered theirs. The Polish armed forces were astonishingly brave but slowly overwhelmed. Molotov, who had boasted to the Supreme Soviet on 1 August that Stalin had outmanoeuvred the ruling classes of Britain and France, was asked by Ribbentrop to participate in the war as promised against Poland on 3 September. Molotov replied on 5 September that the time had not yet come, but the two were clearly working ever closer together. German tanks significantly outnumbered Polish tanks, but the Russians still waited for Warsaw to fall to the Germans. On 17 September, the Polish ambassador in Moscow was told that the Polish state no longer existed and that the Red Army had been ordered by Stalin to protect lives as it started to occupy half of Poland. A German zone and a Russian zone, following secret discussions prior to the war, were established. In the German zone, the SS were responsible for major war crimes, as were the NKVD in the Russian zone of eastern Poland. Russia continued to dominate Estonia, Latvia, and Lithuania.

On 12 October, President Roosevelt wrote to the president of the USSR, Mikhail Kalinin, demanding clarification of the Soviet posture on Finland. Molotov composed Kalinin's response on 15 October, assuring Roosevelt that the talks underway in Moscow had no aim other than 'improving mutual relations between the Soviet Union and Finland'.[27] Still, on 31 October, Molotov could not resist saying in a speech to the

Supreme Soviet that 'it was hard to reconcile America's meddling in these questions with her profession of neutrality'.[28]

That same day, the British War Cabinet discussed 'Soviet Aggression Against Finland or Other Scandinavian Countries'. The chiefs of staff report read:

> At present the sincerity of France and Great Britain is being questioned, and force is being added to German propaganda, particularly in Italy and Spain, because we have not declared war on Russia in spite of the fact that she had already interfered with the liberty of small states in much the same way as Germany ... The question thus seems to resolve itself into whether any advantage which might accrue from the support of neutrals, consequent upon a stand by us against Russian aggression, will outweigh the disadvantage which we should incur by the undoubted increase in our military commitments and by the probability that we should weld Germany and Russia more firmly together.[29]

The conclusion was: 'We and France are in no position to undertake additional burdens.'[30]

It is on the basis of this meeting that McMeekin has built his case for Britain committing its armed forces to fight the Finnish cause. I do not share his views and believe he exaggerates the likelihood of any other country coming to the defence of Finland in military terms. Moral and financial support might have come, but no armed forces. He develops his 'what if' theory in interesting ways and weighs up the possibilities of gaining the open support of the United States or Turkey joining the war against the USSR at that stage. I do not believe that was ever a credible possibility. The phenomenal bravery and relative early success of the Finnish fighting forces are used to buttress McMeekin's theory, and it has some superficial attractions. But I have not been able to find any real evidence of any country, other than Finland, rallying to the cause. Certainly not Italy. In diary entries for the period when he was in No. 10 supporting Chamberlain in 1939 before Churchill came to power, John Colville summed up the arguments. While relatively young, Colville was also fully aware of all the manoeuvrings to involve Sweden against their wishes by linking them to British naval operations in Norway. Colville wrote:

> Personally, I am against our interference: (i) it would be dangerous and might involve disaster or withdrawal and the consequent blow to our prestige; (ii) the idea of wilfully extending the war to Scandinavia, and involving the northern countries against their wishes, is a callous contradiction of those very principles for which we are fighting.[31]

The diaries of Alexander Cadogan are also revealing. On 6 March 1940, having been asked 'what we propose to do to help the Finns' over lunch with Archbishop Lang of Canterbury, Cadogan wrote, 'telegram coming in from Helsinki which seems to show Finns are throwing up the sponge. Secretly, I should be glad. I believe ours is a hair-brain scheme which hasn't been thought out properly by anyone and I am shocked at the levity and stupidity of our General Staff.'[32]

Finland asked Russia for an armistice on 11 March, their army having suffered 25,000 deaths, one tenth of their eligible manpower, though barely a tenth of Russian losses.

What is absolutely clear from a study of Roosevelt's position is that, while on 1 December 1939 he expressed his shock over

Soviet air and naval bombardment of Finland, he had no intention whatsoever of involving the United States.[33]

In my book *The Cabinet's Finest Hour*, I wrote of Churchill's return to government at the start of the Second World War, initially as first lord of the Admiralty, then, following growing cross-party discontent with Chamberlain, as prime minister at the head of a coalition government. As Churchill tried to woo, cajole, and persuade Roosevelt to enter the war in 1940 and 1941, no one was listened to and respected more by Roosevelt – but he was determined not to bring the US into a second war on the European continent until he had the people with him. Even off Newfoundland, when he and Churchill met to sign the Atlantic Charter on 14 August 1941, Roosevelt was certain he had first to win re-election, and he was still not confident of carrying public opinion to the extent he wanted until Pearl Harbour, when the US fleet was attacked by Japan.

Returning to Russia, Churchill appointed Stafford Cripps as ambassador to Moscow. Cripps was considered by most Conservative MPs to be on the extreme left of the Labour Party, which, based on his record until that date, was not an unreasonable label; indeed, he had been expelled from the Labour Party for his views. But he had a complicated and brilliant mind. Cripps wanted the job as a 'special envoy', but the Russians were under no illusions that he was not truly representative of the government, and Molotov insisted that he simply be an ambassador rather than a special envoy. It was not, as things turned out, a successful appointment, and Churchill later regretted it. The following vignette of Cripps's way of thinking shows why.

On 3 April 1941, Churchill sent a personally drafted message for Cripps to deliver direct to Stalin. It was Churchill's first communication with the leader for nine months, and it was based on decrypted German messages received from Bletchley Park, the secret communications establishment that had cracked the Germans' 'Enigma' cipher system. Only Churchill and a very few select individuals were privy to these interceptions of German intentions. Their messages had to be wrapped up as coming from other sources. Churchill's message was therefore brief and talked of information from a trusted agent to conceal that the German code had been broken.[34]

> Prime Minister to Stafford Cripps. Following from me to M. Stalin, provided it can be personally delivered by you.
> 'I have more information from a trusted agent that when the Germans thought they had got Yugoslavia in the net – that is to say after March 20 – they began to move three out of the five Panzer divisions from Roumania to Southern Poland. The moment they heard of the Serbian revolution this movement was countermanded. Your Excellency will readily appreciate the significance of these facts.'

Churchill's foreign secretary, Eden, then added three paragraphs of explanatory text for the ambassador, as if he thought Cripps might miss the inner military meaning. Cripps replied on 12 April that, just before receiving the telegram, he had addressed a long personal letter to Molotov's deputy, Vyshinsky. He argued that: 'Were I now to convey through Molotov the Prime Minister's message, which expresses the same thesis in very much shorter and less emphatic form, I fear the only effect would be probably to weaken impression in letter by me to Vyshinsky.' Eden minuted the prime minister: 'I think there may be some force in Sir Stafford Cripps's arguments against the delivery of your message.' Churchill was not mollified, and correctly insisted that his letter be delivered.

After the war, Churchill wrote: 'I was vexed at this and at the delay which had occurred. This was the only message before the attack that I sent Stalin direct. Its brevity, the exceptional character of the communication, the fact that it came from the head of the government and was to be delivered personally by the Ambassador, were all intended to give it special significance and arrest Stalin's attention.'[35]

Meanwhile, German intentions were becoming clearer. Churchill cabled the South African prime minister, Smuts, on 16 May: 'It looks as if Hitler is massing against Russia. A ceaseless movement of troops, armoured forces, and aircraft northwards from the Balkans and eastwards from France and Germany is in progress.'[36] While Churchill was alert to the threat to Russia from Germany, it is widely thought that Stalin ignored warnings of an impending attack. The true story has emerged from secret Soviet archives and is covered by the brothers Zhores and Roy Medvedev in their book *The Unknown Stalin*.[37] It is true that, on 17 June, the commissar for state security warned that military action was about to begin, and Stalin memorably replied: 'Comrade Merkulov. You can tell your "source" from Ger. Air Force headquarters to go f— his mother. This is not a "source" – it's someone spreading disinformation ... J.St.' Indeed, the authors think Stalin was right; this was disinformation. But military intelligence received on 15 June *was* taken seriously by Stalin, and on 19 June Generals Timoshenko and Zhukov gave orders – approved by Stalin – to camouflage airfields and create dummy sites in preparation for a 1 July attack. The Soviet intelligence resident in Sofia reported on 20 June that the attack would come on the 21st or 22nd. On

21 June, Stalin telephoned the commander of the Moscow military district to put anti-aircraft batteries on immediate alert. At 2 p.m., Stalin had been handed a telegram from his ambassador in London saying that he had been told by the Foreign Office that the Germans would attack on the 22nd, the following day.

At 4 a.m. on Sunday, 22 June, Ribbentrop delivered a formal declaration of war to the Russian ambassador in Berlin. As his standing instructions were that he was only ever to be woken up in the case of a German invasion of England, Churchill only learnt of the German action at 8 a.m. Hitler's Operation Barbarossa involving a three-million-man invasion of the Soviet Union was underway – unanticipated by Stalin despite many warnings. Churchill's reaction was as follows. He immediately set to work on a speech to be delivered in a radio broadcast that evening – his way of talking to Russia directly (and indeed parts of his broadcast would be printed in *Pravda*). He worked all day on his speech, finishing at 8.40 p.m. for delivery at 9 p.m., with only a break for lunch with Cripps (who by chance was not in Moscow), Beaverbrook, and the Marquess of Salisbury. Andrew Roberts reveals that Churchill told them that the invasion was the fourth 'climacteric', the first three being the Fall of France, the Battle of Britain, and the passing of the Lend-lease Act in the US (which allowed it to lend war supplies to other countries).[38] Churchill reminded his lunch guests that King Charles XII of Sweden had invaded Russia but come to grief at the Battle of Poltava a century before Napoleon's 1812 campaign. Over dinner that night, Eden and Salisbury argued that the alliance with Russia 'should be confined to the purely military aspect ... half the country would object to being associated too closely'. Churchill was simply not ready to accept their views and 'was extremely vehement'.[39] He believed that only whole-hearted support for Russia would have military significance.

I have quoted below at some length from Churchill's speech – in effect directed at Russia – as it is largely unknown but a magnificent example of his oratory.[40] After referring to the three 'climacterics' mentioned above, he turned to the invasion itself, pointing out that it had not come as a surprise to him and that he had given 'clear and precise warnings to Stalin of what was coming'. In highly emotive language, he portrays Hitler as 'a monster of wickedness, insatiable in his lust for blood and plunder' who was carrying 'his work of butchery and desolation among the vast multitudes of Russia and of Asia'. The 'blood-thirsty guttersnipe' was setting out on a campaign of 'slaughter, pillage and devastation'. And Russia would only be a 'stepping stone' to China and India.

Churchill then delivers a carefully crafted message – the very essence of his speech – aimed directly at the Russian people. He opens by setting out his personal views on both the Nazis and Communists.

> The Nazi regime is indistinguishable from the worst features of Communism. It is devoid of all theme and principle except appetite and racial domination. It excels in all forms of human wickedness, in the efficiency of its cruelty and ferocious aggression. No one has been a more consistent opponent of Communism than I have for the last twenty-five years. I will unsay no words that I've spoken about it.

But that was the past and, turning to the present, and switching his focus from politics to people, he continues.

I see the Russian soldiers standing on the threshold of their native land, guarding the fields which their fathers have tilled from time immemorial. I see them guarding their homes; their mothers and wives pray, ah yes, for there are times when all pray for the safety of their loved ones, for the return of the breadwinner, of the champion, of their protectors.

And then my mind goes back across the years to the days when the Russian armies were our Allies against the same deadly foe when they fought with so much valour and constancy and helped to gain a victory, from all share in which, alas, they were, through no fault of ours, utterly cut off.

... Any man or State who fights against Nazism will have our aid ... It follows, therefore, that we shall give whatever help we can to Russia and to the Russian people. We shall appeal to all our friends and Allies in every part of the world to take the same course and pursue it as we shall, faithfully and steadfastly to the end.

Then, speaking directly to the British people, Churchill makes it clear that Hitler's:

invasion of Russia is no more than a prelude to an attempted invasion of the British Isles ...

The Russian danger is therefore our danger and the danger of the United States just as the cause of any Russian fighting for his hearth and home is the cause of free men and free peoples in every quarter of the globe.

Following his broadcast, Churchill heard nothing from the Russian government except for a request to receive a Russian Military Mission, so he sent a telegram to Stalin on 7 July 1941 saying, 'we shall do everything to help you that time, geography, and our growing resources allow ... we hope to force Hitler to bring back some of his air power to the West and gradually take some of the strain off you ... We have only to go on fighting to beat the life out of these villains.'[41] On 19 July, Maisky called on Churchill with a message from Stalin. It contained the first of many pleas – which would continue until 1944 – for Britain to launch a second front against Germany. Stalin proposed establishing this second front in northern France, while also proposing joint action on the Northern Front in the Arctic. Stalin did acknowledge the difficulties in opening a western front, but he stressed the importance of speedy action.[42]

Churchill replied to Stalin's message on 20 July, setting out the realities of the situation based on the assessment of his chiefs of staff, and the challenges posed in attacking the heavily defended coast of northern France.

> To attempt a landing in force would be to encounter a bloody repulse, and petty raids would only lead to fiascos doing far more harm than good to both of us. It would all be over without their having to move or before they could move a single unit from your front.

Churchill signed off saying, 'This is the most we can do at the moment. I wish it were more.'[43]

I have written in some detail about Russia's entry into the war and Churchill's readiness to respond generously because Eden and Salisbury advocated a more limited response, a view unsurprisingly shared by many other politicians in Westminster. Yet Churchill's approach struck a chord with the British public in their homes. From 1945 onwards, however, public opinion in Britain and the US has consistently downplayed the fact that if any one country defeated Hitler, it was Russia. The key campaign was not the D-Day invasion in 1944. One figure sums up the imbalance. For every US soldier killed fighting the Germans, eighty Soviet soldiers died doing the same. Considered from the German position, the Nazis suffered three-quarters of their wartime losses fighting the Red Army. It is a salutary fact that the battle for Stalingrad and the battle at Kursk, which was the biggest tank battle in history, have no parallel in the Western European campaigns. In his book *Inferno: The World At War, 1939–1945*, Max Hastings makes much the same point: 'It was the Western Allies' extreme good fortune that the Russians, and not themselves, paid almost the entire "butchers bill" for [defeating Nazi Germany,] accepting 95 per cent of the military casualties of the three major powers of the Grand Alliance.' Two great books by the military historian John Erickson tell it all: *The Road to Stalingrad* and *The Road to Berlin*.[44] From what was then the Centre for Defence Studies in Edinburgh, Erickson provided much knowledgeable insight about Russia, and his legacy lives on. (One Russian general told me in Moscow in 1982 that 'Erickson knows more about the Russian military than we do.') Informed debate about Russia is much needed in the years ahead and the UK must retain and develop respected experts equipped to address all the complexities of today's Russian Federation.

As a former MP for a naval constituency, I have long been interested in the Arctic Convoy effort as an example of Anglo-Soviet cooperation. This is still remembered to this day in Russia. When I was in business there from 1995 to 2015 and I was invited to give speeches, I would remind my audience of this period, when the navies of Britain, Canada, and the United

States escorted merchant ships carrying critical supplies to the ports of Archangel and Murmansk. A surprisingly large number of the older Russians remembered, but the story was less familiar to the younger generations.

There were seventy-eight convoys between August 1941 and May 1945. Some 1,400 merchant ships delivered supplies, including tanks, fighter planes, fuel, ammunition, raw materials, and food. One of the most important destinations for supplies from the convoys was the besieged city of Leningrad. Air attacks launched from bases in German-occupied Norway extracted a huge toll in terms of ships sunk or damaged. The famous Convoy PQ 17 was the first large joint Anglo-American convoy, and it suffered the most severe casualties. Due to a misunderstanding of intelligence, the convoy was ordered to scatter to avoid a perceived threat from a German naval force headed by the feared battleship *Tirpitz*. Without their escorts, the merchant ships became much easier for the German U-boats to pick off. Only eleven of the thirty-five merchant ships reached their destination, and 163 merchant mariners lost their lives. Churchill, however, remained a strong advocate of continuing the convoys, and the next convoy was provided with a constant escort of sixteen destroyers.

My friend and colleague in the business of Russian steel, Alisher Usmanov – who besides his investment in OEMK also had a business in Archangel – paid tribute to the efforts of British sailors by making a large donation to the restoration of the Merchant Navy memorial on the Cutty Sark following the devastating fire in 2007. He has also helped Britons visit Archangel in commemoration of relatives involved in the Arctic Convoys. It took until 2013 for the Arctic Star Medal to be awarded to those who had been involved in the Arctic Convoys.

Usmanov was sanctioned in 2022, which he challenges.

On Friday, 11 July 1941 in Washington, before the US had entered the war, President Roosevelt drew a line on a small map of the Atlantic Ocean that he had torn out of the *National Geographic* magazine. In doing so, he set in motion an important change in policy. The line showed the area of the Atlantic Ocean that the US Navy would assume responsibility for policing, in order to free up British escort ships for service elsewhere, particularly on the Murmansk route.[45] He gave the map to his adviser, Harry Hopkins, who was going to Britain en route to Moscow. Hopkins, in turn, showed the map to Churchill, who recognised it for what it was: a profound shift in the president's position. Hopkins went on to meet Stalin, flying back to Scotland in time to join Churchill on board HMS *Prince of Wales*, which was heading for Newfoundland. He had a personal message for Roosevelt from Stalin, who had said:

> It would be very difficult for Britain and Russia combined to crush the German military machine. The one thing that could defeat Hitler, and perhaps even without firing a shot, would be the announcement that the United States was going to war with Germany.[46]

Stalin also asked Hopkins to tell the president that he would welcome US troops on any part of the Russian front under the complete command of the US Army.

Churchill and Roosevelt's meeting began on 9 August 1941 without any pre-publicity, initially on the American cruiser USS *Augusta*, during which Churchill handed President Roosevelt a letter from King George VI. While the meeting failed to deliver Churchill's objective of getting the United States to enter the war, it did result in a joint statement on 14 August that would become known as the 'Atlantic Charter'. The charter set out their aims for the post-war settlement, and it was a key precursor to the establishment of the United Nations.

On 10 June 2021, President Biden and Prime Minister Johnson signed what has been called the New Atlantic Charter. It was intended to reflect the shifting threats facing the world eighty years later – not least from Russia and China, as implied by references to cyber warfare, though neither is singled out. This charter seemingly demonstrated that the withdrawal of the UK from the European Union would not damage US–British relations. Since the 1950s, the US State Department – and particularly Secretary of State Dean Acheson – has believed that EU membership was an essential element in future British–US relations, a belief which underpinned President Obama's unwise acceptance of Prime Minister Cameron's foolish plea for him to visit the UK during the EU referendum campaign. Private polling later showed that Obama's intervention had the opposite effect to that intended and in fact boosted the 'Leave' vote by some 3 per cent.

Roosevelt made only a few changes to the draft wording of the first Atlantic Charter, but they were of great historic significance. Point three of the charter, drafted by Churchill himself, stated: 'They respect the right of all peoples to choose the form of Government under which they will live.' But, after Roosevelt's changes, points four and five referred to 'all States, great or small' and to 'all nations' respectively. This applied, and was meant to apply, to people in India, Burma, and Malaya. Roosevelt had thus deliberately and surgically separated the US from Churchill's post-war imperial dreams and, doing so, set the scene for Indian independence under Attlee's Labour government.

Relations with Russia and particularly Stalin after 1941 were never going to be easy for either Churchill or Roosevelt, and they contemplated abandoning Moscow. A reader can obtain a sense of these differences in *The Kremlin Letters: Stalin's Wartime Correspondence with Churchill and Roosevelt*.[47] For important issues, Molotov, a wordsmith who had been on the editorial staff of *Pravda*, would prepare a first draft for Stalin who would then approve with the words 'Agree' or 'Agree with amendments', often adding whole paragraphs, before they were dispatched by telegram. The Politburo was a collective decision-making body throughout the war. Though Stalin's personal power grew ever stronger, he was in no sense a dictator at that stage. Indeed, there is some evidence that Stalin lost his nerve on military matters for a few days in 1941 when German tanks entered the outskirts of Moscow.

Churchill's letters, too, were the product of more than his pen, and his private secretary Colville commented how difficult it would be for future historians to be sure what was the real Churchill and what was the 'school of'. The British cabinet also functioned on the basis that Churchill was *primus inter pares* or 'first among equals'. On military matters, however, he was in a special position, as he was also minister of defence. Fortunately, the chief of the imperial general staff (later field marshal) Alan Brooke, whom Churchill had appointed in 1941, was a force to be reckoned with, and he frequently challenged Churchill. The exceptional character of Churchill was summed up by General Hastings Ismay, his chief military assistant.

You cannot judge the P.M. by ordinary standards: he is not in the least like anyone that you or I have ever met. He is a mass of contradictions. He is either on the crest of the wave,

or in the trough: either highly laudatory, or bitterly con-
demnatory: either in an angelic temper, or a hell of a rage:
when he isn't fast asleep he's a volcano. There are no half-
measures in his make-up. He is a child of nature with moods
as variable as an April day, and he apparently sees no difference between harsh words spoken to a friend, and forgotten
within the hour under the influence of friendly argument,
and the same harsh words telegraphed to a friend thousands
of miles away – with no opportunity for 'making it up' ...

I think I can lay claim to having been called every name
under the sun during the last six months – except perhaps
a coward; but I know perfectly well in the midst of these
storms that they mean exactly nothing, and that before the
sun goes down, I shall be summoned to an intimate and
delightfully friendly talk – to 'make it up'.[48]

As for Stalin's view of Churchill, he told Tito's number
three, Milovan Djilas, in June 1944: 'Churchill is the kind of
man who will pick your pocket of a kopeck if you don't watch
him ... Roosevelt is not like that. He dips his hand in only for
bigger coins.'[49] Revealingly, the Russians had nicknames for the
two Western leaders: Roosevelt was 'Kapitan' (captain) and
Churchill was 'Kaban' (wild boar). Apart from Stalin's letters,
the book *Behind Closed Doors*, which draws on archives only
released since the collapse of the Eastern Bloc in 1990, shows
the extent to which the Nazi–Soviet Pact was written out of
much of Soviet history of the period, and how many Russians
never knew about it.[50]

Stalin wrote to Churchill on 3 September 1941, 'I believe
there is only one possibility to remedy the position – it is to
establish already this year a second front somewhere in the

Balkans or France which would be able to divert from the Eastern Front some 30–40 German divisions...'⁵¹

The main disharmony between Churchill and Stalin over the second front had been difficult to deal with and lurked in the background at Churchill's face-to-face meetings with Stalin. The first of these meetings took place in Moscow in August 1942. Churchill flew there via Cairo and Tehran, with Roosevelt's representative, Averell Harriman. On landing, Churchill was met by Stalin, who was informally dressed in a khaki shirt, blue trousers, and half-length boots. Churchill opened their two-hour meeting that night saying, 'I would not have come to Moscow unless I felt sure I would be able to discuss realities', and he told Stalin direct that a second front in Europe was impossible in the near term, whereupon 'Stalin's face crumpled up into a frown'.⁵² At one stage, having difficulty with the translation, Stalin said, 'I did not understand, but I like the spirit.' The next day, Stalin presented Churchill with a tough memorandum demanding a second front. Thereafter, he needled Churchill unsuccessfully, even implying cowardice in not continuing with Convoy PQ 17, whose losses had been too high to launch another. In four days of talks, Churchill's opinion of Stalin turned from 'evil and dreadful' to calling him – after drinking a lot of vodka – 'that great man'.⁵³ Three days later, Churchill faced the aftermath of the disastrous Dieppe Raid, when a mainly Canadian force suffered massive casualties in an amphibious assault. Attacking Dieppe was intended to placate the Russians but, in the end, it showed just how difficult a landing on the French coast would be.

Within six weeks of the Moscow visit, Churchill freely talked of liking Stalin and, though he saw him as uncouth, claimed they had much in common. Their next meeting would be in

Tehran in November 1943, and this time Roosevelt himself attended. In Tehran, Roosevelt stayed in the Russian Embassy to woo Stalin and get to know him better. Churchill, in a very revealing exchange, later told Violet Bonham Carter: 'I realised at Tehran for the first time what a small nation we are.'[54] On his return, via Cairo, Churchill tried to convince the president of Turkey to declare war against Germany but to no effect.

On 11 June 1944, after the D-Day landings, Stalin wrote a surprisingly generous letter to Churchill.

> My colleagues and I cannot but admit that the history of warfare knows no other like undertaking from the point of view of its scale, its vast conception and its masterly execution. As is well known, Napoleon in his time failed ignominiously in his plan to force the Channel. The hysterical Hitler, who boasted for two years that he would effect a forcing of the Channel, was unable to make up his mind even to hint at attempting to carry out his threat. Only our Allies have succeeded in realising with honour the grandiose plan of the forcing of the Channel. History will record this deed as an achievement of the highest order.[55]

Churchill's third meeting with Stalin took place on 9 October 1944 in Moscow, though without an American presence. The mood was very good; so good, in fact, that Churchill made a proposal on a scrap of paper dividing post-war Europe into Western and Soviet spheres of influence. Stalin examined the paper, pondered it for a moment, then wrote a large tick in blue pencil and handed it back to Churchill. The original 'spheres of influence' that Churchill proposed to Stalin in percentages were as follows.

Roumania: Russia 90%, the others 10%
Greece: Great Britain (in accord with the USA) 90%,
   ~~The Others~~ [sic] Russia 10%
Yugoslavia: 50/50%
Hungary: 50/50%
Bulgaria: Russia 75%, the others 25%

Afterwards, Churchill said: 'Might it not be thought rather cynical if it seemed we had disposed of these issues, so fateful to millions of people in such an offhand manner? Let us burn the paper.' Stalin replied, 'No, you keep it.'[56] The whole exchange was never recorded in the official British record. This was certainly not Churchill's finest hour, and when he later complained about the realpolitik of the Yalta Conference, which in February 1945 discussed the post-war reorganisation of Germany and Europe, his complaints rang hollow for those in the know, given that he had already legitimised a carve-up. Churchill never told Roosevelt about it, and all the signs suggested that he was more than a little ashamed of it, calling the scrap of paper a 'naughty document'.[57]

'Naughty' was a strange word for Churchill to choose; 'embarrassing' might have been more appropriate. But the document brought to Churchill's mind the need to learn from Yugoslavia and Greece, and his preoccupation with their fate.

In April 1941, Germany attacked Yugoslavia and the Luftwaffe bombed Belgrade, killing an estimated 5,000 to 17,000 civilians. The dismemberment of the country was brutal. Croatia's fascist leader, Ante Pavelić, was a puppet ruler. Later, Nuremberg would judge that what Pavelić and the Germans did to the Serbs was genocide. (No one knows exactly how many Serbs were killed. The Serbs say 750,000; the Germans

estimate 350,000. Such was the background to the wars of disintegration that Cyrus Vance and I faced in the International
Conference on the Former Yugoslavia in the early 1990s.) Back
in 1942, Churchill had supported the Serbian nationalist resistance leader, Colonel Draža Mihailović. But, by early 1943,
it seemed the Allies had been backing the wrong horse, and
Churchill switched to the Russian-backed guerrilla Communist leader, Tito. On 6 April 1944, learning that the Americans
were about to send an intelligence mission to Mihailović at the
very moment Britain was withdrawing the last of its support,
Churchill cabled the British forces in Cairo, asking them to
delay 'by every reasonable means' any arrangements to fly the
American mission into Yugoslavia, 'the greatest courtesy being
used to our friends and in every case, but no transportation.'[58]

Then, in October, Greece was very much on Churchill's mind
following the withdrawal of German troops and his earlier
decision to move 10,000 men into Athens on 26 September
1944 under the command of British General Ronald Scobie.
Churchill wanted, above all, to restore democracy in the fullest
Greek sense of the word. But he also wanted, from his experience in Yugoslavia, for it to be different; for him, unlike for
many Greeks, that meant the restoration of the monarchy.

In Greece in 1944–5, Churchill and General Scobie faced a
difficult situation. Just as Tito's Communists were the dominant resistance movement against the Germans in Yugoslavia, the Greek Communist-controlled EAM and its military
component, ELAS, had played a somewhat similar role in
Greece. Now with the Germans out, the British forces were
linking up with the security forces loyal to the Greek government. On 3 December, some 200,000 people in Athens protested such a move, and serious violence erupted. Tanks and

British paratroopers moved into the centre of Athens. Officially, twenty-eight protesters were killed, but it is believed to be more. Martial law was imposed on 5 December, with right-wing groups battling on against ELAS forces. Soon, both sides were seeking to control Athens and the country. On 25 December 1944, reinforced by his agreement with Stalin, Churchill flew to Athens with Anthony Eden, the British foreign secretary, to exercise British influence and bring an end to the armed clash known as 'Dekemvriana'. Churchill wanted to influence negotiations with EAM and the Greek government, form a provisional government, and avoid a civil war. The first round of negotiations started in Lebanon focused on how to keep Greece free of Communist control. Even in 1943, the national liberation EAM–ELAS movement was bigger than the right-wing, mainly republican, EDES resistance group.

On arriving at the conference in Athens, which was chaired by Archbishop Damaskinos, Churchill faced a dilemma. He did not want to shake hands with the EAM delegates, but he did not want to cause offence. Instead, he chose to bow his head before them – so low that, in the event, his head nearly touched the floor. In his speech, Churchill emphasises his wish for a political settlement, but he knew that he had the support of both Stalin and Roosevelt to resolve the issue militarily as a last resort. It was suggested that Damaskinos serve as regent while the return of King George II of the Hellenes would be decided by a plebiscite to determine the people's wishes, and Greece should become a member of the United Nations. The press reports in Athens on 26 December stressed that the British would enforce the rule of law and rid the capital of ELAS forces. Unfortunately, Churchill's visit did not resolve the immediate conflict, and its resolution took many years.

On 30 November 2014, *The Observer* published a long article called 'Athens 1944: Britain's Dirty Secret' by Ed Vulliamy and Helena Smith. In it, the journalists call Churchill's decision to turn on the partisans, who had fought during the war on the British side, on 3 December a 'shameful decision' that sowed the seed of the far right in Greece and the coup d'état of the junta on 21 April 1967.[59] Yet while some people today feel that Churchill could have handled the Greek Communist resistance more generously, as Britain did in Yugoslavia, hindsight is all too easy; the situation in Athens was combustible.

It took Greece some time to put the civil war behind it, but this is not surprising. In England, you can still come across attitudes and events that revive memories of our civil war in the seventeenth century. Plymouth, the city I represented in the House of Commons, was a Cromwellian city surrounded by Royalists in Cornwall and Devon. The politics of the West Country reflect this. I, personally, would have been for Cromwell. The United States also still faces the impact of its civil war, particularly in the south. My own experience of spending time in Greece over the last twenty-two years has shown me how individual families in villages and towns have overcome bitter memories. I doubt scapegoating anyone, least of all Churchill, was ever justified. Tragic mistakes were made, but the underlying truth is that Greece has now come together within the EU, and all its many friends delight in its new stability and prosperity. I hope that something similar can come for Serbia, Bosnia-Herzegovina, and Ukraine.

It is also important to recognise the value of exuberance in leaders. As the French essayist La Rochefoucauld wrote: 'Passions are the only orators which always persuade. They are like an act of nature, the rules of which are infallible; and the simplest man who has some passion persuades better than the most eloquent who has none.'[60] Churchill was a passionate, exuberant personality. Woundingly once described in the 1930s as a 'beached whale', he was fortunately not finished, for as he said of himself, 'we are all worms but I do believe I am a glow-worm.'[61] Churchill has never easily fitted into conventional classification.[62]

By the last stages of the war, Churchill's decisions were no longer the vital ones. Churchill also gave the impression at times that he would have had the Allies take Berlin before the Russians, but the casualties would have been so great that I suspect he sensibly shrank from the prospect. In any case, he knew that the United States, which would have borne the military brunt, saw no strategic need.

Given the state of his heart, Roosevelt should not have run again for the presidency in 1944. Nevertheless, the country wanted him, and a new US president would not have made much difference to the actual operation of the war in those few months between Roosevelt's inauguration on 20 January 1945 and his death on 12 April, aged sixty-three.

In Europe, from early 1944, it was General George Marshall and the other US chiefs of staff – along with General Dwight D. Eisenhower, Marshall's choice as supreme allied commander – who had been taking the key military decisions. In effect, Marshall, with Roosevelt's agreement, had been controlling the lead into D-Day and its follow-up. In early 1945, Marshall and the US military were the most reluctant to race the Soviet Union to Berlin, a view expressed in March by Eisenhower in a telegram to Stalin, in the latter's capacity as marshal of the Soviet forces. The telegram confirmed that the Allied armies under his (Eisenhower's) command would not try to take Berlin. In his diaries, Field Marshal Sir Alan Brooke reveals that he told the British chiefs of staff that Eisenhower 'had no business to address Stalin direct, his communications should be through the combined Chiefs of Staff', and that 'what was implied in it appeared to be entirely adrift and a change in all that had been previously agreed on'.[63] Yet, in part, it was a praiseworthy wish of the Americans to save the lives of Allied soldiers under their leadership, based on the judgement that Hitler would insist on fighting to the last man, while Stalin was ready to take Berlin, irrespective of the cost. That Eisenhower wrote without specifically consulting the military and political authorities in London was probably both a reflection of the delegation of power by Roosevelt and the fact that Eisenhower already knew that Roosevelt and Churchill held different views.

For the next meeting with Stalin, in February 1945, Churchill and Roosevelt travelled separately to Yalta on the Black Sea coast. Here, the future shape of Eastern Europe was settled, involving particularly tough discussions about Poland. By this stage, Roosevelt was increasingly ill, but this does not seem to have hampered his performance. Charles E. Bohlen, then the State Department's liaison officer to the White House, acted as the president's interpreter. He was certainly no sycophant, but, in 1969, he wrote about Roosevelt's performance at Yalta: 'I do not know of any case where he really gave away anything to the Soviets because of his ill health.' He added: 'He seemed to be guided very heavily by his advisers and he took no step independently.'[64] Certainly, an interpreter is uniquely placed to see the role of advisers because often, to assist them and let them know what to expect, they are given advance copies of the speaking notes prepared by officials for the head of government. The American historian Arthur M. Schlesinger Jr wrote to Valentin

Berezhkov, Stalin's interpreter, to enquire about Soviet perceptions of Roosevelt's health at Yalta, especially compared with the previous meeting in Tehran, in November 1943. Berezhkov replied that it 'was certainly worse than in Tehran, but everybody who watched him said that in spite of his frail appearance his mental potential was high. Before he got tired, he was alert, with quick reactions and forceful arguments.'[65] He also noted that 'Stalin treated Roosevelt with great esteem.'[66]

A European perspective of Yalta must remember that Roosevelt's primary objective from the meeting was, above all, Stalin's pledge to come into the war against Japan within two to three months of the end of fighting in Europe – and he did indeed achieve this. As things turned out, however, Stalin decided to come in only a matter of days before the Japanese surrender in August. At the time, Russia's entry into the war with Japan was thought to be crucial. It is easily forgotten how costly the war in the Pacific was becoming in terms of US lives, and at this stage there was no guarantee that the atomic bomb development project would be successful. The Soviet Union was strategically positioned, with a naval fleet in Vladivostok and a border with China. That said, Roosevelt was never under any illusion about his negotiating partners' strengths and weaknesses. He knew, as he said to Admiral William Leahy at Yalta, that 'it's the best I can do for Poland at this time.'[67]

The account given by Bohlen, in a conversation with the historian Richard Neustadt, suggests that in late March 1945 the president was still focused.[68] According to Bohlen, the president was acutely conscious that Yalta was a test of Soviet intent to preserve Big Three comity after the war, and he felt that Moscow had reached the point of failing the test. Bohlen further believed that, had Roosevelt returned to Washington in

April, he would have joined with Churchill in an Allied refusal to withdraw from the Elbe to their previously agreed zones of occupation. Also, since Roosevelt was due to travel to London in May after a German surrender, Bohlen felt a tripartite emergency meeting would have been held then, substituting for the later Potsdam meeting. With Edward Stettinius installed in the State Department – far more tractable than his predecessor, Cordell Hull – it is clear Roosevelt envisaged playing a bigger, not a lesser, role; indeed, his appointment of Bohlen to his personal staff to help assert his authority was not really the action of a man reconciled to dying. Yet within a few weeks, on 12 April 1945, Roosevelt passed away in Warm Springs, Georgia. Ever since contracting polio, Roosevelt had fought off ill health and, even though his doctors knew his days were numbered, it would have been in character for him to plan forward, ignoring his health. There are good grounds for arguing that Roosevelt should not have stood for re-election in November 1944, but Yalta is not one of them.

After leaving Yalta, Churchill made a stop at Athens on 22 February where, with the regent, Archbishop Damaskinos, he received a rapturous welcome, and which he was to describe in parliament as the 'high spot of the whole journey'.[69] Churchill's reception in London, however, was not so positive. Concerns were growing over the Polish settlement, spurred on by the Polish government in exile in London, who were sceptical of Stalin's undertakings.

At the debate on the Yalta Conference in the House of Commons on 27 February, Churchill opened by speaking of the difficulties in even organising the conference.[70] He described the Polish question as 'the most difficult and agitating part of the statement which I have to make', arguing that ensuring an independent, sovereign Poland was more important than the actual frontiers.[71] In his view, the Russian proposal on the borders was 'just and right' given the 'chequered and intermingled' history of the two countries.[72] As regards the issue of the freedom of Poland:

> Most solemn declarations have been made by Marshal Stalin and the Soviet Union that the sovereign independence of Poland is to be maintained, and this decision is now joined in both by Great Britain and the United States. Here also, the world organisation [the proposed United Nations] will in due course assume a measure of responsibility.[73]

As for his view of Stalin, Churchill stated:

> The impression I brought back from the Crimea, and from all my other contacts, is that Marshal Stalin and the Soviet leaders wish to live in honourable friendship and equality with the Western democracies. I feel also that their word is their bond. I know of no Government which stands to its obligations, even in its own despite, more solidly than the Russian Soviet Government.[74]

With an unwitting foretaste of what was to come, he continued: 'Sombre indeed would be the fortunes of mankind if some awful schism arose between the Western democracies and the Russian Soviet Union.'[75] He also pointed out that the situation Britain was facing in 1945 was very different from the early stages of the war and recognised the challenges this caused when taking such decisions as those at Yalta: 'Now we are entering a world of imponderables, and at every stage occasions for self-questioning arise. It is a mistake to look too far ahead. Only one link in the chain of destiny can be handled at a time.'[76]

Before long, the cracks over Yalta started appearing. At the War Cabinet meeting of 6 March, 'a very unsatisfactory discussion' with Molotov was reported, in which he had refused to accept the list of nominees to the Polish government presented by Britain and the US, and in particular had made 'a determined effort to exclude' the head of the Polish government in exile, Stanisław Mikołajczyk.[77] The Russians were also to flex their muscles in Romania. By the War Cabinet meeting of 3 April, Churchill reported that: 'Relations with Russia, which had offered such fair promise at the Crimea Conference, had grown less cordial during the ensuing weeks. There had been grave difficulties over the Polish question.'[78] Stalin had played a good hand brilliantly at Yalta – very attentive to Roosevelt but respectful of Churchill – and ultimately secured his objectives, resulting in Soviet control over wide swathes of Europe.

Comparisons between Hitler and Stalin have often been made to determine which was the greater villain. If the measure is the number of deaths of innocent people each caused, Stalin emerges as the worse figure. But, on instinct, the deliberate nature of Hitler's genocidal crimes cast him in a worse light. Churchill never doubted that, in qualitative rather than quantitative terms, Hitler was the more evil of the two. Both Stalin and Hitler used mass murder, deportation, labour camps, and terrible privation as weapons of suppression. In preserving his authority, Stalin would unleash all these forces on large ethnic groups within the Soviet Union, as, for example, the Muslims in Grozny in 1944 (which returned to haunt both Yeltsin and Putin).

At Potsdam the Red Army was now an occupying force, numerically superior to the Allies moving in from the West.

Since the Allies had no appetite for a war against the Soviet Union, the Russians were not going to be rolled back at any talks. And, with the A-bomb now successfully tested, President Truman – who was more sceptical of Russian intentions – did not need Russian military support against Japan. Prime Minister Attlee, newly elected, was focused on bringing the troops home and ensuring they were better treated than after the First World War in terms of jobs and retraining.

After the Second World War, Churchill remained in the House of Commons as leader of the opposition. Most of his time was spent writing; indeed, he said, 'For my part, I consider that it will be found much better by all parties to leave the past to history, especially as I propose to write that history myself.'[79] Churchill did, however, make a very important speech at Westminster College, Fulton, Missouri, on 5 March 1946, commonly known as the 'Sinews of Peace' speech. Missouri was Truman's home state, and he travelled there with Churchill by train from Washington. First, Churchill praised the United Nations, with its 'prime purpose of preventing war', as 'a force for action', and which would have its own international armed force made up of units delegated to it by member states and under its direction.[80]

Moving on to the situation in Europe, Churchill said, 'Nobody knows what Soviet Russia and its Communist international organisation intends to do in the immediate future, or what are the limits, if any, to their expansive and proselytising tendencies.'[81] He nevertheless went on to recognise the contribution the Russians had made to the defeat of Germany and noted that Russia had a 'rightful place among the leading nations of the world'.[82] But that was only a prelude to his memorable description of the Iron Curtain falling, which warrants quoting at length.[83]

From Stettin in the Baltic to Trieste in the Adriatic, an iron curtain has descended across the Continent. Behind that line lie all the capitals of the ancient states of Central and Eastern Europe. Warsaw, Berlin, Prague, Vienna, Budapest, Belgrade, Bucharest and Sofia, all these famous cities and the populations around them lie in what I must call the Soviet sphere, and all are subject in one form or another, not only to Soviet influence but to a very high and, in many cases, increasing measure of control from Moscow. Athens alone – Greece with its immortal glories – is free to decide its future at an election under British, American and French observation. The Russian-dominated Polish Government has been encouraged to make enormous and wrongful inroads upon Germany, and mass expulsions of millions of Germans on a scale grievous and undreamed-of are now taking place. The Communist parties, which were very small in all these Eastern States of Europe, have been raised to pre-eminence and power far beyond their numbers and are seeking everywhere to obtain totalitarian control. Police governments are prevailing in nearly every case, and so far, except in Czechoslovakia, there is no true democracy.[84]

Churchill portrayed Communists as constituting a very 'peril to Christian civilisation'.[85] The old anti-Bolshevik rhetoric was back. Comparing the mood to the high hopes post-Versailles, he did not 'see or feel that same confidence or even the same hopes in the haggard world at the present time'.[86] That said, he did not see another war as either inevitable or imminent. Rather than war, he saw the Russians desiring 'the fruits of war and the indefinite expansion of their power and doctrines'.[87] This would require a firm response. Based on what he had seen of the Russians during the war, he was convinced: 'There is nothing they admire so much as strength, and there is nothing for which they have less respect than for weakness, especially military weakness. For that reason the old doctrine of a balance of power is unsound.'[88] Wise words still in view of the 2022 war against Ukraine.

Churchill made another important speech in September of that year in Zurich, turning his attention to Europe – 'this noble continent', which had been reduced to a region where 'over wide areas ... a vast quivering mass of tormented, hungry, careworn and bewildered human beings ... wait in the ruins of their cities and homes and scan the dark horizons for the approach of some new peril, tyranny or terror'.[89]

Churchill called on Europe to move quickly. He flagged the danger brought about by the advent of the A-bomb and its potential acquisition by countries other than the United States. A future war could lead not just to the end of civilisation, but the possible destruction of the world itself. He ended by saying:

> In all this urgent work France and Germany must take the lead together. Great Britain, the British Commonwealth of Nations, mighty America – and, I trust, Soviet Russia, for then indeed all would be well – must be the friends and sponsors of the new Europe and must champion its right to live and shine.

It was clear from this that he saw Britain's role as a supporter of this effort rather than a participant in it – a theme that played out over the coming years and decades and is still with us today after UK's referendum decision in 2016 to leave the EU. Likewise, the role of Russia in post-war Europe continues to evolve, as the following chapters will show. Churchill's wish that Russia would be a friend of the new Europe was not to be fulfilled, but the fact that he expressed that wish reflects his passionate desire that Russia had a critical role to play in Europe's future.

Churchill was to return to lead his country one more time, becoming prime minister in October 1951 at the age of seventy-six, but it was a very different premiership, both on a personal level and in relation to Britain's position in the world. The task facing him in 1951 was 'to make this Island solvent, able to earn its living and pay its way'.[90] But the spectre of Russia also continued to loom large. The Communist grip on the countries of Central and Eastern Europe had tightened during his years in opposition, though the West's position had been strengthened through the establishment of NATO in 1949.

Further east, British troops were fighting the Soviet-backed forces of North Korea. Churchill inherited Attlee's cabinet's decision of 25 July 1950 to send a brigade of about 9,000 men to serve under US command in the Korean War, following the North's invasion of the US-backed South on 25 June. The situation in the Korean Peninsula was complex. Having been occupied by Japan since 1910, it was divided at the 38th Parallel when Soviet and US armies drove them out at the end of the Second World War. And it remained divided despite UN efforts. Politically, South Korea was led by the US-backed Syngman Rhee, and North Korea by Kim Il-Sung, widely regarded as a Soviet puppet. Given the challenges seen in securing UN authorisation for military intervention in recent years, it is interesting to note that authorisation had only been achieved in this case as the Soviet Union was not in a position to wield its veto. The Soviet Union had walked out in January 1950 because of the UN's continued recognition of Chiang Kai-shek's government in China rather than Mao's Communist government. This was, in fact, a major area of disagreement between Britain and the US. Attlee's foreign secretary, Bevin, had intended to support Communist Chinese representation on UN bodies until the Korean War started but, given the strength of US feeling, he had agreed to hold back once the war was underway.

Taking the decision to support intervention had been a difficult one for the Labour government, not least because on 6 July the Defence Committee, chaired by the prime minister, had accepted advice from the chiefs of staff that it would be 'militarily unsound to make available any land or air forces for the Korean campaign'.[91] In their view, Britain was already stretched by significant overseas deployments in Germany and the Middle East, and in the counter-insurgency effort against the Communists in what was then British-administered Malaya. Although he disagreed with the US on many other issues, Bevin advocated supporting American-led military action, as to do otherwise could have discouraged them from supporting Britain in Malaya and France in Indochina.

Lurking in the background were tensions over the US suspension of tripartite talks with Britain and Canada on sharing technical nuclear weapons information following the 1950 arrest of Klaus Fuchs, a Soviet spy working at the UK Atomic Energy Authority. There were to be further tensions as details emerged about the extent of the penetration achieved by other well-placed Soviet spies such as Kim Philby and others of the Cambridge Five spy ring, which did considerable damage to MI6's and MI5's standing with the FBI and CIA in the US.

Ultimately, however, there was never any doubt that the majority of the cabinet would support the prime minister and Bevin's wish to send troops. Shinwell, the defence minister, told the cabinet that Soviet armed forces had forty fully equipped divisions that they could, if they wished, very quickly move into a position to attack South Korea. Aneurin Bevan, the minister of health, who might have been expected to object given his position as leader of the left in the Labour Party, had asked at an earlier cabinet meeting on 17 July for the evidence that the Soviet Union had a mission helping the North Korean troops. The chief of the imperial staff replied that the information came from captured prisoners of war, though nothing at present indicated Russians were actually fighting alongside the North Koreans. At the cabinet meeting on 25 July, Bevan not only supported sending ground troops to Korea but suggested it would be worth sending a larger force. This was an early sign that Bevan had strong views on foreign policy; by the late 1950s, this was on public display, hence his famous Labour Party Conference speech calling for negotiated nuclear arms reductions with the plea to not 'send him naked into the conference chamber'.

The other person who might have presented problems was Sir Stafford Cripps, the wartime ambassador in Moscow, who was now the chancellor of the exchequer. He had already argued against the UK developing its own atomic bomb and was more worried about the British economy. He had told a meeting of ministers on 4 May that he looked forward to 'the day when this country could free herself from the hegemony, political and economic, of the United States'.[92] He had initially argued against any British contribution to the Korean War other than naval support, yet he too was very sensitive to the danger of giving the American public the impression that the British were leaving everything to them, because he knew how much the nation would continue to rely on US financial support. In the debate in the House of Commons on 26 July, Shinwell announced that Britain would send a force to Korea.[93]

When Churchill returned to Downing Street in 1951, Britain was militarily engaged in a major way against the Soviet Union for the first time since 1919. By then, China had also become heavily involved, deploying increasing numbers of troops in support of North Korea. Eisenhower, who had succeeded Truman as US president in January 1953, set about fulfilling an election promise by ending the conflict through a combination of diplomacy and blunt threats. He asked his secretary of state, on a visit to India, to pass on a message to Prime Minister Nehru to warn Chinese premier Zhou Enlai that, if the peace negotiations were not successful, he would detonate a nuclear device over an unpopulated area north of the Yalu River, the border between China and North Korea. If that did not persuade China to accept a negotiated settlement, he would not hesitate to use another tactical nuclear bomb against China.[94] Eisenhower's efforts were greatly helped by the death of Stalin. He suffered a fatal stroke on 5 March 1953, but no doctor was called to see him for twelve hours, at the orders of the still-terrified senior political figures around him. The new Soviet leadership called for a quick end to hostilities in North Korea and, while no formal peace treaty was signed, an armistice was declared on 27 July, establishing the Military Demarcation Line which remains to this day.

Churchill also suffered a stroke in 1953, though in his case it was not fatal. He had given up his position as minister of defence following a cerebral artery spasm in February 1952, but he ignored his doctor's advice to also step down as prime minister. Then, on 23 June 1953, Churchill suffered a major stroke. He initially managed to disguise the fact by saying little when chairing the morning cabinet. He left Downing Street for Chartwell the next morning; speaking became very difficult, and he lost the use of his left arm. A conspiracy of silence followed, and not just for the three weeks he was seriously incapacitated. Not a word appeared in the newspapers controlled by the 'Press Barons', Beaverbrook, Rothermere, Bracken, and Camrose. Eight weeks after the first medical signs, Churchill was back chairing the cabinet. By 24 July, he was talking about 'bringing something off with the Russians and ... the idea of meeting Georgy Malenkov [Stalin's successor] face to face'.[95]

In December, Churchill travelled to Bermuda to meet President Eisenhower, where he tried but failed to convince both Eisenhower and his secretary of state, John Foster Dulles, that he should fly to Moscow to meet Malenkov. At the first plenary session he talked of an 'easement' with the Soviet Union. Eisenhower was brutal in his response. The Soviet Union, he said, was 'a woman of the streets and whether her dress was new, or just the old one patched, it was certainly the same whore underneath'.[96] The French supported the US position, and it was an open secret that Churchill's foreign secretary, Anthony Eden, was also firmly against a visit by the prime minister to Moscow. Nevertheless, Churchill continued to press the case for engagement. Speaking in America in June 1954, Churchill used the expression 'meeting jaw to jaw is better than war'. Sadly, common parlance rendered it 'jaw, jaw is better than war, war', a phrase without the edge of verbal conflict that is often the essence of tough detailed negotiations. The mere act of negotiations is not weakness; it is what is said and how it is backed militarily that is important, particularly so with Russia and Serbia.

Churchill still planned for an August visit to Moscow, where he intended to propose arms reductions. He had admitted to his old private secretary, Colville, who had returned to No. 10 with Churchill, that he was prepared to adopt any methods necessary to get a meeting with the Russians arranged. The cabinet was, as Andrew Roberts describes it, 'collectively opposed to making an approach to Moscow'.[97] Salisbury, as lord president of the council, threatened to resign over the matter; Churchill privately remarked that 'he didn't give a damn if he did'.[98] Salisbury was not the only one who resented Churchill's attempt to bounce the cabinet on the issue. At the cabinet meeting of 23 July, both Salisbury and Harry Crookshank, the leader of the House of Commons, threatened to resign if Churchill asked the Russians for a meeting. Two days later, the Russians pre-empted the cabinet discussions by summoning thirty-two foreign ministers to discuss a pan-European security plan.

Churchill returned to the charge over Russia in February 1955 when Malenkov was forced to resign and was replaced by Khrushchev's nominee, Nikolai Bulganin. In his last Commons speech on 1 March, introducing the annual Defence White Paper and announcing the government's decision to manufacture a British hydrogen bomb, he opened by speaking of a world divided 'between the creeds of Communist discipline and individual freedom' and living with the threat of nuclear weapons.[99] He then posed the question: 'Which way shall we turn to save our lives and the future of the world?'[100] Churchill followed these words by setting out the conundrum the West faced in seeking peace and security now that nuclear weapons were held by both sides.

The best defence would of course be *bona fide* disarmament all round. This is in all our hearts. But sentiment must not cloud our vision. It is often said that 'Facts are stubborn things.' ... We must not conceal from ourselves the gulf between the Soviet Government and the N.A.T.O. Powers, which has hitherto, for so long, prevented an agreement.[101]

Churchill then reiterated the differentiation he had made in the past between his views on the Russian people and how he regarded their rulers.

The House will perhaps note that I avoid using the word 'Russia' as much as possible in this discussion. I have a strong admiration for the Russian people – for their bravery, their many gifts, and their kindly nature. It is the Communist dictatorship and the declared ambition of the Communist Party and their proselytising activities that we are bound to resist.[102]

He ended: 'The day may dawn when fair play, love for one's fellow men, respect for justice and freedom, will enable tormented generations to march forth serene and triumphant from the hideous epoch in which we have to dwell. Meanwhile, never flinch, never weary, never despair.'[103]

Churchill thus never underestimated the important role Russia had played and would continue to play in European – and global – affairs. He was ready to adapt his approach according to the circumstances and, critically, to what he saw as being in the best interests of Britain. In particular, he recognised the value of maintaining a dialogue and working for change. Having taken a hard-line view over the Bolsheviks, by 1939 Churchill was ready to work with the Russians when Litvinov made his offer. He seized the moment after the Germans attacked Russia in 1941 to help Stalin with the Arctic Convoys. In 1943, he flew to Moscow. At the talks in Tehran, Yalta, and Potsdam he was always looking for a way to improve relations, to negotiate constructively, while acknowledging the realities of the position he was negotiating from. And here he was in 1955, at his last opportunity – and long after he should have stepped back from the frontline of politics – just as motivated to find a way of ensuring nuclear weapons would never be used. Churchill's political and strategic legacy is something no serious politician in the twenty-first century should ever forget. We still live under the shadow of an accidental nuclear weapons exchange.

The fear of an accidental nuclear incident has concerned me throughout my political career, and I feel that anyone wondering why a medical neuroscientist should have spent so much of his political time and energy on Britain's nuclear deterrent deserves an explanation. My concern first took form after I was told that a nuclear-powered Royal Navy submarine HMS *Warspite* had collided underwater with a Soviet nuclear-powered Echo II-class submarine in the early hours of the night in October 1968 when both were creeping submerged across the floor of the Barents Sea. The best description after a long period of necessary secrecy is in the *Daily Telegraph*'s obituary for rear-admiral John Hervey.

In a Cold War game described by one expert as like two knights in armour fighting each other in a darkened room, where one could only hear the other by the occasional clink of armour, Hervey was tracking his foe by listening passively on *Warspite*'s sonars. Quite unexpectedly, Hervey's quarry shut down one of its propellers: the effect was to slow the Soviet boat and to make it even quieter. Hervey was deprived of range information when suddenly there was 'an awful bang, crushing and scraping', alarm bells rang and red lights flashed while *Warspite* rolled on to her starboard side and passed under the Soviet boat.[104]

As *Warspite* bobbed up again she once again struck the Soviet boat and was flung back on her side. She surfaced in the dark. The conning tower of the boat was skewed sideways, and a large part had been chewed off by the Soviet boat's propeller. Much later, a Russian source admitted that the collision had made a hole in the outer casing of their boat which could easily have been done by 'a three-ton truck'. Hervey received a letter expressing the Admiralty's severe displeasure, but he took *Warspite* on its next patrol and had a distinguished career ending up as a rear-admiral.

This type of close trailing of hunter-killer submarines was reduced when the nuclear missile deterrent submarine class emerged, but a new type of shadowing developed: trying to track each other from their bases to the point where they would settle in deep water, making little to no noise and able to fire a nuclear-armed missile at Moscow, Washington, or London. As the *Warspite* incident showed, such tracking is potentially very dangerous. As indeed are many other aspects of the nuclear deterrent, which were demonstrated during the 1963 Cuban Missile Crisis. What's more, there are numerous well reported incidents on both the US and Russian sides where nuclear warfare has very nearly been triggered accidentally. Yet still we do not take risks for disarmament that we routinely take for armament.

In nearly sixty years of watching this, my belief that there will be an accidental nuclear incident has grown not diminished.

The Non-Proliferation Treaty has slowed but not stopped the spread of nuclear weapons. Somehow, we must get heads of government to focus on that reality. The problem is that only a very few have an overall view of the dangers. When I became foreign secretary, Prime Minister James Callaghan asked if I would like to be one of the two senior cabinet ministers designated to take up responsibility for the British nuclear deterrent if at any time he was not able to discharge his responsibilities. During Tony Crosland's illness, he had appointed someone he knew well, so two people had been already designated. I therefore told Callaghan that there was no need to make a change. I had inadvertently been told and shown all the details of the British nuclear deterrent control system back in 1968 when I was a new minister for the navy. I therefore knew, and was satisfied by, the arrangements and was content not to assume this responsibility. Indeed, foreign secretaries are not necessarily the right people to be involved as they are out of the country so much.

We need not only the most modern and fast communications between nuclear-weapon-state leaders but also a determined personal commitment to reducing the risk of a nuclear accident. A fibre-optic-based communication system was introduced in 2008 between Washington and Moscow, but the same cannot be said for all nuclear-weapon states. This is now particularly important between Beijing and Washington. After a lot of discussion, Indian and Chinese foreign ministers agreed to a political hotline in February 2021, and this owed much to China's own 2020 border crisis. The European Leadership Network, of which I am a member, is working together with the UK-based Institute for Security and Technology on nuclear technology, and CATALINK is ready for testing.

Russia, Britain, and China should by now be using fibre-optics, but North Korea, Pakistan, and Saudi Arabia, as well as Iran and Israel, need attention in this area.

6

Face-Off in Europe

Shortly before Churchill delivered his 'Iron Curtain' speech, in March 1946, the US diplomat in Moscow, George Kennan, had sent what was to become known as his 'long telegram'.[1] Kennan had already reported that the Soviets sought to advance the limits of Communist power wherever possible. Soviet power, he argued:

> ... unlike that of Hitlerite Germany, is neither schematic nor adventuristic. It does not work by fixed plans. It does not take unnecessary risks. Impervious to logic of reason, and it is highly sensitive to logic of force ... Thus, if the adversary has sufficient force and makes clear his readiness to use it, he rarely has to do so.

Just a week before Churchill's speech, the US joint chiefs of staff concluded that Soviet aggression and consolidation was the single greatest military threat to world peace.[2] Kennan's advice was to underpin the US response to that threat from then on.

The handling of the Soviet threat by the US and its allies was to develop gradually. An early example was its handling of freedom of navigation through the Bosporus – a worrying forerunner, perhaps, of what we are seeing today in the South China Sea as the US faces an ambitious and nuclear-equipped China over Taiwan. The USSR had challenged the Turkish readiness to allow foreign naval vessels through the Bosporus. It was particularly angered by the arrival of the battleship USS *Missouri* in April 1946, ostensibly to repatriate the ashes of the late Turkish ambassador to Washington but, in reality, as Truman had told Churchill, who relayed the message to Attlee, to demonstrate their intentions clearly to the USSR. Later that year, the USSR stepped up its pressure on Turkey through increased naval and military activity, and Turkey requested US assistance. Truman dispatched a US naval force, and the Soviets ultimately backed off, demonstrating the validity of Kennan's analysis.

All these years later in the summer of 2022, during the Russia–Ukraine war when NATO was supporting Ukraine, one of the most controversial questions was whether NATO ships should escort grain-carrying ships through the Black Sea to the Bosphorus to supply the world grain market, which was showing dangerous signs of not being able to feed millions of people in different parts of the world. It was vital that an end to the Russian blockade of Ukrainian ports be found. On 20 July a UN-led agreement was reached with Ukraine, Turkey, and Russia that should allow the resumption of maritime grain exports from Odesa, Chornomorsk, and Pivdennyi Ukrainian ports. All parties would be represented at a coordination centre in Istanbul to monitor vessels and assess threat levels, and a commitment was made not to attack merchant or other civilian vessels or port facilities covered by the agreement. Whether this deal holds remains to be seen given that on 23 July Odesa was struck by a Russian cruise missile. But on 1 August the first grain ship departed Odesa destined for Lebanon. Potential risks to the agreement remain high, particularly if Ukrainian vessels out in the Black Sea are harassed by Russian naval ships.[3]

The last time US warships were deployed in the Black Sea before the war started was in April 2021, in a show of support for Ukraine after Russia annexed Crimea in 2014, and in that same period the British sailed through Soviet-claimed waters after visiting Odesa and Ukraine's navy. But the gravity of the 2022 situation over a year later calls for special measures if, as is possible, ships from other countries fail to offer their ships and insurance companies refuse to insure at reasonable levels.

Back in 1947, momentum was building to two events of huge significance in eventually securing freedom in Europe. On 21 February, the US under-secretary of state, Dean Acheson, was shown two documents that the secretary of state, George Marshall, would receive personally from the British ambassador, Lord Inverchapel. The message contained in the two documents was that Britain could no longer afford the financial burden of providing support to Greece – which was then in the throes of a fierce struggle with Communist insurgents – or Turkey, facing the Soviet pressure mentioned above. The US had been expecting this news, and the wheels began to move in Washington that weekend. A few weeks later, in a speech delivered to a joint session of Congress on 12 March, Truman announced American aid for Greece and Turkey and launched what was to become the 'Truman Doctrine', designed to contain Soviet expansion. Truman made very clear how he saw the situation facing the world.

At the present moment in world history nearly every nation must choose between alternative ways of life. The choice is too often not a free one. One way of life is based upon the will of the majority, and is distinguished by free institutions, representative government, free elections, guarantees of individual liberty, freedom of speech and religion, and freedom from political oppression. The second way of life is based upon the will of a minority forcibly imposed upon the majority. It relies upon terror and oppression, a controlled press and radio, fixed elections, and the suppression of personal freedoms.

I believe that it must be the policy of the United States to support free peoples who are resisting attempted subjugation by armed minorities or by outside pressures.

I believe that we must assist free peoples to work out their own destinies in their own way.

I believe that our help should be primarily through economic and financial aid which is essential to economic stability and orderly political processes.[4]

This was a bold move from Truman, who was running the risk of an adverse domestic reaction from those opposed to the US making such expensive and expansive international commitments. Indeed, the way the next momentous step in American support for post-war Europe was handled demonstrated the need to manage this balance carefully.

Following his appointment as secretary of state in January 1947, General George Marshall, along with the British, had held lengthy talks with the Soviets over the reconstruction of Germany, but they broke down after the Soviets rejected the proposals. The Americans decided they had to push ahead regardless. Marshall chose the setting of Harvard University – where he received an honorary degree along with the poet T. S.

Eliot and the atomic bomb pioneer Robert Oppenheimer – to deliver a speech for which he had deliberately sought no publicity in the US (though the European media were alerted). This speech, on 5 June 1947, launched the Marshall Plan, which was to play such a critical part in rebuilding Europe. 'Our policy', he said, 'is directed not against any country or doctrine but against hunger, poverty, desperation and chaos'.[5] Everyone was welcome to join this great effort of recovery – although, to be sure, any government that sought 'to perpetuate human misery in order to profit therefrom politically or otherwise [would] encounter the opposition of the United States'. Such a policy could not work on a piecemeal basis, however. 'Any assistance that this Government may render in the future should provide a cure rather than a mere palliative', and so, 'before the United States Government can proceed much further ... there must be some agreement among the countries of Europe as to the requirements of the situation ... The initiative, I think, must come from Europe.' And the programme would need to be 'a joint one, agreed to by a number, if not all, European nations. ... Of course, the United States would be willing, as the Europeans considered just what their needs might be, to offer friendly aid in the drafting of a European programme.'[6]

The response Marshall sought from Europe came instantly from the British foreign secretary, Bevin. He knew exactly how to respond and how to deliver a message from Europe that would help Truman carry America with him in this act of unparalleled generosity. The historian and author Charles Mee brings out the depth underpinning the Marshall Plan, which:

Contributed, more than dollars or credits or goods, the crucial element of confidence – for governments to reach across borders, for entrepreneurs to take new risks, for banks to extend credit, for workers to set aside immediate gains. The most important effect of the plan was as George Kennan had foreseen from the very beginning, essentially, 'psychological'.[7]

The initial Soviet reaction to Marshall's speech was interesting. Bevin had suggested that Britain, France, and the USSR should meet in Paris to consider their response, and at the outset Stalin appeared open to discussion. However, as the terms for the assistance became clearer, the Soviet foreign minister, Molotov, walked out. Only then did France and Britain convene a meeting to discuss the proposals, inviting twenty-two European countries, including the USSR (though it was not expected to attend); Spain, still under Franco's dictatorship, was not invited, nor were the smallest countries. Marshall and Bevin handled this well, with Bevin's invitation to Russia and France as occupying powers in Berlin a subtle and well-judged tactic. This low-key approach covering nearly all European countries helped manage the US domestic audience, where announcing moves that could lead to significant payments to the USSR would have provoked hostile reactions.

On 12 July 1947, sixteen European states[8] met for the discussions that would lead to the European Recovery Program. Despite the initial interest, and following pressure from the USSR, Albania, Bulgaria, Czechoslovakia, Hungary, and Poland did not take part. As a result, in 1948, Congress passed the necessary legislation for Marshall Aid, helping to bolster the market economies of Western Europe. It was a subtle, Kennan-compatible containment policy, the start of defining how to approach the ideological struggle that was an integral part of the Cold War.

It is also important to acknowledge that, between the end of the Second World War and the beginning of Marshall Aid, the US lent very significant sums to Europe: $4.4 billion to Britain, $1.9 billion to France, $513 million to Italy, $251 million to Poland, $272 million to Denmark, and $161 million to Greece. The British loan was particularly high because of Truman's overly hasty decision of 14 August 1945 to cancel lend-lease agreements, triggering John Maynard Keynes's warning to the new Labour government that the UK faced an 'economic Dunkirk'.[9]

The USSR did not take the growing US influence in Europe lying down, particularly when, in early 1948, it learnt of Allied plans to integrate their occupation zones into a new German state. It increased its pressure on the Allies by imposing restrictions on movement in Berlin. Like many Russian initiatives, the blockade's implementation and purpose had not been fully thought through. Everyone knew the USSR could, if it wished, block the roads and railways through the area of Germany it controlled, but did the Soviets seriously believe their action would not provoke a response from the Allies? Tensions continued to build, coming to a climax in June as the Soviets ramped up the blockade by cutting off supplies to the Western sectors. Berlin was in a perilous position.

The Potsdam Agreement had not guaranteed Allied access to ground routes, but fortunately there were agreed air corridors. The Allies' capacity, in terms of the number and size of plans needed to airlift supplies and support into Berlin, was initially in doubt, but logistical problems were overcome and the American and British response (France was not involved at first because of domestic political turmoil) started on 26 June, when the first supply flight of the airlift landed. For eleven months, until 12 May 1949, the Western Allies flew in 2.3 million tonnes of food on 277,500 flights, in addition to coal and oil. Ultimately, the blockade was completely counterproductive for the Soviets. It created two German states and ensured a continued US military presence in Berlin as well as the stationing of US Air Force planes equipped with nuclear weapons in Europe.

Another critical development was the creation of NATO. While such an alliance had been under discussion before the airlift, and with the Truman doctrine contributing significantly to the change in the US approach to European security, the Soviet blockade made it far easier for the general public to see it was essential. By April 1949, the US, Canada, and ten European countries were signed up. Again, it was Bevin on the British side who played a major political role in its creation and structure, adamantly telling his officials not to water down US command authority but rather strengthen it. He wanted a clear-cut command and control structure led by an American supreme allied commander, not some wishy-washy arrangement in which no one knew who precisely was giving the orders. While there was opposition in America to such a close engagement with Europe, which ran contrary to US tradition, America's clear leadership, holding the command position of Supreme Allied Commander, Europe, meant that NATO's launch was approved by the US Senate – unlike the establishment of the League of Nations – and most senators had no doubt their essential sovereignty was not challenged. No other single international structure has developed so effective a command system. The security of Europe and the prevention of a third world war in the tense decades of the 1950s and 1960s owes much to NATO.

Stalin's conduct after taking and occupying Berlin in 1945

had – in the space of four years and against all expectation – ensured a continual American military presence in Europe that remains even today, over seventy-five years since the end of the war. This was a huge blow to Stalin's strategy for increased domination of Europe, despite such confident beginnings. But Berlin was not Stalin's only setback. The USSR was facing problems and challenges elsewhere in Eastern Europe. On 27 March 1948, Stalin and Molotov wrote to Tito saying the Yugoslav Communist Party 'could not be regarded as Marxist, Leninist or Bolshevik'.[10] The date itself was a provocation, as it was the seventh anniversary of the coup d'état spurred on by the Cvetković government's alliance with Hitler, during which the Belgrade crowd attacked German buildings and tore up the swastika. The Yugoslavs consequently refused to attend the meeting of the international Communist grouping, Cominform, in Bucharest, where the expulsion of Yugoslavia's Communist Party was announced to a surprised world for a list of political crimes, one being 'grandeeism'. The expulsion of Yugoslavia was a major mistake by Stalin. It pushed a large European state out of the Soviet orbit, though not totally away from Communism itself. But Tito's skill was to move slowly and maximise opportunities to link with India and Ghana in creating the Non-Aligned Movement. Yugoslavia never became a member of the Warsaw Pact, which was created on 14 May 1955, soon after the formal incorporation of West Germany into NATO. The Warsaw Pact did, however, include the remaining Soviet satellites: Poland, Czechoslovakia, Hungary, Romania, Bulgaria, Albania, and a fully sovereign German Democratic Republic.

The situation in East Germany also continued to give the Soviets cause for concern. Between the spring of 1949 and August 1961 close to three million East Germans passed through Berlin to the West. A very bad harvest in 1952 drove many people from the land to urban areas, where they found life even harder. Over 180,000 people fled the country in 1952. The exodus continued after Stalin's death in 1953, with over 330,000 leaving that year, in a pattern that was to continue.[11] A memorandum from the Soviet Council of Ministers on 2 June 1953 criticised the 'incorrect political line' of the East German leadership under Walter Ulbricht. They were told to halt the collectivisation drive, to stop attacks on small farmers and businesses, to increase the production of consumer goods, and to moderate the use of excessive police powers. The leadership was summoned to Moscow, and the Ulbricht regime was publicly humiliated. On 16 June, construction crews working on Stalinallee in East Berlin went on strike. Between 500,000 and one million people protested across the country. In the early hours of 17 June, the Soviet Twelfth Tank Division entered East Berlin and martial law was declared there and in much of the country. Numerous arrests and some executions followed. While the uprising ultimately fizzled out, the memory remained. Mistakenly, Ulbricht was given another chance, despite all that happened, and he remained East German leader until 1971.

When Khrushchev emerged as first secretary of the Communist Party, he began to address some of the major problems he inherited from Stalin, including making amends with Tito through a visit in May 1955 and again before the Soviet clampdown in Hungary in 1956. The release of political prisoners from the Gulags made Stalin's crimes ever more evident, and in his famous 'secret speech' at the 20th Party Congress of February 1956, Khrushchev denounced the crimes, errors, and 'cult' of General Secretary Stalin, which had trampled on the

Leninist principles of collective party leadership. The speech, although supposedly secret, was widely disseminated both at home and around Eastern Europe. Shortly thereafter, Khrushchev, accompanied by Marshal Bulganin, made a ten-day visit to Britain in April, the first visit by the Soviet top leadership to a Western country since the revolution, in what was seen by the British as a broadly successful attempt to build a working relationship with their Russian counterparts. However, it was in the East rather than the West that the end of the Stalin era was to have its most significant near-term ramifications.

The move towards de-Stalinisation had its greatest immediate impact in Poland, where there were widespread protest and riots, and party reformers pushed for the return of Władysław Gomułka, the veteran Communist and, until relatively recently, prisoner. Though the Soviets did not prevent Gomułka becoming first secretary, the reaction was swift. Khrushchev, Molotov, and Mikoyan arrived in Warsaw for talks on 19 October 1956. Simultaneously, Soviet troops located in Poland started an advance towards Warsaw. Gomułka, in a tough conversation, convinced the Russians that he had no intention of taking Poland outside the Warsaw Pact, let alone demanding the withdrawal of Soviet troops, and his position was secured.

Meanwhile, in Hungary, another apparent reformer, Imre Nagy, who had been prime minister since 1953, was attempting to relax some of the harshest aspects of his Stalinist predecessor, Mátyás Rákosi. Rákosi, who had been demoted to first secretary of the Hungarian Communist Party following the death of Stalin, continued to oppose Nagy, who was eventually pushed out of government in 1955, though he remained popular in the eyes of reformists. Rákosi was forced out of office by the Soviets in July 1956, only to be replaced by his acolyte, the Stalinist

Ernő Gerő. In mid-October, university students started to call for the implementation of a reform package called the 'sixteen-point manifesto', and what began as a protest turned into a much wider revolt. On 24 October, Nagy was back as prime minister, meeting a central demand of the revolutionaries.

With full control of the government, Nagy promised democratic reforms and, by the end of the month, he had declared his intention of withdrawing Hungary from the Warsaw Pact. Initially appearing open to discussions on the level of Soviet troops in Hungary and their withdrawal, Khrushchev then told the Soviet Presidium that Russia would 'take the initiative in restoring order in Hungary'.[12] Yuri Andropov, then Soviet ambassador in Budapest and to whom I shall return later, supported that Soviet military intervention, as did Mikhail Suslov, second secretary of the Soviet Communist Party, who had flown in to assert overall control of the military intervention. On the evening of 1 November, Nagy announced in a radio broadcast that Soviet troops were advancing to the Hungarian border from bases in Romania and Ukraine. He declared Hungary a neutral country and that he had applied to the UN to recognise this.

At 4 a.m. on 4 November, Soviet tanks rolled into Budapest. Just before the final authorisation, Khrushchev flew to the islands of Brijuni to meet Tito at one of his many official houses to tell him of his intentions and to obtain his support, which Tito revealingly readily gave. The visit was a significant indication that Moscow was worried that Yugoslavia could have created trouble.

The Western Allies did nothing. As a student, I joined the protests in a large demonstration in Cambridge. NATO's abdication of responsibility seemed callous against heart-rending cries for help as the radio station in Budapest was surrounded by Russian troops. But containment never meant taking on the Soviet military; its objective was deterring attacks on NATO members or threats to their boundaries by making clear that such actions would be met with a unified military response. While sympathetic to Hungary's plight, the Allied powers under NATO leadership were right not to respond militarily to support Warsaw Pact countries. NATO was not set up to be adventurist or interventionist, and rightly so. Its guiding principles are clearly stated in its charter; it is committed to collective defence and to '[safeguarding] the freedom, common heritage and civilisation of [its] peoples, founded on the principles of democracy, individual liberty and the rule of law', while acting in line with their obligations as members of the United Nations.[13] NATO was in it for the long haul, and Kennan's words were the guiding principles: 'long-term, patient but firm and vigilant containment of Russian expansive tendencies'.[14]

On the yardstick of Europe's progress towards liberation, the Soviet invasion was a clearly a setback for the West, and Hungary remained under Soviet control. Yet it represented a serious ideological defeat for Communism in Britain. The shock and brutal nature of the intervention led to cancellations of party memberships, with some even tearing up their membership cards.

In Britain, it was easy to blame Eden and his handling of the Suez Crisis for encouraging the Soviets to invade Hungary. However, while Britain and France's clandestine support for Israel's invasion of Egypt – an attempt to overthrow President Nasser portrayed as an action to prevent the closure of the Suez Canal – was a serious embarrassment for them, it was not a major factor in the Russian decision to invade Hungary. The Soviets would have reacted as they did in Budapest had there been no Suez invasion. But it did make it harder for the West to moralise, even if NATO had had no intention of responding militarily.

The following decade was to see further dramatic flare-ups in tensions between East and West, both on the fault lines in Europe and further afield. The Soviets initially challenged the charismatic new US President, J. F. Kennedy, who took office in 1961, through the veteran Soviet leader Khrushchev. I analysed the mental health of both these men at some length in my book *In Sickness and In Power*, and I will not dwell on this here.[15] However, I do think it is worth noting that, just before Kennedy's first meeting with Khrushchev in Vienna on 3 June 1962, Kennedy had an injection of amphetamine and steroids from his quack 'Doctor Feelgood' Dr Max Jacobson, probably intravenously rather than into his muscles as is more common. This led to an early high in Kennedy's mood followed by a greater low when the meeting was delayed due to Khrushchev's late arrival. As a result, Kennedy underperformed, leaving Khrushchev badly underestimating the young president. After the two-day meeting, Kennedy himself said off the record to James Reston of *The New York Times*:

> Roughest thing in my life. He savaged me. I think I know why he treated me like this. He thinks because of the Bay of Pigs [the abortive attempt to topple Castro in April of that year which Kennedy had authorised] I'm inexperienced. Probably thinks I am stupid. Maybe most important he thinks I have no guts.

Then on the plane back to America from London, Kennedy found solace in a quotation from Abraham Lincoln.

I know there is a God – and I see a storm coming
If he has a place for me, I believe I am ready.[16]

The storm was not long coming. On the night of 12–13 August 1961, East German security forces erected barbed-wire barriers on the boundary of East and West Germany in Berlin. This was in marked contrast to January of that year when a friend and I had crossed over with no difficulty in my car en route to Prague at the Friedrichstrasse crossing point, better known in the West as Checkpoint Charlie. Gradually, the barbed wire became an actual wall. NATO had decided, once again, that it would not be provoked by Russia. Various anti-Russian measures were taken by NATO, but no thought was given to actual war. As Kennedy was to say, 'It's not a very nice solution, but a wall is a hell of a lot better than a war.'[17]

A much greater storm was brewing a year later, and this fresh clash of wills between the USSR and the West was to be one of the most dangerous moments of the Cold War period. On 16 October 1962, Kennedy was shown satellite and aeroplane pictures of Soviet missiles in Cuba. Fortunately, the president was by then in much better health. In marked contrast to his handling of the Bay of Pigs incident, he imposed a disciplined caution on the decision-making and created the Executive Committee of the National Security Council – ExComm. We now know Khrushchev had decided to put nuclear warheads on missiles in Cuba on 24 May 1962 after asking rhetorically in April, 'Why not throw a hedgehog at Uncle Sam's pants?', not thinking so much of triggering a war but supporting the Communist movements in Cuba and Latin America.[18]

Kennedy chose an old-fashioned naval blockade or 'quarantine', as he cleverly called the armed interception point off

the Cuban coast where the Soviet ship *Bucharest* could expect
to be stopped and searched. When the US ambassador to the
UN, Adlai Stevenson, challenged the Soviet ambassador in the
Security Council to answer his questions on the missile sites, he
added that he was prepared to wait until 'hell freezes over for an
answer'.[19] On 25 October, *Bucharest* was boarded by US forces,
its cargo inspected, and, since no missiles were found on board,
allowed to proceed. We now know that, during the night of
26 October, Soviet troops in Cuba moved three FKR cruise
missiles, with fourteen-kiloton nuclear warheads, to within
15 miles of the US naval base at Guantanamo Bay. That Satur-
day morning, Khrushchev sent an urgent cable to the Soviet
commander to categorically forbid the use of nuclear weapons
without approval from Moscow and requesting receipt of that
message. For a short period of less than twenty-four hours,
nuclear warheads could have been fired into the US nuclear
base in Guantanamo if the US had bombed Cuba that night
without the Kremlin agreeing or even knowing that such a
decentralised decision-making existed.

The world held its breath. At 7.15 p.m. on 27 October, the
day an American U-2 spy plane was shot down over Cuba, the
president authorised his brother, the attorney general, Robert,
to call the Soviet ambassador, Anatoly Dobrynin, and arrange
a secret meeting. This took place half an hour later in Robert's office. Dobrynin was told, 'There is now strong pressure
on the President to give an order to respond with fire if fired
upon. If we start to fire, a chain reaction will quickly start that
will be very hard to stop.'[20] Robert Kennedy went on to say
that the United States would give assurances that Cuba would
not be invaded and that four to five months would be needed
to remove US Jupiter missiles in Turkey, but he warned that

publicly discussing the issue of Turkey posed the greatest challenge to the president. If the Russians revealed this pledge on Turkey, then it would become null and void.

Only the US secretary of state, Dean Rusk, and the two Kennedys knew of this offer to Khrushchev to remove US missiles from Turkey. The following day, Khrushchev responded in a private letter to Kennedy, having also publicly said in a radio broadcast designed to reach the US that the Soviet missiles would be withdrawn. In that letter he wrote:

> I feel I must state to you that I do understand the delicacy involved for you in an open consideration of the issue of eliminating the US missile bases in Turkey. I take into account the complexity of this issue and I believe you are right about not wishing to publicly discuss it. I agree that our discussion of this subject be pursued confidentially through Robert Kennedy and the Soviet Ambassador in Washington. You may have noticed that in my message to you on October 28, which was to be published immediately, I did not raise this question—precisely because I was mindful of your wish conveyed through Robert Kennedy. But all the proposals that I presented in that message took into account the fact that you had agreed to resolve, [sic] the matter of your missile bases in Turkey consistent with what I had said in my message of October 27 and what you stated through Robert Kennedy in his meeting with Ambassador Dobrynin on the same day.[21]

Kennedy's strength was to know not to corner his adversary in international diplomacy without leaving a face-saving line of retreat. This secret diplomacy during the Cuban Missile Crisis was not revealed to Harold Macmillan, the British prime minister, nor to President de Gaulle of France, though both were briefed by a special envoy at the start of the crisis. In the end, most people in Europe, unaware of what had gone on behind the scenes, felt the crisis had resulted in a clear-cut victory for President Kennedy over Khrushchev.

In the wake of the crisis, both Kennedy and Khrushchev stepped up their engagement on arms control issues, nuclear testing in particular. The future Nobel laureate and Soviet dissident Andrei Sakharov, the leading scientist in the USSR's hydrogen bomb programme, had been an early advocate of a nuclear test ban. Indeed, Khrushchev himself had been engaged on this question for a number of years. In the summer of 1963, both Kennedy and Khrushchev spoke publicly on the theme, and a new round of talks began that July in Moscow. These rapidly resulted in the signature on 5 August of the Treaty Banning Nuclear Weapons Tests in the Atmosphere, in Outer Space and Under Water (the Partial Test Ban Treaty) by the Soviet Union, the UK, and the US. In a television address following the signature, Kennedy said 'Yesterday a shaft of light cut into the darkness', marking 'a victory for mankind'.[22]

A year after the ratification of that treaty, in October 1964, Khrushchev was ousted by Leonid Brezhnev, who accused him of having ignored others and being distracted and rude to colleagues. Brezhnev's subsequent long rule is well covered in *Brezhnev and the Decline of the Soviet Union* by Thomas Crump, to which I contributed a foreword.[23] As foreign secretary, I met Brezhnev and Gromyko in Moscow in the autumn of 1977, when Brezhnev witnessed Gromyko and me signing an agreement on the prevention of accidental nuclear war. Brezhnev was visibly ageing. I had been asked by MI6 to assess whether he had cancer of the throat as his voice had changed, but it was impossible to make any such diagnosis. He was friendly but content to let Gromyko do most of the talking.

Brezhnev's life was more than usually representative of the era in which he lived. He was a protégé of Khrushchev and had been brought back to Moscow from serving in Kazakhstan in 1956, becoming a candidate member of the Politburo overseeing the defence, space, and construction industry. In June 1957 – when opposition from Malenkov, Molotov, and Kaganovich to Khrushchev's intervention in Hungary and his denunciation of Stalin led them to attempt to depose Khrushchev – Brezhnev kept his head down. He was to emerge as a Khrushchev supporter, and he became deputy chairman of the Central Committee of the Communist Party before seamlessly being accepted as Khrushchev's successor in October 1964, alongside Alexei Kosygin, who stepped up to become chairman of the Council of Ministers, holding that position until his death in December 1980. Their initial working partnership led to them being called 'B & K' in a popular British newspaper's headlines, and the Brezhnev era was to see a more general return to a collective style of government.

Brezhnev was grounded in industry, agriculture, and the Communist Party. His strength was that he never sought to be a commanding figure like Stalin or Khrushchev. He treated his peers within the party elite as good comrades and colleagues. Once within the inner circle, it was rare to be excluded and, as such, the Soviet Union arguably developed into what the West dubbed a gerontocracy, and one of sclerotic leadership at that. But people like Nixon and Kissinger were able to negotiate with Brezhnev on nuclear weapons and be confident that he would stand by the results. Where he came unstuck, though, was in his relationship with the army, particularly when he awarded himself the Order of Victory. Brezhnev was a rank-and-file chief of the political branch of the army, who exaggerated his military role in the army after Russia was subjected to the Nazi surprise attack in 1941. He was never a frontline military commander of forces. To see him wear this special decoration, hitherto reserved for the renowned Soviet marshals like Zhukov and Konstantin Rokossovsky, was an insult to the military. Zhukov had started his war service fighting against the Japanese in 1939. On the European front, he organised the defence of Leningrad in September 1941; the defence of Moscow from October to December 1941; was a key commander at Stalingrad; and concluded his career with the capture of Berlin. A real military hero in popular eyes. When he died in 1974, he had twenty-seven medals and awards. This was about 10 per cent of Brezhnev's total, most of which he had awarded to himself.

The disastrous performance of Soviet equipment in Lebanon in the summer of 1982 was blamed on Brezhnev's time in office when it became obvious how little had been done to modernise their arms and the defence industries.[24] Brezhnev's record in power from October 1964 revealed him to be an unimaginative Communist administrator presiding over economic stagnation or *zastoi*. He was greatly helped by Suslov and men like Alexei Kosygin and Nikolai Podgorny, who became head of state, in that they never challenged Brezhnev's role and contributed to the stultification. However, he was to make a key personnel move with far-reaching ramifications when, in 1967, he replaced the then head of the KGB, Vladimir Semichastny, with Yuri Andropov. Arguably this was the most important decision he made in influencing Russia's future. The fact that

Andropov was simultaneously promoted to candidate membership of the Politburo showed that he had been given much wider powers, as the Russian political commentator Roy Medvedev made clear in his Political Diary No. 33 of June 1967.

Like Khrushchev before him, Brezhnev was to face unrest in the Soviet satellites, which would generate further tensions in the USSR's relationship with the West. In his case, problems erupted in Czechoslovakia in 1968, where the reformist government of Alexander Dubček had embarked on steps to decentralise the economy and introduce broader reforms aimed at creating a more liberal socialist state, a period called the Prague Spring. Dubček believed there would be no Soviet intervention so long as Czechoslovakia avoided Hungary's decision to leave the Warsaw Pact. The leadership in Moscow, however, saw the reformists' moves as a threat that needed to be dealt with – and dealt with firmly. By the early summer, Andropov, now head of the KGB, was already talking of concrete military measures and the Soviet minister of defence was drawing up plans for Operation Danube. The Soviet ambassador in Prague, Stepan Chernenko, supported such measures.

The Soviets' ideological response to Dubček's actions became known as the Brezhnev Doctrine.

Each Communist party is free to apply the principles of Marxism-Leninism and socialism in its own country, but it is not free to deviate from these principles if it is to remain a Communist party ... The weakening of any of the links in the world system of socialism directly affects all the socialist countries, and they cannot look indifferently upon this.[25]

The practical response was the invasion of Czechoslovakia by

250,000 Warsaw Pact troops and 2,000 tanks on 20 August 1968, with troop numbers eventually rising to around 500,000.

NATO, however, barely stirred. I was duty minister in the Ministry of Defence, responsible for the navy at the time. I left the building at around 9 p.m. with the firm advice that the invasion would not take place that night, only to be called up in the early hours and told it had begun. Unlike with Hungary in 1956, NATO's confidence in its policy of non-intervention was higher by 1968, boosted by the perceived success in facing down the Russians during the Cuban Missile Crisis, so whether to become involved over Czechoslovakia was barely discussed.

The crushing of the Prague Spring was undoubtedly another setback in the freeing of Europe, but it also marked another major crisis for the Communist movements in Western Europe, with many previously hard-line Communists in the UK, France, and Italy giving up their party membership. The invasion of Hungary was hard enough to justify, but to add a second invasion was too much to stomach, and Communism as an ideology in Europe had been very seriously damaged.

The situation for Germany was different, and its future was a strategic factor in the rivalry between West and East. Under Kennedy's successor, Lyndon Baines Johnson – or LBJ as he was known – there was to be a significant change in the US approach. In October 1966, Johnson had made clear that the US would no longer allow its foreign policy to be held hostage to the principle of future German reunification. The message was clear; instead of insisting on the resolution of the 'German problem' as a precondition for détente, a new generation of German diplomats, in concert with the US, would have to be prepared to discuss other policies as well as reunification if they wished to achieve their objectives.[26]

This change in policy was a direct attack on the Hallstein Doctrine. Hallstein was foreign affairs adviser to the former West German chancellor from 1949 to 1963, and the doctrine required third countries be unwavering in their refusal to recognise the East German government, the GDR, or it would otherwise be regarded as an unfriendly act. An exception was made for the Soviet Union. Fortunately, cometh the hour, cometh the man. Willy Brandt, the former mayor of Berlin and leader of the West German Social Democratic Party, became foreign minister in 1966 in Kurt Georg Kiesinger's grand coalition. He introduced a new policy of *Ostpolitik*; working with his close adviser, Egon Bahr, he began to improve relations with Eastern Europe, aiming to bring about 'change through *rapprochement*'.[27] Then, in 1969, Brandt became chancellor, winning a majority in the federal elections. The following year, he became the first leader of the Federal Republic of Germany (FRG) to meet his Eastern counterpart since Germany was divided in 1949.

I only met Brandt once when, as a long-standing friend of Norway, he was invited to speak during their EU referendum in 1972, and I, as a younger supporter of the EU, had been asked by the Norwegian Labour prime minister to speak on the same platform. We were both given a rough time by the Norwegian audience, many of whom were against entry; of course, that was the surprise result: 53.5 per cent voted against and 46.5 per cent for, a result that was reaffirmed in a second referendum in 1994 with 52.2 per cent still voting against. In France during the 2016 British EU referendum, I spoke with the former prime minister Michel Rocard, a great friend; we both agreed the UK should leave the EU.

Through the implementation of the *Ostpolitik*, the GDR

moved into a closer relationship with the West. In 1973, it was recognised by the UN, and in September of the following year it was also recognised by the US and its NATO allies. However, despite the move to recognise the GDR, the leaders of the FDR maintained the goal of unification and worked on various initiatives to encourage integration and correct the economic and social imbalances. One reflection of these objectives was the provision in the EEC constitution for the FRG to treat the GDR in all economic and trading matters as if they were unified.

More broadly, the 1970s were to see several other significant changes in the European political landscape. In 1970, the Portuguese dictator Salazar died, and a period of unrest followed before a new constitution was adopted. In the first elections to be held, Mario Soares became prime minister in 1976. The overthrow of the military junta in Greece, who had been in power from 1967 to 1974, led to the return from self-exile of the former prime minister, Constantine Karamanlis. And in Spain, following Franco's death in 1975, the Spanish monarchy was restored and a reformist prime minister, Adolfo Suárez, installed. Change was also beginning in the Soviet Bloc, where the economic situation was deteriorating, putting pressure on different Communist regimes.

A key moment in the détente era was the signature of the Helsinki Final Act in August 1975, an event attended by senior leaders including Brezhnev, President Ford, and Prime Minister Harold Wilson. This had taken two years to negotiate within the framework of the Conference on Security and Co-operation in Europe, which brought together all European countries (except Albania) along with the US and Canada, with a goal of reducing East–West tensions. The agreements covered four broad 'baskets': political and military issues, including borders; economic issues; human rights; and follow-up and implementation.

Under the first basket, Soviet negotiators were focused on securing agreement that the post-war borders in Europe were 'immutable', though the West negotiated important qualifications, resulting in a declaration that the borders were 'inviolable'. This nuance meant that while borders could not be altered by force, they could be changed by agreement – a critical issue for the West Germans, who had their eye on future unification. The Soviets, and in particular the foreign minister, Gromyko, attached great importance to this clause on the 'inviolability of frontiers', interpreting it as an acceptance by the West of the incorporation of Estonia, Latvia, and Lithuania into the USSR as part of the frontiers agreed at Yalta and Potsdam. Indeed, the acceptance of frontiers more generally was seen as a sell-out by many in the West. For many years, a number of foreign ministers, myself included, had angry exchanges with Gromyko to disabuse him of his interpretation that Estonia, Latvia, and Lithuania were now accepted as part of the USSR. This subject even came up during what was meant to have been a social evening together in Moscow in 1977 when Gromyko forcibly put his case to me and I reiterated that the UK position had not changed.

My visit was the first by a British foreign secretary to Russia for six years. The relationship between the two nations had cooled dramatically in 1971 when, in September of that year, the foreign secretary Sir Alec Douglas-Home expelled ninety Soviet diplomats for spying and refused to accept back into the country another fifteen who were overseas at the time. This amounted to 20 per cent of Soviet diplomats from the total embassy staff of 550. Operation Foot, as it was called in the top-secret papers, remains the largest single expulsion of diplomats. The information on which the large list was based came from a defecting KGB major, who also reported details on what the Foreign Office said on the record at the time 'of Soviet plans for the infiltration of agents for purposes of sabotage'.[28] Alec Douglas-Home's decision, in my view, was correct and justified by subsequent events. Sabotage was a new overt Russian threat and had to be stopped in its tracks.

Against this backdrop, we had no idea how I would be received when my plane touched down, and it was a surprise to find the foreign minister, Gromyko, at the foot of the steps to greet me. I drove with him into Moscow and, as we got closer to the city centre, he pointed out a tank memorial marking the nearest point the German Panzer divisions had reached in the outskirts of Moscow in the Second World War. It was a timely reminder for me, and Gromyko explained that its close prox-imity to Moscow was why Soviet military chiefs were still so cautious in the Mutual and Balanced Force Reductions talks taking place at that time.

The third basket in the Helsinki Final Act – which trig-gered a new emphasis on human rights, including freedoms of movement and the press – was to set in motion changes that had not been anticipated by most of the senior Soviet leader-ship, including Brezhnev himself, who was more focused on the political aspects. In fact, the significance of the third basket measures and the impetus they gave to dissident movements was also not initially fully grasped by many Western leaders.[29] The Helsinki Accords were cited by dissident groups to justify their activities, and they set about monitoring and reporting on breaches of the accords, including in the USSR. In Moscow in

1976, for example, the leading physicist Yuri Orlov established the Moscow Helsinki Group to monitor the USSR's implementation – or abuse, as it turned out – of the Helsinki Accords. When I became foreign secretary in February 1977, I strongly supported the Charter 77 civic movement in Czechoslovakia, which had launched the previous month and which criticised their government's lack of adherence to human and civil rights. The movement received strong support from the UK and other European democracies. One of its leading proponents was Václav Havel, at that time a playwright, who became the country's president following the Velvet Revolution in 1989.

Another specific issue that came to prominence as a result of the Helsinki Accords was that of Jewish emigration from the USSR. While Brezhnev was not interested in religious affairs, Andropov, who was chair of the Committee for Religious Affairs, recognised its considerable political implications in Europe and the US. Throughout his tenure at the KGB, he realised that religion needed to be handled with sensitivity and care, not attributes hitherto associated with the KGB. Soviet Jews were in many cases able to obtain exit visas from the USSR in the 1970s, and this policy was favoured by Andropov for purely pragmatic reasons; a disproportionate number of dissidents were Jewish, and their emigration resulted in a substantial loss to the dissident cause.[30] In 2019, I was reminded of how much time and effort was put into this area of Jewish emigration from Russia when I was contacted by Polina Bayvel, a British engineer. She recalled that in 1978, when I was foreign secretary, I and the Office of the Chief Rabbi had authorised visas for her and her parents to enter the UK from the Soviet Union. Her father, Leopold, became a research scientist at Imperial College, and she became a Fellow of the Royal Society for services to engineering specialising in the next-generation communications network infrastructure. It was a pleasure for me to host her for lunch in the House of Lords to mark the fortieth anniversary of her arrival in the UK. By contrast, Natan Sharansky, a distinguished Jewish Soviet mathematician and chess player, was imprisoned in 1977. Sharansky was the first political prisoner to be released by Gorbachev in 1986 as part of a prisoner exchange, and he and his mother moved to Israel.

By the end of the 1970s, Poland was again causing concerns for Moscow. The public mood was influenced by both external and internal forces, one of which was Pope John Paul II's historic visit to the country, his homeland, in June 1979. His nine-day tour attracted millions of believers – a fact that calls to mind Stalin's derisive military joke: 'How many divisions has the pope?' In this case, the answer was 'many'. It was the first of what became nine pilgrimages to Poland during his twenty-seven years as pope. The pope's engagement in Poland also benefitted wider popular initiatives. During the summer of 1979, Lech Wałęsa, an electrician in the Gdansk shipyard, came to prominence at the head of the independent trade union organisation *Solidarność*, or Solidarity. Opposition to the Polish Communist government's imprisonment of intellectuals and dismissal of workers like Wałęsa had been growing, and this was to prove a turning point in Poland and more widely.

The Soviet government had to consider its attitude to the Solidarity movement and, by April 1980, the Politburo still decided to watch and wait. The Americans believed the Soviets would intervene, and in December President Carter sent a message on the 'hot line' to Brezhnev warning of the very grave consequences to US–Soviet relations of any hostile action. But Brezhnev had already decided with Suslov, the leading

Soviet ideologue, as well as Andropov and the majority of the Politburo, not to send in troops. This was a sign of Andropov's growing influence. When talking to the Politburo on 10 December 1981, he said: 'We do not intend to introduce troops into Poland ... I don't know how things will turn out in Poland. But even if Poland falls under the control of Solidarity, that is the way it will be.'[31] In 1982, Wałęsa was released from internment and, in 1983, he was awarded the Nobel Peace Prize and reignited the Solidarity movement, which went on to play a key role in the fall of Communism in Eastern Europe.

While the Soviets held back on military action in Poland, their military intervention further afield was, as with events in Poland, to have far-reaching implications for global geopolitics. Afghanistan again became a stage on which East–West rivalries played out. With its common border and close ties to the USSR, Afghanistan was treated more or less as a Warsaw Pact country. In 1959, when I first visited Afghanistan, Soviet soldiers were in the centre of the country, and the governor of Herat refused us permission to take the central road across the mountains – an instruction we ignored, simply turning our Land Rover left instead of right, back to Herat. No one stopped us.

In April 1978, the People's Democratic Party of Afghanistan overthrew the Afghan president Daoud Khan. There is little reason for believing Moscow played any major role in the coup. A government was formed under Nur Muhammad Taraki with one of the key organisers of the coup, Hafizullah Amin, taking the role of foreign minister. Brezhnev sent his congratulations on 2 May. Shortly afterwards – and despite the misgivings of Zbigniew Brzezinski, the national security adviser – Cyrus Vance, the US secretary of state, recognised the new government to avoid losing 'the prospect of any influence in Kabul' and, for much the same reasons, I took similar action on behalf of the British government.[32] But the unity between the factions was short-lived, and in retrospect what happened in Afghanistan can be seen as a pivotal issue in the disintegration of the Soviet Union.

In May 1978, Amin visited Moscow and met Gromyko. He came away with a considerable increase in Russian aid money, and many Russian advisers moved into Afghanistan. Radical reforms followed, so much so that, Brezhnev, speaking in Baku in September, was reported by *Pravda* as saying, 'a people's revolution took place; the semi-feudal regime was toppled, and the Democratic Republic of Afghanistan was proclaimed'.[33] But there was a backlash in Afghanistan's provinces against several of the socialist reforms, particularly the land reforms, giving way to armed resistance.

Against the background of insurgent activity in Afghanistan, the situation in neighbouring Iran was also becoming increasingly unstable as the shah lost his grip on power. The shah eventually left Tehran on 16 January 1979, and Ayatollah Khomeini flew into Tehran on 1 February. A brutal revolution followed, resulting in a regime that widely flouted – and still flouts – human rights and began to try to destabilise its neighbours, as it still does today.

On 14 February 1979, the same day that Iranian militants attacked the US embassy in Tehran, taking fifty-two hostages, the US ambassador to Afghanistan was captured in Kabul and subsequently shot dead during a rescue attempt involving Afghan police and Soviet officials. The incident hastened a decline in US–Afghan relations, and the US immediately cut its planned humanitarian and military aid, leaving just a chargé d'affaires in place. In March 1979, an uprising began in Herat, the largest city close to Iran, in which many Soviet advisers were murdered by insurgents. *Pravda* blamed Iran, Pakistan, and China, with their Western 'supporters', for what happened. Seven Russian generals were sent to the scene and reported back that there should be an increase in Soviet arms, aid, and military advisers. The Soviet embassy in Kabul reported to Moscow that 'violent instability will probably remain a fact of life for years to come'.[34]

In the summer of 1979, Amin began to distance himself from Taraki and oversaw a policy of extreme repression in Afghanistan. Both men attempted to oust each other, but Amin emerged as victor with the support of army officers. Taraki was arrested and, according to some sources, the Russians, who did not wish to see him punished, attempted to rescue him. His subsequent death on 8 October at the instruction of Amin shocked Brezhnev.[35] Four major figures in the Politburo – Andropov, Ustinov (minister of defence), Gromyko, and Suslov – pushed for a major military response to the marked deterioration in the security situation in Afghanistan, alleging that Amin was a CIA agent.[36] Brezhnev, who had previously resisted decisions to intervene militarily, was persuaded by key Politburo members to invade, and on 24 December 1979, the Soviet invasion of Afghanistan was launched.

The invasion involved a massive airlift of Soviet forces to the Bagram Air Base outside Kabul, bolstering the already substantial Soviet military presence in the country. By the end of March 1980, there were some 85,000 Soviet troops on Afghan soil. The strongest public criticism came from President Carter, who was facing re-election later that year. He instigated a boycott of the Moscow Olympic Games, which was supported by forty-five to fifty other countries, although in total sixty-seven nations did not participate. The games still went ahead in August 1980, and many British athletes participated in defiance of government objections.

Brezhnev's own explanation for agreeing to invade Afghanistan was that activities on the USSR's southern borders posed a serious threat to the security of the Soviet state. The fact that China, which shared borders with both Afghanistan and Pakistan, was enjoying a period of good relations with India was seen to exacerbate that threat. Where Moscow made a serious miscalculation was in the reaction of the US and Britain. Whereas, as indicated previously, Britain had held back in its response to Soviet action in Eastern Europe, in the case of Afghanistan, it was ready to take concrete action. Britain began to supply the Afghan guerrilla groups, the 'mujahideen', and the anti-Soviet Afghans in particular, with equipment including hand-held missiles that could knock out Soviet tanks. Seven main groups were supported by the British SIS and the US CIA. Far more significant and effective, however, was the Pakistan Inter-Services Intelligence Directorate, with funding coming from Saudi Arabia and other Islamic countries in the Gulf. I got to know some of the mujahideen leaders in Peshawar during visits to Pakistan in the early 1980s and again in 1989 when, at the invitation of Benazir Bhutto, I spoke in Karachi along with Sardar Swaran Singh, a former Indian foreign minister, at an event commemorating the tenth anniversary of the hanging of Bhutto's father, the former prime minister, Zulfikar Ali Bhutto. Afterwards, we visited the family home and then the burial site in the Sindh desert. Benazir and her husband, who later became president, talked of their concerns about their personal safety, and I raised the issue with Prime Minister Margaret Thatcher, who instigated substantive help. Tragically Benazir was assassinated on 27 December 2007 while campaigning for an election.

The story of the Russian intervention in Afghanistan is excellently recounted by Sir Rodric Braithwaite, a distinguished former British ambassador to Moscow, in *Afgantsy: The Russians in Afghanistan, 1979–89*.[37] Braithwaite believes that if any external military power could have conquered Afghanistan, it would have been the Russians, given their political knowledge and large military force. They eventually chose Mohammad Najibullah to lead the country, and with Russian agreement he strove for an Afghan solution. This tactic might have succeeded, but with a weak economy Afghanistan was becoming a costly burden to the USSR which ultimately, as I shall return to later, became unsustainable – shades of President Biden in April 2021.

The pressure for change in the USSR – both from within and from its satellites – was soon to gather momentum, though when I visited Moscow for the third time in June 1981, it was clearly going to be a slow process. At that stage, visible improvements at the airport and in the street lighting and in the restaurants were yet to come; these kinds of more overt signs of change were rather a product of the opening up of the economy and society in the Gorbachev and Yeltsin years. Back in 1981, I was in Moscow at the invitation of the Soviet government for a meeting of the Palme Commission (more formally, the Independent Commission on Disarmament and Security Issues), which led to the publication of its Common Security report[38] in April 1982. I was the group's treasurer. My good friend Cyrus Vance was also a member. I had asked him to join in 1980 on the same day that he publicly resigned as US secretary of state, 28 April. He had resigned privately just before over President Carter's humiliating failed helicopter mission in Iran to rescue

US hostages from the embassy. I was his last visitor in the State Department, and I had gone to seek his advice and assistance on appointing a US member of the commission while Olof Palme, a former prime minister of Sweden, had gone to Moscow to find suitable Russians. After hearing in detail about Vance's meeting with Carter, I said simply, 'When you have time to contemplate other things, why don't you join the Commission?' Fortunately, he did. Other commission members included Egon Bahr, Willy Brandt's close adviser and *Ostpolitik* advocate, and the Norwegian prime minister, Gro Harlem Brundtland, who later became head of the World Health Organization. The Soviet political scientist and long-time adviser to the Soviet leadership, Georgi Arbatov, was an adviser to the commission. Arbatov was close to Andropov and, after he died, became a key adviser to Gorbachev.

During the visit, Palme met personally with Brezhnev while I met Marshal Sergei Akhromeyev, the chief of the general staff, by then one of the most influential people on Soviet nuclear strategy issues. The meeting took place in a vast room in the Ministry of Defence, he and several members of his staff sitting on the other side of a very long table with an interpreter and former GRU military intelligence officer, General Mikhail Milstein, who was also an adviser to the commission. I was on my own and expecting the meeting to last only half an hour, but the discussion was fascinating and went on for so long that I was late for the Bolshoi ballet. It opened my eyes to the seriousness of Akhromeyev's thinking on nuclear weapons and his readiness to grapple with far-reaching disarmament proposals, the full extent of which was revealed later when Gorbachev met Reagan at the 1986 Reykjavik Summit, as I shall cover in the next chapter.

7

Russia on the Road to Reform

While the Brezhnev era was generally seen as the age of stagnation, one of the key figures to emerge from that period, Yuri
Andropov, was to play a critical role in the momentous changes
that followed. A hard-liner in many ways, Andropov was a man
of extraordinary influence, brimming with ideas and involved
in a broad range of decisions on ideological and other issues
from the moment he became head of the KGB in 1967. Moreover, unlike his short tenure at the very pinnacle of the Soviet
system as general secretary, his legacy was long-lasting; Gorbachev took a great deal of inspiration from him. His influence
can also be seen today in the career of President Putin.

The longest-serving KGB chief, Andropov was not corrupt.
He ran it largely unchecked for fifteen years and built it into
the most influential organisation in the USSR, particularly
in strengthening its activities against internal dissidents.
Andropov was well positioned when the Communist Party's
second secretary, Mikhail Suslov, died in 1982. As mentioned
in Chapter 6, he had worked with Suslov during the crushing
of the Hungarian rising and gone on to serve under him as head
of the Foreign (Socialist) Department of the Central Committee from 1959 to 1967. Andropov had 'acquired the reputation

within the Party of being a strong but just man, the guardian of the system. He, Suslov and [minister of defence, Marshal Dmitry] Ustinov were the only Politburo members known to be modest in their personal lifestyle.'[1] Brezhnev's choice for Suslov's successor had been his former personal assistant Konstantin Chernenko, but he soon found there was no support for this move. Gromyko and Ustinov were against Chernenko, and Brezhnev was unable to prevent Andropov's appointment as his number two in the party hierarchy. The background to this man is, therefore, of considerable interest.

Like his protégé Gorbachev, Andropov was a son of Stavropol. His father was a Cossack, his mother, Evgenia Fainshtein, Jewish.[2] By the time he became general secretary of the CPSU, he was a widower with two children. His daughter was married to an actor at the *avant garde* Taganka Theatre, and she worked for the magazine *Theatre*. His son was a delegate to the follow-up conference of the Conference on Security and Cooperation in Europe in Madrid. Andropov spoke English, had tried to teach himself German as a youngster, and was an avid reader; books by Montaigne and Machiavelli were seen on his desk. He did not go to university, but his higher education might have been at the special KGB academy. In later life, he liked the music of Yuri Vizbor and Vladimir Vysotsky, whose songs were often politically incorrect and suspect in the eyes of the ideological guardian but which circulated on tapes hand to hand. According to Gorbachev's biographer, William Taubman, Gorbachev and his wife would sing these together with Andropov.[3]

Andropov had been acutely aware for years that old-fashioned Soviet propaganda was becoming counterproductive and that the nature of the Soviet economy was leading to its persistent economic decline. This KGB realism had become embedded well before the fifteen months of Andropov's own stint as general secretary. He brought on new younger leaders, most notably Mikhail Gorbachev. Gorbachev and his wife Raisa often joined Andropov and his second wife, Tatyana Filipovna, for part of their vacations in the Caucasus. When Gorbachev was promoted to the Central Committee, Andropov recalled a remark he had made about the spectacle of leaders ranged on Lenin's mausoleum, 'there can be no forest without undergrowth', and said with a smile 'Congratulations, Mr Undergrowth. Now you're part of the forest.'[4]

Andropov's leadership style contrasted sharply with that of the rather pompous Brezhnev. He cut back privilege and met workers on the shop floor. Corruption, absenteeism, and alcoholism were high on his list of concerns. And he made a significant number of revealing personnel moves when he took over from Brezhnev in 1982. He promoted the fifty-nine-year-old Heydar Aliyev, a former KGB officer and first secretary of the Communist Party of Azerbaijan, to Politburo membership, and fifty-three-year-old Nikolai Ryzhkov, later chair of the Council of Ministers, to head of the Central Committee's economic department. And as a first step in his anti-corruption campaign, Andropov removed the seventy-two-year-old General Shchelokov from his position as interior minister. According to the author Christian Schmidt-Häuer, 'Altogether nine high-ranking Brezhnev protégés lost their posts during Andropov's thirteen months in office; 19 out of 84 ministers, 20 per cent of all regional party chiefs and several Central Committee departmental heads were replaced.'[5] Recruits for the police had to come from the army because the ranks of the police, or militia, had been depleted and disciplined. Six of Shchelokov's deputies went out, along with a host of Brezhnev's friends and supporters, including his son-in-law. The KGB was the driving force behind these moves. Not a single general other than Akhromeyev had risen in the political hierarchy.

Though Andropov served as general secretary of the Soviet Communist Party for only fifteen months, dying on 9 February 1984 after having been on renal dialysis since 1983, he did his best to influence the choice of his successor. Andropov valued Gorbachev's intelligence and energy, and in December 1983, when very ill in hospital and unable to attend a meeting of the Central Committee, he added a handwritten note to a typed speech prepared for the plenary session, saying that 'Gorbachev (rather than Chernenko) should in his absence chair the Politburo and secretariat'.[6] But Chernenko, now the second secretary of the party, together with Nikolai Tikhonov, the chairman of the Council of Ministers, and Marshal Ustinov, decided that Andropov's addendum would not be read out. Andropov's aide tried to tell Gorbachev what had happened, but he was prevented from getting to him, and he later recounted the story to the American journalist David Remnick. Although Andropov had been unsuccessful in his attempt to secure his immediate successor, there is no doubt that his support was crucial in preparing the way for Gorbachev to succeed Chernenko later. In the interim, the ageing Politburo's choice of the seventy-two-year-old Chernenko as general secretary marked a throwback to Brezhnevism rather than reform. At his inauguration ceremony, which I attended and where I shook his hand, it was obvious the life-long smoker had bad emphysema, a chronic lung disease; I did not expect him to last long.

Whether Andropov, if his health had allowed him longer in office, would have been a major economic reformer is an open question. For many years he had been a supporter of the more liberal economic policies pursued by the Hungarian leader János Kádár, which had brought some moves towards the market and generated a higher standard of living for the population. Given time, it seems likely that he would have backed a greater measure of economic reform in the Soviet Union. Andropov was, however, a reformer only within narrow limits. He believed more discipline, energy, and initiative would turn things around. He remained an 'implacable opponent of overt dissent and of any development in the direction of political pluralism'.[7] He told a KGB conference in 1979, 'We simply do not have the right to permit the smallest miscalculation here, for in the political sphere any kind of ideological sabotage is directly or indirectly intended to create an opposition to our system.'[8] He had earlier said that of the 15,580 people that the KGB had given warnings to in the previous year after acts of 'ideological subversion', only 107 had reoffended.[9]

National dissent was a corrosive issue within the Soviet system. Russians made up a little over half of the total population of the USSR, with the Russian Soviet Federative Socialist Republic (the RSFSR) encompassing around three-quarters of its territory. What's more, national feeling was historically closely connected to respect for the Orthodox Church, and many shared the novelist and philosopher Aleksander Solzhenitsyn's resentment of the way Christianity was persecuted during the Communist years.

Professor Archie Brown, a respected authority on Russia, writes in *The Rise and Fall of Communism* that:

In terms of broad movements of opinion within the CPSU, there was a fundamental division between those, on the one side, who constituted 'the Russian party' and those, on the other, who wanted greater integration with the rest of the world, many of whom could be accurately described as Westernizers. Although both Mikhail Suslov and Yuri Andropov were orthodox enough Communists, Suslov was seen as the protector of the Russian nationalists and Andropov, strange though it may seem, was held to be the patron of the internationalists. Andropov himself never even visited a non-Communist Western country, but he was generally well disposed towards the international institutes, such as the Institute of the United States and Canada (founded early in the Brezhnev era) and IMEMO (the Institute of World Economy and International Relations), which had existed for much longer, in neither of which was there any shortage of Westernizers. Andropov was also a hate figure for many Russian nationalists.[10]

Andropov thus very firmly reasserted the role of the general secretary as a leading authority on the national question. But, in marked contrast to Brezhnev, who in his later years used to distance himself from ideological infighting, his pronouncements ended ambiguity and articulated his own position on the national question clearly, though without setting out specific policies.

Andropov used the occasion of the sixtieth anniversary of the formation of the USSR in December 1982 to speak on the subject of nationalism. This was against the backdrop of an All-Union Conference of the Communist Party, held in Riga in June of that year, on the subject of 'The Development of National Relations in Conditions of Advanced Socialism', which focused on practical aspects of the issue. Brezhnev had preferred the term *sblizhenie*, or rapprochement, which described a process that integrates people while preserving their national uniqueness. He had espoused his position in a speech in 1977.

> In the USSR, as is well known, there is a new community of people, the Soviet people. Several comrades, though it is true they are very few in number, have reached incorrect conclusions from this. They propose to introduce in the constitution the concept of a single Soviet *nation*, to liquidate union and autonomous republics or to curtail sharply the sovereignty of the union republics, depriving them of the right to leave the USSR, and the right to foreign dealings. ... I think that the error of such suggestions is clear. The socio-economic unity of the Soviet people in no way means the disappearance of national differences.[11]

While these views had not been openly attacked at the conference, the view was widely held that the party should do more to stress its commitment to an internationalist and integrationist strategy. In Andropov's December speech, he demonstrated that he shared the concerns of those who advocated such a strategy, while still being sensitive to the argument that national distinctions are long-lasting and potentially volatile. In one striking passage, he warned that national traditions could be negative as well as positive and said that he sought both increased vigilance and greater sophistication in dealing with manifestations of national feeling. This was a clear ideological message to his followers.

> Life shows that economic and cultural progress of all nations

and nationalities is unavoidably accompanied by the growth of national self-awareness. This is a natural objective process. It is important however that the inevitable pride in achieved successes does not turn into national arrogance or conceit, does not give rise to inclinations toward isolationism, to disrespectful attitudes to other nations and peoples. But negative phenomena of this sort are still found. And it would be incorrect to explain them only as survivals of the past. They are fed at times even by our own miscalculations. Here, comrades, there are no minor details. Here everything is important, the attitude toward language and to the monuments of the past, and the interpretation of historical events, and the way in which we transform villages and towns, and how we influence conditions of labour and the lives of people.[12]

Andropov did not overtly challenge the Leninist view of how different nationalities would come together under the Soviet system through the process *sliyanie*, meaning fusion, but his views represented an intellectual distancing from Lenin's viewpoint.

There is no doubt, however, that Brezhnev's conception of the rapprochement of nationalities was to be achieved through economic and social development. As Ben Fowles concludes, Brezhnev's approach 'of corporatist compromise, ethnic equalisation, and masterly inactivity ... was effective enough to preserve the USSR for a couple of decades, although it contained the seeds of its own destruction'.[13] Andropov used the term *sblizhenie* in his speech in the context of the creation of a multinational Soviet culture and paid tribute to generations of Soviet people of all nationalities. However, while he also saw the final goal of Soviet nationality policy as a blending of *sblizhenie* and *sliyanie* over time, he was aware that such a process could not be speeded up and that there would be a 'continued existence of national differences'.[14] Neither he nor the USSR itself was to last long enough for that to happen. The continued pull of nationalism, particularly in the Baltic states, was to play its part in the break-up of the union, following which the argument became less relevant, though the problems of nationalism did not go away, as the Chechen Wars proved.

Andropov did not live to witness the rise of Yeltsin, and he certainly would not have approved of the chaos that was to plague those years. He may well have gone down a path similar to that we have seen in China. Olga Kryshtanovskaya, then head of the Russian Academy of Sciences Institute for Elite Studies, described Andropov's thinking in a 2007 interview: 'Andropov thought that the Communist Party had to keep power in its hands and to conduct an economic liberalisation. This was the path China followed. For people in the security services, China is the ideal model.'[15] Interestingly, in 1987, Gorbachev rejected the advice of his close adviser on economic reform, Oleg Bogomolov, to follow the Chinese economic model, as Gorbachev did with anything Chinese. It is unlikely Andropov would have acted in the same way.

Nevertheless, one of Andropov's main legacies is the esteem in which he was held by Gorbachev and Putin. Putin placed flowers on Andropov's grave in June 1999 to mark the eighty-fifth anniversary of his birth. In 2000, Putin arranged for a plaque to be placed on the Moscow building in which Andropov lived and, on the ninetieth anniversary of his birth, Putin arranged for a 10-foot statue to be erected in the suburb of St Petersburg where Andropov was born. There can be no clearer pointer as to who Putin sees as his intellectual godfather, yet it was Gorbachev who was to build on Andropov's legacy in the first instance.

In December 1984, shortly before he became general secretary, Gorbachev made what would turn out to be a very important visit to London. This was his first visit to Britain, but it was by no means his first visit to the West. That had taken place over a decade before when he and his wife visited Italy in 1971 and 'fell in love with the country and its culture'.[16] Their love for Italy was reciprocated, and Gorbachev remained popular there long after he lost power. The Gorbachevs also toured other European countries by car, including France in 1977, where they were accompanied by an official of the French Communist Party and were reportedly enchanted. Gorbachev later acknowledged that those trips, 'shook our *a priori* belief in the superiority of socialist over bourgeois democracy'.[17]

By the time of Gorbachev's London visit, he was expected to be the next Soviet leader, given Chernenko's failing health. It was following her meeting with him that Margaret Thatcher declared, 'I like Mr Gorbachev. We can do business together.'[18] This was to presage the arrival of a new, positive era in Britain's relations with the USSR and then Russia, lasting until the early years of the Putin presidency. What was particularly important about Thatcher's judgement was that it carried great conviction with the one person in the world – President Reagan – with whom it was essential Gorbachev did do business.

In helping her assess Gorbachev's and wider Soviet intentions, Thatcher had the benefit of what (or rather who) was possibly Britain's most important espionage coup. Back in 1974, MI6 had recruited a high-ranking KGB official, Oleg Gordievsky, as an agent. He went on to serve in key roles in the Russian embassy in London in June 1982, but he eventually suspected that he had been discovered and, in 1985, asked for a special plan to be set in motion to take him out from Moscow through Finland to Britain. MI6 accomplished this with great flair. With Gordievsky stuck in the boot of a car, the driver played Finlandia on the car's radio when it crossed the border to signal to him that he was free. I judge Gordievsky, who was operating while I was foreign secretary, to be arguably the most important spy Britain has ever had. His information was shared, with Thatcher's agreement and at a moment of high tension with Russia, directly with President Reagan in 1983. At this point, the Russians were totally misinterpreting US policies, reading into what was a normal NATO military exercise a degree of US hostility that was never even contemplated and putting on full alert 100 aircraft armed with nuclear bombs.[19] This incident shows how important a role intelligence gathering can have in deepening understanding and avoiding miscalculations that can have disastrous consequences.

I had the opportunity to meet with Gorbachev in my role as leader of the SDP, along with the Liberal leader, David Steel. By seeing him jointly, we doubled our separate time allocation. He had an openness and a readiness to use a different vocabulary to that of the programmed Marxists, and also to think conceptually. He was, however, still a committed Communist. In February 1986, Gorbachev would tell the French Communist newspaper *L'Humanité* that the Communism of Lenin remained, for him, a fine and unsullied ideal. 'Stalinism', he went on, was 'a concept made up by the enemies of Communism and used on a large scale to smear the Soviet Union.'[20]

But that commitment to the Communism of Lenin had not prevented him embarking on the path to reform before he succeeded to the highest office. In 1984, Gorbachev delivered a speech at an ideological conference which was approved, though not without a struggle, by the Propaganda Department.[21] He had worked on the speech with a small group of advisers, two of whom were to become key members of his leadership team: the director of the Institute of World Economy and International Relations, Alexander Yakovlev (Politburo member 1987–90), and Vadim Medvedev (Central Committee secretary and Politburo member). Following the speech, Gorbachev used the terms *perestroika* (reform) and *glasnost* (openness) publicly for first time in June 1984 when attending the funeral of the Italian Communist Party leader Enrico Berlinguer, who in 1973 had committed his party to the defence of Italian democracy.[22]

The Italian Communists were the force behind Eurocommunism, reaching their peak in 1976 when they won 12.6 million votes and 227 parliamentary seats. I wrote about Eurocommunism for a chapter in a book called *Human Rights*, which was published in 1978 while I was foreign secretary. Naturally, great scrutiny was paid within the FCO to my words before publication: 'Western Communist leaders themselves are now using the word Eurocommunism. It is a convenient portmanteau ... Eurocommunism is becoming respectable. It is a term socialists should eschew. It should be given no currency ... In rejecting the term one is refusing to accept that Communism anywhere, particularly in Europe, is a coherent entity.'[23]

On 10 March 1985, Chernenko died and Gorbachev succeeded him. At Chernenko's funeral, Gorbachev was welcoming in the receiving line, and Thatcher's attitude to the USSR had noticeably transformed following her meeting with him in London. For the first time since the Nixon–Brezhnev era, I began to think there might be progress with the US on nuclear disarmament. The Strategic Arms Limitation Talks (SALT-II)

Treaty, however, remained unratified by the US Congress on 3 June 1985 when I was in Washington, and it was due to expire in December. Because of Russian cheating, Reagan, at a National Security Council meeting that morning, before I met him, discussed not dismantling Poseidon submarines as would be required if the US was to comply. When I saw him in the White House that afternoon, I raised this and other nuclear issues. Reagan subsequently wrote in his diary: '[saw the] head of a new party that's coming on like gang busters in old "blighty" ... [he] put in a pitch for continuing to observe the restraint'.[24] Compared to when I previously saw him during my time as foreign secretary in London in 1977, I gained the strong impression that Reagan now wanted nuclear arms controls.

Gorbachev was not to be a pushover, though. When Gromyko had recommended Gorbachev for general secretary, he told party leaders that, 'He may have a nice smile, but he has teeth of iron.'[25] Reagan and Gorbachev met in the Chateau Fleur d'Eau beside Lake Geneva on 19 November 1985. There, the two men agreed on a simple truism – 'a nuclear war cannot be won and must never be fought' – and they agreed to follow-up meetings in Washington in 1986 and in Moscow in 1987.[26] Gorbachev recognised the importance of building a relation-ship with the US, telling the Politburo on 3 April 1986, 'we cannot do anything without them and they cannot do anything without us'.[27]

Reagan, however, appeared to lose interest in the follow-up summit planned for Washington. Soviet troops were still in Afghanistan; Cubans were in Nicaragua; American soldiers had been blown up in a discotheque in West Berlin in April 1986, with the involvement of Libya. Fortunately, Richard Nixon, with no role in government, met Gorbachev in Moscow in July and told him directly that Reagan was impressed by his commitment to peace at Geneva. Gorbachev, in the light of this meeting, then decided to write to Reagan and propose another meeting in London or Reykjavik, halfway between them both, so none of the big other powers would be offended. It was to be a short one-on-one meeting in which they could discuss a concrete schedule, taking account of both his and American proposals for a nuclear-free zone by 2000. The chief of the general staff, Marshal Akhromeyev, later admitted that the proposal originated in the Ministry of Defence.

Reagan, who accepted a meeting at very short notice in Reykjavik on 11–12 October 1986, was hoping to agree on a few measures and then have a major meeting in Washington, but Gorbachev had more ambitious plans. That much soon became clear at Reykjavik where even Paul Nitze, a tough arms negotiator, admitted: 'This is the best Soviet proposal we have received in twenty-five years.'[28] Gorbachev was ready to accept Reagan's proposal for a 'zero option' for Euromissiles and to cut long-range nuclear missiles by 50 per cent, including his massive SS-18 missiles. Furthermore, he agreed to drop from the proposal the inclusion of the British and French missiles, a long-standing Soviet demand that was at this early stage more of an obstruction than a factor in whether the US and USSR would agree reductions. Also discussed at Reykjavik were two five-year periods building up to the complete elimination of thousands of nuclear weapons. While the proposal was certainly not without serious problems – not least how to deal with China, which had acquired nuclear weapons in the 1960s and was fast building more – it was a dramatic and unprecedented offer that George Shultz, Reagan's secretary of state, did not dismiss. To her shame, Thatcher, standing in the wings of the debate, did her utmost to block all references thereafter to complete elimination. The objection that 'you cannot put the genie back in the bottle' can be made for ridding the world of all weapons of mass destruction – chemical, biological, and nuclear. At the Reykjavik meeting, Gorbachev even agreed to Reagan maintaining his Strategic Defense Initiative (SDI), provided it was limited to testing in laboratories.

In his book *The Secret World*, Christopher Andrew reveals how the Soviet Union had earlier interpreted the announcement of the US SDI ('Star Wars') programme in March 1983 as part of the psychological preparation of the American people for nuclear war.

> On 28 September 1983 the terminally ill Andropov issued from his sickbed a denunciation of US policy couched in apocalyptic language unparalleled since the depths of the Cold War ... 'Outrageous military psychosis,' he declared, had taken over the United States ... 'The Reagan administration, in its imperial ambitions, goes so far that one begins to doubt whether Washington has any brakes at all preventing it from crossing the point at which any sober-minded person must stop.'[29]

Now Gorbachev's own Russian scientists had told him that Moscow could 'destroy or neutralise' SDI without spending more than a tenth of the US expenditure.[30] It was tragically the SDI that caused the meeting to fail. Reagan would not give up the concept. His basic idea was very simple, as was often the case with him and as I had learnt from my first conversation with him when he came through London after being governor of California and No. 10 had refused to see him. Of course, the practicalities of actually implementing his ideas were not as simple. Reagan knew that, but he believed that the importance of defending missile attacks was worth the cost of going into space if they allowed sufficient confidence to get rid of incoming missiles. In his autobiography, Reagan describes how at Reykjavik, 'my hope for a nuclear-free world soared briefly, then fell during one of the longest, most disappointing – and ultimately angriest – days of my presidency'.[31] Reagan foresaw a comprehensive network of anti-ballistic missile defences, including some systems based in space (hence SDI being dubbed the 'Star Wars' programme) as being necessary to intercept and destroy incoming nuclear missiles. The criticism ranged from interception being unworkable to it promoting a new phase of the arms race. The SDI was only formally halted after the collapse of the USSR, when President Clinton redirected the focus towards shorter-range missiles and changed the agency's name to the Ballistic Missile Defense Organization. The debate over 'interception' will, I predict, re-emerge when the US faces the prospect of a large Chinese nuclear missile programme and more sophisticated Russian missiles.

Yet the Reykjavik Summit remained very influential in Gorbachev's thinking. It paved the way for the 1987 Intermediate-Range Nuclear Forces (INF) Treaty and the 1991 Strategic Arms Reduction Treaty (START I). In retrospect, the significance of arms control negotiations in US–Russian relations during this period should not be underestimated. Nixon and Kissinger deserve considerable credit for remaining committed to arms control negotiations throughout their long period out of office. Pursuing the SALT agreements even when the Cold War was going through a very difficult period when the US was embroiled in the Vietnam War was the correct policy. In my experience, few politicians who ever get close to the mechanics and capabilities of nuclear weapons ever lose their concerns. We risk a lot by adopting in 2021 onwards a mood of resignation to their dangers. The new generation of politicians around the world must restore the priority given to, first, their reduction and, second, their abandonment through mutual and balanced negotiations.

The planned Washington summit took place in December 1987. Apart from signing the INF Treaty, little serious business was conducted, but the prestige and warmth of the visit mattered to Gorbachev. The next summit was held in Moscow from 29 May to 3 June 1988, with another following in New York in December of that year. Gorbachev was gaining a great deal of respect on the international scene, and the Soviets' relationship with the US was boosted by the signature of the Geneva Accords in April 1988. The accords led to the withdrawal of Soviet troops from Afghanistan, which commenced in May 1988 though did not end until February 1989. It is a tragedy that neither the US nor Britain, especially given the latter's earlier history in the region, did not heed the lessons learnt by Russia. After twenty years of intermittent war, President Biden announced the final withdrawal of US troops from the country in 2021, though he did not rule out attacking from outside.

As a senator, Biden had voted in September 2001 for the US to go into Afghanistan, along with ninety-seven other senators. He also supported the war in Iraq the following year. But during visits to Afghanistan in 2008 as chair of the Senate Foreign Relations Committee, Biden is said to have found confusion at all levels about US strategy and objectives. Robert Gates, the former defense secretary, wrote in his memoir *Duty* that Mr Biden was so frustrated at the Afghan leaders he once threw down his napkin and walked out of a dinner with President Karzai.[32]

It is a fact that, as yet, no country in the 200 years covered by this book has successfully fought politically or militarily in Afghanistan. The CIA – not the Pentagon – masterminded the initial strategy for retaking Kabul in 2001–2. Money in suitcases was used to bribe various tribal leaders to join together and march towards Kabul, while the US Air Force bombed in front of them, guided by special forces on the ground. This unconventional approach was the key to the early US success. After this, US and British special forces went after bin Laden and came very close to capturing him. The problem was that bin Laden had the support of the Pakistani military intelligence, a force that has for years acted independently of the Pakistan Army and the country's political leadership. For them and the mujahideen, the mountain border has no meaning or respect; they criss-cross it routinely.

History has repeatedly shown that no country can defeat the Afghans once those who bear arms in sufficient numbers want foreign forces to leave. That reality must be understood. And when Pakistan puts its weight behind such forces, it is time to get out. Trump and Biden understood that in their different ways, and both chose a withdrawal negotiated with the Taliban – which, somewhat surprisingly, held; the Taliban did not attack US forces as they withdrew. It was an ISIS-K suicide bomber who caused the devastation at Kabul airport.

A practical experience convinced me of this truism, why no external force – Russian, American, British, or NATO – can defy the Afghans. In 1959, I was twenty-one and one of five undergraduates on a Cambridge University expedition to Afghanistan, riding on horseback in the mountains with an

Afghan guide and a local schoolmaster acting as an interpreter. We planned to see the Ghurid Empire city of Firuzkuh and the Minaret of Jam. At that time, there were no roads into that part of central Afghanistan. We had been riding for a few hours, and I left the saddle to relieve myself against a grey boulder. Suddenly, the boulder moved; it was a grey blanket hiding an Afghan with gun and knife in his belt who, unnoticed, had been following us with a now-revealed colleague. No modern army can defeat such resourceful, independent, and brave people. The Russians were forced to leave, as was the US-led NATO.

President Biden decided to set the twentieth anniversary of 9/11 as his target date for leaving. It was necessary to go into Afghanistan, but in retrospect President Obama should have left Afghanistan soon after May 2011 when bin Laden was killed by American special forces in Pakistan and buried at sea. *The New York Times* claims that Biden, then vice president, clashed with the Pentagon, including with defense secretary Robert Gates and secretary of state Hillary Clinton, about troop levels in Afghanistan, arguing for bringing them down to a minimal counterterrorism force. He lost that battle.[33]

The return of the Taliban to power in Kabul in August 2021 will tragically mean a rise in terrorism in many parts of the world. Much will depend on whether the Taliban will choose different policy approaches and, in particular, will not provide havens for ISIS-K or Al-Qaeda. Russia and China have an important role to play.

It is claimed that as many as three-quarters of the population of Afghanistan in 2021 are under twenty-five. It is not impossible that such a significant change in demographics will modify the approach of the Taliban to Afghan women. There is now concrete evidence about the value of women to Afghan society, and there needs to be some form of debate, Afghan to Afghan, about women's status. The UN, NATO, and many voluntary organisations did their very best over this and in other areas to promote a change in attitude. All may not be lost if countries closer to the Taliban, like Pakistan and other Muslim countries, lend their weight to advocating a change of heart on women's roles. Many Muslim countries have changed their attitudes to women in the last twenty years, and the Taliban might just slowly shift their previous behaviour.

What if the pessimists are proven right and the Taliban remain unchanged on the above issues and continue harbouring terrorists? President Biden and Prime Minister Johnson have already said they will not withdraw all US and British involvement. The US should be retaining an active CIA presence in the country and keep ready US special forces with specialist knowledge of drone technology to help any mujahideen movements and to monitor any terrorist training ground activity. Similarly, British intelligence should remain engaged and the considerable military knowledge of Afghanistan in the British Army maintained and not dispersed.

Only the Afghans can remove the Taliban from power. An unreformed Taliban will not, I believe, remain in power indefinitely. Britain should be ready to help hasten the day when a more representative, less corrupt Afghan government can take power, with a better chance of success than before.

The announcement of the Russian withdrawal from Afghanistan was made in a speech delivered by Gorbachev at the nineteenth party conference in June–July 1988. It revealed another critical change in Soviet foreign policy. Here, Gorbachev spoke of the importance of freedom of choice, saying that the time for opposing freedom of choice with force was over. This signalled a shift from the Brezhnev Doctrine (see page 176) and attracted attention in Eastern Europe. He reiterated the message on the international stage at the UN in December 1988. According to Gorbachev, his policy of *perestroika* contained 'a tremendous potential for peace and international cooperation' which he wanted to be 'properly understood'.[34] In a wide-ranging speech, he stressed the changes brought about by the world coming closer together, thanks to improvements in communication and transport, and the response this called for. Approaches had to change; more universal solutions had to be found to critical problems. He was particularly clear, if a little naïve, in his statements on the use or threat of force.

> It is obvious, for instance, that the use or threat of force no longer can or must be an instrument of foreign policy. This applies above all to nuclear arms, but that is not the only thing that matters. All of us, and primarily the stronger of us, must exercise self-restraint and totally rule out any outward-oriented use of force.[35]

Then, echoing the earlier words at the party conference which had been so closely heeded in Eastern Europe, Gorbachev went on to say:

> It is also quite clear to us that the principle of freedom of choice is mandatory. Its non-recognition is fraught with extremely grave consequences for world peace.
>
> Denying that right to the peoples under whatever pretext or rhetorical guise means jeopardizing even the fragile balance that has been attained. Freedom of choice is a universal principle that should allow for no exceptions.[36]

While the West saw a real chance that the Communists' grip on Eastern Europe would loosen, handling the multiple moving pieces was to pose challenges. Experience had brutally demonstrated how periods of change in the region could prove both short-lived and tragic. This time, the risks were compounded as changes were simultaneously under way both at the centre and in the satellites, though at varying speeds. As the failure of Communism to deliver decent lifestyles, both economically and in terms of human rights, became ever clearer, dissatisfaction in Eastern Europe was now fundamentally a reaction against Communism and its record in power. What had changed compared with previous periods of dissent and unrest was that the innate threats and menace that had hitherto ensured Communism's survival now appeared to be evaporating. Gorbachev's pronouncements had given the people living under Soviet rule the hope that, this time, it would be different; this time, there would be no Soviet tanks crushing their aspirations. The tide was turning – slowly but remorselessly – and so it, by and large, has proved. The map of the world is very different today.

The climax came in 1989, and it came in dramatic and unexpected fashion. By the end of the year, the liberation of the Eastern bloc was summed up by the phrase: '10 years in Poland, 10 months in Hungary, 10 weeks in East Germany and 10 days in Czechoslovakia'.[37] Poland had seen major strikes and demonstrations in 1988, which had brought Solidarity back into prominence. Accepting this, in February 1989, the Polish government officially recognised Solidarity as a negotiating partner and round-table talks commenced. These led to parliamentary elections in June and a Solidarity-led government; the Communist monopoly on power was broken.

But the most critical developments were to stem from events

in East Germany, where opposition to the hard-line leadership was growing. There were demonstrations on the East German side of the Berlin Wall in 1987 and again in January 1988, but the government had dealt with them firmly. The East German leader, Erich Honecker, visited Moscow in September 1988 and went out of his way to praise *perestroika*, but demonstrations followed on his return. Municipal elections were held in the GDR in May 1989 and, predictably, in rigged elections, 98.5 per cent of the votes cast were for government candidates, contrasting with what was happening in Poland and even in Moscow. Then, on 2 May, the Hungarian government, which had already relaxed travel restrictions for its citizens the previous year, began dismantling the electrified fence on its border with Austria. Other Communist governments were furious at Hungary for creating this breach in the Iron Curtain, but Moscow did not intervene. East Germans saw a potential hitherto closed route to the West opening up, and they began to travel in large numbers to Hungary and other Eastern bloc countries, hoping to be able to travel onward to the West. Hungary itself had continued its measured reforms and, in June, on the thirty-first anniversary of Imre Nagy's execution, his remains, together with other prominent figures of the 1956 revolution, were reburied with full honours, an event that contributed to the collapse of the Hungarian Socialist Workers' Party regime.

In August, during what was to become known as the 'Pan-European Picnic', a border crossing point was opened to allow Austrians and Hungarians to mix. Several hundred East Germans took the opportunity to flee to Austria, and they were not stopped by Hungarian border guards. On 10 September, the Hungarian foreign minister, when asked on television what his response would be if even more East Germans crossed the

border, said: 'We will allow them through without any further
ado and I assume the Austrians will let them in.' Within three
days, 22,000 East Germans had passed into Austria. The Hungarian authorities felt that they were as acting in accordance
with the Helsinki Final Act, which allowed such movements.
Throughout this revolt of the people up until the loss of life
in Lithuania, Gorbachev, to his great credit (at least from the
West's point of view) stuck by his recently espoused principles
and never contemplated deploying Soviet tanks as his predecessors had done. The Brezhnev Doctrine was well and truly gone.
The Kremlin simply watched and waited.

The East German government made every mistake possible in handling the growing crisis it faced. Many thousands of
people attended demonstrations in Leipzig on 2 October 1989.
On 7 October, Gorbachev arrived in the GDR to much public
support. He was there to celebrate the fortieth anniversary of the
state's foundation, and all he said of substance was 'life punishes
those who delay'.[38] Protests continued with thousands of arrests
and many injured. On Monday, 9 October, the police and military planned to prevent any further demonstrations but, faced
with a huge number of peaceful protesters taking to the streets,
the security forces stepped back from mounting a large-scale
intervention. On 18 October, with demonstrations growing in
strength, Honecker was removed and replaced by Egon Krenz.
In Moscow for talks with Gorbachev in early November, Krenz
spoke of applying the lessons of *perestroika* and submitting a
programme of political and economic change, but he also made
clear that some things remained immutable, including the
Berlin Wall. It was all too late. Demonstrations in Leipzig were
now attracting up to 300,000 people and, on 4 November, half
a million East Germans gathered in Berlin. In an attempt to

stem the tide of protest, Krenz authorised the reopening of the border with Czechoslovakia. This, however, merely resulted in a mass exodus through Hungary. On 9 November, Günter Schabowski, Krenz's unofficial spokesperson, announced that both emigration and travel to West Germany would be allowed, provided prior approval was given, but on seeing no date in his notes as to when the new rules would come into effect, he announced it was immediate. Crucially, in an interview afterwards, Schabowski told reporters, 'It is no question of tourism. It is a permission of leaving GDR [permanently].'[39] Within hours, thousands of East Germans gathered at the wall demanding the guards open the gates. Fearing a stampede, the gates were opened, and some began to demolish the wall itself.

The liberation of Europe had now taken on a completely new dynamic. In Moscow, people began to ask what degree of liberalisation could be introduced in Russia. For Gorbachev, his handling of the changes now underway in the Soviet Empire ultimately served to weaken, not strengthen, his personal authority. On 10 November, Todor Zhivkov, who had been in power in Bulgaria since 1954, announced that he was retiring, and the Bulgarian Communist Party opened negotiations with the opposition and promised free elections. In Prague, demonstrations spread across the country on 17 November, signalling the start of the Velvet Revolution. The entire leadership of the Communist Party resigned, and a coalition government was formed. By the end of the year, Václav Havel was the new president and Alexander Dubček, the veteran reformist from the days of the Prague Spring, was chair of the Federal Assembly. Charter 77 had come a long way.

This dramatic shift in Europe was not to be entirely without tragedy. On 17 December in Romania, President Nicolae

Ceauşescu, who had been in power since 1965, personally ordered his army to shoot on demonstrators in Timişoara, killing dozens of people. On 21 December, a pro-government rally called by Ceauşescu in Bucharest turned into a jeering, angry crowd that he could not control. He and his wife fled the capital by helicopter, but they were captured, summarily tried, and executed by firing squad on Christmas Day. Ceauşescu had met Gorbachev in the Kremlin only twenty-one days previously; neither had envisaged such a breakdown in the authority of Eastern European Communism.

Many theories have been put forward to explain the rapid collapse. Some favour the 'domino' theory; others talk of 'contagion'. A powerful force – as Gorbachev had to some extent foreseen in his 1988 speech – was the ever-present TV cameras, relaying pictures of demonstrations and generating momentum both internally and in neighbouring countries. Fortunately, aside from the events in Romania, violence was limited; too many of the revolutionaries had been on the receiving end before. Youth was often in the lead. Viktor Orbán, the future prime minister of Hungary, was twenty-six and created a party initially for people under thirty-five years old, though this restriction was lifted in 1993. The language of 'returning to Europe' prevalent in the 1960s and 1970s had, by the 1980s, morphed into a new language, that of 'joining the European Community' and even visionary talk of a Europe united in one country.

To some Americans, the fall of the Berlin Wall recalled the image of President Reagan in West Berlin in June 1987 making a heartfelt appeal: 'Mr Gorbachev, tear down this wall...' To some Britons, the imagery of Reagan and Thatcher as the principal architects of the fall of the wall was strong. The truth is more pedestrian, but also more realistic. If a single architect is to be singled out for praise in bringing down the Berlin Wall, it is the American diplomat George Kennan, the inspiration for 'containment'. If there are political leaders to praise, the list is a long one, mainly for making small but important moves. Among the European protagonists, the name Brandt looms larger than most. Among the Americans, Marshall, with his sound military mind and generous nature, should never be forgotten in Europe. In terms of organisations, NATO towers above all others in exercising the right of collective self defence and the pressure it brought to bear on Soviet ideology. The original European Community of six nations showed how the deep-seated enmities that played out in two world wars could be overcome. Even earlier, the bringing together in the European Coal and Steel Community of the very French and German coalmines and steelworks that fuelled both wars demonstrated a new resolve. And in all of this, Europeans must never forget the US military twice crossing the Atlantic to help them defeat German aggression.

But it is only fair to give credit where credit is due and recognise the steady and determined contribution that successive British governments made to the liberation of Europe from Communism. This was particularly evident in their contribution to NATO. Despite Britain's financial weakness after 1945, it was prepared to spend vast sums on defence before NATO was created in 1948 and after in Europe and east of Suez until 1965 – as much as 7 per cent of GDP in 1955–6 and 1956–7 (compared to around 2.2 per cent in 2021).[40] From 1969 until 1988, the year before the Berlin Wall fell, annual defence spending was between 4 and 5 per cent of GDP, substantially more than all NATO allies except the US, and the continuing imbalance in contributions, particularly by wealthy members such as Germany, has remained a thorny issue between Europe and both Democrat and Republican administrations in the US.

In the summer of 1977, during a reception at Buckingham Palace, I settled the phasing out over three years of the German financial contribution to the British Army of the Rhine with the then German chancellor, Helmut Schmidt. Never one to stand on ceremony, when he realised my opposite number, Hans-Dietrich Genscher, was unwilling to commit to the phasing, we traded three figures literally on the back of an envelope under the eagle eye of Jim Callaghan, who was also in the same large room. Even so, the last British troops ceased to be permanently stationed in Germany in 2020.

The key moment when British decision-making in relation to the liberation of Europe might have done very serious damage was over German reunification. Margaret Thatcher was wrong to be concerned about Germany's aims. Modern Germany had learnt from two world wars. But her sentiment was deeply felt, and her most senior adviser on foreign policy in No. 10, Sir Percy Cradock, wrote about her fears.

She had grown up during the second of those wars and for her, as for many of her contemporaries, the concept of Germany was indelibly marked by that experience. The fact that the German leader [Kohl] had a very different vision of Europe from her own, the integrated model rather than her '*Europe des patries*', made it worse. The final twist of the knife was that the American President [Bush], to whose attention she thought Britain had a particular claim, backed the German Chancellor throughout and added warm words about an integrated Europe ... Against that background, our policy was a failure of calculation as well as imagination.[41]

Thatcher thought she might find an ally in the French president, François Mitterrand, and used to talk openly with him about her doubts over reunification. While he acknowledged her concerns in private discussions, his focus on the wider Franco-German relationship meant he never even hinted at this underlying attitude when dealing with Chancellor Kohl. The period in which Thatcher held her views more or less openly was short, but whether she ever changed them in private is an open question. Douglas Hurd, her new foreign secretary and a modest and decent man, gave her words short shrift. For him and Cradock, one of the very best diplomats in the FCO, their main task of rebuilding her relationship with Germany was 'rescue work'.[42]

But Thatcher's relationship with Kohl undoubtedly suffered, and President Bush simply ignored her views. Surprising many, Kohl openly proposed reunification just before the Malta Summit on 2 December 1989, where Gorbachev was to have his first meeting with Bush, who had become president at the start of the year. James Baker, the US secretary of state, was present along with Brent Scowcroft, the national security adviser. Gorbachev was accompanied by Eduard Shevardnadze, his foreign minister, Alexander Yakovlev, his chief adviser, and Akhromeyev, a former chief of general staff, now his military adviser. Some people believe Malta was the moment the Cold War ended. Indeed, in the words of Gorbachev, 'The world is leaving one epoch and entering another. We are at the beginning of a long road to a lasting, peaceful era. The threat of force, mistrust, psychological and ideological struggle should all be things of the past.'[43] Others in Russia, particularly in Andropov's reformed KGB, like Putin, saw increasing humiliation and were determined to restore Russia's power internationally.

Gorbachev felt that, of all the Europeans, the socialist Mitterrand was his closest ally in the construction of a post-Cold War Europe, believing the French president shared his concept of the 'common European home' and the idea of dissolving both military blocs in favour of new European security structures. And to an extent, Mitterrand did share that view. Gorbachev, who was embraced by Europe during 1990 and long afterwards, often used the term 'common European home', though the term's meaning could be fluid. At times, this manifested itself in a wish for Russia to be a member of the Council of Europe, which it became in 1996 and still is in 2021. At other times, it was less specific, though there was talk of joining the European Union.

Gorbachev still hoped to persuade Mitterrand to oppose a unified Germany in NATO, but Mitterrand was quite direct in telling Gorbachev that he could not do that. Nevertheless, Mitterrand did suggest that Gorbachev demand 'appropriate guarantees' from NATO, recognising the danger of isolating the Soviet Union in the new Europe and the need to 'create security conditions for you [Russia], as well as European security as a whole'.[44] Thatcher used similar wording in conversations with Gorbachev: 'we must find ways to give the Soviet Union confidence that its security would be assured'.[45]

Back in Russia itself, Gorbachev's decision in 1988 to create a new, elected Congress of People's Deputies of 2,250 legislators was not a major democratic reform, but it still had within it the seeds of his own downfall. With elections set for March 1989, the congress was to consist of 750 deputies elected in territorial districts, 750 from districts chosen in ethnic territories, and 750 representing social organisations. Of the latter, 100 deputies came from both the CPSU and the Central Council of Trade Unions; 75 each came from Komsomol (the young Communist League), the Soviet Women's Committee, and the War and Labour Veterans Organisation; and 325 came from other organisations, such as the Academy of Sciences. The congress would later elect a smaller number of 542 deputies for the new Supreme Soviet, which would function as the country's working parliament. Of these, the party would nominate 100 seats, dubbed the Red Hundred as they would effectively be nominated by Gorbachev.

Gorbachev was not certain enough of the result to risk putting himself up for democratic election, so he and some his Politburo colleagues were included in the Red Hundred. Leading the Academy of Sciences' list was Nobel Prize-winner Andrei Sakharov, who had become an activist for disarmament, peace, and human rights. Boris Yeltsin, who had resigned from the Politburo in 1987 in protest at the slow pace of reforms, made his comeback in the elections, taking the Moscow district with 89 per cent of the vote, against the Communist candidate. However, this was only after one of the other nominated candidates, the cosmonaut Georgy Grechko, stood down in Yeltsin's favour. Many Politburo members were very anxious about holding these elections and, when challenged, Gorbachev said 85 per cent of those elected were Communists. But Yegor Ligachev, the second secretary of the CPSU and increasingly a critic of Gorbachev, and others were not content saying, 'but what sort of Communists?'[46]

Trouble was indeed to come. On 11 May 1989, the election results in the Baltic States were challenged in the Politburo. This came soon after an anti-Soviet demonstration in Tbilisi, Georgia on 9 April, which caused a reported twenty-one deaths and injured hundreds more. On 25 May, the first session of the new congress opened. A Latvian deputy went to the podium and lodged an official 'deputy's inquiry' into who had given the order 'to slaughter ... with poisonous substances'. Sakharov spoke and warned Gorbachev that his support was only 'conditional'.[47] With TV cameras covering the congress proceedings live, such challenges to the authorities were being watched by ordinary people in their homes. Following the initial session of the congress, Yeltsin started to stress the need for a proper democracy, as did Sakharov. Though Sakharov was actually more friendly to Gorbachev than Yeltsin, he became disillusioned and told the democratic opposition, the Inter-regional Deputies' Group, which he co-led, that Gorbachev 'was leading the country into a catastrophe'.[48] But before Sakharov could have any greater impact, he died on 14 December 1989, while preparing an important speech for the following day's meeting of the second congress session.

Gorbachev tried to avoid tributes to Sakharov and was beginning to show an ambivalence about the logic of reforms leading to a proper democracy. Meanwhile, Yeltsin was starting to build momentum both inside and outside Russia. He had given lectures during a tour in the US in September 1989 about how he saw the future of Russia and, while President Bush was not ready to formally agree a meeting with Yeltsin, he 'dropped in' on a discussion Yeltsin was having in the White House with Brent Scowcroft. One problem that was to resurface throughout his political career, his weakness for alcohol, was already evident when Yeltsin spoke at Johns Hopkins University. As the US press reported at the time:

That he could stand up, let alone be engaging and sound urgent, seemed a little miraculous. It wasn't just the two hours' sleep he was going on. It was the amount of Tennessee sipping whisky he had knocked back overnight ... [He] came swaying and galumphing and bassooning and mugging and hugging and doom-warning through the greater Baltimore-Washington corridor yesterday ... [It was] like watching a circus bear negotiate a skateboard.[49]

Alcoholism destroyed Yeltsin's career and was no minor medical matter. That he could behave like this damaged Russian people's sense of pride in their leader and their country. Any normal politician would not have survived *Pravda*'s coverage of Yeltsin's American tour, but as Yeltsin's career went on to show, Russians have a huge tolerance for alcohol abuse, so many having used it to deaden the harshness of their lives.

The Congress of People's Deputies elected Gorbachev president of the Soviet Union on 14 March 1990, but it was by no means an overwhelming victory. He registered less than 60 per cent of the votes when abstentions were taken into account, revealing serious weaknesses in his power base. He was not worried and began telling his staff, 'All of you are just consultants. Don't forget that.'[50] During the May Day parade, demonstrators, including some from Lithuania and Estonia, waved Soviet flags with the hammer and sickle ripped out.

Western leaders were now faced with the dilemma of how to handle these monumental changes in Eastern Europe and the Soviet Union itself. With the publisher's kind permission, I quote below a passage from the chapter entitled 'The Soviet Union: The Last Act' in Percy Cradock's book *In Pursuit of British Interests: Reflections On Foreign Policy Under Margaret Thatcher and John Major*. He was present at the key meetings and expertly summarises the challenges they faced.

Western governments watching this scene faced a series of questions, almost all unprecedented. They had to form some judgement of where events inside the Soviet Union were leading. They had to balance their investment in Gorbachev against thoughts of his growing vulnerability and against their instinctive support for the 'imprisoned people' of the Soviet Union, above all those in the Baltic states. They had to balance the immense gains already achieved in Central Europe, and the need to secure and fortify these, against the more doubtful prospects further east. Increasingly too, they were having to discuss the question of economic aid for the Soviet Union.

This last issue became active in the summer of 1990. I recall Teltschik, Chancellor Kohl's Foreign Policy Adviser, raising it with me in Bonn in June. He spoke of the need for very large sums, much more than Germany alone could bear, which would not only help preserve Gorbachev and orderly reform, but also help secure Soviet acquiescence in politico-military issues. Western advisers might be supplied to do something to ensure the money was sensibly used.

I said I sympathised with the wish to help. But there were serious objections. There was as yet no framework into which the money could usefully be injected. More advisers would not suffice; what was needed was something much more radical, something like a receivership of the Soviet economy. So far we lacked even the basic commitment on the Soviet side to market development. Without that, or much greater Western control, we would be pouring money into a black hole.

The question was considered by our principals at the G7 meeting of leading industrial countries at Houston in July.

Kohl and Mitterrand argued for some $10 billion in aid. The Russians asked for three times as much over a period. The prime minister was very cautious, as was President Bush. Until the Soviet economy was restructured and Soviet military spending reduced, there could be no confidence that Western funds would be wisely used. There were in any case serious objections, particularly in Congress, to aid for the Soviet Union while the Baltic states were still under thrall and Soviet aid was still being used to back left-wing regimes in Angola and Cuba. But the unreformed state of the Soviet system was the clinching argument.

In the end Gorbachev had to be satisfied with offers of international studies of the Soviet economy as a prelude to possible Western aid. It was a negative answer; but I thought it was the right one. It was a realistic recognition of the limits to our capacity to influence the deteriorating Soviet internal situation. In the end it was probably wiser to use what Western money was available to help the new democracies in Eastern Europe. There we had something to build on and a much higher chance of success.[51]

This long note explains in a very fair way why so little money was passed to Russia under Gorbachev. But what about under President Yeltsin? It is here that the West failed. Business went in with speculative money but never took the long view. Why wasn't more money tied to specific projects? Funds should have been made available for Yeltsin's government. A KGB 'counter coup' was always there. Also, paradoxically, the very changes that were most acceptable to Western democracies were those that had made some interest groups more hostile to Yeltsin: the huge shrinking of Russia as compared to the USSR, the ending of the Warsaw Pact, the privatisation of many economic and industrial industries that had been run hitherto by the central government, as well as a redistribution of spending, with more money spent on ensuring better government and improving the standard of living of the average citizen. These sorts of deep changes had been beyond the political reach of the Marshall Plan over its first thirty years but were suddenly within reach. Yet there were no Western statesmen around to seize the initiative. The West did not 'lose' Russia, but the tied aid that could have helped Russia save itself was never made available.

On 12 July 1990, Yeltsin – who had been elected, against Gorbachev's wishes, to the chair of the Presidium of the Supreme Soviet in May – renounced his Communist Party membership on the grounds that he could no longer submit to party discipline. In October, Yeltsin accused Gorbachev of having gone back on promises made during discussions over Prime Minister Ryzhkov's '500 Days' programme, which was intended to overcome Russia's economic crisis by introducing moves towards a market economy. By November, Gorbachev was being widely criticised by the Russian media. Yakovlev, formerly his closest adviser, was no longer in his inner circle. Then on 20 December 1990, the foreign minister, Shevardnadze, who had personally built up a strong reputation in the West, spoke at the fourth congress meeting, railing against the increasing hard-line influence on Gorbachev, and in announcing his resignation said: 'Dictatorship is coming ... No one knows what kind of dictatorship it will be, what kind of dictator will come, and what order things will take.'[52]

A number of factors had resulted in this undermining of Gorbachev's authority but, for Russian opinion makers, allowing NATO to expand into East Germany was certainly a major one. It can be argued that, during this period, Western leaders were preoccupied by Saddam Hussein's invasion of Kuwait and the subsequent first Gulf War, with President Bush focused on organising and leading a multinational response from August 1990 to January 1991. But insisting on the GDR's entry into NATO was one of the big mistakes Western leaders made at the time.

On 25 January 1991, at a meeting with his key advisers, Gorbachev accepted German reunification and instructed Marshal Akhromeyev to start preparing to withdraw Soviet forces from East Germany. He nevertheless continued to strongly oppose a united Germany being included in NATO, always insisting that he had received assurances on this issue – as indeed he had, though these assurances were only verbal. Certainly, Germany's Hans-Dietrich Genscher never made any secret of his views and, as early as 31 January 1990, he had made a major speech in Tutzing, Bavaria, in which he said, 'the changes in Eastern Europe and the German unification process must not lead to an "impairment of Soviet security interests." Therefore, NATO should rule out an "expansion of its territory towards the east, i.e. moving it closer to the Soviet borders".' The report of the speech by the US embassy in Bonn to Washington also noted Genscher's proposal to leave the East German territory out of NATO military structures, even in a unified Germany in NATO.[53]

In reality, the decisions on NATO expansion were made at the level of Kohl and Bush, as set out in Taubman's book on Gorbachev. When Bush, referring to the idea of giving up too much to Gorbachev, told Kohl, 'To hell with that! ... We prevailed, they didn't ... We can't let the Soviets clutch victory from the jaws of defeat', Kohl said, in that case, they would have to find some other way to placate Gorbachev.[54] 'It will come down in the end to a question of cash', Kohl said. Bush replied that West Germany had 'deep pockets'. Or, as Robert Gates put it later, the goal would be 'to bribe the Soviets out' of East Germany, with 'West Germany paying the bribe'.[55] Kohl's decision to offer parity between the West German Deutschmark and the much less valuable East German Ostmark was a brave but very costly decision. The countries that should have been more generous to Russia were the US, Britain, and France.

It was not just the GDR's membership of NATO that concerned the Soviet leadership at this stage. John Major, who succeeded Margaret Thatcher as prime minister in 1990, met Gorbachev several times, including two visits to Moscow in March and September 1991. During his visit in March, he held a meeting with military officials in which Marshal Yazov expressed his concerns about Eastern European leaders' interest in NATO membership. In his diary, Rodric Braithwaite, the British ambassador, wrote: 'Major assures him that nothing of the sort will happen.' Years later, quoting from the record of conversation in the British archives, Braithwaite recounts that Major replied to Yazov that he 'did not himself foresee circumstances now or in the future where East European countries would become members of NATO'. Braithwaite also quoted the foreign minister, Douglas Hurd, as telling the Soviet foreign minister, Alexander Bessmertnykh, on 26 March 1991 that, 'there are no plans in NATO to include the countries of Eastern and Central Europe in NATO in one form or another'.[56]

I am in no doubt that the way in which President Bush Jnr pushed NATO on enlargement led directly to many of the problems we face in dealing with Putin's Russia today. Angela Merkel had, as German chancellor, refused to let both Ukraine and Georgia become members of NATO (see Chapter 9). Everything that has happened since points to her judgement being right; neither Georgia nor Ukraine should be in NATO until first the Russia–Ukraine war is settled and an overall settlement is reached on all boundary disputes in Europe.

We all have our personal criteria for judging when and why we can no longer support the actions of a political leader whom we had previously held in high regard. For me, Gorbachev, for all his initial bravery and skill, was damaged as a credible reformist leader following the January 1991 massacre in Lithuania. Tensions had been high in the state since its declaration of independence, following free elections, in March 1990, which was subsequently denounced as illegal by Gorbachev. Pressure grew on Gorbachev to take action in Lithuania and elsewhere to rein in the independence movements. On 13 January 1991, events culminated in the Soviet troops storming the TV station in Vilnius, leaving fifteen people dead.

In response, I wrote to *The Independent* newspaper, taking up their editorial with 'The Price of Baltic Repression'.

It is no accident that Mr Gorbachev has never put his own leadership to a proper democratic test in the Soviet Union. Quite simply, he feared he would lose. Mr Gorbachev thinks he can get away with a managed democracy and a managed economy. He has transferred power from the Communist Party to a power elite that grew out of Andropov's KGB. This elite is now in trouble on every front, confounded by its own internal contradictions.

We are being told that President Gorbachev, the Commander-in-Chief, had nothing to do with violence in Vilnius. Yet he threatened Lithuania after General Moiseyev, the Chief of the Soviet General Staff, had told Tass, on 3 January 1991, that 'Not a single additional soldier will be dispatched to the Baltic States in future' and that they might even consider reducing the contingent there. The Lithuanians refused to be lulled. It was the Army that provoked.

We in Britain have for 50 years refused to accept that the three independent Baltic states are part of the USSR. The Union of Soviet Socialist Republics has always been a myth. Professor Kolakowski has been right to deride the 'Union of Soviet Socialist Republics' as being a lie in every word. Never has that been truer than today.

I stand by my criticism. Yeltsin flew to Vilnius and condemned the attack. Demonstrators in the streets of Moscow carried banners reading 'Gorbachev is the Saddam Hussein of the Baltics' and 'Give back the Nobel Prize'. Visiting Estonia, Latvia, and Lithuania later that year as chair of an inter-parliamentary union delegation of UK politicians, I talked to leaders who were negotiating their future separately with Gorbachev and Yeltsin. They had no doubt that Yeltsin was the democrat. Their certainty convinced me too. In my eyes, the coup that was to come exposed Gorbachev even further. Shevardnadze claimed that Gorbachev had in some unspecified way been 'involved'. He later appeared to drop that suspicion. Much later, after he had ceased to be president of Georgia, I visited him in his home in Tbilisi. Of all the members of the Soviet leadership whom I had met over a long period, I had always found him intelligent and genuine. I planned to ask him directly about his suspicions over the coup, but I felt he was too fragile to burden with recalling this sensitive time, and he died soon after my visit.

During 1991, while Gorbachev struggled to hold the union together in the face of growing pressures, particularly from the Baltic Republics, and with Yeltsin's position in Russia strengthening, the Joint Intelligence Committee in London was 'warning, not only of the coming disintegration of the Soviet Union, but also of the danger of a right-wing coup'. In their analysis, however, 'they doubted whether such a coup would hold and prove able to turn back the clock back for long'.[57] They were correct in their assessment. The coup came when Gorbachev was on holiday in Crimea. Led by hard-liners including the vice president, Yanayev, the prime minister, Pavlov, the KGB chief, Kryuchkov, the defence minister, Yazov, and the interior minister, Pugo, it took the world by surprise – and yet more surprises came as it played out, suggesting the plotters were not in full control of events. The morning after they had announced their putsch, on 19 August, Yeltsin flew back to Moscow from Kazakhstan. Rather than being arrested on landing, as might have been expected, he travelled unhindered to the White House, the seat of the Russian parliament. No attempt was made to stop Yeltsin supporters gathering at the White House. As Cradock somewhat laconically noted:

Gorbachev was incommunicado; we had expected no less. But Yeltsin was very visible. According to the normal laws of such operations he should have been eliminated in the first hour. But pictures of him were appearing on local television; he was alive; he was seen on a tank.

Something very odd was happening.[58]

The British prime minister, John Major, phoned Yeltsin to offer his support when the outcome of the coup was still uncertain.

Unlike Mitterrand, Major did not hedge his bets, and this ensured Major and Yeltsin enjoyed very good personal relations.

The plotters did eventually issue an order to storm Yeltsin's stronghold on the third day of the coup, but the key elite KGB Alfa troops refused to fire on the White House. The former armed forces chief, Marshal Akhromeyev, who had worked with Gorbachev but who had been on holiday, quickly went to Moscow to support the coup. After the coup failed, he wrote to Gorbachev and then hanged himself in his office leaving a note, 'I can no longer live when my Fatherland is dying and everything I have worked for is being destroyed'.[59] For his part, Kryuchkov spent three years in jail, was amnestied, and then started to claim that Gorbachev had known about the plot.

Gorbachev's final humiliation came after his return to Moscow. While addressing the Russian Supreme Soviet on 23 August, he claimed that Prime Minister Pavlov's cabinet had resisted the coup. Yeltsin rose from his seat in full view of a large TV audience and advanced on Gorbachev. He shoved in his face a transcript of the cabinet meeting of 19 August at which virtually all the ministers listed had supported the coup. 'Go on, read it now', Yeltsin demanded, stabbing his finger in Gorbachev's face, the moment captured in what was to become a famous photograph. Gorbachev had returned to what he called a changed country, but it was no longer his; its leader was now Yeltsin. Gorbachev had become virtually irrelevant.

In late August, Gorbachev summoned the British ambassador, Rodric Braithwaite. Not in the least prone to exaggeration, Braithwaite described Gorbachev as overwrought, almost incoherent: 'His Southern accent is stronger than ever, his sentences ever more complex and elliptical. I can barely understand him.'[60]

On 1 September, John Major, as chair of the G7, was in

Moscow expressing his relief at the failure of the coup and extolling the strength of President Gorbachev under such pressures. He also expressed his admiration for Yeltsin for the stand he took in facing down the perpetrators of the coup. In his press conference he said:

Fifty years ago this week British ships began to bring food into Murmansk at a time of very great need for the Soviet people. Again this winter we may face the need to help the Soviet people through a period of acute difficulty ... The Soviet Union and the republics face momentous decisions and only they can take those decisions.[61]

During the press conference, Major also welcomed the independence of the three Baltic States; Estonia and Latvia had declared independence in the aftermath of the coup attempt, following Lithuania's declaration of the previous year. Furthermore, he confirmed that Britain would be sponsoring their entry to the UN.

Earlier, on 1 August 1991, President Bush had visited Kyiv and seemed out of touch with the movement of opinion in that he recommended to the Ukrainians that they should stay in the Soviet Union. On 24 August, the Ukrainians voted overwhelmingly to quit the union. Between 24 August and 21 September, Belarus, Moldova, Azerbaijan, Kyrgyzstan, Uzbekistan, Georgia, Tajikistan, and Armenia all followed suit.

These expressions of view from free peoples all over the former USSR should not ever be forgotten in the wake of Russia's two invasions of Ukrainian territory. Nobody should be misled by Putin's propaganda about people wanting to come back to the former boundaries of the USSR; that those who live in Ukraine are tired of democracy or can be labelled as Nazis or, even more outrageous, are being kept in Ukraine against their will. People are already starting to leave Russia as a result of Putin's invasion of Ukraine. I predict a slow exodus will continue until Putin loses power.

On 6 November 1991, Yeltsin ordered the disbanding of the CPSU and the Communist Party of the RSFSR. On 8 December 1992, Yeltsin, supported by the Belarusian president, Stanislav Shushkevich, and the Ukrainian president, Leonid Kravchuk, agreed to establish a Commonwealth of Independent States. The Soviet Union that had existed since 1922 was over, and Gorbachev had no job to call his own.

President Yeltsin's decision had some similarities with that of Lenin's on 3 March 1918 to sign for a separate peace with the Central Powers in the Treaty of Brest-Litovsk (discussed in Chapter 4). He could only do this when Trotsky moved away from Bukharin who wanted an expansionist war. Lenin, like Yeltsin many years later, made the decision to consolidate a smaller Russia ('we need both hands free'). The other country besides Russia to gain from Lenin's decision in 1918, and Yeltsin's in 1991, was Ukraine.

8

Yeltsin: A Free Spirit

The Yeltsin years were to see dramatic changes as Russia emerged from the collapse of the Soviet Union. Having made the break with Communism, he was a genuine reformer. But he was also an alcoholic who had serious heart trouble, a condition he never fully overcame even after major heart surgery. Though very brave, Yeltsin at times was unable, particularly towards the end of his presidency, to provide the steady leadership that was desperately needed in Russia.

Yeltsin felt it was essential that he move fast to secure the reforms the country needed, sensing the Communists were waiting in the wings. He also recognised that he was more likely to ensure further change if he focused on the Russian Federation alone. He thus immediately and commendably ditched Gorbachev's idea of trying to hold on to the Soviet Empire under another name. Smaller was better, as Lenin had known. Yeltsin had already abolished the CPSU, and on 25 December 1991 the Russian tricolour flag replaced the Soviet hammer and sickle. He allowed his young deputy prime minister for economic policy, Yegor Gaidar, and his team of advisers to make rapid moves towards introducing a market economy. He knew he risked criticism for moving too fast; indeed, his haste to tackle the immense challenges of the Soviet economy and its political legacy was to prove a major contributor to the situation the country finds itself in today.

The scandals and failings surrounding the Yeltsin presidency, which I shall return to, should not, however, be allowed to obscure his achievements in securing the independence of the former Soviet republics, and in particular his handling of the three Baltic states. While his close relationship with President Clinton was to be one of the enduring images of his time as president, the early years of his presidency also saw a close relationship sealed with Britain, building on the support John Major offered during the coup attempt. In January 1992, Yeltsin made a first visit to London for talks with the prime minister, where they agreed a fifteen-point declaration. This was followed on 10 November by a full state visit to Britain, the first by an elected Russian leader. Yeltsin met the queen, addressed a joint session of parliament, and signed a new Russo-British Treaty of Friendship. In October 1994, the thaw in the relationship between Britain and Russia was completed when the queen visited Moscow, putting behind her seven decades of estrangement between the Kremlin and Europe's royalty following the murder of the tsar and his family. Yeltsin also made significant contributions on the wider international stage, not least in helping achieve and then sustain a peace settlement in Bosnia-Herzegovina. In my role as the EU co-chair of the International Conference on the Former Yugoslavia (ICFY) from September 1992 to May 1995, I worked closely with the Yeltsin administration. There was an active partnership. Russian troops served in light-blue berets or helmets in the UN peacekeeping forces in the region and Russian civilians worked alongside them, as well as in the specialist agencies, such as the UN Refugee Agency.

Professor Sharyl Cross's important study on Russia and NATO in the twenty-first century published in August 2001 provides a balanced and broadly understanding account of what happened in Bosnia and Kosovo, and I draw from it here.[1] The Russians come out quite well from the study, given the difficult circumstances in which they found themselves. Yugoslavia had emerged as a country from the Versailles settlement, bringing together a disparate group of peoples with very different histories under one umbrella. Communist since the Second World War, Yugoslavia's post-war politics had been dominated, until his death in 1980, by the former partisan leader Marshal Josip Tito, who skilfully managed a country consisting of six separate republics and two autonomous regions. With Communism collapsing elsewhere in Eastern Europe, and with increasing economic inequality between its republics, a burgeoning nationalism emerged in the country. The republics of Croatia and Slovenia in particular sought to lessen the influence of the larger Serbia, whose president, Slobodan Milošević, was equally determined to maintain it. With the backing of Germany, who had broken ranks with their EU partners, Croatia and Slovenia declared independence in June 1991, leading to conflict with the Yugoslav Army. Macedonia followed with a declaration of independence in September. The situation in Bosnia-Herzegovina, because of the particularly diverse make-up of its population, was even more complex. There, Serbs held a referendum in the areas they controlled to set up their own republic, which they intended to remain aligned with Serbia and Montenegro. This was declared unconstitutional by the Bosnian government, who held their own national referendum in early 1992. The vote was overwhelmingly for independence, although turnout was low because of a boycott by many Serbs. This triggered the

declaration of a breakaway Bosnian Serb republic, soon followed by war.

Both at a political level and in the wider population, the Russians were more sympathetic towards the Serbs than could be
justified by the Serbs' behaviour, given a deep-seated historical
relationship and their shared Orthodox Christian religion (the
Croatians and Slovenes were predominantly Catholic; Kosovo
was mainly Muslim, and Bosnia and Macedonia had large
Muslim populations). But despite these traditional ties with
the Serbs, Yeltsin wanted Russia to demonstrate its readiness
to move beyond the divisions of the Cold War and to cooperate with NATO. NATO, meanwhile, realised that, thanks
to those connections, Russian involvement could help secure
Serb cooperation and reassured the Serbs that someone would
protect their interest in any settlement.

I found the Russian foreign minister, Andrei Kozyrev, a true
partner in the Balkan peace negotiations. Kozyrev, quite correctly, also conducted himself as a partner with the other four
permanent members in the Security Council. China, however,
did not play a major role in the Balkan discussions.

In retrospect, the nearest we came to gaining US acceptance
of the Vance–Owen Peace Plan for Bosnia (the VOPP) was in
December 1992. Vance and I had gone to address an extraordinary session of the Organization of the Islamic Conference
in Jeddah on 1–2 December 1992. At a meeting in Geneva on
16 December with Lawrence Eagleburger, the US secretary of
state for the outgoing Bush administration, it was clear that
they supported the VOPP – as the former US ambassador to
Yugoslavia, Warren Zimmerman, had done.[2] But both Americans believed that the world was losing confidence in the West
over Bosnia and encouraged us to move as fast as we could to

end the siege of Sarajevo. The US government was prepared to act over some 'no fly' violations but not support enforcing peace.

The siege continued for three times as long as the siege of Stalingrad and one year longer than that of Leningrad. A force of around 13,000 Bosnian Serbs, situated in the hills that surrounded the city, fired down on the inhabitants below, day in, day out, with no regard for humanitarian law. In the words of the prosecution's opening statement in the International Criminal Tribunal for the former Yugoslavia vs Stanislav Galic, 2003:

> One must go back to the Second World War to find a parallel in European history. Not since then had a professional army conducted a campaign of unrelenting violence against the inhabitants of a European city so as to reduce them to a state of medieval deprivation in which they were in constant fear of death.[3]

Vance had gone back to the US, working with some apparent success at getting endorsement for the VOPP from Anthony Lake, who had been designated Clinton's new national security adviser. I flew into Sarajevo and entered intensive discussions with General Morillon, the commander of the UN Protection Force, and all other parties. One night, a Serbian anti-aircraft gun round was fired at Morillon's headquarters while we were both sleeping there, as it also served as his residence. The Croatian newspaper, *Novi Vjesnik*, made a play on my name, calling me 'Ovan' – a ram – and saying that I was the 'only international politician to have come to the devastated city who did not flee from it hastily at the first hint of darkness'. Morillon was a delight to work with in meeting after meeting, and we came very close to a settlement between 18 and 20 December 1992.

The key problem we faced in negotiating the demilitarisation and cessation of hostilities was that, although the Bosnian government troops were greater in number than those of the Bosnian Serbs, the government troops lacked the critical tanks, artillery, and other heavy equipment of the Serbs. The Serbs were also not ready to withdraw unless the UN forces that would take their place were substantial and sufficiently well-equipped to prevent any breaches of the agreement. Morillon wanted to deploy British Warrior armoured vehicles to Sarajevo and believed that was more important to the UN than controlling Bosnian Croatian forces outside Sarajevo. I sent an urgent message to John Major, then British prime minister. But, on 26 December, he told me that such a deployment was unlikely, and to some extent the British reluctance was justified when, in the New Year, the Bosnian Croatians in the south substantially increased their activity and ethnic cleansing. No other country had armoured forces available for use by the UN. The Russians were not acceptable to the Bosnian government; the French already had UN troops on the ground in Sarajevo; and Germany was politically not yet ready to contribute forces to the UN anywhere. Nevertheless, it was a heavy blow to Morillon and me that we could not force the Serbs to withdraw their heavy weaponry north of the airport and lift the siege of Sarajevo, which had started on 5 April 1992. Tragically, the siege would continue until 29 February 1996, when it was lifted under the terms of the Dayton Accords.

In May 1993, Vance and I faced another major setback in our negotiations. We had spent many months negotiating the VOPP and had travelled to Athens for a plenary negotiating session. Following an all-night meeting chaired by the Greek prime minister, Konstantinos Mitsotakis, the final signatures to the agreement were secured on 3 May from the president of Serbia, Slobodan Milošević, the president of Montenegro, Momir Bulatović, and the leader of the Bosnian Serbs, Radovan Karadžić. On that same day, 3 May, unconnected to the VOPP, Warren Christopher arrived in Britain as the first stop of a European tour to announce President Clinton's new policy to lift UN sanctions on arms supplies to Bosnia-Herzegovina and authorise more extensive NATO air strikes, a policy in shorthand called 'lift and strike'. Within days, European leaders found Christopher's presentation incoherent and unconvincing. Only later did they discover that Christopher knew, in the words of the US defense secretary, that President Clinton had 'gone south on this policy. His heart isn't in it.'[4]

On 5 May, I visited the secretary general of NATO, Manfred Wörner, and was surprised to be given a detailed, politically and socially sensitive implementation plan for what was agreed in Athens. NATO had clearly been following our talks in detail for months. It was only the refusal of the Clinton administration to have anything to do with that NATO plan that meant we could not proceed to detailed discussions with the UN secretary-general and the specialised UN agencies, as well as Serbia and Montenegro, whose presidents had signed the Athens Agreement.

As later cover for their refusal to accept the VOPP, the US cited the rejection of the Athens document by the Bosnian Serb assembly meeting in Pale. This was despite the fact that, at that stage, Presidents Izetbegović and Tudjman were also supportive of the Athens Agreement; indeed, they were more enthusiastic for it knowing that the Serbs were split. Underlying the split

was Milošević's exasperation with General Mladić, the Bosnian
Serb army leader. Mladić had support in Belgrade, but Milošević
was firmly in control. Of course, once US opposition to any
involvement became clear, NATO was effectively blocked. This
block on NATO stemmed from President Clinton and Vice
President Gore, and for two and a half years it was the source
of incoherence and disagreement in Washington's attitude to
the Balkans. It continued unabated after I had stepped down
as EU negotiator in May 1995 to be succeeded by Carl Bildt
and right up until Mladić rolled tanks into the so-called safe
area of Srebrenica and committed a flagrant act of genocide
in July 1995. Until then there was never any spirit in London,
Paris, or Berlin to take a military role in the Balkans without
the US. That should not be a surprise. NATO is founded on the
involvement of the US, and with it comes a presidential veto on
US involvement in any major action.

By 6 May 1993, the Bosnian Serbs in Pale had rejected the
Athens Agreement, despite Milošević, Bulatović, and Mitsotakis all going to Pale to urge them to support it.

Stoltenberg, who succeeded Vance after the Athens meeting,
and I decided to fly to Moscow on 15 May to see if any additional pressure could be placed on Milošević to ensure, despite
this setback, the progressive implementation of the VOPP.
Over lunch on 16 May, Kozyrev said he totally agreed with
our phrase 'progressive implementation' of the VOPP, and he
proceeded to use it extensively in the press conference that followed. He also accepted that the Russian Federation should
monitor the Serbian–Montenegrin border. We raised the possibility of 2,000 Russian troops as a contribution to implementing the UN resolution on safe areas and asked for them to be
deployed rapidly. Kozyrev promised to discuss this with Yeltsin,

whose approval would be required, and stated his intention to table a framework resolution for Security Council decision at a ministerial-level meeting on 21 May. After the meeting, he gave the press the strong impression that Russia would contribute both monitors and peacekeepers.

Kozyrev met Clinton and his secretary of state, Warren Christopher, in Washington on 21 May, but by this point there had been an incredible volte-face in the US position. In marked contrast to their previous criticism that the VOPP rewarded Serb aggression and wasn't generous enough to the Bosnian Muslims, the Americans now hinted that they felt the VOPP was too hard on the Serbs. In fairness to Kozyrev, at his meeting with Christopher, the Americans had baited the trap to win over the Russians to their position with great cunning. The Russians had always believed that Vance and I had been too tough on the Serbs in terms of territory, and it was inconceivable that the Russians would reject an offer from the US of more land for the Serbs. Also, at that time, Russia understandably valued the opportunity to be accepted as a fully fledged partner in a 'Big Four' initiative to resolve the Yugoslav problem.

The text that eventually emerged from Washington did contain references to the 'Vance–Owen peace process', but the VOPP itself was not mentioned – a significant omission. The British and French foreign ministers managed to resist the American attempt to abolish the ICFY itself, but they understandably wanted a new structure capable of ending the widening Atlantic rift. The outcome was to effectively ditch the VOPP, replaced by Washington's so-called Joint Action Programme (JAP) on Bosnia, which would involve Russia. The JAP was, however, destined to fail; in essence it proved to be a JIP, a joint *in*action plan. Its inherent flaw was that it declared five 'safe areas' in the knowledge that the US was not prepared to send any troops in blue berets or allow a NATO force to back up the claim that the areas would be safe.

Two years later, in July 1995, the almost inevitable happened at Srebrenica, a supposed safe area, with a terrible genocidal massacre of over 8,000 Bosnian Muslims. Perhaps the JAP's one redeeming feature was its commitment to establish the Yugoslav War Crimes Tribunal, which tried the perpetrators of such crimes. What the JAP also showed was that senior UN figures must be prepared to say 'no' to the Security Council, and in this case, Kofi Annan, who was in charge of peacekeeping, should have done so. The professional advice from respected military figures, many of them NATO officers then in blue berets, involved on the ground in Bosnia, was that 31,500 well-equipped soldiers were necessary to guarantee the safety of the five so-called 'safe areas'; the UN could only muster 6,000. The Clinton and Christopher policy was doomed from the start, and Vance and I warned them both and the secretary-general of the UN, Boutros-Boutros Ghali, who agreed with us, that the Security Council should not proceed given such a grave short-fall in troop numbers.

The European and American media saw the JAP as an endorsement of the Serbs' territorial conquests, a view shared by the Bosnian leader, Izetbegović, who said it would also prevent displaced populations from returning to their homes and turn safe areas into reservations. He declared the plan absolutely unacceptable. For the Bosnian government, the VOPP was the minimum they could accept, and they would not waste any more time in futile negotiations. Izetbegović called upon all citizens who loved Bosnia to unite and defend, with all permissible means, its integrity and freedom. I agreed with his criticism, and I felt very sorry for his predicament. The US, who had for the last few months been posing as his strong supporter, had totally let him down.

Nevertheless, the quest for peace had to continue, and a less formal 'contact group' structure, which I had advocated, was established to take forward negotiations with the US, Russia, Britain, France, Germany, and later Italy as members. Yeltsin's government was cooperative throughout and went even further, in effect, never challenging NATO's use of force after the Srebrenica genocide when the four permanent members (China was not involved) agreed to combine to use their military to help implement the Dayton Accords. These were successfully negotiated in November 1995 by Richard Holbrooke, who was the most realistic senior US diplomat throughout the Bosnian Wars. Russia agreed to work alongside the NATO-led Implementation Force (IFOR) and joined NATO's Operation Active Endeavour in the Mediterranean. Russia subsequently provided 1,200 of the 20,000 peacekeepers in the Stabilization Force (SFOR), which took over the mandate in December 1996.

At this point, the Russian representative changed. In December 1996, Yeltsin appointed Yevgeny Primakov as foreign minister in Kozyrev's place. Yeltsin had previously appointed Primakov as head of one of the successor organisations of the Soviet KGB, the SVR or Foreign Intelligence Service, which had been trying to check Kozyrev's power for the past five years. It was a revealing appointment, which Yeltsin had marked in September 1991 with a visit to Yasenevo, the KGB's foreign intelligence and espionage headquarters. When the first volume of the Mitrokhin Archive (a vast amount of documentary evidence of KGB activities smuggled out of Russia by a former KGB archivist, Vassili Mitrokhin) was published in 1999 it caused some embarrassment for Primakov personally, who always tried to present himself as a diplomat, not a spy, 'because it contained a number of references to him as a KGB co-optee, codenamed MAKSIM, who had been sent on a series of missions to the Middle East and the United States. There were also references to the role of Primakov's deputy and successor, Vyacheslav Trubnikov, as a KGB officer in India.'[5]

Securing the archive had been a major coup for British intelligence when Mitrokhin defected in 1992. Indeed, it was described by the FBI as the most complete and extensive intelligence ever received from any source.[6]

Russian cooperation in the former Yugoslavia was to continue under Primakov, with Kosovo becoming the focus of international attention. The population of this autonomous region of Serbia was predominantly Albanian Muslim, though there was a Serb minority and, for historic reasons dating back to the 1389 defeat of the Serbs at the battle of Kosovo Polje by the Ottomans, it was considerably important to Serb nationalists. Against the wider backdrop of the break-up of Yugoslavia, opposition to Belgrade rule in Kosovo had grown in the 1990s, as the Kosovars felt increasingly discriminated against. Discontent ultimately descended into guerrilla warfare against the forces of the rump Yugoslavia, spearheaded by the Kosovo Liberation Army. Again, the international community worked to broker a settlement, but talks broke down in March 1999 when the Yugoslav delegation did not sign up to the Rambouillet Accords, paving the way for a NATO bombing campaign that would run until June 1999, much longer than Western leaders had anticipated.

The arguments for military intervention in the affairs of

another state were set out in Prime Minister Tony Blair's 21 April 1999 speech in Chicago, which is discussed on pages 17–19 of this book. His speech was delivered just before a NATO meeting in Washington celebrating its fiftieth anniversary. NATO, meanwhile, was worried that its air bombing campaign against President Milošević's forces had so far showed few signs of success. It was a worrying time, particularly for President Clinton, who was against putting in NATO ground troops. Blair wanted Clinton to consider this strategy.

Kosovo was a critical moment for NATO–Russian relations. Though in many ways it was a humanitarian intervention, it was a political bridge too far for President Yeltsin to support NATO's decision to take military action via the UN. Recognising this, and rather than provoking a Russian veto in the Security Council, NATO tried to limit its actions by applying the humanitarian intervention criteria of proportionality when choosing bombing targets. But NATO's action was still never lawful in terms of the UN Security Council authority. It stretched the elasticity of the UN Charter too far, as the Russians (among others) were to remind the West on many subsequent occasions.

Sadly, too, well before then, Russian–NATO diplomatic cooperation was cooling. The bombing campaign itself triggered widespread public and parliamentary outcry in Russia, culminating in the suspension of relations with NATO. Indeed, Primakov cancelled a trip to Washington mid-flight. When I spoke with Russian diplomats early on in the Kosovo conflict, they correctly predicted that bombing alone would not succeed. But they were also very clear that it was not the moment for an early political intervention by Russia. They would wait and intervene diplomatically when the time was

ripe. But despite this internal opposition, Yeltsin was not prepared to completely turn his back on the relationship with the
West – and the US in particular – over Kosovo, and in mid-
April 1999, he shrewdly appointed Viktor Chernomyrdin, the
former chair of the energy company Gazprom and Russian
prime minister until 1998, as his special envoy for Yugoslavia.
A realist, Chernomyrdin was respected by many countries bordering Kosovo.

The true story of why Milošević agreed to withdraw his
troops from Kosovo has never been told. The best account is
in *Winning Ugly*, which details the hectic period of shuttle
diplomacy that followed Chernomyrdin's appointment.[7] This
resulted in the agreement on 1 June between Chernomyrdin,
the EU envoy (Finnish president Martti Ahtisaari), and the
US representative (Deputy Secretary of State Strobe Talbott)
in Bonn that all Yugoslav forces would have to leave Kosovo.
Milošević would be given reassurances in the form of Russian
participation in the implementation of the agreement. The
negotiators then travelled to Belgrade and when, on 2 June,
Milošević asked Chernomyrdin, 'Is this what I have to do to
get the bombing stopped?' the reply was simply, 'Yes'. Milošević
knew the game was up. Agreement on the details of the withdrawal was finally reached on 9 June, and the following day the
Security Council authorised the deployment of the NATO-led
peacekeeping force, Kosovo Force (KFOR).

We may never know what Chernomyrdin told Milošević in
their crucial earlier one-on-one meetings. Chernomyrdin was
of a generation that zealously protected Gazprom's then much-
prized reputation for not being used as a diplomatic tool by
closing gas pipelines. That inhibition has long since gone under
Putin, and Russia more or less overtly threatens cutting gas

supplies. I suspect that, on one of his five visits to Milošević in Belgrade during this period, Chernomyrdin warned the Serbian president that when he returned with Ahtisaari he would be demanding Serbia's military withdrawal from Kosovo and that if this was not done there would be a total cut-off of Russian gas to Yugoslavia. Can I prove it? Certainly not. But the fact that Yeltsin's new prime minister Sergei Stepashin (who replaced Primakov in May 1999) rang Clinton immediately after Chernomyrdin's visit on 27 May 1999 to say that Moscow wanted to settle all differences with the US as soon as possible, before the G8 Cologne Summit on 18 June, is very telling.

The most important military-political lesson for the future, though much neglected, was China's role in the defence of Belgrade during the NATO bombing. China had been a political and military supporter of President Milošević for some time. On 7 May 1999, five US Joint Direct Attack Munition guided bombs hit the embassy of the People's Republic of China in the New Belgrade district, killing three Chinese journalists. The US defense secretary, William Cohen, took two days to make an announcement that the US plane had bombed the wrong target because the bombing instructions were based on an outdated map. The Chinese Embassy was not surrounded by many buildings; it stood alone. It is politically significant that at no stage did the Chinese government come anywhere close to accepting the US explanation. Very openly, President Xi Jinping visited the site with the Serbian president during a trip in June 2016. From a military point of view, it is also note-worthy that every other US air attack on the night of 7 May 1999 was on a Serbian command-and-control centre.

Having dealt with Milošević over three and a half years, I am sure that an ultimatum from Yeltsin would have been more important in clinching the deal than any speech by Blair or Clinton. Although I was no longer involved in the former Yugoslavia, Blair called me while I happened to be in Berlin. I suggested calling a major NATO exercise in Hungary on Serbia's northern border as the best way of applying powerful pressure. When I pointed out to Blair that we were talking on an open telephone line, he said words to the effect that it did not matter since he wanted everyone to know that he was looking at all options. He knew that entering from what is now North Macedonia would be difficult because of adverse ground conditions. In the end, Milošević was forced to order an extremely reluctant Yugoslav military to withdraw from Kosovo, despite having successfully withstood eleven weeks of NATO bombing involving almost 10,500 strike sorties. Milošević's agreement to pull back set the Serbian Army against him. It also caused his failure in the subsequent election in Serbia and, ultimately, his extradition from Belgrade to be tried in The Hague, having been indicted on 24 May 1999 for crimes in Kosovo. Milošević was to die in prison in March 2006, just before the inevitable guilty verdict was due to be passed. I cannot prove it, but I believe he was never ready to spend years in prison, and he knew that Russia had agreed to look after his wife, which they did.

The most important military lesson from Kosovo is put very frankly by the authors of *Winning Ugly*. 'Bomb and pray' strategies, combined with the tendency to be satisfied with 'degrading' the military capacity of an opponent in vague and limited ways, were shown to have little – if any – strategic impact on the Serbs. Indeed, NATO's reliance on such strategies had eventually undermined 'the credibility of threatening force'.[8]

After the NATO war was over, some 3,600 Russian soldiers were eventually to serve as part of the 40,000-strong KFOR.

However, their initial deployment heightened, rather than reduced, tension. A contingent of Russian troops from Bosnia entered Kosovo in their armoured vehicles to take control of Pristina Airport on 11 June, the day before the negotiated withdrawal and KFOR deployment was due to commence. This was a provocative act that once again raised the political temperature between Russia and NATO members. The then Supreme Allied Commander Europe (SACEUR) Wesley Clark recalls that he immediately contacted the NATO secretary-general, the former Spanish foreign minister Javier Solana, saying, 'Javier, have you seen the TV? The Russians are in Pristina.'[9] In response, Clark ordered the securing of Pristina Airport by sending in British and French troops by helicopter. He wanted to stop the Russians receiving additional reinforcements and taking control of a sector in the north, which he feared could have led to the partition of Kosovo. To some extent, Clark's attitude could in fact have provoked the Russian action, as they were aggrieved not to have been given their own sector in the planning of KFOR.

Clark's order was, however, rejected by the KFOR commander, British general Mike Jackson, who, according to Clark, offered the following reply: 'Sir, I'm not starting World War III for you.' Jackson's position was then, rightly, in my view, supported by the British chief of defence staff, General Sir Charles Guthrie. When Guthrie appealed to General Hugh Shelton, chair of the US Joint Chiefs of Staff, he evidently agreed too and told Clark by phone that they 'didn't want a confrontation'.[10]

Wesley Clark explained why he wanted Jackson to act quickly.

I didn't want to face the issue of shooting down Russian

transport aircraft if they forced their way through NATO airspace. If they were able to land a large force, then we would be in the position of having to contain them, which could force a confrontation where the odds were less favourable to us.[11]

Jackson was right to refuse and to appeal against SACEUR's instructions to his own British senior officer, allowed for under NATO rules, because he was in effect being asked to break the very complicated phased Serb withdrawal plan. In doing so, he felt he would have given the Serb generals, who had been bullied into agreeing a withdrawal by Milošević, the chance to renege on the whole settlement. One reason NATO has held together is the formal right of appeal within NATO's command-and-control procedures, as outlined above. Jackson's handling of the issue proved to be successful and ended with him, a Russian speaker, sharing a bottle of whisky with the Russian commander at the airfield the following day. It was also made much easier by Bulgaria, Romania, and Hungary supporting NATO's request to deny Russia aeroplane access to their airspace. This blocked the Russians from flying in reinforcements to their small force, the very response Clark had feared.

Ultimately, the decisions surrounding Kosovo's future and the arrangement for the deployment of peacekeepers were finalised at the political level. In that process, Yeltsin and his generals got a lot of support from the Russian media by showing that they were not controlled in all circumstances by NATO. While the Russians did not put their forces under NATO command, they agreed carefully worked out command-and-control arrangements, as they had in Bosnia. Russian liaison officers at the Supreme Headquarters Allied Powers Europe

(SHAPE) coordinated issues in KFOR, with the Russian battalion commander on the ground working closely with NATO counterparts. All in all, Russia was involved in a more consultative process than other non-NATO nations participants, with bilateral planning meetings held between the Russian head of delegation at SHAPE and SACEUR.

In the US, views on Russian involvement in the Bosnian and Kosovan peacekeeping efforts were varied. For his part, Wesley Clark claimed that the Russians showed partiality towards the Serbs in Bosnia and had similar concerns for Kosovo. In his book *Waging Modern War*, he writes:

> I had closely observed the double standard the Russians had applied while working for us in the Bosnia mission. They took care of the Serbs, passing them information, tipping them off to any of our operations, and generally doing their best to look after their 'fellow Slavs' while keeping up the full pretence of cooperation with us. And in Bosnia we hadn't given them their own sector. If they had their own sector in Kosovo, they would run it as a separate mission, and Kosovo would be effectively partitioned.[12]

Others, however, spoke in favourable terms. Major General William L. Nash, former US commander of the multinational force in Bosnia, who was charged with enforcing the Dayton Accords, describes several factors contributing to success with the Russians:

1) our nations had common strategic objectives
2) we were professional soldiers fulfilling our nations' mission

3) after fifty years of studying each other, we were very knowledgeable about each other; and

4) frankly, we did not get too much help from Washington or Moscow. Our leaders gave us a job to do, and for the most part, left us alone to do it.[13]

Similarly, US Brigadier General John Craddock, who worked with the Russians in Kosovo, said that there had been 'a significant disinformation campaign against the Russian unit', and despite there being a 'preconceived' idea among the Albanians that the Russians would 'favour the Serbs' in Kosovo, he had not seen it. The Russians had in fact 'shown restraint and control' in some inevitable confrontations with ethnic Albanians.[14] Professor Cross, in her study, concluded that 'if the Russian-NATO peacekeeping missions, SFOR and KFOR, are to be assessed in terms of the capacity of former adversaries to cooperate, then these instances must be deemed a success'.[15] Watching Kosovo, from my perspective of witnessing Russian behaviour in Bosnia, I find this retrospective study rings true.

On 18–20 June 1999, Yeltsin was in Cologne for the G8 meeting. Commenting on Yugoslavia, he said: 'We need to make up after our fight.'[16] However, Yeltsin was never to receive the financial support inside Russia he was looking for in the aftermath of their Kosovo peacekeeping. He did receive assurances that the International Monetary Fund would be pressed to release $4.5 billion of Western aid that had been blocked after Russian financial markets had collapsed in August 1998, and discussions did take place concerning Soviet-era debt relief. But Yeltsin never got any upfront funding, which he desperately needed and, in my view, deserved.

Having chosen to cooperate with NATO in Bosnia and later

Kosovo, Yeltsin found himself facing a fundamental dilemma, one that still dogs relations between Russia and the West to this day: NATO enlargement. Despite NATO's attempt to address the issue through its 1994 Partnership for Peace initiative, which was designed to respond to the demands of former Eastern bloc countries for membership while not granting it, and also build a new relationship with Russia, the question of enlargement continued to hang in the air. In February 1997 in *The New York Times,* George Kennan warned very clearly of the risk of NATO stretching to the boundaries of the Russian Federation when he stated in blunt terms that 'expanding NATO would be the most fateful error of American policy in the entire post-cold-war era'. He could clearly see that it would 'inflame the nationalistic, anti-Western and militaristic tendencies' in Russia. He also predicted that it would 'have an adverse effect on the development of Russian democracy' and change 'Russian foreign policy in directions' that the Clinton administration would not like.

Over a year later, Kennan returned to the charge in a May 1998 interview with Thomas L. Friedman of *The New York Times* in which he commented on the US Senate's agreement on NATO expansion.

I think it is the beginning of a new Cold War. I think the Russians will gradually react quite adversely and it will affect their policies. I think it is a tragic mistake. There was no reason for this whatever. No one was threatening anybody else. This expansion would make the founding fathers of this country turn in their graves. We have signed up to protect a whole series of countries, even though we have neither the resources nor the intention to do so in any serious way.

[NATO expansion] was simply a lighthearted action by a Senate that has no real interest in foreign affairs.

I was particularly bothered by the references to Russia as a country dying to attack Western Europe. Don't people understand? Our differences in the Cold War were with the Soviet Communist regime. And now we are turning our backs on the very people who mounted the greatest blood-less revolution in history to remove that Soviet regime.[17]

NATO's fiftieth anniversary, in Washington, saw the Czech Republic, Hungary, and Poland welcomed as NATO's newest members. The expansion process continued and, unsurpris-ingly, Russia started to perceive the US, or US/NATO, as constituting a 'bloc' seeking to exercise unipolar global and regional dominance. Over the years, the atmosphere became so sour that on the twentieth anniversary of the Srebrenica geno-cide, Putin's Russia was the only country on the UN Security Council to vote against – and indeed veto – the resolution con-demning the genocide.

If, under Yeltsin, foreign and military cooperation was broadly successful, the same cannot be said for economic coop-eration. Much has been written about why Yeltsin allowed Yegor Gaidar, who was to become his acting prime minister (the Congress of People's Deputies, opposed to Yeltsin's choice, never approved his appointment) to move so fast on economic reform. A proponent of the 'shock therapy' championed by Columbia University economist Jeffrey Sachs, his measures included liberalising prices, cutting subsidies, and privatising large swathes of business. The rationale behind this approach was a deep-seated determination to take unpopular decisions as quickly as possible and to take irrevocable steps towards a market economy. The coup against Gorbachev had shown that certain elements in Russian society would contest each and every small step towards a genuine market economy. A broader concern was that, although the Communist Party had been formally abolished, much of the Russian population remained comfortable with living under the familiar control of the state and did not like major changes. The young reformers feared that, by the time of the next election, a party of Communists would exist – either in effect or under that name – and that it would strongly oppose their plans.

While it was right for the G7 at the Houston meeting in 1990 to withhold major financial support, it was a mistake for the G7 summit meetings not to fund targeted and strictly controlled support in 1992 and 1993. That's not to say that to do so would have been easy. By that time, the consequences of the shock therapy were all too apparent. Inflation was rampant, crippling pensioners in particular, but also others whose wages did not keep pace. Privatisation was not the panacea promised. Unemployment was rising, but transferring state monopolies into the private sector did not bring with it an automatic move to efficiency and profitability. All too often, assets ended up in the hands of well-placed insiders and those best placed to exploit the voucher privatisation schemes.

Gaidar was replaced by Chernomyrdin in December 1992, but even so Yeltsin continued to face real opposition from the Congress of People's Deputies, 86 per cent of whom had been members of the Communist Party.[18] The stand-off between president on the one hand and congress on the other deteriorated dramatically over the course of the next year. On 21 September 1993, Yeltsin announced that he was dissolving parliament. This move was challenged by the parliament, who in turn declared it unconstitutional and announced the impeachment of Yeltsin. By 28 September, clashes had broken out between police and anti-Yeltsin protesters, and Interior Ministry troops sealed off the parliament building from protesters and the White House. Having declared a state of emergency, Yeltsin fatefully ordered tanks to fire on the White House, and the building was retaken on 4 October 1993. Yeltsin had won, but at the cost of many lives – and making powerful enemies in the process. Later, in his retirement, Yeltsin most feared being taken to court for shelling the White House.

To consolidate his position, Yeltsin put in place a new constitution and set up the Duma, a new lower house of parliament, which took the name given to the first Russian legislature by Tsar Nicholas II in 1906. But by 1994, it was hard to convince the US and the British public to find large sums of money for a country that still lacked a proper legal framework. Strobe Talbott tried to convince his close friend Clinton, but in US terms it was never a political runner for the president. Kennan, ever the realist, wrote in *Foreign Affairs* as long ago as 1951, 'change would have to flow from the initiatives and efforts of the Russians themselves'.[19] I share this view today in 2022.

After being involved in commercial business in Russia from 1995 to 2015, I became familiar with the profoundly adverse consequences of not having a legal framework within Russia for commercial business. During the Gorbachev and Yeltsin years, Western business leaders did not hold firm enough in the EU or the OECD in insisting on doing more to support the building of a comprehensive legal framework for doing business in Russia. When, as I hope, we start to engage more with Russia again commercially, Britain must make the case in every international forum that Russia needs to overhaul its commercial and banking system and put in place an independent judiciary to handle disputes. And we should stand ready to provide assistance in achieving that. Without such reform, it is difficult to envisage Russia reaching its true economic potential and its citizens enjoying the better quality of life they deserve. And while the Russian marketplace urgently needs reforming, we must acknowledge that malpractice is not only present in Moscow, but also in London, Frankfurt, Zurich, Paris, Luxembourg, Valletta, and Nicosia, to name only a few financial centres in Europe. We must do our utmost to counter money laundering, probably the biggest source of corruption in Russia, and to ensure the full enforcement of economic sanctions for those who continue the practice.

Another aspect of the Yeltsin era increasingly being revealed is how the KGB's successor organisations and former KGB officers exploited the changes underway. Andropov's KGB had started to involve Russia in international financial schemes. The extent to which this was known by Yeltsin, Gaidar, Anatoly Chubais (the deputy prime minister who led the privatisation programme and served as Yeltsin's chief of staff), and his successor as chief of staff Valentin Yumashev (who later married Yeltsin's daughter), has never been fully acknowledged. Nor has the fact that many of Andropov's men privately saw Yeltsin as a transitional figure to use as they had used Gorbachev. Large sums of money were stashed away over the years by the KGB in countries outside the Soviet sphere, a process that Andropov started. It has taken some time for this axis of power to be identified and exposed in the Putin era. Two recent books have tried to unravel the dynamics of the KGB's involvement, and the involvement of the Russian mafia at home and in Italy and America. *Putin's Kleptocracy: Who Owns Russia* by Karen

Dawisha is one source and, more recently, Catherine Belton's *Putin's People: How the KGB Took Back Russia and then Took on the West*.[20] This excellent book saw libel cases taking place in British courts, where rich Russians had some minor changes made.

Andropov's KGB was more sophisticated than the Russian mafia, and perhaps the reason why this was missed by Western democracies is that many of us had grown up with these initials, KGB. As a consequence, we had our own ideas about the KGB. First and foremost, to many they were on the losing side and we in the West were the winners. This image was reinforced by former naval intelligence officer Ian Fleming's books and the James Bond films, in which the KGB was always, after a great struggle, being outwitted. Even those who did not read the books or watch the films were generally aware of Bond as a cultural icon, the slim, muscular 007 who thwarted the KGB's plots.

In February 1992, it has been claimed that:

the Yeltsin-Gaidar government signed an agreement with an American corporate private investigation firm, Kroll Associates, to track down and help repatriate money illegally held or taken abroad by former Communist Party and Soviet government agencies, including the KGB. The money had allegedly left the country prior to the attempted coup in August 1991 against the reformist-oriented Gorbachev by conservatives in the highest echelons of the ruling Communist Party and the KGB.[21]

As early as 3 March 1992, *The New York Times* reported that one estimate for the sums of money involved was $50 billion, and Kroll was reported to have 'found that thousands of mostly offshore bank accounts, real estate holdings and offshore companies had been set up to launder and shelter these funds and what had been the Soviet Union's gold reserves'. The Kroll findings were reported to the Yeltsin government in 1993, but, it is claimed, they were not followed up. Apparently neither Gaidar nor Chubais pushed for the revelations to be made public, and Kroll, sensing this, produced nothing incriminatory on the KGB.

Money transfers increased considerably when the then head of the KGB, Kryuchkov, convinced Gorbachev to use KGB-trained economists to stimulate and control an opening for Western investors in the USSR and increase Soviet investments abroad. It also appears that the KGB was involved in exploiting the opportunities offered by the economic reforms of the Gorbachev and the Yeltsin years, which led to a distorted ownership model far removed from what the reformers had intended. Indeed, the process saw a number of individuals who had been close to the KGB, and benefitted from those connections, make such fortunes that they were no longer prepared to answer to their former patrons or submit to the control of the Yeltsin government, particularly in its last few years.

In fairness, the Yeltsin government, particularly Gaidar and Chubais, had to manage their inheritance. Yeltsin had watched, like everyone else in Russia, the statue of Felix Dzerzhinsky, founder of the KGB's notorious antecedent, the Cheka, winched off its base by protestors in front of the feared Lubyanka Square headquarters after the 1991 coup attempt. He had signed the order breaking up the KGB into several separate agencies, although he stopped short of initiating the necessary wholesale reforms. The new Foreign Intelligence Service, the

SVR, emerged under Primakov, preserving much of the old KGB apparatus.

Chubais, a strong supporter of Gaidar, was creating time to put in place the mechanisms of a market economy and significantly reduce state ownership of industrial assets. The pair brought in a privatisation scheme through which Russian citizens received vouchers that they could use to acquire shares in companies that were being privatised, spreading, they hoped, both wealth and ownership. It was a good idea in principle, but it failed to achieve the reformers' admirable objectives, and the economic situation deteriorated.

On top of the economic challenges, Yeltsin's health became a serious problem, affecting his ability to govern from as early as 1994, when the nitroglycerin that he had initially found alleviated the pain from his heart condition stopped working. Yeltsin began to rely more and more on a combination of painkillers and alcohol, and he also started to restrict his inner circle, losing the attractive openness of the early years of his presidency. All this affected his popularity. The Russian public did not like seeing him very clearly drunk at a televised ceremony in Berlin in August 1994 to mark the departure of the last Russian troops. On that occasion, he famously snatched the baton from the conductor's hand and conducted the Berlin Police Orchestra himself, before singing a Russian folk song. A month later at Shannon Airport in Ireland, Yeltsin failed to disembark his plane, despite the entire Irish cabinet being assembled at the foot of the stairs to greet him. One explanation is that he had fallen into a drunken sleep after heavy drinking on the flight back from a summit meeting with President Clinton in the US; Yeltsin later said his officials had not wanted to wake him. However, many think he suffered a serious heart attack on the flight but that it was thought preferable for the rumours of drunkenness to persist, rather than news of a heart attack to come out. Indeed, it was revealed in 2004 that he suffered five serious heart attacks while in office – two of which, in July and October 1995, had been serious.

By January 1996, only 10 per cent of Russians told pollsters they would vote for Yeltsin in the presidential election due on 16 June. They were disillusioned with the economic situation and a prolonged and brutal war in the breakaway republic of Chechnya, which had by then cost the lives of many thousand Russian soldiers and tens of thousands of civilians. The spectre of a Communist revival was looming, under their leader and rival presidential candidate Gennady Zyuganov. If he was going to win the election, Yeltsin believed he needed very large sums of money – and he managed to obtain these from a group of wealthy businessmen who had risen to prominence through the privatisation years in the now notorious 'loans for shares' scheme which secured the fortunes of the so-called oligarchs.

The Western democracies and their politicians, like myself, turned a blind eye to this corruption of the democratic process, so desperate were we for Yeltsin to win. I think this was a misjudgement on our part. The moral high ground over holding out for free and fair democratic processes once ceded is very hard to restore. Justified criticisms of undemocratic developments in Russia existed before Putin. Criticisms of Putin are now open to accusations of hypocrisy. Writing with the benefit of hindsight, it would have been better to let democracy take its course in Russia and accept the greater chance of the Communist candidate, Zyuganov, winning particularly since near the end of the campaign Yeltsin found a new lease of life.

However, Yeltsin did sign a decree allowing valuable strategic assets still owned by the state to be sold through an auction rigged in favour of the future oligarchs, a number of whom were not Andropov men, and ending the employee voucher scheme. The future oligarchs raised the money by borrowing from their own banks and then made massive loans to the government, which were secured on shares in key companies that the government then passed on to the oligarchs after the election. All concerned knew that the state would never repay the loans and the oligarchs would keep the shares.

When Yeltsin found renewed strength to campaign, he did so with surprising skill and managed to persuade Russian people to vote for him by constantly pointing out the Communist record of power, supported by Zyuganov. In a defiant campaign speech on 15 February at Yekaterinburg, Yeltsin warned the Russian people of returning to the past. He was hoarse and coughing as he quoted Solzhenitsyn's famous words about perishing 'under the red wheel'. In Moscow, wits recalled the old proverb '*Masterstvo propit' nel'zya*' (you cannot completely lose your talent, no matter how hard you drink).[22] What started to come through was Yeltsin's drive as a politician who had recovered the will to win. Slowly, this new factor made the crucial difference. Some of his flamboyant performances may also have been helped by his doctors discovering that Yeltsin had been suffering from obstructive sleep apnoea. They gave him oxygen at night, resulting in a proper sleep, which helped increase his energy significantly during the day.[23]

Even so, Yeltsin only just won the first round against Zyuganov, and neither had over 50 per cent. The charismatic General Alexander Lebed, who ran third, agreed to be co-opted by Yeltsin into his team before the run-off. Despite another heart attack on 3 July 1996, Yeltsin beat Zyuganov by a big margin of

15 per cent. Could he have won without the oligarch's money? We can never know for sure. But what we do know is that by his inauguration on 9 August, Yeltsin was hardly able to walk, had slurred speech, and was clearly very ill.

In September 1996, it was announced that Yeltsin would have open heart surgery, and President Clinton arranged for him to be seen by Dr Michael DeBakey from Houston. He was also found to have hypothyroidism, which is likely to have contributed to his coronary artery disease and to his puffy face, as well as to his inability to metabolise excess alcohol. DeBakey recommended a delay to the operation and more preparation before Yeltsin had surgery. On 7 November, he underwent a seven-hour quintuple bypass operation in Moscow, and the German chancellor, Helmut Kohl, told the Americans that the two German doctors who had participated in the operation thought that Yeltsin would not last until the presidential election in 2000. This prediction proved to be wrong, but Yeltsin was not fit enough to remain president, and it is to his credit that he knew it and did not cling to office.

So, on health grounds alone, it was not altogether surprising that Yeltsin began to consider how he could choose his successor and step down. Having defaulted on its debt in August 1998, Russia was now facing serious economic problems. By the middle of 1999, Yeltsin had dismissed his government for the fourth time in seventeen months and sacked two prime ministers. First to go was Primakov, though a poll showed that 81 per cent of Russians did not approve of this decision. Yeltsin was in a hurry to find a president who would protect him personally when retired, and he became convinced that Primakov would not. Yeltsin then chose Sergei Stepashin as prime minister, clearly a stop gap, lasting only three months. Chubais, though a loyalist, was not seen by Yeltsin's family as tough enough to guarantee their personal safety and position in retirement. At this time, Boris Nemtsov, once seen as the potential liberal successor to Yeltsin, declared that 'The people have grown tired of watching an ill leader who is not capable of doing his job.'[24] Yeltsin then made a surprise choice for his next prime minister: Putin.

He also indicated that Putin was his preferred candidate to succeed him as president. Suddenly, on 16 August 1999, the forty-six-year-old Vladimir Putin, who had headed the Federal Security Service, the FSB, since the previous year, took office. An even bigger surprise was to come on New Year's Eve 1999, when Yeltsin unexpectedly resigned and chose Putin to become acting provisional president, which helped him win the subsequent necessary election.

Why did Yeltsin, a very shrewd man, draw Putin into his circle? Political analysts and historians will no doubt be asking themselves this question for a long time. Yeltsin and his advisers were fully aware of Putin's earlier KGB connections. But Yeltsin was always confident that he could manage the KGB; had his health held up, he might have done so. After leaving the KGB, Putin had carved out a career in the St Petersburg administration and become one of the deputies to Anatoly Sobchak, the first democratically elected mayor of the city. Critics have alleged that it was during this period, when Putin was one of those responsible for the everyday management of the city, that corruption took hold and he started to build KGB structures on which he rose to hold supreme power.

After Sobchak narrowly failed re-election as mayor in the summer of 1996, Putin moved to Moscow and was appointed, with Yeltsin's knowledge, deputy chief of the Presidential

Property Management Department, where he was responsible for the state's foreign properties. In March 1997, he was appointed deputy to Yeltsin's new chief of staff Valentin Yumashev, who had succeeded Chubais. Yumashev said in a BBC interview that Chubais had recommended Putin as 'a strong manager who would make a good deputy'. In the same interview, when asked if he thought at the time Putin could be president, Yumashev replied:

> Yeltsin had several candidates in mind, like Boris Nemtsov, Sergei Stepashin and Nikolai Aksenenko. Yeltsin and I talked a lot about possible successors. At one point we discussed Putin. Yeltsin asked me: 'What do you think about Putin?' I think he's a superb candidate, I replied. I think you should consider him. It's clear from the way he does his job that he's ready for more difficult tasks.[25]

It appears that Yeltsin had also been advised by Yumashev that Putin would best protect his family's interests in a pending investigation by Swiss authorities into corruption charges related to contracts for a major renovation of the Kremlin. The need for presidential protection was becoming ever starker for Yeltsin in retirement.

In the event, Putin proved the correct choice for the Yeltsin family. But this was also a victory for the inheritors of Andropov's KGB. I have met Yumashev only twice and very briefly, first in London and then in Moscow, so I cannot claim to know him. But while Yumashev is many things, including clever and charming, he is not naïve. Serving as Yeltsin's chief of staff, he must have been fully aware of the Andropov school of KGB influencers. Nor had Yeltsin, though ill, lost his own judgement about people, and he had wrestled with the KGB long before becoming president. I believe both Yumashev and Yeltsin realised they were restoring KGB influence when they selected Putin.

Putin, the acting president, won the election in March 2000 after a major clampdown in Chechnya where terrorist attacks in Moscow and elsewhere threatened to destabilise the election process. That night, the Yeltsin family was shown watching television, and there is an agonisingly embarrassing moment when Yeltsin is urged to ring Putin to congratulate him. Yeltsin resists but then does so, only to be told the president is busy. Yeltsin then waits, expecting Putin to ring him, but the telephone remains ominously silent. Putin was brutally showing Yeltsin that he was now his own man. Perhaps at this moment Yeltsin realised what he had created. Nevertheless, the Yeltsin family has been protected by Putin and he has kept his word. The first presidential decree that Putin signed was a guarantee for the former president and the members of his family protecting his property and finances. Yumashev never claims other than that Putin has fulfilled all his commitments to the family.

Yeltsin went on to enjoy a peaceful retirement, watching Putin win again by a large margin in 2004 with genuine popular support. When he died from heart failure on 23 April 2007, aged seventy-six, Yeltsin was the first Russian leader to have a Russian Orthodox burial for over 100 years. This was perhaps no surprise, given the important gesture he made while president in acknowledging the relevance of the Orthodox Church in Russian history by ordering that the bones of the murdered Romanov royal family be reinterred in St Petersburg's Saint Peter and Paul Cathedral alongside earlier tsars. Indeed, against the advice of his own entourage, he flew to

St Petersburg without any warning on the day of the funeral, 17 July 1998 – the eightieth anniversary of their murders – to attend the church service. Reputedly, he justified his presence on the grounds that his mother, who remained a practising churchgoer through the Communist period, would never have forgiven him if he had not gone. It is worth noting that Putin's mother also remained a believer and he, even more so than Yeltsin, continues to support an increased role for the Patriarch of the Russian Orthodox Church and the church generally. Both Yeltsin and Putin have encouraged the restoration of churches left in a very poor state and the recruitment of a much higher standard of clergy than had been the case in the Communist era.

I have called Yeltsin a free spirit and that spirit will, I believe, remain in the Russian people and will someday reassert itself.

9

Putin's Russia

Putin is now in his third decade as the driving force behind Russian politics, with a referendum in 2020 having paved his way to remain in power until 2036. Today, the world is much more aware of the complex internal and external influences that have shaped his rise to power and his ability to stay at the pinnacle for so long. The man once characterised as a typical, grey KGB apparatchik has himself emerged from the shadows, but that is far from saying we now know much about him and, what's more, about his associates.

How far is Putin steeped in the culture of Andropov's KGB, which he joined in 1975 when Andropov was still in charge? That is still a difficult question to answer. Early on in his KGB career, Putin formed a friendship with Sergei Ivanov, whom, when at the FSB, he appointed head of one of its six director-ates and who was later to serve as his chief of staff. This pattern of bringing former associates into his administration was also evident in his St Petersburg days.

Putin's career in Dresden is deliberately cloudy, but there is little dispute he was there from 1985 to 1990. Andreas Förster, the editor of *Berliner Zeitung*, claims that Putin was accredited to the GDR from 1982 to 1986 under the alias Aleksandr Rybin, with a birth date of 9 February 1947.[1] In Dresden, it appears that 'he was involved in espionage designed to steal as many of the West's technological secrets as possible'.[2] Putin himself has described his work 'as gathering information about NATO, the "main opponent"'.[3] Once he moved to Moscow and started working in Yeltsin's private office, he rose quickly through the ranks before becoming head of the FSB in 1998.

Putin's extensive experience within the security apparatus has surely influenced his authoritarian instincts, and he has always acted to uphold the authority of the FSB. He uses the GRU, the military's foreign intelligence agency, to kill those he calls 'spies' or 'traitors' – as we saw in Britain with the murder of Alexander Litvinenko and the attempted murder of Sergei Skripal and his daughter. Yet the sheer incompetence of the killers and the publicity that followed does not seem to concern Putin. Why? Because he believes the consequent publicity acts as a powerful deterrent. He does not appear to want these killings to pass unnoticed, as would once have been the case.

Putin undoubtedly wants Russia to be a unified autocratic state. Rather than taking the reformist Gorbachev and Yeltsin as models, he looks further back for inspiration. Andropov is a key model, but his legacy is by no means the sole influence. Indeed, as Mark Galeotti suggests in his book *We Need to Talk About Putin*, the austere anti-corruption campaigner Andropov would not have been enamoured by Putin.[4]

But Andropov was a realist as well as a reformer; he would have seen merit in some of Putin's reforms. Other figures from deeper in Russia's past, before the Soviet era, also seem to have influenced Putin, as he works to build the image of a renewed Russia. He appears to accept Khrushchev's policies of de-Stalinisation and does not seem to want to turn the clock back to Stalin; he does, however, recognise Stalin as a great historical figure whose legacy cannot and will never be wiped out. For Putin, history creates facts both to live with and to adapt. New histories by Russian writers, said to be encouraged by Putin, show only certain aspects of Stalin's legacy, while other aspects of Russia's past are conveniently dismissed. Out go anti-Semitic pogroms, the gulags, and the annexation of the Baltic states, all events that have supposedly been corrupted by Western historians to denigrate Russia.

Yet Antony Beevor's new book shows how complex the situation was and its relevance to what is happening today: 'Red forces had recaptured both Kharkov and Kiev in January 1919 and Ataman Grigoriev, who had joined them, took Kherson in March' (the names of these three places in 2022, during the Russia–Ukraine war, were to become all too familiar to the British people). Beevor goes on: 'fighting in the Ukraine produced anti-Semitic pogroms of unprecedented scale by Grigoriev's horde and Petliura's Ukrainians'.[5]

It was no accident that Putin celebrated anew the 1812 Patriotic War against Napoleon. Russian history now proudly recognises the abolition of serfdom on private estates in 1861 by Alexander II.

In 2009 Putin paid for the graves of the counter-revolutionary 'White' generals, including Anton Deniken and Vladimir Kappel, to be brought back to Moscow and transformed into the 'Memorial of the White Warriors'. Admiral Alexander Kolchak, who was briefly declared Russian supreme leader before being executed by the Bolsheviks, had a statue erected in his honour in Irkutsk in 2004. By these acts, Putin revealed that he has a broad view of Russian history and its greatness, even when it comes to its bloody civil war. Unfortunately, as he's demonstrated over Ukraine, it is also a distorted view.

Another aspect that Putin has brought to the fore in defining the new Russia is the role of the Orthodox Church, again harking back to the days of the tsars and the height of Russia's imperial past, as well as providing an anchor for policies based on 'traditional values'. Indeed, Putin talks of the 'vertical of power', expressed through appointed governors, an obedient judiciary, a rubber-stamping Duma, and an established religion recognised by the state but operating within its ordered constraints. In the 2012 trial of the feminist punk band Pussy Riot, who had staged a protest performance in Moscow's Cathedral of Christ the Saviour, it was telling that the three women were convicted of 'blasphemy', a crime not previously mentioned in the Russian Criminal Code.

In a series of articles for *The Interpreter*, Matthew Dal Santo describes the dominant position of the Grand Duchess Elizabeth and Tsar Nicholas II inside Moscow's Christ the Saviour Cathedral following their public rehabilitation under Putin. Inside the Moscow cathedral, demolished by Stalin in 1931 and amazingly rebuilt in its entirety in the 1990s by Yeltsin, a prominently displayed icon of the 'Imperial Passion-bearers' shows Tsar Nicholas II and his son Alexei wearing military uniform with the empress and her daughters wearing elegant dresses. Across the nave, an icon of the 'Assembly of the New Russian Martyrs and Confessors' depicts Nicholas II, Alexandra, and their five children at the centre of a mass of bishops, priests, monks, and men martyred by the Communist government between 1918 and 1941. To the family's left is another sainted Romanov, Grand Duchess Elizabeth, who, after being widowed by Socialist revolutionaries in 1905, founded a home for poor women and children in Moscow. She too was executed by the Bolsheviks. The home she founded has now reopened.

In his article, Dal Santo also quotes a well-connected former editor of a Moscow newspaper as saying, 'Putin doesn't want to be seen as merely continuing the USSR. The Soviet Union failed and for him that indicates that there was something wrong with it.' Putin, he said, 'isn't interested in being remembered as some kind of Communist Party General Secretary. He thinks of himself as a Russian General de Gaulle or a Franco, head of a "self-consciously transitional regime" aimed at restoring a semi-traditional political and social order.'[6]

Having secured a change in the constitution that will allow him to remain in power for the foreseeable future, Putin does indeed appear to see himself as a father of the nation, entitled to his position and unwilling to accept criticism or challengers as he fulfils what he believes is his historic destiny. That said, Putin has always wanted to be seen as a popular leader, and he has clearly focused on building a domestic and international image of a strong 'action man' capable of restoring Russia to its rightful position in the world. Retaining that popularity is important to him, particularly domestically. He was anxious before his 2012 election, and commentators felt that his public tears when speaking of his victory indicated genuine relief. Initially, many Russians respected his 'strong man' image, emphasised by the 2014 invasion of Crimea. However, since the second invasion of Ukraine and his initial attempt to seize the capital, Kyiv, he has increasingly begun to be seen as aloof, ruthless, and dictatorial, inclined towards stamping out any overt public criticism, whether this be written, spoken, or in the form of demonstrations against his style of government.

Is this aloofness a reflection of his attachment to autocratic tsarist antecedents? Galeotti goes so far as to say that Putin has created 'a system that, at least at the top, functions in a similar way to a royal court'.[7] He describes this corrupt system, on top of which sits the Kremlin, as follows.

> The way this corruption works is through favours, access, lucrative contracts and the authorities turning a blind eye to flat-out embezzlement. The Kremlin doesn't pay people – it simply grants them opportunities that they can milk. In return, rather than handing over suitcases of cash, they invest in projects, donate to charities, grant stakes in businesses and look after friends.[8]

Galeotti mentions that this also includes officials taking advantage of their positions, recalling what was known in tsarist times as *kormleniye*, or 'feeding'.[9] Claims of Putin's wealth and luxurious lifestyle have become a key feature of opposition leader Alexei Navalny's attacks on the president – of which, more later. Once elected president, Putin showed the same determination and ruthlessness he had previously displayed over Chechnya in establishing his position. An initial target were oligarchs whose media interests had been critical of him. After his inauguration on 7 May 2000, Putin wasted no time. Four days later, the second-most-popular TV channel, NTV, was raided by armed and masked police who searched the offices of its owner, Vladimir Gusinsky, the founder of the Media-Most holding company.

On the eve of the presidential inauguration, Gusinsky had openly questioned whether the FSB were behind a number of deadly explosions in apartment blocks the previous year that had been blamed on the Chechens. A month later, Gusinsky was arrested on corruption charges. After much pressure, and probably in return for his freedom, Gusinsky sold his business at a knockdown price of $300 million to Gazprom Media and left Russia never to return. Putin had also been severely stung by the media criticism of his performance following the sinking of the submarine *Kursk* in August 2000, and he went after the ORT television network of Boris Berezovsky. In spite of his efforts to retain control, Berezovsky and his partner sold their stakes in ORT to another oligarch, Roman Abramovich, in February the following year.[10]

Putin also turned his attention to the critical oil and gas sector, where several oligarchs had made their fortunes. In the early 1980s, oil production was the mainstay of the Soviet economy, producing almost 20 per cent of the world's oil and the biggest percentage of the state's export revenues. The connection between the collapse in Russian oil production by almost one half in 1990–4 and the state of the economy Putin inherited was all too obvious. In his dissertation for a Candidate of Economic Science degree, which he submitted to the St Petersburg Mining Institute in 1996, Putin had written that natural resources would be the basis for Russia's entry into the world economy. In 1999, in an article for the institute's journal, he restated the importance of the resource sector, adding that it was too important to be left entirely to market forces. He followed this conclusion through in dramatic fashion during his presidency. Indeed, it is worth noting that this approach has respectable antecedents in Britain's Labour Party, in their desire to control the commanding heights of the economy.

Battles for control of Russia's natural resources were to be a constant theme in the post-Communist era. A major player in the sector was another oligarch, Mikhail Khodorkovsky, an entrepreneurial ex-Komsomol member who had rapidly built up the oil company Yukos. In building his business, Khodorkovsky had taken over VNK, or Eastern Oil Company, which had links to the FSB through their involvement in trading its oil, though he claimed to have been unaware. As a result, Khodorkovsky ran up against Andrei Akimov, who had traded VNK's oil through an Austrian company, IMAG. At the time, Akimov was an intelligence officer who, at thirty-four years old, had been appointed to head the USSR's Austrian-based Donau Bank. Khodorkovsky's deal affected Akimov's VNK's business.

It was against this background that, at the end of July 2000, Putin met with the leading oligarchs, including Khodorkovsky, and told them to 'stay out of politics'. From Putin's point of view, this was not an unreasonable demand, given their earlier corrupt political involvement in funding Yeltsin's re-election and achieving great wealth and influence through the infamous 'loans for shares' scheme. Whatever the oligarchs thought about Putin's own election campaign at that time, he was sending the clear sign that he did not see an ongoing role for them in the political arena. The choice was business or politics, not both. Khodorkovsky, however, went on to want both. Another significant development was the appointment in 2001 of Alexey Miller to the role of chief executive of Gazprom, one of the most important companies in Russia for many decades. Miller had previously been Putin's deputy on the Foreign Relations Committee of the mayor's office in St Petersburg. Gazprom had long had a special place in Russia; few were surprised or deeply offended when the organisation that had previously enjoyed close ties with Yeltsin was then firmly linked to Putin.

In February 2003, at what was becoming a regular event,

Putin again met Russia's leading oligarchs. This time, Khodorkovsky delivered a presentation on corruption in Russia, in which he claimed that corruption in the country had reached 10 per cent of GDP, or $30 billion a year. The discussion was broadcast live. It was brave for Khodorkovsky to assert that the state-controlled oil company Rosneft had overpaid by $300 million in its acquisition of another oil company, Severnaya Neft, and that there should be an investigation into the overpayment. But given Putin's earlier clear warning about mixing politics with business, it was also folly. It also brings to mind the old English saying, 'people in glass houses should not throw stones'. Belton claims that, in response, Putin pointed out that as a state company Rosneft needed to increase its reserves. What's more, Yukos had too many reserves, and how it came to have them would be discussed, as well as tax non-payment.[11] Putin then used an ice hockey term – he was then still an active player – and, looking at Khodorkovsky, he challenged him live on TV: 'I return the puck back to you.'[12] Had Khodorkovsky been content to stay a businessman, Putin might well have been prepared to live with Yukos as a very successful independent commercial company, merely clipping its wings from time to time. However, Khodorkovsky had sealed his own fate.

I watched these events particularly closely because, in March 2002, I had been appointed for a three-year term as chair of Yukos International UK, headquartered in London, with the remit to guide the company in its accelerated programme of expansion outside Russia. But I had no role in Yukos' decision-making inside Russia. Yukos International UK was then the holding company for John Brown Hydrocarbons (bought for $100 million in November 2001), Davy Process Technology, and Yukos Services. Other assets were also added, including the

Lithuanian oil refinery AB Mazeikiu Nafta, on whose supervis-
ory council I served, and Intelligent Energy, a fuel cell engineering company. It was a good portfolio of businesses, proving that
Khodorkovsky was a highly intelligent businessman. But he
was no politician; he'd flagged up his links with three of the
opposition parties for all to see: the Communist Party and two
small liberal parties.

In May 2003, shortly after the merger of Yukos and Abra-
movich's Sibneft had been announced (a transaction that was
later annulled), Putin invited Khodorkovsky and Abramo-
vich to dinner at his country residence to discuss their negotiations with two separate American companies, ExxonMobil
and Chevron. Both were vying to acquire shares in Yukos. It
was odd that Putin would even contemplate a sale with a US
company, but there appeared to be a genuine misunderstanding: Putin had been told by his staff that only a 25 per cent
shareholding was involved, while Yukos knew the Americans
wanted much more than that. Indeed, Putin may have seen the
transaction as a route for another Russian company to take a
stake in one of the US majors, as he had already agreed could
be done between TNK-BP and Rosneft. Khodorkovsky did not
heed Putin's warning, however, to stay out of politics.

A report in *Putin's People* alleges that during a meal together,
Putin ordered Khodorkovsky to stop funding the Communist
Party.[13] When Khodorkovsky said Putin's chief of staff, Alexander Voloshin, and his deputy, Vladislav Surkov, had approved
the funding, Putin reportedly warned him off, saying that he
was too busy with his company and other business.[14]

Just before Putin left for London in the summer of 2003 to
undertake an important state visit hosted by the queen, he held
a press conference at which he said, 'We must not allow certain

business interests to influence the political life of the country in their group interests.'[15]

Shortly after Putin's visit, the joint venture between TNK-BP and Rosneft was agreed. It was a time when Britain, under Prime Minister Tony Blair, had been pursuing very similar policies towards Russia to those that had been followed by John Major. Relations were good, though they had begun to fray because of Bush and Blair's ill-judged invasion of Iraq. I attended the Buckingham Palace State Banquet, having been doing business in Russia since 1995 as chairman of a small company called Middlesex Holdings, with a shareholding in OEMK,[16] the modern steel plant in Stary Oskol, as well as being chairman of Yukos International. The chairman of the political Leningrad Region approached me during the evening with a terse message, 'Tell Khodorkovsky to stay out of politics.' I did relay such a message, and I believed it was vital for himself and Yukos that he did as he was told, but to no avail. Khodorkovsky was arrested a few months later, tried, and imprisoned. Yukos was a very well-run commercial company and it was a great sadness for those who worked in it and a huge setback for shareholders that it was broken up and made part of Rosneft. The Yukos employee who had passed that message on for me a few days before I myself spoke to Khodorkovsky in Moscow was Ray Leonard. His long and factual article 'Khodorkovsky, Yukos, and Putin' is now required reading in many graduate schools in their post-Soviet Union studies.[17] I strongly recommend it for its demonstration of how much Russia lost in the Putin-led destruction of Yukos. The American finance director of Yukos, Bruce Misamore, has persisted over many years in demanding justice for Yukos shareholders, resulting in the European Court of Human Rights' record verdict against Russia for about $2.6 billion, which

Russia has not paid. In a 5 November 2021 judgment, the Dutch Supreme Court rejected Russia's claims that it was not bound by the Energy Charter Treaty (ECT), thereby confirming the arbitral tribunal's jurisdiction in the decade-long Yukos arbitration.

The Supreme Court further dismissed several other grounds for annulling the Yukos awards (which were in excess of $50 billion) as rendered in 2014. However, the court accepted Russia's argument that the lower courts should have reviewed Russia's claims that there was sufficient evidence that the Yukos shareholders had committed fraud during the arbitration proceedings. Therefore, the Supreme Court referred the matter back to the Appeal Court of Amsterdam, further extending the Yukos saga, which has been keeping the Dutch courts busy in recent years.

Through his handling of the oligarchs, Putin had sent early messages about how he would deal with internal opposition and challenge, but his behaviour in the international political arena took longer to develop. Much has been made of Putin's love of judo and the influence the sport has had on his approach to leadership. Galeotti says:

> Much of the art is in using the opponent's strength against him to seize the moment when it appears. In this respect, in geopolitics as in judo, Putin is an opportunist. He has a sense of what constitutes a win, but no predetermined path towards it.[18]

Given Putin's track record over the last twenty years, this assessment seems more realistic than those that characterise him as a mastermind, plotting each and every move on a global chessboard. If Putin does have an overarching goal, it would appear to be repositioning Russia as a significant international player with an acknowledged sphere of influence. This throwback to the days of the Great Powers is not how many in the West saw relations with Russia developing in the twenty-first century, and in view of his invasions of Ukraine in 2014 and 2022 it has caused – and continues to cause – huge concern. There can be no objection to Russia trying to become a powerful nation again. It is how Putin is going about it that is unacceptable.

In the early period of his presidency, there were encouraging signs that Putin was seeking to engage with the West as a partner. At his first meeting with Putin in Slovenia in June 2001, President George W. Bush famously said:

> I looked the man in the eye. I found him to be very straight forward and trustworthy. We had a very good dialogue. I was able to get a sense of his soul, a man deeply committed to his country and to the best interests of his country.[19]

Putin himself talked of 'counting on a pragmatic relationship', and that the US and Russia bore 'a special responsibility for maintaining common peace and security in the world – for building a new architecture of security in the world'.[20] Following the 9/11 attacks, Putin was quick to call President Bush to offer his support. He also announced, against the wishes of his own personal advisers, that Russia was giving up its bases in Cuba. Perhaps in part he hoped this would lead to greater support from the US in Russia's fight against Chechen separatists, an issue over which there had been differences at their summit meeting. Putin's support was also important in securing access to Central Asian airbases used by the US in the early stages of its war against the Taliban in Afghanistan.

It comes as no surprise that fear of Islamist fundamental-ism has been an important driver in Putin's foreign policy given the large Muslim population in Russia itself, particu-larly in its southern border regions, and in neighbouring coun-tries. Following the break-up of the USSR, the strict Wahhabi sect, closely connected with Saudi Arabia, moved in with a deep-seated motivation – and deep pockets – to spearhead an Islamic revival in former USSR territory such as Uzbekistan, which, seen from Moscow, was potentially threatening. The Russians claim that Arab fighters were called into their two wars in Chechnya by two figures leading the separatist guerrilla campaigns: Ibn al-Khattab and Shamil Basayev. The Russians also cite the civil war in Tajikistan and the secessionist conflicts in the South Caucasus as attracting Wahhabi money. These claims have deepened what has always been a fairly widespread view in Russia: that religious conflict underlies a great swathe of international terrorist activity, and that the Islamic faith is the biggest element in this form of international terrorism. That said, Putin, to give him credit, constantly stresses that, inside Russia, counterterrorism action is aimed at infiltrators, not Russian Muslims. Still, the problem of Islamist extremism remains in Russia on a significant scale, and maintaining stabil-ity in and around Russia's borders is a key element in Putin's policy both in this region and further afield.

For too long, the Western democracies that were trading and dependent on oil from Saudi Arabia were reluctant to call out this Wahhabi activity. Even the 9/11 Commission, chaired by the former Republican governor of New Jersey Thomas Kean, dealt far too circumspectly with this issue in its 2004 report. In 2020, a US federal judge directed the Saudi Arabian govern-ment to make twenty-four current and former officials available for depositions about any knowledge of events leading up to the 9/11 attacks. The depositions included the Saudi Prince Bandar, who was the former ambassador to the United States, and his chief of staff. This is a thorny issue for the Saudi Crown Prince Mohammed bin Salman, particularly after his alleged involvement in the assassination of the journalist Jamal Khashoggi in the Saudi Consulate in Istanbul in 2018. But the FBI has also identified, in recently discovered documents, individuals from the Saudi Arabian embassy at the time who are suspected of helping and supporting the plane hijackers.

In July 2022 President Biden, with the US at last self-sufficient in energy, tried to grapple with these complex but interrelated issues. Russia, subjected to international sanctions on oil and gas exports because of Ukraine, tried to influence Saudi Arabia not to increase production levels to alleviate record high world energy prices. Saudi Arabia wanted an OPEC decision to step up production. Even so, Russia sold at lower prices to India and China and other countries. Iran wanted higher prices and offered help to Russia to avoid US sanctions.

Politically and economically the two invasions of Ukraine have damaged Russia, but not in oil and gas revenues to the extent predicted.

Putin's early desire to cooperate with the West, and NATO in particular, came less than a year after the Bush–Putin meeting in Slovenia at the NATO Summit in Rome in May 2002. It was at that meeting that the NATO–Russia Council was established.[21]

President Putin said in his statement at the Slovenia summit that Russia had no alternative to developing its ties with NATO.

For Russia, given its geopolitical position, the deepening of equal interaction with NATO is one instance of its multi-vector approach to which there is no alternative and to which we are firmly committed. We cannot imagine ourselves outside Europe, as we have told some of our colleagues just now. But we believe it is equally inconceivable to underestimate the role of the time-tested mechanisms of cooperation in the CIS and Asia. Only a harmonious combination of actions in all these areas opens broad opportunities for creating a common security space from Vancouver to Vladivostok.[22]

This built on NATO's founding act and set out to provide 'a mechanism for consultation consensus-building, cooperation, joint decision and joint action ... on a wide spectrum of security issues of common interest'.[23]

I believe that NATO failed to exploit the potential of this forum in the early years, in particular when Medvedev, as president, did not exercise the Russian veto in the UN Security Council over the invasion of Libya. Instead of consulting the Russian military in the NATO–Russia Council, Prime Minister Cameron and French President Sarkozy went ahead on their own in dealing with the vexed question of how to handle Gaddafi and Obama, with the US distancing itself from the whole venture.

The deterioration in relations between NATO countries and Putin's Russia after Libya cannot be divorced from other tensions over NATO enlargement. Strobe Talbott's excellent book *The Russian Hand* demonstrates that President Clinton learnt just how sensitive the issue of NATO enlargement was when, as early as the start of his second term in February 1996, he held a serious discussion with the new NATO secretary-general Javier Solana. Talbott, who was deputy secretary of state, was present and writes of Clinton's summing up: 'We need to walk a tightrope. We should be methodical, even bureaucratic, almost boring. We need as much as possible to take the emotional energy out of this whole thing. We should just smile and plod ahead.'[24] But in reality Clinton went on supporting NATO enlargement, as did his successor, Bush, who at the 2008 NATO summit strongly supported Ukraine and Georgia joining.

Yevgeny Primakov, the Russian foreign minister, who sometimes recognised the NATO realities of living with some enlargement, likened it to 'sleeping with a porcupine – the best we can do is to reduce its size and keep its quills from making us too miserable'. He also said it helped make enlargement 'merely unacceptable rather than insulting', and gave the impression that the US was also holding open, in theory at least, the possibility of Russia itself being eligible for NATO membership someday. While these intimate discussions were going on, Talbott was engaged in public discussion in America with enlargement's most powerful critic, George Kennan, mentioned previously, who on 5 February 1997 in *The New York Times* wrote a powerful article arguing against it.[25]

President Clinton, aware of this article, asked Talbott, 'Why isn't Kennan right? Isn't he a kind of guru of yours going back to when you were at Oxford?' to which Talbott responded, 'Yes... Kennan had been and always would be someone I admired, but not as a source of all wisdom. Kennan had opposed the formation of NATO in the first place, I said, so it was no great surprise that he opposed its enlargement.'[26] Also part of that public US debate was the late Fritz Stern, German-born and a famous historian of Europe, who influenced Talbott in supporting the principle of NATO enlargement.

I had also talked with Stern, having been introduced by a mutual friend in New York. Another influential voice on my own thinking on enlargement was Chancellor Kohl, whose opinion I encountered in a wide-ranging discussion with him when I was in Bonn in 1997 to talk about the German edition of my book on the Balkans.

Personally, I am a qualified supporter of enlargement, though I changed my mind on Georgia, which for complex reasons I am no longer in favour of admitting to NATO. I did not support NATO's enlargement to include Ukraine until Russia's second invasion in 2022. Now I support Ukraine's membership in NATO, if they apply, and that of Finland and Sweden, who have already applied. The reason is that there must be penalties for Russia having attacked a democratic country and flouted international law. I judged it appropriate for Ukraine not to become a NATO member before 2014, but after Crimea was annexed NATO membership became a possibility. After 2022's second invasion NATO membership has become a matter for them to decide, particularly once it became clear they would become candidate members of the EU, although there is no telling how long this may take.

Edward Glover and Sir Roderic Lyne wrote an article in *InsideOut*, an FCO Association magazine for retired diplomats, in the spring of 2021 describing how, a month after Kennan reported to Washington, a British diplomat called Frank Roberts also submitted his own views to London.[27] Roberts reported at slightly greater length than Kennan and, specifically, he reported to the then foreign secretary Ernest Bevin. Roberts later became UK permanent representative to NATO in 1957–60, ambassador to Moscow in 1960–2, and ambassador to Bonn in 1963–8.

Sir Roderic Lyne, British ambassador to Russia from 2000 to 2004, and who later served with distinction on the long-delayed Iraq Inquiry, believes the arguments used then are still very important today in analysing Russia's reactions. He argues, 'If you delete "Marxism" and replace "the Soviet Union" with "Russia", there is much in the Kennan and Roberts analyses which remains relevant seventy-five years on.'[28] There are striking parallels between Kennan's and Roberts's writing from Moscow in 1946. Both were running their respective embassies while awaiting the arrival of new ambassadors at this crucial juncture. Each, though young men, were asked by their home departments to provide updated assessments of the nature and aims of Stalin's foreign policy. Kennan, as a direct result of his February 1946 cables, was in April appointed deputy commandant for foreign affairs at the soon-to-be-inaugurated National War College in Washington, and just over a year later he was appointed the first director of the State Department's Policy Planning Staff. Roberts's suggestion of establishing a Foreign Office Committee on policy towards Russia was taken up in mid-1946, and it subsequently met weekly. On his return from Moscow in 1947, he became principal private secretary to Ernest Bevin.

There had been general agreement in official circles in London since October 1945 with the Joint Intelligence Committee (JIC) assessment that Russia's geographical situation was 'strategically relatively invulnerable'.[29] But that was not how it looked from the Kremlin. Russia felt both vulnerable and insecure and, as it had done in the past, it sought to establish a protective territorial buffer and to use 'acquiescent or subservient near neighbours to exert influence further afield'.[30] A key element of Soviet strategy was ensuring they could never again be threatened by a resurgent Germany, and that post-war Germany should look

East instead of West. Where Russia's interests were not threatened, Western interests and objectives could be accommodated; but any perceived encroachment would be resisted with force if necessary. As Roberts wrote in 1946:

> Russia's first priority was security ... The frontiers of Russia have never been fixed and have gone backwards and forwards with defeats or victories in war. But even after her greatest victories in the past, Russia has somehow found herself deprived of many of the fruits of those victories.[31]

Roberts also emphasised the importance of ideology in Soviet policy, together with Russian national tradition. Stalin supported this approach for domestic political reasons as well as ideological ones; it was useful to give the impression that the Soviet peoples were 'surrounded by a hostile world composed largely of reactionary capitalists and their willing tolls in the social democratic movement'.[32] Yet, though Soviet policy was fundamentally hostile to Western liberal, democratic capitalist, and imperialist conceptions, Roberts thought it 'possible, though difficult' to reconcile British and Soviet aims, 'granted the right mixture of strength and patience and the avoidance of sabre-rattling or the raising of prestige issues'.[33]

According to Glover and Lyne, the constant theme is that Roberts's advice from Moscow undoubtedly influenced the way the foreign secretary approached policy towards the Soviet Union. Bevin and Attlee took a much less rigid ideological approach than the US government. Stalin, however, disliked Britain's bourgeois liberalism much more than naked American capitalism; Roberts reported that Bevin was seen like Trotsky – as a 'very important but dangerous and hostile personality'.[34]

In telegrams on 21 March 1946, Roberts wrote that 'although Soviet intentions may be defensive, tactics will be offensive'.[35] Roberts was clear that 'all Soviet tactics are short-term, but their strategy, although flexible, is definitely long-term'.[36] While the Soviet regime was dynamic and still expanding, it did not want to achieve that expansion by armed conflict unless forced to, or if it occurred through miscalculation.

This historic background helps put into context how events were to play out following the NATO summit of November 2002, when four more former Warsaw Pact members, Bulgaria, Romania, Slovakia, and Slovenia, and the Baltic republics Estonia, Latvia, and Lithuania were invited to begin accession talks. The following year, the US and Britain invaded Iraq. They toppled Saddam Hussein but found no weapons of mass destruction, which was the UK's supposed justification for the intervention. Both the US and Britain were damaged by their intervention and still are today. Russia was far from alone in its opposition to an intervention that had not been recently approved by the Security Council. In 2004, NATO agreed the accession of all seven applicants mentioned above. The same year also saw the EU expand significantly eastwards, with the Czech Republic, Estonia, Hungary, Latvia, Lithuania, Poland, Slovakia, and Slovenia all joining (along with Cyprus and Malta); Bulgaria and Romania were to follow in 2007. This was not how Russia had envisaged a partnership with the West developing – and Gorbachev, Yeltsin, and Putin believed they had been seriously misled about NATO expansion.

To understand President Putin, we need to carefully examine some of his key concerns about the loss of defence in depth. George Friedman has written compellingly about the loss of strategic depth faced by Russia since NATO expansion.[37] In

2005, in a speech delivered in front of Russia's Federal Assembly, President Putin said that the fall of the Soviet Union was the 'greatest geopolitical catastrophe in Russia's history'.[38] He is also reputed to have said, 'Anyone who does not regret the collapse of the Soviet Union has no heart. Anyone who wants to see it restored has no brains,' although a similar remark had been attributed in earlier years to General Alexander Lebed, who ran for president in 1996 against Yeltsin and Zyuganov.[39] One of the key themes of Putin's speech was his belief that the fragmentation of the Soviet Union had cost Russia the element that had allowed it to survive foreign invasions since the eighteenth century: strategic depth. For a European country to defeat Russia decisively, it must capture Moscow. Hitler and Napoleon both launched attacks in which their armies covered great distances to reach Moscow, and they arrived exhausted. Both were beaten by a combination of distance and 'General Winter', having to fight at the end of stretched supply lines, against defenders fighting on and for their home territory. During the Cold War, St Petersburg was about 1,000 miles and Moscow about 1,300 miles from the nearest NATO forces in the West. In 2022, St Petersburg is about 100 miles away and Moscow about 500 miles from NATO forces positioned in the Baltic states. From the Russian point of view, this is a significant change. NATO in a wider negotiation could respond with mutually agreed confidence-building measures and some could well involve Finland as a new NATO member.

Having the former Baltic republics join NATO was bad enough for many Russian strategic thinkers, but the prospect of the former Soviet republics of Ukraine and Georgia joining was a bridge too far. On this, all Russian leaders had made their concerns clear to all NATO countries. In 2007, Russia deliberately suspended its observance of its obligations under the Treaty on Conventional Armed Forces in Europe, or CFE Treaty, which in turn concerned NATO. Russia, of course, knew NATO members themselves were not in agreement on further expansion. The US support for Ukrainian and Georgian membership was countered by France and Germany, and in 2006 Angela Merkel, as already mentioned, made it clear this was not acceptable. At NATO's Bucharest summit in April 2008, while it was agreed to begin accession talks with Albania and Croatia, the decision on Ukraine and Georgia was postponed. Unfortunately, the official communiqué made the intention clear: 'We agreed today that these countries will become members of NATO.' President Bush argued in favour of this while Prime Minister Gordon Brown and Chancellor Merkel acquiesced, the latter not pushing her previous objections. In retrospect, this might have been the best time for Ukraine to apply for membership.

On 29 July 2022 the *Financial Times* carried an interview with Dmitry Firtash which, if true, throws an important light on Ukrainian decision-making. Firtash, a billionaire Ukrainian oligarch, made his fortune trading gas with Russia and is still being pursued by the US Department of Justice. He recounted a tale from 2006 when he was chair of the Federation of Employers of Ukraine, when the then newly elected president and strong European Viktor Yushchenko called a meeting with Yanukovych, a pro-Russian politician who would become president in 2010, and some senior ministers to say he wanted Ukraine to join NATO and needed their support. According to Firtash, Yanukovych baulked at the notion, and Yushchenko lost his temper: 'He turned to us and said: "Remember this moment, because while we still have time, and Russia is still regaining its strength, we can do this. But if we don't join NATO soon and Russia gets stronger, eventually they will invade." Then he looked at Yanukovych and said: "This is going to be on your head,"' before storming out.[40]

By 2008, Putin had stepped down as president at the end of his second term, in accordance with the constitution. Probably no one, apart from Putin, knows why he did agree to step down in 2007. Before it was announced, knowing Kissinger was meeting Putin in Russia in a few weeks, I arranged to see Kissinger in New York. Over lunch, he was surprised that I had only one major subject to discuss: a request to raise the issue with Putin of whether it was wise to change the law so he could have a third term. Kissinger's regular meetings with Putin will one day make a fascinating record, but wisely he keeps the details very close, and I have deliberately never asked him since about what, if anything, happened in his meeting with Putin about stepping down.

Perhaps Putin saw engineering a further term in 2008 as behaving too like numerous presidents around the world who appoint themselves 'president for life' to much justified ridicule. Now, in 2022, Putin has to win in 2024 before becoming president for life. Predictably, having gone down that route, he has been the subject of quiet derision and ridicule even in Russia, and not just by his declared opponents. If by 2024 he is unpopular because of the war in Ukraine, Putin will change his title, perhaps to 'tsar', and pass some powers to a new president, thereby avoiding election but retaining control of the armed forces.

When Putin stepped down in 2008, he agreed as presidential candidate Dmitry Medvedev, a lawyer who had served as his deputy in St Petersburg and was his prime minister. In February of that year, the situation in the Balkans had again come to the fore with Kosovo's unilateral declaration of independence from Serbia. It was duly recognised by the US, Britain, France, and Germany, among others, though Russia unsurprisingly did not follow suit. Nor, revealingly, did the EU countries of Cyprus, Romania, Slovakia, and Spain. Medvedev was duly elected president in March 2008 and, in a switch of roles, Putin became prime minister, theoretically no longer responsible for foreign policy. Medvedev was to face some immediate challenges on the foreign policy front.

Before the outbreak of full-blown hostilities in Georgia, Medvedev had already taken his own stance in relation to foreign policy, and in a speech in June in Germany he reinforced the point that Russia wanted to be seen as an equal partner in the new Europe. With continued NATO expansion, he highlighted the need for 'genuinely equal cooperation between Russia, the European Union and North America' and criticised those in the West who simply wanted 'to bring Russia's policies closer into line with those of the West' as Russia did 'not want to be "embraced" in this way'.[41] Medvedev was to develop these themes in a new 'Foreign Policy Concept of the Russian Federation' and in various speeches during his presidency.[42] Tensions rose, and there were clashes between Russian and Georgian troops in August 2008.

The Russian Duma called on the government to establish diplomatic links with Abkhazia and South Ossetia, which had broken away from Georgia, as well as with the breakaway Moldovan region of Transnistria. As on its European frontier, Russia saw its buffer zone on its southern border weakened, now that the states of the South Caucasus – Armenia, Georgia, and Azerbaijan – were independent; and, in its own territory of the North Caucasus, Russia faced unrest from Islamist separatists in Chechnya and Dagestan.

The Independent International Fact-Finding Mission on the Conflict in Georgia, established by the EU to investigate the situation, concluded that Georgian shelling had triggered the wider conflict, but the Russian response, while initially justified, had subsequently been disproportionate and a violation of international law.[43] The Russians gained small, but for them crucial, territorial adjustments as a result of the war, retaining land on the southern side of the strategic tunnel under the Caucasus mountains. This has made it easier for them to project their military influence into the region and beyond. It is worth reflecting that if Georgia had become a member that April, NATO would have been obliged to intervene, and it is questionable whether NATO could have remained united.

The arrival of Barack Obama in the White House was seen as another opportunity for an improvement in the relationship between Russia and the West. What worried the US and its allies was the divergence between Russian statements of principle and the reality of their behaviour. It appeared that Russia was simply paying lip service to global norms while continuing a campaign of disruption and destabilisation in what it regarded as its sphere of influence. There were some positive developments, particularly on arms control, where Obama and Medvedev got on well and negotiated directly; a new START Treaty was signed in 2010, they cooperated on Iran and North Korea, and they made progress on trade relations. Unfortunately, developments following the 2010–11 Arab Spring took hold in North Africa, and President Gaddafi found himself facing increasing public opposition, which he and his sons set about crushing in a brutal way. With the spectre of another

Rwanda or Srebrenica looming, and following a specific request from the Arab League for a no-fly zone, the Security Council passed UNSCR 1973 on 17 March 2011. This authorised UN members to 'take all necessary measures ... to protect civilians and civilian populated areas' in Libya. Crucially, neither Russia nor China vetoed the decision. Medvedev was helped in his decision by Obama saying publicly on 28 March: 'Broadening our military mission to include regime change would be a mistake ... If we tried to overthrow Gaddafi by force our coalition would splinter'.[44] After engaging in the initial series of strikes, which focused on destroying Libyan air defences, the US stepped back, leaving the British and French to take the lead. President Obama was later to criticise Britain and France for failing to stop Libya becoming what he called, in an interview with *Atlantic* magazine in 2016, a 'mess', singling out Cameron for allegedly becoming 'distracted by a range of other things'.[45]

Whatever the rights or wrongs of handling Gaddafi over the years, a large section of global opinion believes France and Britain were intent on removing him. Much of what President Sarkozy and Prime Minister Cameron said publicly at the time fed the impression that their goal was to capture Gaddafi dead or alive. Yet when he was killed, neither country was ready to take a sustained role in finding and fully supporting a successor. President Medvedev of Russia deserved better from the US, Britain, and France in particular, as he had made it possible for their military intervention to be approved by the Security Council and thus legal. As it was, Libya created a public rift between Medvedev and Putin, whose comparison of the UN resolution to 'medieval calls for crusades' drew Medvedev's retort that 'under no circumstances is it acceptable to use expressions which essentially lead to a clash of civilisations, such as "crusade" and so on'.[46] The Libyan military intervention still hangs over Putin's attitude to both Britain and France, as well as the US; he believed Medvedev was wrong to abstain in the Security Council vote, and Russia should have voted against. Russia was not involved through the NATO–Russia Council in consultations on target selection and other relevant issues.

This was a great mistake. The British and French reluctance to keep Russia involved over Libya contributed to the failure of Cameron and Sarkozy's intervention. Libya collapsed into chaos. It became a major trafficking hub for migrants seeking to cross into Europe, and there appears, as yet, no end to this sad saga. While the initial intervention to save Benghazi from the air was sound, the resultant follow-through nationwide meant that full NATO and US involvement was essential. The US secretary of defense, Robert Gates, made it clear from the outset his lack of enthusiasm for the whole intervention, making no secret of his view that the destruction of Libyan ground-to-air missile systems and implementing a no-fly zone was a declaration of war, not a half-way house. Politicians more widely in Europe continue to forget this fact. While a few ground troops from Qatar made an important contribution in ground-to-air targeting in Libya, aided by British and French special forces, relying on no-fly zones as an instrument of intervention is never enough. There must be a continuing and meaningful presence on the ground, which neither Britain nor France were ready to provide in Libya. Some of those lessons were learnt in the joint Russian, US, British, and French air action targeted on ISIS in Syria and Iraq where the Kurdish armed forces provided troops on the ground.

Although there had been some speculation that Medvedev

would run for a second term, ultimately it came as no surprise when, in September 2011, Putin announced he would stand for re-election for president in 2012. In January 2012, Kissinger met up with Putin again in Moscow and, not long afterwards, according to the former *New York Times* bureau chief Steven Lee Myers, Kissinger said of Putin, 'He's a little less buoyant now.'[47] Myers reported that the elder statesman of realpolitik had met regularly with Putin ever since he came to power, and that according to Kissinger, 'Putin is not a Stalin who feels obliged to destroy anyone who might potentially at some future date disagree with him. Putin is somebody who wants to amass the power needed to accomplish his immediate task.'[48]

Putin duly won the election, which, because of constitutional changes, meant a further term of six years rather than four. But Putin right up to the end feared losing, having been convinced that the CIA, under instructions from the secretary of state, Hillary Clinton, was interfering inside Russia to deprive him of votes. Whether that was true or not, there is no doubt that Putin retaliated with a quantitative increase in Russian interference in US elections. CIA sources are still reluctant to provide chapter and verse of Putin's intervention in the presidential election in which Donald Trump beat Hillary Clinton in the electoral college, despite her polling some three million more votes overall.

By the end of 2013 it should have been no surprise to the EU in Brussels that Ukrainian–Russian relations were deteriorating. President Viktor Yanukovych, whose electoral strength lay in the Russian-speaking parts of Ukraine, was starting to shy away from the actual terms of the EU Association Agreement with Ukraine, which aimed to promote and assist Ukraine's gradual convergence towards the EU's Common Security and Defence Policy.[49] Those parts which built up EU defence agreements were strongly disliked by Russia, and even today we don't know enough about the line-by-line negotiations. Under pressure from Russia, Yanukovych started to reject EU defence implications and tried to establish closer ties with the Russian Federation's plans for a trade and economic agreement with countries that had formerly been in the Soviet sphere of influence. This was the more prudent alternative for him personally, as well as for his main supporters in Ukraine's Russian-speaking regions. But a wave of demonstrations and civil unrest against President Yanukovych, dubbed the Euromaidan protests, then began to underline the importance of the agreement to the pro-European parts of Ukraine, including some out-and-out nationalist elements. These protests escalated in January 2014 when Yanukovych's government came forward with new anti-protest laws aimed at consolidating his grip on power. The ensuing violence and riots, starting on 18 February, resulted in 100 deaths and thousands injured.

What then followed was called EU diplomacy – but it involved few EU countries. Britain, under Prime Minister Cameron and with William Hague as foreign secretary, was virtually absent – a very strange omission, since Britain was a signatory along with Russia, the US, and France of the 1994 Budapest Memorandum, a treaty promising to uphold the territorial integrity of Ukraine and which formed the basis of Ukraine's decision to forego its arsenal of nuclear weapons (the world's third largest arsenal when Ukraine was part of the Soviet Union).[50] The only other state to follow their example was South Africa, at a time when de Klerk and Mandela came together to create a new South Africa.

The negotiations in Kyiv consisted of the German, French,

and Polish foreign ministers and Yanukovych's government, followed by the signing of a document on 21 February between Yanukovych and opposition leaders. The extent of the involvement of the EU's Common Security and Defence Policy and the External Affairs Secretariat in this initiative is still not clear. On 19 February, the EU's high representative, then Catherine Ashton, did ask the Polish foreign minister, Radek Sikorski, to undertake a diplomatic mission to Kyiv. Given the history of Polish–Russian relations, this in itself was an inflammatory choice for many Russian speakers in Ukraine and for Russia itself. But on whose authority was the request made? Was it the EU Council of Ministers? Britain appeared not to be involved or even represented, although France, its fellow Budapest Memorandum signatory, was, along with Germany. Was Britain deliberately omitted, or did Cameron and Hague not want to be involved? The US, another signatory to the memorandum, was also not formally involved in any way, but President Obama did speak to President Putin to press on him the need for a Russian presence at the negotiations and for a helpful Russian who could work with the EU negotiating team to join the diplomacy.

The ink was barely dry on this so-called EU-brokered agreement when Yanukovych felt forced to flee from the capital and, on 22 February 2014, members of parliament found him unable to fulfil his duties. The EU's credibility and authority were openly shredded overnight. They have yet to be fully re-established. Watching the EU's disgraceful diplomatic performance – which paved the way for Putin to invade Crimea in 2014 – hardened my growing belief that Britain's EU membership should cease, and that we should regain control of our own UK foreign policy. Winning the referendum to leave the EU has, in relation to the UK's handling of the Russia–Ukraine war of 2022 through NATO, been justified in every respect and will continue to be so under Prime Minister Liz Truss. On this key security question vis-à-vis Russia, this grouping of EU nations posed as a sovereign power and was exposed. Much the same happened in Macron's personal diplomacy with Putin in 2022.

In fairness, the European Commission president since 2019, Ursula von der Leyen, created a tough sanctions package on Russia in retaliation for its invasion of Ukraine in 2022 in concert with the US and NATO, and slowly pressurised Germany to go further on gas and oil sanctions than many energy experts believed possible.

Putin's second invasion of Ukraine has had many adverse consequences for Russia, but none more so than over defence. Three days after Russian forces invaded Ukraine, the German government announced it would spend €100 billion on modernising its army, the Bundeswehr. Speaking in the German parliament the defence minister, Christine Lambrecht, just before NATO held a major training exercise on the moors and forest of Luneburg Heath, said the army was out of ammunition and had a massive shortage of combat-ready equipment. 'For years all we did was make savings ... We have to put an end to that.' As Chancellor Scholz told parliamentarians, the goal was 'a powerful, cutting-edge, progressive Bundeswehr that can be relied upon to protect us'.[51]

Angela Merkel was the prime target of President Obama's jibe in 2016 about NATO's 'free riders'. President Trump was more direct: 'Angela, you've gotta' pay your bills!' As the *Financial Times* wrote:

Trump's logic was simple. At a NATO summit in 2014, Germany had promised to move towards paying 2 per cent of GDP on defence, but it never achieved that goal; the current level hovers at about 1.5 per cent. The result: a perception that Berlin never really pulled its weight.[52]

On the day of Putin's second invasion of Ukraine, Alfons Mais, the chief of the German army, said the Bundeswehr was 'broke'. Now it has a commitment in terms of euros, not GDP. Only 150 of its 350 Puma infantry fighting vehicles were actually operational; only nine of its fifty-one Tiger helicopters could fly. A Munich-based think tank has revealed that the number of German battle tanks fell from 6,779 to just over 806 over the last thirty years, and the number of combat aircraft and helicopters from 1,337 to 345.

Anything supplied to Ukraine was bound to compromise Germany's own defence. Putin's invasion of Ukraine has achieved what no amount of talk could do: a German contribution to NATO at long last worthy of its proven democratic and political development. The opposition Christian Democrats reject the idea that the €100 billion fund can just be used to reach the 2 per cent target figure. They are demanding that the fund, which requires a two-thirds majority as a constitutional amendment, means a long-term commitment to higher military outlays than 2 per cent of GDP. Putin's invasion of Ukraine has brought about a response from NATO he least expected.

President Macron's attitude to NATO – describing it as 'brain dead' – has had to change. Now without a majority in the French assembly, he has no chance of creating his wished-for smaller federal union of perhaps as few as seven to nine nations initially, with a sovereign economic, foreign, and defence force akin to what the US created. Such nations within the EU would control its currency, back it with their money, and have a smaller but more powerful Central Bank. Other EU countries would continue to use the euro and all would continue as part of the wider overall European Union. The logic of such a development is overwhelming from a global perspective; over thirty countries going into the next decade cannot negotiate and implement complex arrangements, let alone defence, as if they are a sovereign power. I wrote about such arrangements in *Europe Restructured*, first published in 2012.[53] President Macron's proposals for a confederation were leaked to the *Daily Telegraph* in an article by Ambrose Evans-Pritchard on 13 May 2022. But they are now diminished.

Whatever happens over the coming months, we in the West must ensure Ukraine comes out of the war with Russia as a viable state, is given substantial help to rebuild and join the EU and, if it wishes, can become a member of NATO.

Meanwhile, let us remind ourselves of what Putin started to do in Crimea on the night of 22–23 February 2014, against the background of what became known as the Euromaidan revolution in Ukraine, when Putin discussed with his security team the extrication of the deposed President Yanukovych. Putin then started to implement his policy of returning Crimea to Russia, claiming he feared that agreements on their key Sevastopol naval base would be rescinded by the new Ukrainian government. On 23 February, pro-Russian demonstrations were held in the city of Sevastopol and, by 27 February, Russian troops without insignia – the so-called 'little green men' – took over the Supreme Council of Crimea. A hastily organised referendum was held in March 2014, resulting in an overwhelming vote in favour of Crimea returning to Russia. The vote was widely condemned as illegal and illegitimate, including by the EU and US, who started to impose very weak sanctions on Russia. Shortly afterwards, President Putin issued a decree 'on the recognition of the Republic of Crimea'. He remained intransigent, making comparisons between the Crimea referendum and Kosovo's declaration of independence in 2008 (which Russia had never accepted), saying: 'We keep hearing from the United States and Western Europe that Kosovo is some special case. What makes it so special in the eyes of our colleagues?' Putin went on to reinforce the message about how Russia saw itself in the world: 'Russia is an independent, active participant in international affairs; like other countries, it has its own national interests that need to be taken into account and respected.'[54]

He began to see Russia invading Ukraine as akin to the US invasion of Iraq: controversial in its own right, but necessary to legitimise Russia's activity in an area where their longstanding interests were being challenged.

Meanwhile, the situation in Ukraine deteriorated further, with armed clashes in eastern Ukraine and the pro-Russian Donetsk and Luhansk regions declaring independence. Despite the signature of a second peace agreement in Minsk in February 2015 (Minsk II), the fighting continued, with numerous ceasefires being negotiated only to be broken.

After Russia's seizure of Crimea, I decided to retire from all my business commitments in Russia. From 1995 to 2015, I was involved, as described earlier, in business in Russia, initially in steel, and later oil. I eschewed any attempt to combine this commercial life with my previous one from 1966 as a British politician. On 16 November 2017, by now free from all Russian business connections, I made my last public speech in Russia to the Moscow State Institute of International Relations, speaking mainly about the Middle East.[55] I described the times when relations between Britain and Russia were strong and mutually advantageous. I also talked about Putin's state visit to the UK in the summer of 2003. To my mind, the seizure of Crimea made the containment of Russia now ever more vital. It was right that the invasion was met with economic sanctions. But the sanctions were designed to ensure they didn't harm the national interests of those countries applying them, and they were too weak to deter Putin – an example of 'gesture politics' that by definition wills the end but fails to provide the means towards achieving that end. Russian–British relations were bound to deteriorate and, I feared, business in Russia would become ever more corrupt. Of course, business would continue between Britain and Russia as it had with the Soviet Union during the long Cold War. Yet, for me, the optimism engendered by the Yeltsin era was over; it was better to retire and avoid any personal conflict of interest. A real market economy needs to take root inside Russia, but this will only happen if there is a major overhaul of the corporate legal environment, including a genuinely impartial court system. This, I judged, was not going to happen under Putin after the first invasion of Ukraine, but I did not predict the second invasion.

I believe in the separation of politics and business. I hoped that after 1989, when Yeltsin emerged as a political force, he would develop a truly mixed economy in Russia and that commercial relationships would build up trust between Russia and the rest of the world, and the Russian Communist command economy would never return. Commercial relationships did lead to a better intergovernmental relationship for twenty years and gather in its wake personal relationships that still bind businesspeople together. I remain of the view that this will be the dynamic for the rebuilding of Russia's very strained relationship with NATO countries now. It has been mooted that 70 per cent of the Russian economy is, in effect, controlled by the Russian government. If correct, this figure is much too high, and is surely rising. One of the many consequences of the sanctions NATO countries and others have imposed upon Russia is that they have pushed many people in Russia back into the command economy of the past, with all its diseconomies and threats to freedom of choice. Yet I am convinced most Russians do not want this. Russia will revisit, I hope, the Yeltsin reforms, but in a more coherent way.

Yet at times we who represent the Western economies have not been the best practitioners of our market economy. The first warning sign I had that commercial relations with Russia would not be smooth came with rouble devaluation in August 1998. I had been somewhat involved with the negotiation of a US $100 million loan from the European Bank of Reconstruction and Development for the OEMK steel plant. We had even exchanged 'tombstones' to mark the completion of the deal, but a technical cancellation of the contract took place immediately after devaluation. It was an outrageous decision. Never again could I engage with Russian managers on the need for the honouring of commercial obligations and acting in good faith with conviction. Fortunately, OEMK overcame this shock decision and in the years that followed joined up with the iron ore mine Lebedinsky GOK as part of Metalloinvest, whose iron ore flows down a water pipe into the steel mill with virtually no transport costs. The combined business is now a profitable modern-equipped plant selling iron briquettes around the world and raising private finance from many different countries.

Here it may be worth reflecting for a moment on the impact of the sanctions imposed on Russia in 2022, which were purportedly much tougher. In all the writings and conversations about Putin's mistakes, and there were many following his handling of Russia's second invasion of Ukraine, there has not been enough realism about Putin's calculating mind. We are not dealing with a Gorbachev or a Yeltsin. First and foremost, Putin is not a great government spender: he builds up Russia's financial resources before embarking on foreign adventures. In his first ten years he used high oil prices to pay off debts. He built up his foreign currency reserves. He anticipated there would be Western economic sanctions for seizing Crimea and reacted rationally, accepting a rouble devaluation. He has, by common consent, employed sensible economists. The chair of Russia's Central Bank, Elvira Nabiullina, and his finance minister, Anton Siluanov, have combined into an effective team – they actually increased the country's budget surplus during the Covid pandemic. They have also been fortunate in that, with surging oil prices, Russia has earned about $97 billion during the first 100 days of the war with Ukraine, as calculated by the Helsinki Centre for Research On Clean Energy and Clean Air – a record windfall. Despite criticism, the European Commission did reduce the EU's purchases of Russian gas and oil during the first 100 days: gas was down by 23 per cent and crude oil by 18 per cent. Overall, China was the largest purchaser of Russian fossil fuels, edging out Germany, Italy, and the Netherlands. The initial economic package of sanctions was not tough enough on Russia and needs to be toughened. It looked as if the US finance minister, Janet Yellen, wanted the formation of a cartel that would set a cap on the price of Russian oil, roughly equal to the price of production. That would be a serious economic sanction, just the realistic prospect of which might concentrate Putin's and OPEC's minds. Yet nothing came out of the G20 finance meeting that discussed the issue, nor from President Biden's summer meeting in Saudi Arabia. We need sanctions to match the gravity of Russia's offence of trying to seize the Ukrainian capital Kyiv by force of arms, as well as the disruption of Ukraine's grain harvest, which will have consequences for many countries across the globe.

President Obama's description of Russia as no more than 'a regional power' still rankles with Putin, and it has proved wrong in relation to Russia's influence in the Middle East.[56] Yet the poor shape of the Russian armed forces as exposed in Ukraine has led to many questions about where the extra money for the military budget has been spent, aside from building hypersonic cruise missiles. In July 2022 Putin threatened to start using these missiles.

Let us for a moment shift our focus from Putin's actions in Ukraine and look at his record in the Middle East. Russia had not been a significant player in the Middle East since Kissinger was in office, and then under President Carter with the Camp David Accords in 1978. After the events in Libya, Putin appears to be pursuing a policy – supported by China – of never letting a UN security resolution pass if it could provide a precedent for UN action that would damage President Assad's position. This blanket veto has proved a very serious blow to resolving the prolonged Syrian Civil War. The one moment of hope was in 2013, when Russian Foreign Minister Lavrov and US Secretary of State Kerry negotiated over ending the use of sarin gas in Syria. There is little doubt that a very large part of that stock was removed and destroyed under UN supervision. This was not an easy thing to do during a war. Regrettably, gas has continued to be used in Syria, although initially it was much reduced.

Having observed the consequences of the West's limited military interventions, Putin learnt that any successful military intervention on Russia's part requires full commitment and the involvement of ground forces as well as air power. In the summer of 2015, Assad visited Moscow and warned President Putin that the road link between Damascus and the Mediterranean was in danger of being blocked militarily by anti-Assad rebels. Putin responded swiftly and intelligently. In September 2015, the Russian naval base in Syria, which it has occupied since 1971, was quickly reinforced by adopting a nearby Syrian airfield. Russian planes began a bombing campaign to tilt the balance back in favour of Assad, while claiming the action was primarily to attack ISIL (the Islamic State of Iraq and the Levant). Russia was helping to militarily control an area of Syria in the west, just as the Turks had wanted – and should have been helped – to do in the east. Though some Russian special forces were deployed, they relied on Syrian ground troops for most of the fighting, assisted by some forces coming in from Iran who were targeted by Israel very effectively. President Obama could have welcomed President Putin's initial response, as it tackled a real rather than theoretical threat to Damascus. Had Damascus, a multi-religious centre not dissimilar to Jerusalem, been captured by ISIL, then already ensconced in the suburbs, it would have been devastating. President Obama could, and I believe should, have suggested to Putin that while Russia focused on the defence of

Damascus and the Alawite Mediterranean stronghold, the US would help protect Aleppo and, using its air power, work with Turkey to create a haven for some two million Syrian refugees on Syrian territory. Such an action, long advocated by Turkey, would have meant the US helping a NATO partner, and would have gone some way to stabilise Syria – admittedly at a high risk of seeing it split permanently into two parts, but saving a lot of lives in the process. It would also have been a welcome sign to President Erdoğan that NATO was ready to act intelligently in support of Turkish interests, as well as helping Turkey deal with its share of the refugee crisis, which has severely stretched its economy.

Instead of reaching a solution to the ongoing war in Syria, there has been successful cooperation with Russia in destroying ISIL's military capabilities in the region. In the airspace over Syria in particular, military-to-military coordination has been unparalleled. The US, Russia, Turkey, Britain, and France attacked ISIL targets very successfully. We reached the point where there was no longer a declared and organised ISIL grouping in Syria. However, a long-unanswered question is what to do with those who rose to prominence as a result of a very necessary ground fight, namely the Kurds. US and NATO discussions with Erdoğan on how to deal with the Kurds in Syria have made no progress.

The Kurds provided the crucial ground forces that were ready and able to deal with ISIL. The Kurdish population is spread across Iran and Iraq, as well as Turkey and Syria. As a result of the collapse of the Ottoman Empire and the post-First World War settlement, the Kurds still invoke the promise in Paris after World War I for an independent Kurdish state. That has been, and continues to be, formally opposed by other states in the region. This deadlock can only be resolved if an independent Kurdish homeland is carved out of Syria, supported by Russia.

Putin has, however, focused on the stresses within NATO and hitherto has tended to exploit them as an opportunity to drive a wedge between Turkey and its NATO allies. He struck an important blow by securing Erdoğan's agreement to share intelligence and to purchase the sophisticated S-400 defence system from Russia. President Trump had little alternative but to reluctantly apply modest sanctions against Turkey in December 2020 in response to the deal, despite warnings. Turkey had already been removed from NATO's F-35 fighter jet programme, but the US has banned export licences in accordance with the Countering America's Adversaries Through Sanctions Act. The sanctions were applied to the Turkish government agency, the SSB, which handles military purchases and defence exports. Erdoğan's bark can be worse than his bite. He initially indicated he would block Finland and Sweden joining NATO, but that now appears to be resolved.

NATO should not take any pre-emptive step to deprive Turkey of membership. A Turkey in NATO that works with Russia and the US can be a stabilising factor. A Turkey outside NATO that exclusively links with Russia will be destabilising. Turkey has never fitted in any historical relationship with Russia for long. But Turkey is entitled to want to have working relations with both NATO and Russia, and this should not be incompatible with NATO membership. Indeed, Russia and Turkey have been involved in monitoring the ceasefire after the 2020 conflict between Azerbaijan and Armenia over the disputed territory of Nagorno-Karabakh.

The major new factor in the Middle East is the Arab–Israeli

'Abraham Accords'. Its present signatories, soon to be joined by Saudi Arabia, are determined that Iran should never develop a nuclear warhead for its supersonic cruise missiles. Since the revolution, Iran has annually held a national Quds Day, or Jerusalem Day, when people come out to chant 'Death to Israel'. It continues to try to infiltrate men and missiles through Syria into Lebanon. Beirut has never been in a worse state. After an eleven-year war in Syria the danger of ISIL returning still exists. The humanitarian crisis remains huge in Syria, with over 14.5 million people still dependent on aid and 90% of the Syrian people classified as living in poverty. Overcoming this legacy will be very difficult, and there can be no going back to the old pattern of untrammelled rule by the Assad family. Syria needs the checks and balances that have developed on the ground and in the air if it is to attract the financial backing to rebuild its cities and infrastructure, let alone restore the capacity to feed its people.

Turkey has a close relationship with Qatar, with a large military base there. It is intent on being an important player in the wider region, having a military involvement in Libya in support of the UN-recognised leadership. Erdoğan's offer to Biden, when they talked together on the fringe of a NATO meeting, was for Turkey to be prepared to guarantee the security of air access to Kabul when the US and other NATO armed forces withdrew from Afghanistan in August 2021. It was a bold offer, and it was accepted by NATO and tolerated by the Taliban.

When the far-right junta took over in Greece from 1967 to 1974, many argued that Greece should be thrown out of NATO. I was – I admit – sympathetic to this cause, but wiser heads prevailed. Denis Healey, then secretary of state for defence, whom I served under from 1968 to 1970 as minister for the navy in

Harold Wilson's government, argued that democracy would be restored quicker in Greece if a military dialogue was maintained, and fellow soldiers were telling Greek generals and colonels to abandon politics and return to democracy. That proved to be the correct analysis. As an individual protest, I personally stopped visiting Greece during the seven-year rule of the 'junta'. President Macron, while being very friendly towards Greece, has adopted an openly hostile stance to Turkey, so Britain, along with Germany, must remain fully engaged with both Turkey and Greece. However frustrating President Erdoğan's behaviour is at times, we must demonstrate patience and persistence.

As for President Erdoğan's apparent dream of a new Ottoman Empire, that world ceased in Paris after the end of the First World War. Its return would be in no one's interest. Erdoğan is, nevertheless, involved in Libya and Nagorno-Karabakh, and is supporting the Uighurs in China. He is also challenging the interpretation under the Law of the Sea of Greece's and Cyprus's claims to exploitable gas and oil reserves and, related to these, Erdoğan has made claims on Libyan waters. Many of these issues will not be easy to resolve, but if there is any risk of armed conflict, then no commercial oil and gas company will likely bid for the rights. Turkey, meanwhile, asserts that it has companies well able to exploit any finds.

Putin's Russia is playing the field of countries bordering on the Mediterranean, and Britain must, therefore, also engage with a broad range of partners, especially now that it is no longer tied to the EU's foreign policy. Britain has retained its close relationship with Israel and the Palestinians, not forgetting the double commitment in the 1917 Balfour Declaration. The circumstances are different now, however, even if the core issues remain. The coalition government in Tel Aviv, contrary to most predictions, lasted for a year and started to pay more attention to genuine Palestinian concerns than Netanyahu ever did as prime minister, and deserves to come back after the elections with a working majority.

Russia's traditional relationships in the Middle East have been in the Arab world, but Putin has embedded Russia as a strategic player in the region. He has recognised the need to cultivate relationships across all countries and he has handled Israel well. The freeing up of emigration has ensured that Russian-speaking Israelis now make up an influential 15 per cent of Israel's total population. And to give him credit, Putin has changed Russia's diplomatic attitude to Israel. He has cultivated a good relationship with all Israeli prime ministers, meeting them with the same regularity as other leaders in the Middle East.

President Biden is unlikely to want to talk to President Putin directly about the war in Ukraine; that is for the presidents of the two warring countries to engage in. But just as he met with the Crown Prince of Saudi Arabia, so at some stage might he be ready to talk to Putin about the Middle East. Putin's visit to Iran in July 2022 was interesting given they compete for oil sales, and they probably exchanged information on how to evade sanctions.

The then president of Iran Mohammad Khatami, visited Russia in March 2001 and went to Tatarstan and the Islamic university in the capital, Kazan. Ever since, Russia has tried to build closer relations with Iran, which is also deeply engaged in the war in Syria. Against that background, it was a significant diplomatic victory to secure Russia's cooperation with Security Council partners and Germany (the P5+1) in reaching the Joint Comprehensive Plan of Action with Iran (JCPOA) in 2015, which may have somewhat limited Iran's nuclear development activities. The agreement was enshrined in UN Resolution 231. President Trump's withdrawal of the US from the agreement in 2018 was replaced in 2021 with renewed engagement under the Biden administration. However, JCPOA can only continue if there is meaningful engagement on the Iranian side.

A negotiated settlement in Syria remains very difficult to achieve. There is a delicate balance to strike as to whether President Assad is to be accepted internationally as the leader of Syria according to its previous boundaries, or whether permanent adjustments are made to these boundaries to accommodate the realities of a long and distressing war. The Golan Heights will have to stay with Israel. The Kurds will also need a portion of Syrian territory, and Turkey will need land. For the world to accept Assad continuing in power, viable arrangements will also need to be made to prevent Iran's military passing through to Lebanon. This will take time and imagination.

Few predicted the Abraham Accords being signed by some Arab countries in a ground-breaking initiative to normalise relations with Israel. Saudi Arabia has taken the initiative over economic cooperation and involvement with Egypt. Egypt, in a stand-alone relationship, could rent to Gaza territory on its Sinai border. The chances of Israelis and Arabs working together in this way looked impossible for many years until Camp David under President Carter. President Trump too deserves credit for the substantive change in attitudes that helped make the Abraham Accords possible.

Britain's bilateral relationship with Russia, which got off to a positive start in the early days of Putin's presidency, was affected by the dangerous tensions that developed after he authorised the use of polonium and novichok on former members of the Russian security services living in Britain, Alexander

Litvinenko and Sergei Skripal. This took relations to the lowest level for many decades, and has since been exacerbated by Britain's unequivocal support for Ukraine.

In his inquiry into the poisoning of Litvinenko with polonium, a radioactive substance, the distinguished judge Sir Robert Owen found that the FSB operation to kill Litvinenko on British soil 'was probably approved by Mr Patrushev [Director of the FSB] and also by President Putin ... Moreover, President Putin's conduct towards Mr Lugovoi [one of the suspected killers] suggests a level of approval for the killing of Mr Litvinenko.'[57] As for 'Mr Kovtun's [the second suspected killer] boast that he was planning to kill with a "very expensive poison"', Owen states, 'there is a wealth of independent evidence before me that shows this is exactly what he was planning to do'.[58] As for Lugovoi and Kovtun's motivation, Owen found no evidence of 'any personal reason' for murder. Someone else had directed the 'protracted and costly operation'.[59] In chapter twelve of the report, entitled 'Russian State responsibility – involvement of Nikolai Patrushev and President Vladimir Putin', the concluding paragraph states: 'Taking full account of all the evidence and analysis available to me, I find that the FSB operation to kill Mr Litvinenko was probably approved by Mr Patrushev and also by President Putin.'[60]

In Salisbury in March 2018, Sergei Skripal and his daughter, Yulia, were victims of an attempted murder. Skripal had been a Russian military intelligence officer who had worked as a double agent for the British. Having been imprisoned for treason in Russia, he had been freed to come to the West as part of a prisoner exchange agreement. In his case, a Russian-produced nerve agent, novichok, was the weapon of choice. Within days of the incident, the British government deemed it 'highly likely' that the Russian state was responsible. Britain expelled twenty-three diplomats, and Russia, as is typical, responded on a tit-for-tat basis. Both sides also took other punitive measures against one another. In what the then foreign secretary Boris Johnson described as an 'extraordinary international response' on the part of the UK's allies from within and beyond NATO and the EU, concerted action on 26–27 March 2018 saw over 140 accredited Russian diplomats expelled, with the US alone expelling sixty. Three months later, the same novichok that had been sprayed on the Skripals' front door caused the death of Dawn Sturgess, a totally innocent victim, who by chance came into contact with a discarded perfume bottle in which the nerve agent had been transported some distance from Salisbury. Somewhat unusually for a former cabinet secretary, Sir Mark Sedwill wrote in the *Daily Mail* on 18 January 2021 about the Salisbury poisoning. He explained how Britain had placed financial sanctions on Russians close to Putin and expelled twenty-three agents known to be working covertly in London for the Russian foreign military agency, the GRU, and that a signal had been sent to Moscow to indicate that we knew what was going on and that they weren't hiding it as well as they perhaps thought they were. Sedwill also met his counterpart in the Kremlin to reinforce in person the message that such an attack could not be repeated, and certainly not on British territory.[61]

Putin and his spokespeople claim such killings are reserved for those they call 'ex-patriots', and he has publicly pledged to eliminate any Russian double agent, however long it may take and wherever in the world they may be. The Duma has provided legislative authority for this in the form of the foreign agent law of 2012 and the undesirable organisation law of 2015.

Yet it is clear from the British investigations that the Russian use of polonium and novichok in London and Salisbury killed one innocent British citizen, Dawn Sturgess, and could very easily have killed many more. Whether one likes it or not, government spies and secret intelligence gathering have been with us for centuries. What is new is this blatant disregard of the risk to innocent lives through the indiscriminate use of deadly, state-produced poisons. The fact that President Putin has continued to authorise the use of novichok in circumstances where innocent civilians, including his fellow Russians, could be killed must not go unchallenged under international law, and it is Britain's responsibility to pursue this.

Britain, like many other countries, has also been the victim of cyberattacks from Russia, and its National Cyber Security Centre (NCSC) has identified the GRU as the likely perpetrators of attacks on institutions such as the Foreign and Commonwealth Office and the UK Defence and Science Technology Laboratory.[62] The year 2020 saw attacks on institutes involved in research on the Covid-19 virus and vaccine development.[63] In April 2021, in light of the NCSC's assessment that the SVR was likely responsible for a major international hacking incident known as SolarWinds, the British government issued a statement condemning 'Russia's pattern of malign behaviour around the world – whether in cyberspace, in election interference or in the aggressive operations of their intelligence services – [which demonstrated] that Russia remains the most acute threat to the UK's national and collective security.'[64]

The US, for its part, expelled ten Russian diplomats and imposed sanctions on several individuals and companies in response to the SolarWinds incident and for its interference in the 2020 presidential elections.

Russian interference in the democratic process in the West has become a prominent issue, particularly since the 2016 presidential elections in the US. It has also caused serious concern in the UK, with allegations of Russian interference in the EU referendum. In July 2019, in one of his first big decisions on foreign and security policy, Prime Minister Boris Johnson in my view wisely blocked publication of the Intelligence and Security Select Committee Report on Russia until after a general election had been held. The country was at that time deeply divided over Brexit and was in no position to discuss Russia rationally.

In 2020, a new select committee was formed, and it ordered the report to be published after a long wait. The new government made the wise decision to substantially increase defence spending with Russia in mind.

The new committee prudently made no changes to what the press by then called the 'Grieve' Report after its previous chair, who had lost his seat at the election, and so what became important was not the report itself so much as what the new government, again led by Boris Johnson, would say on Russia. The response was both balanced and concise in its future assessments.

The UK's free and open democracy is one of the nation's greatest strengths. However, we know that certain states seek to exploit our open system to sow division and undermine trust in our democracy, and those of our allies, through disinformation, cyberattacks and other methods. We have made clear that any foreign interference to the UK's democratic processes is completely unacceptable. It is, and always will be, an absolute priority to protect the UK against foreign interference, whether from Russia or any other state.[65]

The government report also said: 'Specifically the UK has worked with international partners to call out the malign influence and activities of Russia's Military Intelligence (widely known as the GRU).' It was noted that the then foreign secretary Dominic Raab 'is quite enthusiastic about sanctions against individuals because we are all quite sceptical that sanctions against countries have a huge effect and they often hurt the very people they are trying to help'. This last point referred to the twenty-five Russian government officials who were sanctioned for their involvement in the death in custody of the lawyer Sergei Magnitsky, who was working with US investors and investigating major tax fraud. His death was seen as one of the very worst cases of human rights abuse by Russia, and it led to the passing of the Magnitsky Act in the US, which provides for the sanctioning of individuals for infringing human rights. The law does not just apply to Russia; recently, for example, a number of individuals involved in the murder of Saudi journalist Jamal Khashoggi have been sanctioned under it.

Interference in the US presidential elections was a highly controversial issue, particularly in 2016, and indeed it had a major impact on President Trump's ability to develop an appropriate working relationship with President Putin, who consistently denied the allegations. Special Counsel Robert Mueller published a 448-page report into the alleged interference in April 2019, which stated that: 'The Russian government interfered in the 2016 presidential election in sweeping and systematic fashion.'[66] The interference, the report revealed, took two forms.

First, a Russian entity carried out a social media campaign that favored presidential candidate Donald J. Trump and disparaged presidential candidate Hillary Clinton. Second, a Russian intelligence service conducted computer-intrusion operations against entities, employees, and volunteers working on the Clinton campaign and then released stolen documents.[67]

Thirteen Russian nationals and three Russian entities, including the Internet Research Agency, were indicted for interfering in the elections, and GRU officers were charged with 'conspiring to hack into various U.S. computers' in association with the Clinton–Trump presidential campaign and others. The interference continued in the Biden–Trump 2020 presidential campaign, according to a March 2021 report by the US National Intelligence Council.[68] The report stated:

We assess that Russian President Putin authorized, and a range of Russian government organizations conducted, influence operations aimed at denigrating President Biden's candidacy and the Democratic Party, supporting former President Trump, undermining public confidence in the electoral process, and exacerbating sociopolitical divisions in the US. Unlike in 2016, we did not see persistent Russian cyber efforts to gain access to election infrastructure. We have high confidence in our assessment.[69]

The report also highlighted that Russia was not the only country to attempt to interfere in the elections, with Iran, Cuba, and Venezuela all mentioned.

In addition, we are dealing with flagrant and systematic

breaches of international agreements and norms by both Russia and China. This undermines the rule of law and heightens levels of distrust across a whole field of international affairs. Addressing the threats such actions pose must be foremost in the minds of British decision-makers as they develop Britain's foreign policy in the post-Brexit era. This cannot be done without much greater realism – the element, above all, that has been missing from British politics for twenty years. Cabinet government started to eke away in 2001 when Blair's second term in office began. The culture of politicians, civil servants, and military commanders all working together has also been slowly eroded: scapegoating and disloyalty in Whitehall has been accompanied by leaks of sensitive information on a new and worsening scale. No British prime minister in war time – not Asquith, Lloyd George, Churchill, let alone Major during the first invasion of Iraq – made strategic decisions outside cabinet as Blair did over Iraq. Yet when the Inquiry Report was published on 6 July 2016, after eleven years of delay, Blair commented, 'If I was back in the same place with the same information I would take the same decision.'[70]

Many of the same criticisms of the handling of the invasion of Iraq can be made of Cameron's handling with President Sarkozy of the intervention in Libya. What the UK needs is a mechanism to learn from our mistakes. We were warned as long ago as 2010 by Sherard Cowper-Coles, ambassador to Afghanistan, about the Herculean task we and NATO faced in promising to rebuild the Afghan nation and state.[71] We failed in that task and Biden decided to stop any further nation-building military interventions and accept the Taliban's readiness to halt attacks on NATO troops while they withdrew. The Taliban kept to that agreement but in other respects human and women's rights have seen a reversion to when they were last in control and giving sanctuary to Al-Qaeda before 9/11. Europe unwisely condemned Biden's actions, ignoring the fact he had offered to leave all US weaponry behind in Afghanistan if the European members of NATO wished to continue the fight, which of course they had no wish to do.

As I ponder Ukraine and its evolution towards embracing a remarkable democracy after President Volodymyr Zelensky won power in an anti-corruption campaign in 2019, and its current fight against the invading Russian forces, I have read more about its true history – a counterpoint to the distorted version of history peddled by President Putin, and on which he has justified his two invasions. Serhii Plokhy, whose book *The Gates to Europe* I have already referred to, claims that:

> the rise of Ukraine to honorary second place in the hierarchy of Soviet republics and nationalities began in January 1954 with all-union celebrations of the tercentenary of the Pereiaslav Council (1654). Official party propaganda hailed the Council, which approved the passing of the Cossack Hetmanate under the protection of the Muscovite tsar, as the 'reunification of Ukraine with Russia'.[72]

Crimea was not given, as is widely believed, by Nikita Khrushchev to Ukraine when drunk in the small hours of the night but following a visit to Crimea in the autumn of 1953. He experienced an economically depressed region with distressed settlers demanding assistance. He travelled directly to Kyiv to start negotiations on the transfer of the peninsula to Ukraine, whose agricultural experts were more capable of making improvements. By February 1954 the Ukrainian, Russian, and all-union Supreme Soviets had signed off on the deal and Crimea became part of Ukraine. Between 1953 and 1956 the production of electricity increased by almost 60 per cent, its production of wine doubled, and the construction over several years of the Crimean Canal brought Dnieper water to the region, providing a major irrigation boost to agricultural land.

Khrushchev's secret speech at the Twentieth Party Congress in Moscow in February 1956 heralded, according to Plokhy, a new era in the life of the Soviet Union and its constituent republics. Its theme of de-Stalinisation, nevertheless, did not mention Stalin's role in the Great Famine of 1932–3 and the persecution of many millions of Ukrainians. Khrushchev never saw Crimea or Ukraine as a great strategic asset. Similarly, neither did Yeltsin, who blocked Gorbachev's wish to keep the concept of a greater Russia intact and instead settled on Ukraine and Belarus separating from the Russian Federation. In December 1991, following a remarkable turnout, 92.3 per cent voted overwhelmingly for independence in Ukraine. In 2022, we witnessed Putin trying by force of arms to turn around the basic restructuring of Russia and its neighbours, which by common consent had stood for thirty years and been recognised by the UN and every international organisation. In retrospect, the decision of Prime Minister Cameron not to be involved in the Minsk negotiations was a blessing since it meant that Prime Minister Boris Johnson was not circumscribed by what had gone before in those negotiations in the same way that Germany and France were. He was free to identify the UK with President Zelensky's determination to fight to maintain the independence of Ukraine.

That determination had deep roots in three Maidan

demonstrations ('Maidan' is Ukrainian for 'square'). The first was on 2 October 1990 when students from Kyiv, Lviv, and Dnipropetrovsk began a hunger strike in Kyiv, demanding the resignation of Prime Minister Vitaliy Masol, and the withdrawal from the new union treaty, which was Gorbachev's attempt to save the union by giving its constituent republics greater autonomy.[73] Encouraged by Kravchuk and moderate parliamentarians, the Communist majority retreated. The second Maidan protest – also known as the Orange Revolution – occurred in 2004, during which Yushchenko and Yanukovych, the latter being Putin's choice of candidate, faced each other in the most strongly contested presidential election. During the campaign Yushchenko fell ill and his face was disfigured. It was subsequently confirmed he had been poisoned by some form of dioxin. After treatment he returned to the election campaign and exit polls showed him clearly in the lead, but the official results placed Yanukovych in the lead. Thousands protested the election fraud and eventually the president, under pressure too from European politicians, announced a new election. On 26 December 2004 Yushchenko became president and set about bringing the country closer to Europe. Unfortunately, having already accepted ten countries as new EU members, including seven which were former Soviet satellites, the EU was cautious about any further enlargement, and instead of accession only offered Ukraine a plan for closer cooperation. Political turmoil marked much of Yushchenko's presidency, and in 2010 Yanukovych narrowly beat Yulia Tymoshenko in a run-off poll. In April 2010, following a fractious parliamentary debate, Ukraine agreed to extend Russia's lease of the port at Sevastopol, originally set to expire in 2017, until 2042. In exchange, Ukraine would receive a reduction in the price of Russian natural gas.

The Yanukovych administration continued its pivot towards Moscow when it officially abandoned its goal of joining NATO. The third Maidan took place in 2013 and 2014 in the wake of the unfulfilled expectations of the Orange Revolution. Protests began in late 2013 demanding reform, the end of corruption, and closer ties to the EU. On 20 February 2014 Bohdan Solchanyk, a budding poet, travelled to Kyiv to join the protests. He and others were killed by sniper fire and became known as the 'Heavenly Hundred', with more than one hundred being killed during the first two months of 2014.

Many eminent foreigners over the years have, in good faith, warned Ukraine to abandon the path of resisting Russian claims on its territory and independence. One such person was President George H. W. Bush, who, on 1 August 1991, taking Gorbachev's side, flew from Moscow to Kyiv to try to persuade Ukraine to stay within the USSR. His unwise intervention was forever called, by US journalists, his 'Chicken Kiev' speech. Another was Henry Kissinger, who spoke to the rich and supposedly influential people at the Davos conference in May 2022 arguing that some kind of peace must eventually be negotiated and stating that the dividing line between Ukraine and Russia should return to the 'status quo ante',[74] meaning the situation before 24 February 2022 when parts of the Donetsk and Luhansk provinces were under the control of pro-Moscow separatists and Crimea was part of Russia, as had been the case since 2014. In the midst of war, it is wiser for those leaders not from the countries involved to avoid wading in on the exact details of the compromises necessary to bring an end to the conflict; the best compromises are hammered out in the negotiating room between the two warring countries.

In writing the earlier hardback version of this book in

September 2021 I did not foresee that Putin would take military action and invade Ukraine a second time. Nor that the Ukrainians would put up such a magnificent resistance. Wiser now, I've come to know two wider truths. Firstly, never underestimate a Russian leader's capacity to lie unchecked. Secondly, for Ukraine, hope is the spirit's youth. NATO must ensure their country remains defiant and undefeated.

10

Britain, Russia, and the Wider World

Russia is no longer a Communist state – that was Yeltsin's great achievement – and Putin has not sought to bring back Communism and the rule of the Politburo. Even during the Soviet Communist era, Churchill, once a scourge of the Bolsheviks, worked as a partner with Stalin during the Second World War. Even when he became prime minister again in the early 1950s he wanted to resume contact. The dialogue with Russia continued, albeit with varying intensity, with Eden, Macmillan, Home, Wilson, Heath, Callaghan, and Thatcher all dealing with their Communist counterparts through the depths of the Cold War: Khrushchev, Brezhnev, Andropov, and Chernenko. It became much easier to engage with Russia under Gorbachev and Yeltsin. Initially, this continued with Putin, but it has undoubtedly become much more difficult for Western leaders to deal with President Putin the longer he has stayed in office. Russia is now identified by the UK officially as posing 'the most acute threat to our security' in the British government's *Integrated Review of Security, Defence, Development and Foreign Policy*,[1] and even the usually balanced *Economist* is describing it as a 'thuggish kleptocracy'.[2] Finding a starting point again for future engagement will not be straightforward. Still, common interest remains, not least in tackling the world's two great challenges: climate change and nuclear arms control.

Any British prime minister should work to build a dialogue with Russia, even if at times adopting a very minimalist position. It will be for Ukraine to determine in direct talks the nature of any settlement, but UK influence on Ukraine will reflect the very considerable levels of support that we have given through NATO, at G7 meetings, and in the UN. Russia's disregard for international norms is not new, but Putin's Russia has shown its disregard in unprecedented and extensive international campaigns of misinformation and disinformation. What the Ukrainians have bravely demonstrated is the limited nature of the power of Putin's armed forces. They are nowhere as strong as those of Stalin in 1948 when NATO was created as a defensive alliance against the USSR. NATO must now avoid an inadvertent World War III and yet stop any dreams Putin might have of becoming a superpower again. China is a superpower and understands the realities of Russia's power base, but from time to time it fosters Russian illusions that suit China. Against the background of the Russia–Ukraine war is an opportunity for the US to reassess China, and for China to reassess the US. There is nothing inevitable about a US–China military clash. The post-Brexit UK is right to be part of the Indo-Pacific initiative.

Successive British governments, during a headlong race to cultivate commercial relationships, took a long time to understand the true measure of President Xi's China over the past decade, which regrettably involved turning a blind eye to a multitude of flagrant breaches of international laws and norms. These include the appalling treatment of the Uighurs, which is increasingly being brought to light, and which serves as a reminder of what China did to the Tibetans in the 1950s, their reneging on treaty obligations over Hong Kong, their increased military threat to Taiwan, and breaches of the Law of the Sea in the South China Sea. Sir Alex Younger, the former head of MI6, told BBC Radio 4's *Today* programme on 16 March 2021: 'There's no doubt that China represents the generational threat, and the reason for that is that the idea that China will become more like us as it gets richer, or as its economy matures, is clearly for the birds.' As yet, wisely, despite this threat, there has been no complete abandonment of political dialogue, nor of business contacts with China. Instead, Britain's *Integrated Review* report makes it clear that efforts will be made to better understand China. The review states:

> We will invest in enhanced China-facing capabilities, through which we will develop a better understanding of China and its people, while improving our ability to respond to the systemic challenge that it poses to our security, prosperity and values – and those of our allies and partners. We will continue to pursue a positive trade and investment relationship with China, while ensuring our national security and values are protected. We will also cooperate with China in tackling transnational challenges such as climate change.[3]

For its part, the US is now devoting much more political and military time and effort to dealing with China, and rightly so. Henry Kissinger has described tensions with China as 'the biggest problem for America, the biggest problem for the world'.[4] I am not yet convinced, as some are, that China is inexorably fixed on developing on a hostile trajectory towards the US or the UK, if for no other reason than that Xi believes in a law-based economic structure (as long as those laws have been made by the Communist Party). He may lose that respect for a Chinese law-based economy, but as yet he's shown little sign of the disrespect for all international laws that is so prevalent now in Putin's Russia.

Some influential Russian commentators in the West argue that if we had not taken the NATO decision in 2008 to expand further and had recognised the problems our actions were causing for Russian pride, not to mention genuine fears for their security, we might have stopped relations with Russia from sliding so far into hostility. I had some sympathy with these arguments prior to the second invasion of Ukraine. There are real problems that Russia now poses for its neighbours. Under Putin, Russia has chosen the force of arms to deal with the successful democratic and economic transformation of the previously Communist countries surrounding Russia. Those already in NATO and those aspiring to become NATO countries are now prepared to counter Russian attacks, and NATO has wisely chosen to help them fight to defend themselves. Where Russia failed was in making so little progress on its democratic reform agenda and only very little progress on economic market performance. Not helping Yeltsin deal with the raw capitalism that became a feature of the 1990s in Moscow and St Petersburg was a mistake made by NATO countries. One of the roots of Russia's fear of NATO expansion is the strength of some neighbouring countries' economies. The aspiring NATO member countries did not shirk from making the necessary reforms to become members of the EU, and though it took time, most accepted the discipline necessary to be able to adapt to the EU's *acquis communautaire*. To its credit, this is the course Ukraine had wanted to embark on but was blocked from doing so by Russia.

Russia now faces Ukraine being an EU candidate member, and possibly even a member of NATO. There were serious people in Yeltsin's government who wanted real market reforms, but some did not recognise that law reforms for the marketplace were an essential element. Putin's KGB hated putting into place legal market reforms. Putin's Russia thought its oil and gas reserves would shield its unreformed economy, and to some extent that has happened, but increasingly this will not be the case as even China is accepting in part the environmental pressure to reduce dependence on oil and gas.

Putin's authoritarianism took a harsher tone after he resumed the presidency in 2012, and sadly during the four years of President Medvedev too little progress was made on market reforms. Nevertheless, Russia did open up internationally. Putin's unique structures of government, it is important to recognise, differ considerably from those of the USSR even on the economy. Yet Putin has never wanted legal constraints to apply to him or his government. Putin appears to be focused on developing an ever more authoritarian system, built to some extent on the foundations of Andropov's KGB. However, Andropov was not corrupt, nor was he inclined towards prolonging and preserving power and privileges for himself and those around him. Putin's brand of personal corruption would have been anathema to Andropov.

Any semblance of collective control ended after Yeltsin. There is no proper law enhancing the Russian parliament's authority. It is a tamed Duma, which is elected but answerable to Putin's wishes, with a regional system of government controlled by Putin's single-voice decision-making. While an increasing number of Russians are critical of Putin's lengthening rule, many had regard, before his invasion of Ukraine, for his overall record in raising Russia's global profile. Putin probably thought, with some justification, that he had personally restored the credibility of the armed forces following their decline under Yeltsin. But in the initial stages of Russia's second invasion of Ukraine it became obvious that Russian military effectiveness was not what many in the West thought it to be, and its equipment was nowhere near as good as expected. As yet there are few signs in the Kremlin of Putin's power base weakening as a result of failures in Ukraine, but outside the Kremlin there are rumblings sufficient to develop into serious criticism following such obvious mistakes and false starts. Whether that will develop into a serious challenge to Putin remains to be seen, and continuing to tighten economic sanctions is vital.

To further embed his position of power, Putin has created a much bigger role for the Russian Orthodox Church, which he clearly uses to bolster his form of nationalism. As with Yeltsin, Putin was a genuinely popular leader for a period, and he still commands a measure of respect. But the Russia that is emerging is in some ways more akin to that of the tsars' authoritarian rule. For most of the tsarist era Russia was not cut off from the rest of the world. Isolation was a feature of Soviet Communism. In Putin's Russia, prior to recent sanctions, the wealthy and business leaders used to travel extensively, but they had to acknowledge their subservience to Putin's rule – as happened under the tsars. While Putin today wants Russia to be as globally expansionist as it once was under the tsars, it is likely to prove far harder to expand beyond the limited boundaries that Yeltsin set for the Russian Federation. Yet Putin is clearly focused on an expansionist agenda for rebuilding his sphere of influence and bringing areas that he sees as traditionally 'Russian' back under his control. But he underestimates the extent to which these areas have rejected his authoritarianism. Tearing up maps, as in the tsars' time, ended with the First World War. Then came Hitler, after which the practice continued under Stalin and Khrushchev, and to some extent Brezhnev, but ended with Andropov.

Putin fails to understand the lack of appeal to Russians generally of further extensions of war and being bogged down in a conflict with Ukraine. He really does seem to believe he can become a land-grabber on the scale of Peter the Great. That is a delusion in 2022, and it is why President Biden and NATO must not shift from the praiseworthy stand of defending Ukraine short of triggering World War III.

Peter the Great was born in 1672 in Moscow and died in 1725 in St Petersburg. He is known for having fought for Russia to grow into a major European power. He was both cruel and tyrannical. He founded St Petersburg in 1703, and in a victory at the Battle of Poltava in 1709 he cemented the demise of Sweden as the dominant Northern European power and assured Russia's access to the Baltic Sea. He went on to establish Russia's first navy. Putin's alignment of himself with Peter the Great is a ludicrous comparison when one considers what Russia has achieved under Putin's rule. It does not square with what the more realistic Russians know to be true. Putin is showing all the signs of acquired 'hubris syndrome', about which I have written in some detail over the years.[5]

'Hubris' is not a medical term. The most basic meaning, developed in ancient Greece, was simply a description of an act: a hubristic act was one in which a powerful figure, puffed up with overweening pride and self-confidence, treated others with insolence and contempt. He – and it was usually but not invariably a male – seemed to get kicks from using his power to treat others in this way. Such dishonouring behaviour was strongly condemned in ancient Greece. In a famous passage from Plato's *Phaedrus*, a predisposition to hubris is defined: 'But when desire irrationally drags us toward pleasures and rules within us, its rule is called excess (*hubris*).'[6] Plato saw this 'rule of desire' as something irrational that drags men into doing the wrong thing through acts of hubris. In his *Rhetoric*, Aristotle picks up the element of desire Plato identifies in hubris and argues that the pleasure someone seeks from an act of hubris lies in showing himself as superior. 'That is why the young and the wealthy are given to insults (*hubristai*, i.e. being hubristic); for they think that, in committing them (acts of hubris), they are showing superiority.'[7]

But it was in drama rather than philosophy that the notion was developed further in ancient Greece to explore the patterns of hubristic behaviour, its causes and consequences. A hubristic career proceeded along something like the following course. The hero wins glory and acclamation by achieving unwanted success against the odds. The experience then goes to his head: he begins to treat others, mere ordinary mortals, with contempt and disdain and he develops such confidence in his own ability that he begins to think himself capable of anything.

This excessive self-confidence leads him to misinterpret reality and make mistakes. Eventually he gets his comeuppance and meets his nemesis, which destroys him. 'Nemesis' is the name of the goddess of retribution, and often in Greek drama it is the gods themselves who arrange this retribution, because a hubristic act is seen as one in which the perpetrator tries to defy the reality they ordained. The hero committing the hubristic act seeks to transgress the human condition, imagining himself to be superior and to have powers more like those of the gods.

But the gods will have none of that, so it is they who destroy him. The moral is that we should be wary of allowing power and success to go to our heads. In Putin's case, his self-confidence was boosted by the 'success' of annexing Crimea. Then, in the run up to invading Ukraine, his self-imposed isolation from fear of contracting Covid arguably heightened his tendency to only listen to himself.

The theme of hubris has fascinated playwrights, no doubt because it provides the opportunity to explore human character within highly dramatic action. Shakespeare's *Coriolanus* is a study in it. But the pattern of the hubristic career is one that will immediately strike a chord in anyone who has studied the history of political leaders. The historian Ian Kershaw aptly titled the two volumes of his biography of Hitler *Hubris* and *Nemesis*.[8]

Together with contempt for others, another character trait of Putin's that has clearly intensified over the years is aggression. It could be that the muscles on display in his bodybuilding photographs – which are clearly narcissistic – are facilitated by anabolic steroids, which are well known to help increase one's pectoral muscles while also increasing one's innate aggression. They are also addictive.

Can Putin find a way to ease himself out of day-to-day political control while preserving privileges for himself and those around him? In Russian history, change has either been imposed from above or – more worryingly for Putin – as a result of revolution from below, as in 1917 and 1991. But Putin may be so hubristic that he cannot detect that he is losing support. Keeping other visiting presidents at a distance at the end of a grotesquely vast table was just one example of his self-aggrandisement.

It is interesting how Roderic Lyne, in the *InsideOut* article quoted earlier, depicts Putin's regime:

> the Kremlin has developed a doctrine largely underpinned by the ideology of the Orthodox Church which has antecedents in both Communist and Tsarist rule – a doctrine of a strong State and a Great Power which is authoritarian, nationalist, xenophobic and strongly opposed to the corrosive influence of Western liberalism.[9]

Assertive nationalism has always struck a chord with Russians. We in the West have not yet fully absorbed the fact that the annexation of Crimea was by far the most popular act of Putin's in over twenty-one years in power. Yet the first invasion does not compare to the second, which has involved the brutal killing of many, many more people, including ethnic Russians living in Ukraine and co-religionists from the region.

The stirrings of a democratic movement in Belarus were no doubt a factor in bringing on the second invasion of Ukraine. Until the invasion of Ukraine there was an international Orthodox Church spanning Russia and Ukraine which had its roots in their Christian faith. But the Ukraine Orthodox Church has now cut its ties and declared independence from the Russian Orthodox Church. Orthodoxy is also strong today in Greece and Cyprus and is reviving, after the Balkan Wars, in Serbia, parts of Bosnia-Herzegovina, Montenegro, and Macedonia, along with Catholicism in the new EU countries of Romania and Bulgaria.

Military expansion is clearly a high priority for Putin, who is hinting at further 'operations' in the future in Georgia, Moldova and Transnistria, South Ossetia, and even Lithuania in relation to the Russian enclave of Kaliningrad. The three Baltic states worry with good reason that they could be next if Putin succeeds in Ukraine. The conflict in Ukraine has shown that countries do not have to be members of NATO to be defended and supported by NATO, but in the case of the Baltic states their NATO membership carries an absolute commitment in Article 5 for other NATO members to come to their military assistance if attacked. In the wake of Ukraine there are far fewer questioning NATO will do precisely that.

Churchill was right to focus attention on what Russia sees as its national interest. Is it in the interests of Putin's Russia to become an ever-closer ally of China? You have to travel across Russia to Vladivostok, crossing eight time zones, to realise how perceptions start to change about China as you reach the Siberian oilfields and see Chinese people working where no Russians appear to want to work. The Russian population is falling. In 2020 the Russian Federation was 144.1 million, but according to the latest UN population projection it could fall to 139 million by 2040. Russia has, however, new territory within the massive Arctic zone, with global warming opening up new and potentially very important shorter maritime routes for commerce and for armed naval vessels (see map on pages x–xi), enhancing Russian influence.

I find it hard to believe that Putin or the Russian power elite under him will ever accept a relationship in which Russia plays 'second fiddle' to China any more than to the US. As we in the Western democracies seek to constrain China, we need to ask a strategic question: is it in our interest to push Russia away from Europe and closer to Xi's Communist China? That, I believe, would be a very undesirable result. Now more than ever before, having ignored the true nature of President Xi's China for too long, we need to take a long view of the true nature of Russia, as I have tried to do in this book, over the last 200 years. Russia may replace Putin, but it will never be an easy partner. In its own eyes it will always be a great power. Helping Ukraine in its battle against Russia does not mean we in the West should demean Russians' own assessment of their greatness.

Tolerance and a broader perspective are great virtues in international politics. They help to bridge divisions. We need in the West to demonstrate that we still believe in the value of being good neighbours, and that we respect nationhood. The tragedy is how much the West was beginning to respect Yeltsin's chaotic Russia and wanted to believe in Putin's slowly maturing nation. That evolving Russia can return with greater efficiency and an inbuilt respect for the laws of a market economy, but it necessitates Putin stepping back from his current position of absolute power.

History can lift one's sights as well as lower them. Britain is now standing at a turning point in its own history, one that will allow it to define its future relationships with the EU, Russia, and China, as well as the wider world. A different framework is already emerging in relation to Russia compared to that which ran from 1973 to 2020 while we were a member of the EU. The indifference with which the Cameron government, and to some extent the British people, regarded the first invasion was unfortunate. As was the inaction on the part of Germany and France in the Minsk negotiations to stop the fighting in the pro-separatist areas of the Donbas region. The Russia–Ukraine war is opening up the UK's capacity to make our own decisions again as a self-governing nation. This is something Boris Johnson as prime minister and Ben Wallace, the secretary of state for defence, seized on to the advantage of NATO and Ukraine. The UK has been involved in Ukraine over military training and later in supplying arms since 2014, which was little spoken of at the time but a wise decision. The US and UK within NATO have a rapid decision-making structure that has been able to respond far more quickly than most other EU states. The most notable EU contribution by far has come from Poland, which has responded magnificently over armaments to Ukraine and in welcoming Ukrainian refugees. In 2022 it has been easier for the UK and its people to respond more wholeheartedly without the cumbersome structure of the EU. Brexit was a policy driven by a deep-seated feeling that what began as a common market had become an ever more overarchingly intrusive European Union. After the Maastricht Treaty, though the UK opted out of the single euro currency, we were, nevertheless, affected by its restrictive procedures and rules. Once again, the eurozone is showing troubling bond spreads and the ECB president has brought forward proposals designed to deal with potential fragmentation. The UK has an independent Bank of England but the governor reports direct to the chancellor of the exchequer on inflation targets set by the chancellor. The bank's failure to come anything close to the inflation target has brought the system into disrespect; Chancellor Sunak should have demanded that the target figure was either brought down or changed it to a more realistic figure. The sight of the monthly reports missing the inflation target led to widespread indiscipline on financial matters throughout the government and a weak pound. For that the government has no one to blame but itself, and as a result it gave signals worldwide that the UK was relaxed over inflation post-Covid.

Covid-19 also showed a nation sorely ill-prepared for a pandemic. In part because of Brexit, however, the UK was able to react quickly to the urgent demand for an effective vaccine; we adopted new national procedures and had faster decision-making, as well as cooperation going far beyond national boundaries, with no EU putting outside constraints on our pharmaceutical industry. It is a great shame that the same combination of urgency and competence has not been more widespread in other areas, and it is troubling that Kate Bingham, appointed by Boris Johnson to steer the procurement and deployment of vaccines and who did so well on post-Covid pharmaceutical innovation, spoke, after she left, of Whitehall inertia and risk aversion stifling initiative.[10]

But the greatest benefit of Brexit foreign policy so far has been in the area of defence and decision-making within NATO, having put to bed false dreams of a purely EU defence. It owes much as a policy to Johnson as prime minister and Wallace as defence secretary. In the aftermath of the 2019 election – which had decisively rejected the disgraceful democratic proposition of a second referendum – there quickly emerged a post-Brexit foreign policy. NATO became the pillar of that policy. Immediately the defence budget was expanded at the temporary expense of the aid budget. It would be churlish to deny that there was a climate of opinion crossing the political divide and stemming from Brexit that drove that shift. It has resulted in a UK assertiveness in NATO that had been missing since the Suez debacle under Anthony Eden. The mood change inside the UK was recognised by John Bolton as having restored the nation's scope for independent action on the world stage; the long-serving security adviser to Republican presidents commented in Washington in June 2022 that UK policy was, 'In many respects, I say with some envy, taking a stronger and more effective view than the USA.'

The UK, no longer a member of the European External Action Service, like other members of the EU, has greater freedom to help the US develop a policy to constrain China. This came up when Australia wanted to switch from its conventional-powered submarine-building programme with France and approached the US and the UK, knowing of the two countries' close cooperation in its programme of nuclear-powered SSN attack submarines. Such a programme for the Australians would enable their navy to travel long distances in the Pacific without having to come near to the surface and expose themselves to Chinese aerial reconnaissance. Whilst Australia has no wish for such submarines to carry nuclear warheads, they will carry conventional torpedoes and possibly cruise missiles with conventional warheads. Unfortunately, and not surprisingly, the Australian decision to cancel the billion-dollar order with France triggered a diplomatic crisis in which President Macron hit out wildly, even blaming the UK.

A welcome change in the wake of Russia's second invasion of Ukraine was the new German social democrat coalition under Chancellor Scholz which replaced Angela Merkel's Christian Democrat-led coalition. Scholz made a big shift in German defence spending, as already discussed, and, despite a little backtracking, seems to have settled on a much-needed and overdue decision to have a step-like increase in German defence spending, thereby to play a bigger role in NATO.

President Macron, by contrast, before his re-election made much of his frequent discussions with Putin. Since failing to secure an overall majority in the French Assembly elections he has become a much louder critic of Putin. France, I am sure, will be able to find a majority in the Assembly to work closely in NATO with Germany, the UK, and the US to challenge Russia fighting inside Ukraine. If there is one major lesson to be learned so far from Ukraine, it is how much it still matters that the US under President Biden has been a solid NATO member, with his secretary of state, Blinken, a frequent traveller to NATO discussions in Europe – and long may that remain. Loose talk of EU defence has been destabilising NATO for far too long and should now cease.

The Afghanistan withdrawal by the US, long foreseen and spelt out by Presidents Trump and Biden, did not weaken America's attitude to NATO. American public opinion, divided on so much, was united on withdrawal, across both Democrats and Republicans, and on the wish to end 'forever wars' – not that this stopped later criticism of Biden. European NATO members were offered all the US equipment they wished for if they decided to stay but, as expected, they declined. The Biden administration and NATO's secretary general, Stoltenberg, have kept NATO united during the Russia–Ukraine war. NATO's unity has reinforced the thinking of all those who have remained loyal supporters of NATO and highly sceptical of the concept of European defence as advocated by President Macron in particular. It is that sense of solidarity that has persuaded Finland and Sweden to apply for NATO membership.

A critical advantage of having American resources behind NATO is that it gives Europeans a huge intelligence advantage over the Russian Federation, something on display day after day in the Russia–Ukraine war. It is an inconvenient fact for President Macron that French intelligence told him throughout the early stages that Putin was not going to attack Ukraine. It was US intelligence, and President Biden personally, who continuously told Europe that the Russians were going to attack Ukraine.

Russia under Putin has displayed an appalling readiness to use lethal substances such as novichok inside Russia. That readiness was extended to a Russian dissident, Alexei Navalny. On 20 August 2020, Navalny fell ill on a flight from Tomsk to Moscow. He owes his life to the pilot, who insisted on landing at Omsk airport, despite being told it was closed, so that Navalny could obtain urgent medical treatment. We now know that Navalny was in grave danger of dying from novichok poisoning.[11] Putin, somewhat surprisingly, accepted Chancellor Merkel's plea to allow Navalny to fly to Berlin for treatment. After this was agreed, German intelligence sources believe that Navalny was given a second dose in the full expectation that he would die before arrival in Germany. In Berlin, he was proven to have novichok in his body. He spent eighteen days in a coma and had to convalesce for months in Germany. In January 2021, Navalny decided to fly back to Russia.

Navalny's case has attracted worldwide attention, not least because of his courageous decision to return to Russia after months of treatment in Germany following the poisoning. In doing so he was sent straight to prison, where he continues to face ever-increasing sentences and a risk to his life. Navalny knew that to leave Russia and live abroad is exactly what President Putin wanted him to do. In deciding to return, he thus recognised a crucial point: that change in Russia must be driven from within. Many prominent Russians who have opposed the Putin regime have been threatened with similarly long and unjustified prison sentences unless they leave Russia.

Aside from his bravery, Navalny has the rare ability to make people laugh at Putin, which, while pretending to pay little attention, the president undoubtedly hates. By 2021, Navalny had a track record of posting videos exposing stories of corruption among officials and businessmen, leading street demonstrations, and risking arrest. He upped the stakes by releasing sophisticated – and lengthy – video footage revealing a luxurious palace allegedly owned by Putin in all its excess. Captured using drone technology launched from an offshore rubber dinghy, despite the estate being surrounded by a no-fly zone and a maritime buffer zone, the aerial footage of the estate was a major public relations coup for the opposition. The sheer size and unthinkable extravagance of the palace and grounds on the Black Sea, equipped with a covered landscaped ice hockey rink, was on a scale bound to anger the millions of Russian citizens whose own standard of living is being squeezed. The video circulated worldwide, and we know it has been seen by millions of people in Russia. This was coupled with a hilarious recording of Navalny tricking an FSB employee into detailing the poisoning of his underpants while posing as his superior officer. More films are likely to be released, and Putin will find it very hard to prevent their circulation without resorting to ever more intrusive blocking mechanisms for digital media. Younger Russians have enjoyed digital freedom too much to easily accept its removal.

Navalny will be lucky to come out of this alive and he knows it, as do his wife and young supporters. President Biden was right in his first foreign policy speech to strongly criticise Navalny's imprisonment. It was reminiscent for me of the criticism President Carter persistently made of Sakharov's imprisonment after he took office in 1977. In a visit to Moscow in the autumn of that year on behalf of the British government, I raised Sakharov's case with Gromyko. He brushed it aside. Sakharov, a distinguished Soviet nuclear scientist, survived hunger strikes and forced feeding, and he lived to take part in public debates with Gorbachev, sadly dying before Yeltsin, his choice for president, took office.

I profoundly hope Navalny, too, will prove to be a courageous survivor. His use of humour is very clever, and the public has clearly responded to it. But no dictator likes being ridiculed. Looking back, will Putin's imprisoning of Navalny be recognised as the moment he started to lose authority and control inside Russia? Or will it be the news of the increasingly large loss of life being suffered by Russian soldiers fighting in Ukraine that turns the tide against Putin?

We in the UK must continue to support those at all levels of Russian society who are brave enough to put their freedom and potentially their lives at risk for the cause of a more open and free society in Russia, and indeed elsewhere in the world. It is no coincidence that discussions on threats to undermine democracy, freedoms, and human rights were on the agenda of the G7 foreign ministers' meeting in London in May 2021, and their joint communiqué rightly condemned Russia's activity in these areas, including the treatment of Navalny and its behaviour in relation to Ukraine.[12] Nevertheless, the G7 correctly reiterated their interest in 'stable and predictable relations' with Russia, and they repeated their commitment to 'engage with Russia in addressing regional crises and global challenges of common interest such as climate change; arms control, disarmament and non-proliferation; and peaceful, sustainable economic development and environmental protection in the Arctic'.[13]

Unlike some authoritarian leaders, Putin prides himself on being popular in opinion polls and holding power through 'genuine' elections, but that model, initially successful, is looking increasingly hard for him to sustain, hence his efforts to neuter any real opposition. His first two terms in power went well. The US and Britain were foolish enough to invade Iraq, which proved a major distraction for them both. It forced oil and gas prices high, enabling Putin to improve living standards. Compared to the Yeltsin years, Putin also brought much-needed, and indeed much-wanted, stability. Russians felt a renewed pride in their country. As Mark Galeotti points out, many Russians 'still revere Putin for making them feel that their country matters in the world again'.[14] But he also highlights a 2017 poll carried out by the Levada Center which asked Russians about their views on reform. This revealed:

> massive differences in opinion about what kind they wanted, and how quickly it should come, and how far it should go, and the Kremlin is able to capitalise on this lack of any consensus. But at the same time it must also be deeply concerned, as while 42 per cent wanted dramatic reform and 41 per cent preferred incremental change, only 11 per cent wanted to retain the status quo.[15]

Where does this leave Putin at a time when the economy has gone into reverse due to sanctions and Russia is increasingly isolated as a result of his second invasion of Ukraine? The answer is: vulnerable.

Some Russians do still like Putin and believe that Russia needs an authoritarian leader. Putin tried the compromise of stepping down to a prime ministerial role, but he clearly did not feel comfortable playing second fiddle to Medvedev, notably during the Georgian war. Could Putin be ousted in 2022–3 if Ukraine fights on successfully and he fails to establish himself as the clear victor? Yes, in theory. Perhaps it will be the Russian economy, aided and abetted by sanctions, that forces change.

In response, Putin might decide to change his power base and assert himself as titular head of state, moving away from exercising day-to-day executive powers. But he would most certainly wish to remain commander-in-chief of the armed forces. Could Putin, backed by the Orthodox Church and the armed forces, become Tsar Vladimir? It would be a profound step to go back to that period of Russian history, but perhaps there is a halfway house, with Putin as tsar but no longer all-powerful, and the Duma developing a bigger role as part of a complex system of managed democracy. Some will scoff at Putin ever making any such changes, particularly now he has the option to remain president for life. And perhaps those who scoff will be proved right. But I have a nagging suspicion that Putin is clever enough to recognise that his present policy faces a dead end.

One thing is clear. Ukraine is Putin's personal war. In some ways Putin's position of power may make it easier for Ukraine to reach a settlement when the time comes. But in essence it can only be a deal between Ukraine and Russia. NATO has no right to suggest when and how this war should end. We must go on doing what we can but, as previously stated, we are not participants in this war. Some people find this a distinction without a difference but, in my view, it is a vital one.

But whatever path Putin chooses to go down, if there is to be any real rapprochement with the West, he needs to reassess his attempts to weaken our democracies through sophisticated cyber techniques and use of the media to disseminate blatant misrepresentations and denials of the truth. He does this, I suspect, because of what he believes the US – and in particular the then US secretary of state Hillary Clinton – did to him in his 2012 election by supporting opposition groups and criticising the electoral process. President Biden and Secretary of State

Blinken have told Putin bluntly and truthfully that his actions will hold back improved relations, whereas greater commercial contacts, trade, and mutual economic activity after a settlement in Ukraine will expand relations. The benefits of continuing down the hostile path are meagre for Russia, and it might be possible, now that Hillary Clinton's power base in politics has dwindled, for Putin to quietly drop hostile political activities in the US and other democracies.

Putin must be held to the statement he delivered to the seventy-fifth session of the UN General Assembly in September 2020, in which he spoke of the 'timeless principles ... enshrined in the UN Charter', which include 'the equality of sovereign States, non-interference with their domestic affairs, the right of peoples to determine their own future, non-use of force or the threat of force, and political settlement of disputes'.[16] Currently, Russia seems far from upholding these principles itself, and even further from being ready 'to hear and appreciate the concerns of people over the protection of their rights, such as the right to privacy, property and security', which Putin went on to talk of in that speech.[17]

Even if Putin steps back from the cyber campaigning, he will not give up spying. It has become an accepted part of international relations, and no international law can inhibit such activities. Indeed, there is a positive case to be made for spying in terms of intelligence gathering, as I mentioned earlier, if it can help reduce misunderstandings and help defuse confrontations. But that is just one aspect of espionage activities, and others are certainly much more threatening and disturbing, such as the April 2021 revelations by the Czech government that they had connected the GRU with the explosions at an arms depot which had killed two people. This was followed by the expulsion of eighteen Russian diplomats. What remains unacceptable, and cannot be allowed to go unchallenged, is espionage activity that results in collateral damage, and the threat to innocent people with no links whatever to spying. In recognition of this, we in Britain must continue building up our counter-espionage capabilities against Russian spies operating in Britain. They certainly proved very effective in investigating both the Litvinenko and Skripal cases. As a statement of intent, there is an overwhelming case now for mounting a legal challenge over the use of novichok, not just in respect of the British citizen who died but over the attack on Navalny. Britain should be actively involved, but the action needs to be sponsored by as many countries as possible, and particularly Germany because of its involvement in the Navalny case.

While the Navalny case in Russia is not an exact replica of the Sturgess case in the UK, in that he was deliberately targeted while she was an innocent casualty, they are both cases which involve individual citizens, and both attacks could have endangered other innocent citizens – particularly those travelling on the same flight as Navalny from Tomsk to Moscow when he was poisoned. It is time legal action was taken to seek a judgment that condemns state-sponsored use of such agents.

The best recent example of international action taken in similar circumstances is the decision of the Dutch government in July 2020 to sue Russia at the European Court of Human Rights for its alleged role in the shooting down of the Malaysian airliner MH17 carrying 283 passengers and fifteen crew over eastern Ukraine in 2014.[18] After six years of careful investigation, the Dutch foreign minister said that achieving justice for the 298 victims was the government's highest priority. A Russian foreign ministry spokesman, perhaps unsurprisingly given its track record in denying culpability in this and the poisoning cases, said the decision was 'another blow to Russian–Dutch relations', but such steps have to be taken if Russia is to recognise that its flaunting of international norms will not go unchallenged.[19]

The European Court of Human Rights, established in Strasbourg in 1959, is not an EU organisation but is based around the member states of the Council of Europe who signed the European Convention on Human Rights. Britain is a founder member, and Russia became a member in the late 1990s. However, in June 2022 the Russian parliament passed bills breaking ties with the Council of Europe and ending the jurisdiction of the European Court of Human Rights in the country.

Nevertheless, the use of weapons of mass destruction, WMD, in day-to-day life and their effect on individual human rights is a matter that could be put on the agenda of the UN General Assembly, which is perhaps a better world forum for exploring issues of this kind.

Equally, war crimes committed in a war zone must be tried. There have been many cases in the Russia–Ukraine war where the Laws of War have been broken: women have been raped, innocent civilians killed, houses and hospitals bombed, and inhabitants killed and wounded. There should be no general amnesty. Ukraine has already started to bring cases to trial during the war: one Russian soldier who was filmed shooting and killing a civilian has been tried and found guilty.

In considering how Britain deals with Russia in the wider foreign policy arena, it will be important to find a balance with other priorities, not least the challenges posed by China. Russia is rightly, along with four other countries, a permanent member of the UN Security Council, and it has an influential position in international diplomacy. But Russia is no longer a superpower. Arguably the most relevant criterion is whether the other superpowers – the US and China – regard Russia as a great power. It is a hard fact of life for President Putin that US presidents from George H. W. Bush onwards, after the fall of the Berlin Wall, have no longer regarded Russia as a superpower, which it undoubtedly was in the early Brezhnev years based on its military might alone. After a brief period when the US appeared unchallenged as a sole global superpower, China has risen to fill the superpower seat vacated by Russia, but with the crucial difference that it is both an economic and military power. Like Britain in the middle of the Second World War, Russia needs to accept that it is no longer a superpower and adapt accordingly.

This does not mean Russia is only a regional power. President Obama's assessment was wrong. Russia today, in my view, remains a considerable power, though primarily on the basis of its nuclear weapons strength. Russia could reinforce that position if it made serious efforts to overhaul its moribund economy. I would rank Germany similarly as a considerable power, but only because of its economic strength; France and Britain are also considerable powers because of their combined military and economic strength. Japan is beginning to assert itself internationally, and it could quite quickly match France, Britain, and Russia. So too may South Korea, and India is another contender, as the largest democracy in the world, though its economy still disappoints. India, facing increased tensions along its huge shared border with China, has started to increase its military spending. It is important that India is part of a South Asia initiative over China, a change of policy that has followed the steady improvement of US–India relations. India will always keep its relationship with Russia as long as its continuation does not damage its new improved relations with the US, and it is entitled to try for relations with all three, the US, China, and Russia. For the UK there is room for improving our relationship with India, which would fit well with our need to diversify out of the EU market.

It is likely that historians will judge the year 1976, and the death of Chairman Mao, as the start of a turnaround in China's world standing. Deng Xiaoping, the wisest yet of Chinese leaders, said, 'hide your strength, bide your time'.[20] Gradually, after far-reaching economic reforms, China's military spending started to increase. In fact, China was becoming an economic superpower before Xi became president. But what changed under Xi was his close relationship with the military, which shared his desire to see China become a military superpower. Xi has also focused on his own personal power and, like Putin, has overseen constitutional changes that effectively pave the way for him to become president for life. Xi's military power is now, in all but nuclear weapons, the second strongest in the world after the US, but in terms of nuclear capability, Russia remains stronger for now. President Biden wanted to restart negotiations with Russia on nuclear weapons and, despite China hitherto refusing, trying to involve China as well. The British government too must rediscover a greater interest in nuclear weapons reductions as part of its non-proliferation treaty obligations.

The impact of Xi on China as a superpower can scarcely be overemphasised. Under him, China has become an aggressive economic and military superpower. Its aggression has so far been confined to industrial espionage, flagrant abuse of international laws connected with fishing rights, and the creation of military bases out of rocks and reefs in the South China

Sea with no regard to the international Law of the Sea. President Xi's actions in 2020 over Hong Kong are particularly ominous. They are undoubtedly illegal in international law, breaching the terms of the international treaty Deng Xiaoping made with Margaret Thatcher enshrining the principle of 'one country, two systems'. And the pace at which President Xi has dismantled Hong Kong's democracy through the purging of pro-democracy lawmakers points to serious trouble ahead for Taiwan. UK policy on Hong Kong has been sound and honourable, and offering Hong Kong people the right to come to the UK will bring technological expertise that will add value in every respect to the UK.

China presents new and far-reaching challenges, above all, for President Biden, who started to shift his position markedly during the presidential election campaign and, for better or for worse, called Xi a 'thug'. Some claim the chances of the Chinese military invading Taiwan have now increased following the Russia–Ukraine war, and the US military has embarked on a wide-ranging strategy to deter such an act. This builds on developments over the past few years that have seen the beginnings of what promises to be a massive shift in US defence attitudes to preparing to deal with a rival military nuclear superpower in the form of China.

How to deal with China's rise in power was high on the agenda of the G7 meeting hosted by Britain in 2021, which was in effect a D10 meeting, bringing together ten democracies: the original G7 plus India, Australia, and South Korea. The ten will all be involved in a new Indo-Pacific strategy, but reaching consensus on action will be a challenge as the three EU members – Germany in particular, but also Italy and, hopefully to a lesser extent, France – will be hesitant over the risks to their trading relationships with China. This is also a challenging aspect for Britain, which saw increased trade with China as a major post-Brexit opportunity. The EU pushing ahead in December 2020 with a trade arrangement with China, after being asked by the incoming Biden administration to reassess, was a sign of how trade priorities can differ between NATO countries. The situation is delicate, and delicacy – so much the hallmark of the former president of the European Commission Jacques Delors – is not present in today's Commission, which has become far too large.

The US Department of State published a report entitled 'A Free and Open Indo-Pacific: Advancing a Shared Vision' in November 2019 under President Trump. It has developed since and will continue to develop under President Biden. This relatively new policy in Asia, which has broad-based support in the US Congress, will need all the political unity it can in constraining and, if need be, confronting China, particularly as China has already set out its stall in terms of its view on the US. In March 2021, at a round-table meeting in Alaska, China's top foreign affairs policymaker Yang Jiechi, speaking directly to his US counterparts, said: 'The United States does not have the qualification ... to speak to China from a position of strength.'[21] That statement could not have been made by any other country to the US president's team of senior advisers. China was not claiming superiority in any specific area, but rather expressing its confidence in its own position and giving an objective evaluation of how it sees that position developing. China is inevitably going to seek a greater role beyond East and South-East Asia, and the UK should be ready to engage with it on major global initiatives.

Like the Western democracies, Russia also faces problems

over how to respond to Xi's China. It is even clearer than in the case of the US that China does not consider Russia an equal, and even less so following Russia's military performance in Ukraine. It is a new experience for Russia to watch China – a latecomer to Communism – now replace it as a superpower and start to pull further away. At the same time, Chinese Communism, having developed a vibrant economy, must maintain its dynamism to stay ahead. China watches Russia with some apprehension, remembering how Russia suffered massive disruption as its Communist system imploded following the collapse of the Berlin Wall. Despite its continued authoritarian model, Russia has failed to make anything like the economic progress China has, remaining very dependent on the exploitation of natural resources. But Russia will never fit easily into a junior relationship with any country in the world. If the Biden administration could become more sensitive to deep-seated Russian views than the Obama administration was then geopolitics might start to rebalance. An independent Russia, not under Chinese dominance, is the preferable outcome for both the US and for Britain.

As I hope I have made clear, Britain's commitment to helping Ukraine has so far been very well judged, and this must continue under the new Conservative prime minister, Liz Truss. In the first few months of the war starting, Britain supplied anti-tank weapons, long-range rockets, short-range missiles, armoured vehicles, drones, and air defence systems. It also supplied 200,000 non-lethal assistance items including body armour, helmets, night-vision equipment, and GPS jamming devices. In his second visit to Kyiv in June 2022, Boris Johnson also announced a major expansion of our training programme for Ukrainian forces whilst warning that 'we need to steel ourselves for a long war, as Putin resorts to a campaign of attrition, trying to grind down Ukraine by sheer brutality. The UK and our friends must respond by ensuring that Ukraine has the strategic endurance to survive and eventually prevail.'[22]

Besides increasing spending on the armed forces substantially, Britain is participating politically and militarily to the fullest extent in NATO. At the same time, it has reversed its late 1970s retreat from 'East of Suez' with a renewed Indo-Pacific naval orientation. This will strain our defence budget, but it will also help the US maintain its NATO commitment and so is a positive development. Similarly, France is doing much the same with its ties to islands in the Pacific. Post-Brexit commitments to help British business open up commercial markets outside the EU are making progress, but they still have a long way to go given the considerable potential. In concrete terms, a vital defence contribution continues under the intelligence partnership developed over many years between the 'Five Eyes' countries: the US, Britain, Canada, Australia, and New Zealand. Britain, however, now has two new aircraft carriers whose overseas base was always planned to be in Oman, and they should remain based there for the present. In November 2020, the government announced that it would give priority to the extra escort vessels needed for those carriers to operate in a hostile environment far from British waters, a critical enhancement to its ability to deploy these powerful new additions to its fleet flexibly. The Royal Navy has long been involved in helping prevent interference to the free movement of ships in the Straits of Hormuz at the mouth of the Gulf. Now, if necessary, the UK aircraft carriers can free up a US carrier normally positioned there if it is required more in the South China Sea or, indeed, a British carrier may well be able to deploy to the South

China Sea on a longer-term basis.[23] In addition, Britain will be building up an operational relationship with the Indian Navy. Pakistan, despite its long-term relationship with China and its irresponsible contribution in the past to nuclear weapons proliferation, should not be ignored. Past tensions over Pakistan's military intelligence activities in relation to Afghanistan will ease now British troops are no longer involved on the ground.

It will require discipline within British defence and foreign policy to ensure we allocate resources to Asian security priorities that do not damage our primary task, which is to strengthen NATO. Deploying a British carrier to the South China Sea permanently would stretch our naval resources, though undoubtably the US navy would from time to time help provide some of the necessary escort vessels, along with Australia, New Zealand, Japan, and South Korea. Realistically the UK will no longer take a leading political role since President Xi tore up our mutual international treaty over Hong Kong, but we should maintain our long-held trading presence in Hong Kong.

It is essential, as I have repeated several times in this book, that Britain's primary post-Brexit vehicle for foreign and security policy remains NATO. The UK's mission must be focused on reviving and strengthening, by example, the European input into NATO. We should not get drawn into any involvement with an EU military organisational headquarters separate from NATO. Hopefully, after events in Ukraine, the EU will be adjusting its thinking on this. In 2017 NATO chose to adapt its command structure. Its key elements include a new Command for the Atlantic to ensure that sea lines of communication between Europe and North America remain free and secure; a new Command to improve the movement of troops and equipment within Europe; reinforcing logistics elements across NATO's command structure in Europe; and a new cyber operations centre to strengthen cyber defences and integrate cyber capabilities into NATO planning and operations.

Few people in Europe know how far the military in France and in the UK have gone in honouring the Lancaster House Treaties of 2010 between David Cameron and Nicolas Sarkozy with a view to enhancing military interoperability. Nothing underlines this more than the fact that a French brigadier general, Jean Laurentin, for a period commanded one of the UK's elite army divisions. It is an extraordinary example of Anglo-French military cooperation and friendship that would astonish naysayers of our relationship on both sides of the Channel. I have sailed from the West Country into too many French ports over the years to believe that Anglo-French relations will remain as strained as at present. President Macron's 'Jupiter' phase has come unstuck. He will move to build better relations between Paris and London as his dream of one country called Europe within the EU is blocked by a French Assembly he no longer controls.

With Keir Starmer announcing Labour will not return to the EU single market or the customs union nor allow free movement of people from the EU, Brexit is a settled cross-party reality. Germany will remain France's essential friend, but the UK's relationship with both of them will develop an enduring quality across a number of international forums. Brexit was never a policy for the short term but a major repositioning on the same scale as the Reformation.

Post-Brexit, the Conservative government has been far too slow in changing the climate in relation to the EU and finding an acceptable and lasting dispute procedure. The EU's European Court of Justice (ECJ) was always going to be unacceptable to the UK. An alternative could be part of the Vienna arbitration procedures, or what the EU once offered Switzerland, to 'dock' alongside the EFTA Court without joining the EEA. Sometime, hopefully sooner rather than later, an acceptable form of resolving disputes will be agreed and the EU and UK will then find it much easier to develop a closer and respectful relationship with the EU as a whole, the individual countries within it, and those countries aspiring to be members.

The British government led by Boris Johnson was right, in its first major foreign policy decision since leaving the EU, to find extra funding for an exceptional four-year commitment to the defence budget amounting to 2.2 per cent of our GDP, even amid Covid-19. Such a decision could only have come from a government determined to prioritise defence and face up to the threats posed by President Putin and President Xi. The relevant extract from the spending review states:

> Defence is a central pillar of the government's ambitions to safeguard the UK's interests and values, strengthen its global influence, and work with allies to defend free and open societies. SR20 provides Defence with additional funding of over £24 billion in cash terms over four years, including £6.6 billion of R&D, to maintain a cutting-edge military. This settlement means that the Defence budget will grow at an average of 1.8 per cent per year in real terms from 2019–20 to 2024–25. This reaffirms the UK's commitment to its allies, making the UK the largest European spender on defence in NATO and the second largest in the Alliance.

Even so, the chair of the Public Accounts Committee has warned, given the financial mess in which UK defence procurement finds itself, that this money is going to be insufficient. Even without the challenges of the procurement system, it will not be possible to continue to help Ukraine militarily as much as we have so far without additional funding, and the new Conservative prime minister, Liz Truss, must recognise this in the autumn of 2022. At the G7 meeting in Madrid in June 2022 Boris Johnson pledged an additional £1 billion in military aid to Ukraine, saying, quite rightly, that the cost of freedom was worth paying for. He also pledged defence spending would rise to 2.5 per cent by 2030. But we must be realistic: that commitment may only be sustained if our economic performance improves. The then chancellor Rishi Sunak was right to call for overseas aid spending to contribute as part of an overall new realism in the wake of unprecedented government borrowing during the pandemic. This helps, but does not meet our continuing extra expenditure on Ukraine. The legislative requirement of 0.7 per cent of gross national income, fixed by parliament for the aid budget, has always had built into it the flexibility to be reduced in exceptional circumstances. The year 2022 will be, by any practical test, such a year, as will 2023 and I suspect 2024. When our economy hopefully recovers by the end of 2024, we should aim to continue our long-term 0.7 per cent commitment to overseas aid.

With the Foreign, Commonwealth and Development Office (FCDO), to give it its new full title, having rightly regained control of that overseas aid budget, just as was the case when I was foreign secretary, I am glad to see that it is starting to develop a much greater realism to fit within the government's overall global strategy. The UK must improve its economic performance in order to proceed on both the 0.7% aid spending and make a quantum leap in defence spending. We must reassess how our support is delivered to countries, some of them in the Commonwealth, that do not live up to reasonable expectations in terms of good governance. There should be little aid to governments who have, in effect, 'presidents for life'. This deeply damaging concept shows signs of growing again, and our aid risks becoming a fig leaf behind which such presidents abuse human rights. In such countries, and other countries with poor human rights records, aid might best be delivered through independent NGOs rather than through government-controlled infrastructures. The FCDO must also try to spend more on promoting poor countries' economic growth while also promoting British trade and products, with a new emphasis upon building an Indo-Pacific policy. Closer to home, we should continue to consider assisting some EU countries, as well as other European countries currently outside the EU, such as Albania, Bosnia-Herzegovina, Kosovo, North Macedonia, Moldova, Montenegro, and Serbia, and it should make no difference that many of these countries are candidate countries to join the EU – including Ukraine and Moldova, who recently gained candidacy approval following Macron, Scholz, and Draghi's welcome visit to Kyiv in June 2022. Where possible, aid should also be considered for Kazakhstan, Mongolia, and Uzbekistan, countries that are becoming increasingly worried about a more assertive Russia and China. These countries can help us to influence the Taliban in Afghanistan.

On 25 April 2021, the *Observer* carried an article under the title 'UK aid cut seen as unforced error in a "year of British leadership"'. The article focused on the £4 billion cut in the aid budget being matched by an extra £4.4 billion for defence in 2021–2, commenting that, 'As choices go, this could not have been a clearer endorsement of traditional hard power over Joseph Nye's soft power.'[24] Subsequent events have shown that the UK chose wisely. Traditional hard power has been neglected by successive British governments in recent years. We must learn from the past: the UK did not rise to the challenge of the new and growing defence threat from Putin's Russia nor of President Xi's China. Hard power can be supplemented by soft power, but it cannot be replaced by soft power.

With its excellent secretary-general Jens Stoltenberg, NATO has demonstrated in Ukraine that it can operate in circumstances of great political difficulty. What NATO needs to develop is not emergency power so much as a continuing power in areas of dispute and priority. Eventually dialogue between NATO and Russia will need to develop to cover all border disputes in Europe. There is room too to develop a framework for a collective dialogue with China, complementing the separate arrangements that some NATO countries are already making for security in Asia. Stoltenberg is also commendably using the NATO framework to address the problems in the east Mediterranean economic zone, in particular helping to build a Greek–Turkish–Cypriot dialogue, especially in the light of disputes over their oil and gas reserves. The UK should support this dialogue, while working broadly to help keep Turkey within the NATO fold. A settlement in Cyprus is still feasible. What went on during the Greek Cypriot takeover in 1963, followed by a Greek-backed coup in 1974 and, soon after, the Turkish invasion and occupation of Northern Cyprus, is not fixed in concrete. I visited the island in 1976 as minister for Europe and met all its leaders, including Archbishop Makarios. I have never stopped believing that a negotiated settlement can be reached if all parties take a common-sense and logical approach.

The essence of NATO is that it was built on Kennan's concept of 'containment'. When we look at building what some dub an 'Asian NATO', we should start from a different basis. We cannot 'contain' China as we did Russia. China is integrated into the global economy in a way that Stalin's Russia was not in 1948 and nor is Putin's Russia still in 2022. China is a critical element in international supply chains in ways that Russia will never come close to matching. A better word is to 'constrain' China. We are thankfully still some distance from calling China the adversary, a word NATO has regretfully had to reapply to Putin's Russia over Ukraine. We have serious disagreements with China, but there are some grounds for believing that with luck and persistence these can be, if not overcome, then 'constrained'. There are plenty of international forums in which we work constructively with China and should continue to do so.

As for Russia, it will remain a force to be reckoned with militarily, as it seeks to emphasise and to enhance its missile capabilities and test NATO's defences. Its military expenditure spiked in 2016 to a staggering 5.4 per cent of GDP, and in 2019 it was still at 3.8 per cent. President Putin has admitted that he considered putting Russian nuclear forces on full alert during maximum tension over Crimea, demonstrating that Russian nuclear strategies are nowhere near as cautious as ours in NATO. It is also true that President Putin has threatened to base nuclear forces in Crimea and has deployed missiles capable of carrying nuclear warheads in Kaliningrad, the Russian military enclave on the Baltic Sea that continued even after the collapse of the Berlin Wall. Since 2019, Russia has also invested in seven military bases on its Arctic coast, part of the opening up of a new military sea route due to global warming, where the Arctic Ocean is becoming ice-free. The Russian war against Ukraine has shown we should never underestimate the military threat Russia can pose to NATO. But we should still do all we can to avoid becoming inexorably locked into an arms race with Russia. There is, however, no escaping genuine concern over Russia's military focus on Estonia, Latvia, and Lithuania in the wake of Ukraine. Hitherto, there was a belief among informed NATO military personnel that Russian forces could punch a hole in NATO's defences in the Baltic region in a limited conventional conflict. This concern is perhaps slightly less in view of Russia's poor military performance in Ukraine, but Putin's ambitions concerning this region remain a threat. Britain, as part of NATO, must therefore continue to deploy extra troops on the ground in the Baltic States and, if appropriate, be ready to further increase them.

Russia has also rapidly developed its capabilities under Putin in the field of hybrid warfare. In this arena, Russian activity has been characterised by misinformation, unconventional activity, and ambiguity, at a level deliberately kept below the threshold that would involve conventional conflict and carefully planned to avert political and economic sanctions. The situation in Ukraine has involved hybrid warfare techniques which could now escalate beyond its confines. The ongoing danger of Russia's strategy over Ukraine is that it could undermine confidence in deterrence, and that in itself is destabilising.

All nuclear-weapon states have a duty to try to restore dialogue and negotiation. Hopefully President Biden will return, albeit with caution, to the type of nuclear weapons negotiations that made significant progress under Nixon, Reagan, and Clinton. Reagan and Gorbachev's nuclear negotiations in particular were both surprising and successful. But the long-standing risks of nuclear accidents, of overreaction and misunderstanding, have not gone away. The absence of any real dialogue on such matters, a hallmark of the recent past, is neither wise nor sustainable. It is encouraging that Biden, in one of his first decisions on taking up office, had proposed to Russia a five-year extension to START, which limits each country's number of nuclear warheads and to which Russia had given an initial welcome. Britain should also try to develop a better bilateral relationship with Russia over nuclear, chemical, and biological weapons. To have no dialogue is simply too dangerous. Furthermore, arms control discussions are not incompatible with spending on nuclear weapons; Britain has successfully followed this strategy of minimum nuclear deterrence for half a century.

As I alluded to earlier, I think it is important for Western leaders to try to put themselves in the shoes of, if not Putin himself, then the wider Russian population and to try to understand how their actions look from their perspective. In that regard, I have found Andrew Monaghan's book *The New Politics of Russia: Interpreting Change* a thought-provoking examination of how we all might start to readjust attitudes. He writes about 'strong linguistic dissonance, both in terms of translation and different interpretation of terminology', suggesting that the crisis in Ukraine has revealed that the West and Russia are speaking different dialects on security.[25] In Western terms, for instance, Crimea was 'annexed' by Russia, but in Russian terms, Crimea was 'reunified' with Russia. Similarly, NATO's policy is of an 'open door' or 'enlargement', whereas the Russian term is 'expansion'. These issues were also highlighted in the conclusions of the House of Lords 2015 report on the crisis in Ukraine.

While we are clear that NATO is a defensive alliance, for the Russians NATO is seen as a hostile military threat, and successive rounds of NATO's eastern enlargement have, as the Russians see it, brought it threateningly close to the Russian border. EU enlargement, as it has become conflated with NATO enlargement, has also taken on the aspect of a security threat. These views are sincerely and widely held in Russia, and need to be factored into Member States' strategic analyses of Russian actions and policies.[26]

Trying to understand what lies at the root of these differences in nuance and interpretation may help lead to a more constructive dialogue. There are, however, no excuses for Putin's military conduct in Ukraine. We are now seeing violence against civilians on a massive scale and indiscriminate bombing of civilian homes and shopping centres. The worldwide consequences of the destruction and looting of much of Ukraine's food exports is a scandal. The famine in Ukraine in 1932–3, which Stalin viciously exploited, as hauntingly explained in Anne Applebaum's recent book, has a renewed resonance today in many parts of Ukraine.[27] Little did many realise famine could be exported from Ukraine to the wider world in 2022. Global supply lines are a vital part of any settlement and Ukrainian retention of the port of Odesa is of world concern.

NATO's key differences with Russia are not simply the result of differences of perspective. Russia, by any objective standard, has repeatedly flouted international law in both its invasion of Ukraine and conduct in the war. In so doing it has exposed its own conventional military weaknesses, and as a result Moscow may feel more strategically vulnerable than the USSR did at any stage during the Cold War. NATO should recognise and seek to address this feeling of Russian vulnerability urgently without giving Russia any explicit veto on NATO's decision-making or Ukraine's. Boundary dispute settlement procedures across Europe and future membership of NATO could be on the political agenda. President Biden and his secretary of state, Blinken, may need time to weigh up and fully develop a coherent policy within NATO and with Ukraine before engaging with Russia on these fundamental issues.

At a time when the US has growing problems with China, any NATO decision must also be set in an overall geopolitical strategy of geographically limiting the areas of potential confrontation with Russia. Such NATO decisions cannot be expected to happen quickly. There is a lot of history to revisit and resolve, some of which is covered in the previous chapter, and it will be important to try to understand how it all looks from a Russian standpoint. There should be an open discussion about what lies behind Russian fears of NATO membership being extended to cover Georgia, for example, the prospect of which Biden raised in his presidential race against Trump. NATO's dilemma regarding Ukraine is obvious. Belarus is also becoming an immediate subject for discussion, with missiles coming directly from here into Ukraine. There is growing dissent in Belarus with its present president's performance. Fears over Sweden and Finland joining NATO may have heightened Moscow's feeling of being surrounded, but these are the unforeseen consequences of Putin's attack on Ukraine. Politics has its own dynamics and, as we have seen, so has Russia.

It is inevitable and right that economic sanctions related to the two invasions of Ukraine will remain while negotiations proceed. The Minsk I and II format involving Ukraine, Russia, and the Organization for Security and Co-operation, represented by Germany and France, never gelled and now it must be a bilateral negotiation between Ukraine and Russia. Russia may only be constructive as part of a search for an over-arching solution in which it might be felt appropriate to address disputed boundaries and recognition issues, such as Transnis-tria, Kosovo, and Georgia. While challenging, all these dis-putes have the potential for trade-offs that could make success more likely. In the short term, however, there can be no replac-ing a direct dialogue between the president of Russia and the president of Ukraine to bring the second military invasion to an end.

The Ukrainian government accepted becoming a non-nuclear state in 1994 and in return the Budapest Memorandum signed that year by the US, Britain, and Russia, with separate agreements too with China and France, provided security assurances to Ukraine. That Memorandum was reconfirmed as recently as December 2009 by the US and Russia. It is yet another example of how Putin's Russia has complete disregard for international agreements.

I have argued earlier in this book that it will also be import-ant to see how constructive Russia is in other areas where it has an influence, notably the Middle East. President Putin has made his mark in this region and follows developments there closely. I hope Prime Minister Liz Truss and President Biden will start to talk seriously to Putin, both on addressing the threat posed by Iran and on generating a renewed impetus for a broader negoti-ated settlement of issues across the Middle East.

In coming to the end of this book, I would like to take a step back and look at the wider issues facing the world today. History certainly did not end with the fall of Communism in Europe. What was once seen by many as an unchallengeable universal aspiration, liberal democracy – as so defined in the West – has been challenged, and harshly so. The world is seeing a rise in authoritarianism, including in the heart of Europe, where leaders such as Hungary's Viktor Orbán are posing fundamental challenges for the EU, which commendably has always been ready to embrace the countries emerging from the ruins of Communism.

The commentator on anti-democratic trends in Europe Anne Applebaum gives an excellent account of this in her recent book *The Twilight of Democracy*.[28] Against the present backdrop, the writings of a foremost proponent of liberal internationalism, John Ikenberry, are valuable. In his new book *A World Safe for Democracy*, he writes about how liberal internationalism 'is not a fixed doctrine but a family of evolving – and often conflicting – ideas, doctrines, projects and movements'.[29] He points out that, since the Cold War ended, 'a set of bargains that held this core grouping together has slowly weakened',[30] and that the changing internal politics of the US, which made possible the Trump presidency, has unsettled the liberal order. During the Cold War, Ikenberry claims that the economic foundations of this security community were organised around what John Ruggie, the Harvard professor on human rights and international affairs, calls 'embedded liberalism'.[31] But market expansion, he admits, created 'new, sharp economic divides between winners and losers in Western societies, while weakening embedded liberal supports and protections'.[32] Indeed, we have seen the growing divides between economic winners and losers in Russia and other post-Communist states as they tried to adopt the Western market model, and these are at the root of many of their – and our – problems.

The Western democracies cannot stay fixated on an outdated

model of economic liberalism that in some instances has failed. We need to develop a new combination of capitalism and community, a model that I have often called in the British political debate a social market economy. We have allowed great inequalities of income distribution, job opportunities, and life chances under Western capitalism, in particular in its Anglo-Saxon form. In the aftermath of the Covid-19 pandemic, Britain and the US need to look again at adapting the model of capitalism that we have both championed for decades to better address the complexities of our modern world. Social concern and social market attitudes need to be designed into a new economic world model. There are some encouraging signs from the Biden administration, helped by the former head of the Federal Reserve Bank Janet Yellen, now secretary of the treasury, and Senator Bernie Sanders, too often decried, that its policies are pointing in this direction. Yet Americans are likely, for their own historical reasons, to eschew the word 'social' let alone 'socialism', which for many in the United States is considered almost inseparable from Communism. Russia, on the other hand, might accept 'social market' but would eschew 'liberal order'. China seems all too happy to stay with the word 'Communism'. In the Lisbon Treaty, meanwhile, the EU has accepted 'social market' into its constitution. While the direction must not be lost in a debate around semantics, what relevance does the word 'communism' now have? It went without anyone really noticing in Cuba and in North Korea. It went under Yeltsin in Russia and was eroded under Deng Xiaoping in China. Now neither President Putin nor President Xi are practising Communism in the traditional sense of the word, but authoritarianism is very much in evidence. In effect we are seeing sole decision-makers eroding collective decision-making, hitherto one of the main distinctive features of Chinese and Russian Communism. The world will have to wait to see if authoritarianism succeeds in China and Russia. The omens are not good.

We must be ready, therefore, to think afresh on many issues in a post-Covid-19 world. This horrendous pandemic has shaken the world up. There seems to be some agreement at least on concrete proposals to prevent damage to our environment. Hitherto, environmental protection has been divisive and resisted. The UN Climate Change Conference (COP26), held in Glasgow in November 2021, contained many new pledges and commitments in its final statement, but within it many compromises could be found – not least a weakening of target deadlines. What's more, the biggest consumers of polluting fossil fuels – the US, China, and Russia – refused to sign the Global Coal to Clean Power Transition statement. One of the important initiatives to be achieved was for the US and more than 100 other countries to reduce methane emissions by 30 per cent by 2030 compared to 2020. There is no doubt President Biden wants to raise global ambition during this decisive decade of climate action, but it may not always be possible to carry Congress with him. The ruling by the Supreme Court in June 2022 to constrain the Environmental Protection Agency's authority to regulate emissions from existing coal- and gas-fired power plants will have dealt quite a blow to Biden's, and in particular Senator John Kerry's, efforts to persuade the rest of the world to do more. Unfortunately, Russia is a bystander in this debate. A huge challenge exists in the old rust-belt industrial areas in many countries, not least in the US and Britain, as well as in the EU, Russia, and India. Nowhere near enough financial support is yet available to tackle their environmental legacy. The key question, particularly for the old industrialised economies, will remain how to balance environmental concerns while staying competitive in a world that is slowly abandoning the structures that allowed free trade to dominate.

Free trade must not be abandoned; to do so would be to threaten technological development, scientific discovery, and improved standards of living. Instead, we need a much wider acceptance of the concepts that underpin social harmony and living well alongside each other as nations and communities with different income levels – but not different opportunities – for the younger generations. Ikenberry argues that the unique interest and values that bring liberal democracies together mean that:

> They need each other in order to act together in a way that gives them a critical mass in world politics. But in the twenty-first century, the storms of modernity are also global. Liberal internationalists will need to gather their two hundred years of ideas and projects into a grand effort – illuminated by ideals but grounded in pragmatism – to ensure not just the future of democracy but the survival of the planet.[33]

These are wonderful words, but they are narrowed in the eyes of many readers by the associated qualifying words. Here, words do matter. I would prefer new thinkers, whether they live in Britain, the Russian Federation, China, the US, or the EU, to accept that most of our citizens see their lives in terms of birth and death. The hope is that more and more people, as over the environment, will see their lives also in terms of international wellbeing. For that to begin to happen in all countries, we would be wise to stop using qualifying terms internationally, like 'liberal order' or 'social market' and others like them

– such as 'private capital' or 'religious values' – when discussing internationalism. Most such qualifying words have different connotations in different countries. We should settle for simply 'internationalist' alone. 'Democracy' too. We know both when we see them in practice. The same applies to 'order' or 'market'. I do not see the need for controversial qualifications to be attached to these four very basic words when used in an international context. Let the four words stand also in domestic national debate – internationalism, democracy, order, markets. We must constantly explain in speeches and writing what these four words mean and, in the process, clarify their breadth of meaning and the importance of achieving them. 'Communism' is not a word Xi's China shies away from using, yet authoritarianism maybe a better description for Xi's and Putin's styles of government. To let a qualifying word predetermine what is a democracy, what is internationalism, weakens both words. Let the qualities of internationalism and democracy be encapsulated internationally in a single word as well as order and the market. What we need post-Covid-19 is global engagement, tolerance of different viewpoints, and a readiness amongst states to learn from and help each other.

In closing, I shall return to the central theme of this book and pose the question: what does the future hold for Russian–British relations under President Vladimir Putin and our new British prime minister, Liz Truss? I see many key common factors. Both countries have long, proud, and entwined histories, influenced by strong religious traditions. Both are major European countries outside the EU. Both are permanent members of the UN Security Council, with complementary relationships, Britain closest to the US, and Russia to China. Both have an interest in settling all disputed territorial boundaries between members of the Conference on Security and Cooperation in Europe and the final geographical boundaries of NATO. Both need to strive for agreement on global environmental issues, particularly at the next UN Climate Change Conference in November 2022 in Sharm el-Sheikh. Both are nuclear-weapon states.

With such common ground and so many shared concerns, as well as deep disagreements, a continued dialogue between our two nations, even when they disagree, is not just a necessity – it is a duty.

Notes

Introduction
1. Winston Churchill, BBC broadcast (1 October 1939).
2. Andrew Roberts, *Churchill: Walking with Destiny* (London, 2018), 473 and 472.
3. Ibid.
4. 'Vladimir Bukovsky Obituary', *The Times* (5 November 2019).
5. 'Putin in Heading for "Economic Oblivion"', *The Times* (4 August 2022).

1 George Canning and the Path to Navarino
1. Wendy Hinde, *George Canning* (London, 1973), 65.
2. Ibid.
3. Henry Kissinger, *Diplomacy* (New York, 1994), 75.
4. John Bew, *Castlereagh: The Biography of a Statesman* (London, 2014), 246–7, 259–67.
5. 'The Castlereagh Memoirs and Correspondence', *The New Monthly Magazine and Humorist*, 84 (1848), 358–70.
6. Bew, *Castlereagh*, op. cit., 411.
7. Harold Temperley and Lilian M. Penson, eds, *Foundations of British Foreign Policy From Pitt (1792)*

to Salisbury (1902), or Documents Old and New
(Cambridge, 1938), 48–63.

8. Augustus Granville Stapleton, *Intervention and Non-Intervention; or, the Foreign Policy of Great Britain from 1790 to 1865* (n.p., 2008), 6.

9. Hansard, HC vol 175, cols 527–45 (20/5/1864).

10. Charles Guthrie and Michael Quinlan, *Just War. The Just War Tradition: Ethics in Modern Warfare* (London, 2007).

11. Lawrence Freedman, 'Force and the International Community: Blair's Chicago Speech and the Criteria for Intervention', *International Relations* 31/2 (2017), 107–24.

12. Lord Butler, House of Lords Hansard, 22 February 2007.

13. Quoted in Mark Jarrett, *The Congress of Vienna and its Legacy: War and Great Power Diplomacy after Napoleon* (London, 2016), 307.

14. Special Collections, Firestone Library, Princeton University, 'The Hanging of Gregory V in Constantinople', *Graphic Arts Collection* (2019), accessed online 25 August 2021.

15. Will Humphries, 'Byron's Big Greek Loan Discovered', *The Times* (2021), 16.

16. Robert Castlereagh, *Correspondence, Dispatches and Other Papers*, vol XII, ed the Second Marquess of Londonderry (n.p., 1848–52), 403f.

17. Jarrett, *The Congress of Vienna and its Legacy*, op. cit., 301–7.

18. H. Montgomery Hyde, *The Strange Death of Lord Castlereagh* (London, 1959), 52–3.

19. Sir Charles Kingsley Webster, *The Foreign Policy of*

Palmerston Vol II (London, 1969), 342, 348. See also Jarrett, *The Congress of Vienna and Its Legacy*, op. cit.

20. For those interested in learning more, an excellent account is recorded by Flora Fraser in her book *The Unruly Queen* (London, 1996), 122.

21. Harold Temperley, *The Foreign Policy of Canning 1822–1827: England, the Neo-Holy Alliance, and the New World* (London, 1925), 320.

22. David Owen, *Balkan Odyssey* (London, 1995).

23. Arthur, Duke of Wellington, *Despatches, Correspondence and Memoranda of Field Marshal Arthur Duke of Wellington*, vol I, ed his son, the Duke of Wellington (London, 1867–80), 284.

24. Allan Cunningham, 'The Philhellenes, Canning and Greek Independence', *Middle Eastern Studies*, 14/2 (1978), 151–81.

25. Paul Jacques Victor Rolo, *George Canning: Three Biographical Studies* (London, 1965), 263.

26. Epaminondas (*c.*410 BCE–362 BCE) was a Greek general and statesman who transformed the balance of power between Greek city states, leading the city of Thebes out from Spartan dominance to political prominence.

27. In the nineteenth century, 'belligerent' in a civil war referred to a protracted armed conflict, with insurgents administering large portions of country. This recognition was not equivalent to what we would now call diplomatic recognition, but it was nevertheless seen as an unfriendly act by the Ottoman rulers and perhaps the first sign of a new toughness in Britain's dealing with the Ottoman Empire.

28. The second loan was concluded in 1825 for thirty-six years at 55.5 per cent of the nominal value of £2,000,000.

29. George Finlay, *History of the Greek Revolution*, vol 2 (Cambridge, 2016), 24–8.

30. Gary Jonathan Bass, *Freedom's Battle: The Origins of Humanitarian Intervention* (New York, 2008), 102.

31. John Cam Hobhouse, who wrote *Travels in Albania and Other Provinces of Turkey in Europe and Asia, to Constantinople, during the years 1809 and 1810* (London, 1833), was a friend of Byron since their Cambridge days and was frequently his travelling companion.

32. Tina Krontiris, 'Henry V and the Anglo-Greek Alliance in World War II', in Clara Calvo and Ton Hoenselaars, eds, *European Shakespeares*, a special section of *The Shakespearean International Yearbook* (London, 2008). Krontiris cites from an address Churchill made to parliament.

33. John Arthur Ransome Marriott, *The Eastern Question: An Historical Study in European Diplomacy* (Oxford, 1969), 210.

34. Alexis Heraclides and Ada Dialla, *Humanitarian Intervention in the Long Nineteenth Century* (Manchester, 2015), 116.

35. Ibid.; Temperley, *The Foreign Policy of Canning*, op. cit., 320.

36. Pushkin's poem, *To V. L. Davydov*, 1821.

37. Demetrios J. Farsolas, 'Alexander Pushkin: His Attitude Toward the Greek Revolution 1821–1829', *Balkan Studies*, 12/1 (1971), 67.

38. H. W. V. Temperley, 'The Foreign Policy of Canning 1820–1827', in A. W. Ward and G. P. Gooch, eds, *The*

Cambridge History of British Foreign Policy 1783–1919, vol II: 1815–1886 (Cambridge, 1923), 89, note 5.

39. Temperley, *The Foreign Policy of Canning*, op. cit., 340–7.
40. Ibid.
41. Ibid., 345–7.
42. Ibid.
43. Ibid.
44. Ibid., 329.
45. Ibid.
46. Christine Sutherland, *The Princess of Siberia: The Story of Maria Volkonsky and the Decembrist Exiles* (London, 1984).
47. Sean Cannady and Paul Kubicek, 'Nationalism and Legitimation for Authoritarianism: A Comparison of Nicholas I and Vladimir Putin', *Journal of Eurasian Studies*, 5 (2014), 1–9.
48. David Brewer, *The Greek War of Independence: The Struggle for Freedom from Ottoman Oppression* (London, 2011), 256.
49. Temperley, *The Foreign Policy of Canning*, op. cit., 354–5.
50. Ibid., 354–5.
51. Hansard, HC vol 16, cols 350–98 (12/12/1826).
52. Augustus Granville Stapleton, *George Canning and His Times* (London, 1859), 528.
53. Harold Temperley, 'Princess Lieven and the Protocol of 4 April 1826', *The English Historical Review*, 39/153 (1924), 55–78.
54. C. M. Woodhouse, *The Battle of Navarino* (London, 1965), 27. There are other major books written about the Battle of Navarino, but the Woodhouse book surpasses them all. Three are noteworthy nonetheless

– two in French and one in Russian: Fleuriot de Langle, *L'affaire de Navarin: autour de la journee du 20 Octobre 1827* (Société d'éditions géographiques, maritimes et coloniales, 1930); Georges Douin, *Navarin: 6 juillet–20 octobre* (La Societe Royale de Georgraphie Degypte, 1927); E. V. Bogdanovitch, *Navarin* (Moscow, 1877).

55. Woodhouse, *The Battle of Navarino*, op. cit., 41.
56. Dutch by birth, Heiden had somewhat surprisingly served in the Royal Navy before transferring to the Russian Navy and becoming a Russian citizen in 1810.
57. Woodhouse, *The Battle of Navarino*, op. cit., 43.
58. Ibid.
59. Ibid., 42.
60. Lady Janet Bourchier, *Memoir of the Life of Admiral Sir Edward Codrington: With Selections from his Public & Private correspondence*, vol I, ed his daughter, Lady Bourchier (London, 1873), 510–12.
61. Temperley, *The Foreign Policy of Canning*, op. cit., 403.
62. United Nations Office on Genocide Prevention and the Responsibility to Protect, 'Responsibility to Protect' (n.d.), accessed online 2 August 2021.
63. Stapleton, *Intervention and Non Intervention*, op. cit., 31–2.
64. Owen, *Balkan Odyssey*, op. cit., 146.
65. Bass, *Freedom's Battle*, op. cit., 136.
66. Ibid., 151.
67. David Owen, *Seven Ages: Poetry for a Lifetime* (London, 1992).
68. Byron's words used by Bass in his frontispiece to his book *Freedom's Battle*. These words come from *The Giaour* (1813), line 123.

69.   John Bew, '"From an Umpire to a Competitor":
      Castlereagh, Canning and the Issue of International
      Intervention in the Wake of the Napoleonic Wars', in
      Brendan Simms and D. J. B. Trim, eds, *Humanitarian
      Intervention: A History* (Cambridge, 2011), 134.

70.   W. A. Phillips, 'Great Britain and the Continental
      Alliance, 1816–1822', in A. W. Ward and G. P. Gooch,
      eds, *The Cambridge History of British Foreign Policy 1783–
      1919, vol II: 1815–1886* (Cambridge, 1923), 64.

71.   Bew, '"From an Umpire to a Competitor"', op. cit., 135–6.

72.   Ibid.

73.   Simms and Trim, eds, *Humanitarian Intervention*, op.
      cit., 133.

74.   John Arthur Ransome Marriott, *George Canning and His
      Times: A Political Study* (London, 1903), 142–4.

75.   Augustus Granville Stapleton, *George Canning and His
      Times* (London, 1859), 604–5.

2   The Untoward Event

1.   Stanley Lane-Poole, *The Life of the Right Honourable
      Stratford Canning, Viscount Stratford De Redcliffe KG
      GCB GCL LL D& C* Vol 1 of 2 (n.p., 2019), 449.

2.   Ibid.

3.   Ibid.

4.   C. M. Woodhouse, *The Battle of Navarino* (London,
      1965), 60.

5.   Ibid.

6.   Ibid., 75–7.

7.   Ibid., 92.

8.   Ibid., 94.

9.   Ibid., 95.

10. Ibid., 100.

11. Ibid., 105.

12. Bourchier, *Memoir*, vol II, 68–9.

13. Woodhouse, *The Battle of Navarino*, op. cit., 116.

14. Brewer, *The Greek War of Independence*, op cit., 333–4.

15. Douglas Dakin, *The Greek Struggle for Independence: 1821–1833* (Berkeley, CA, 1973), 230.

16. Lane-Poole, *The Life of the Right Honourable Stratford Canning*, op. cit., 452–3.

17. E. V. Bogdanovich, *Navarin* (Moscow, 1877), 126.

18. Woodhouse, *The Battle of Navarino*, op. cit., 152.

19. Hansard, HL vol 18, cols 1–4 (29/1/1828).

20. Hansard, HC vol 18, cols 69–83 (31/1/1828).

21. David Brewer, *The Flame of Freedom: The Greek War of Independence, 1821–1833* (London, 2001), 335.

22. Woodhouse, *The Battle of Navarino*, op. cit., 167. See also *Memoranda of Field Marshal Arthur Duke of Wellington*, vol IV, ed his son, the Duke of Wellington (London, 1867–80), 344.

23. Hansard, HC vol 24, cols 496–513 (17/6/1834).

24. The second-highest rank in the Royal Navy.

25. Bogdanovich, *Navarin*, op. cit.

26. Ibid., 126–30.

27. Ibid., 134–6.

28. Ibid., 138.

29. Alexis Heraclides and Ada Dialla, *Humanitarian Intervention in the Long Nineteenth Century* (Manchester, 2015), 119.

30. Bogdanovich, *Navarin*, op. cit., 164.

31. John Arthur Ransome Marriott, *George Canning and His Times: A Political Study* (London, 1903), 135.

32. Ibid.

3 British and Russian Relations with the Ottoman Empire, 1825–1914

1. Henry Kissinger, *Diplomacy* (New York, 1994), 25.
2. Hansard, HC vol 14, cols 1030–71 (2/8/1832).
3. Hansard, HC vol 97, cols 66–123 (1/3/1848).
4. Ibid.
5. Ibid.
6. H. A. Gibbons, *Foundation of the Ottoman Empire* (Oxford, 1916).
7. Kissinger, *Diplomacy*, op. cit., 24.
8. G. D. Clayton, *Britain and the Eastern Question: Missolonghi to Gallipoli* (London, 1971), 126.
9. David Fromkin, 'The Great Game in Asia', *Foreign Affairs* 58/4 (1980).
10. Edward Ingram, *The Beginning of the Great Game in Asia 1828–1834* (Oxford, 1979), 32.
11. Ibid., 39.
12. Ibid., 44.
13. Ibid., 5.
14. Ibid., 17.
15. Ibid., 219.
16. Sherard Cowper-Coles, *Cables from Kabul: The Inside Story of the West's Afghanistan Campaign* (London, 2011), xx.
17. Clayton, *Britain and the Eastern Question*, op. cit., 98.
18. Orlando Figes, *The Crimean War: A History* (New York, 2011), 36–7.
19. Roy Jenkins, *Gladstone* (London, 1995).
20. Richard Shannon, *Gladstone and the Bulgarian Agitation*

1876 (London, 1963); M. S. Anderson, *The Eastern Question 1774–1923: A Study in International Relations* (London, 1966).

21. W. E. Gladstone, *The Bulgarian Horrors and the Question of the East* (London, 1876).

22. David Owen, *The Hidden Perspective: The Military Conversations 1906–1914* (London, 2015), 187–97, deals with how British relations with Germany were moving to a friendlier footing in early 1914, and how the feared revival of Russian power from 1912 in the Foreign Office had provided the context for the foreign secretary, Edward Grey, to agree that his private secretary, William Tyrell, should meet the kaiser's new state secretary for foreign affairs, Gottlieb von Jagow, in April 1914. Unfortunately, delay followed delay, and they never met.

23. J. S. Koliopoulos and Thanos M. Veremis, *Greece: The Modern Sequel, From 1821 to the Present* (London, 2007), 68–70.

24. Andrew Roberts, *Salisbury: Victorian Titan* (London, 1999), 647.

25. Ibid.

26. The analysis of Gladstone's position draws on the following sources: Richard T. Shannon, 'The Conservative Version: Disraeli's External Bid 1874–80', *The Crisis of Imperialism 1865–1915* (London, 1974); Martin Swartz, *The Politics of British Foreign Policy in the Era of Disraeli and Gladstone* (London, 1985), 31–50; W. E. Gladstone, 'The Hellenic Factor in the Eastern Question' and 'Montenegro 1877', in *Gleanings of Past Years 1844–78*, vol II, (London, 1879).

27. Jenkins, *Gladstone*, op. cit., 505–6.

28. T. G. Otte, *Statesman of Europe: A Life of Sir Edward Grey* (London, 2020), 301.

29. H. J. Mackinder, 'The Geographical Pivot of History', *The Geographical Journal*, 23/4 (1904), 421–7.

30. Edward Grey of Fallodon, *Twenty-Five Years, 1892–1916*, vol I (London: 1925).

31. Kissinger, *Diplomacy*, op. cit., 181.

32. Steven L. Burg and Paul S. Shoup, *The War in Bosnia-Herzegovina: Ethnic Conflict and International Intervention* (London, 1999), 17.

4 Winston Churchill and the Russian Revolution

1. G. D. Clayton, *Britain and the Eastern Question: Missolonghi to Gallipoli* (London, 1971), 222.

2. David Fromkin, *A Peace to End All Peace: The Fall of the Ottoman Empire and the Creation of the Modern Middle East* (New York, 2001), 54–76.

3. Sean McMeekin, *The Berlin–Bagdad Express: The Ottoman Empire and Germany's Bid for World Power 1898–1918* (London, 2010), 48.

4. Andrew Roberts, *Churchill: Walking with Destiny* (London, 2018), 196–7.

5. Barbara W. Tuchman, *The Guns of August* (London, 2000), 192–5.

6. Roy Jenkins, *Churchill: A Biography* (London, 2017), 272.

7. Ibid., 274.

8. Ibid., 275.

9. Martin Gilbert, *Winston S. Churchill Vol 4 1917–1922* (London, 1975), 8–13. Incidentally, the author sent me an inscribed copy of the book on 2 May 1977 after I told him I was planning to visit Russia as foreign secretary in

a few months' time. When I last saw Martin Gilbert in 2010, he admired the two prints of the Battle of Navarino on my office wall, confirming it was a most important battle.

10. Clayton, *Britain and the Eastern Question*, op. cit., 226.

11. Michael Llewellyn Smith, *Ionian Vision: Greece in Asia Minor 1919–1922* (London, 1973), 3.

12. Clayton, *Britain and the Eastern Question*, op. cit., 226.

13. Ibid.

14. Winston Churchill, *The World Crisis, Vol IV, The Aftermath 1918–1922* (London, 1929).

15. Martin Gilbert, *Winston S. Churchill Vol 4 1917–1922* (London, 1975), 219.

16. Ibid., 220.

17. Ibid., 219–20.

18. John Wheeler-Bennett, *Brest-Litovsk: The Forgotten Peace, March 1918* (London, 1966).

19. Orlando Figes, *A People's Tragedy: The Russian Revolution 1891–1924* (London, 1997), 550.

20. Gilbert, *Winston S. Churchill Vol 4 1917–1922*, op. cit., 220.

21. Ibid., 221.

22. Barnes Carr, *The Lenin Plot: The Unknown Story of America's War Against Russia* (New York, 2020).

23. Gilbert, *Winston S. Churchill Vol 4 1917–1922*, op. cit., 224.

24. Victor Sebestyen, *Lenin the Dictator: An Intimate Portrait* (London, 2017), 405–9.

25. Gilbert, *Winston S. Churchill Vol 4 1917–1922*, op. cit., 224.

26. Ibid., 225.

27. Ibid., 226.
28. Ibid., 226.
29. Appendix to the Minutes of the Meeting of the War Cabinet (502), 14 November 1918, National Archives CAB 23/8/23.
30. Gilbert, *Winston S. Churchill Vol 4 1917–1922*, op. cit., 226–7.
31. Ibid., 227.
32. Ibid.
33. Ibid., 227.
34. Ibid., 227–8.
35. Ibid., 228.
36. It first met on 16 March 1917. In addition to being a member of the Imperial War Cabinet, General Smuts became a member of the British cabinet and the War Cabinet, living in the Savoy Hotel, London.
37. Ibid., 229.
38. Minutes of the Imperial War Cabinet (48), 31 December 1918, National Archives CAB 23/42/20.
39. David Owen, 'The Shah's Secret Illness', in *In Sickness and In Power: Illness in Heads of Government, Military and Business Leaders since 1900* (London, 2016), 211–40.
40. David Owen, *Balkan Odyssey* (London, 1995).
41. Gilbert, *Winston S. Churchill Vol 4 1917–1922*, op. cit., 229.
42. Figes, *A People's Tragedy*, op. cit., 86.
43. Gilbert, *Winston S. Churchill Vol 4 1917–1922*, op. cit., 234.
44. Lauri Kopisto, *The British Intervention in South Russia 1918–1920* (Helsinki, 2011), https://core.ac.uk/download/pdf/14920703.pdf.

45. Gilbert, *Winston S. Churchill Vol 4 1917–1922*, op. cit., 233–4.
46. Ibid.
47. Ibid., 235.
48. David Owen, *The Hidden Perspective: The Military Conversations 1906–1914* (London, 2015). See pages 204–11 for an outline of the written and verbal exchanges between Churchill and Lloyd George in the cabinet.
49. Gilbert, *Winston S. Churchill Vol 4 1917–1922*, op. cit., 235–6.
50. Ibid., 238.
51. Ibid., 244.
52. Ibid., 246.
53. Ibid., 249.
54. Ibid., 256.
55. Ibid., 257.
56. Ibid., 260.
57. Ibid., 268–9.
58. Ibid., 271.
59. Ibid., 272.
60. Ibid., 275–6.
61. Ibid., 277.
62. Ibid., 277–8.
63. Hansard, HC, vol 116 (29/5/1919).
64. Gilbert, *Winston S. Churchill Vol 4 1917–1922*, op. cit., 295.
65. Ibid., 306.
66. Ibid., 331.
67. Ibid.
68. Ibid., 332.
69. All quotations in this paragraph: ibid., 330–5.

70. All quotations in this paragraph: ibid., 335.

71. Figes, *A People's Tragedy*, op. cit., 437–8.

72. Ibid., 480.

73. Jenkins, *Churchill: A Biography*, op. cit., 352.

74. Gilbert, *Winston S. Churchill Vol 4 1917–1922*, op. cit., 487–8.

75. Ibid., 497.

76. Norman Stone, 'Turkey in the Russian Mirror', in Ljubica Erikson and Mark Erikson, eds, *Russia: War, Peace and Diplomacy* (London, 2005), 86–100.

77. Ibid.

78. Gilbert, *Winston S. Churchill Vol 4 1917–1922*, op. cit., 775.

79. Ibid., 776.

80. Fromkin, *A Peace to End All Peace*, op. cit., 551–4.

81. Owen, *In Sickness and In Power*, op. cit., 16.

82. Lord Beaverbrook, *The Decline and Fall of Lloyd George: And Great Was the Fall Thereof* (London, 1963), 10–11.

83. Roy Jenkins, *Churchill: A Biography* (New York, 2001), 350.

84. Winston Churchill, *The World Crisis, Vol IV*, op. cit., 263.

5 Churchill and Stalin: World War to Cold War

1. Gabriel Gorodetsky, ed, *The Maisky Diaries: Red Ambassador to the Court of St James's 1932–1943* (London, 2015), 164.

2. Tim Bouverie, *Appeasing Hitler: Chamberlain, Churchill and the Road to War* (London, 2019), 199.

3. CAB 27/624, 18 March 1939.

4. Hansard, HC vol 345, col 2415 (31/3/1939).

5. Hansard, HC vol 347, col 1834 (19/5/1939).

6. Gorodetsky, *The Maisky Diaries*, op. cit., 170.

7. Hansard, HC vol 345, col 2502 (3/4/1939).

8. Ibid.

9. Gorodetsky, *The Maisky Diaries*, op. cit., 172.

10. Hansard, HC vol 346, col 36 (13/4/1939).

11. William Manchester, *The Caged Lion: Winston Spencer Churchill 1932–1940* (London, 1988), 453.

12. Ibid., 454.

13. Sean McMeekin, *Stalin's War: A New History of World War II* (London, 2021), 73–4.

14. Ibid., 75.

15. Alexander Cadogan, *The Diaries of Sir Alexander Cadogan 1938–1945*, ed David Dilks (London, 1971), 175.

16. Manchester, *The Caged Lion*, op. cit., 455.

17. Ibid.

18. Andrew Roberts, *The Holy Fox: The Life of Lord Halifax* (London, 2015), 213.

19. All quotations in this paragraph: Manchester, *The Caged Lion*, op. cit., 455.

20. McMeekin, *Stalin's War*, op. cit., chapter 5. See also, Albert Resis, ed, *Molotov Remembers: Inside Kremlin Politics* (Chicago, IL, 2007), 192.

21. Hansard, HC vol 347, cols 1809–86 (19/5/1939).

22. Roberts, *The Holy Fox*, op. cit., 216.

23. Ian Johnson, 'Sowing the Wind: The First Soviet-German Military Pact and the Origins of World War II', *War on the Rocks* (2016), accessed online 3 August 2021.

24. Xenia Joukoff Eudin and Harold H. Fisher, *Soviet Russia and the West, 1920–1927: A Documentary Survey* (Stanford, CA, 1957).

25. McMeekin, *Stalin's War*, op. cit., 58.

26. Bouverie, *Appeasing Hitler*, op. cit., 366–78.
27. McMeekin, *Stalin's War*, op. cit., 121–2.
28. Ibid.
29. 'Chiefs of Staff Report', CAB 104, 27 October 1939.
30. Ibid.
31. John Colville, *The Fringes of Power: Downing Street Diaries 1939–1955* (rev edn, London, 2004), 49.
32. A. Cadogan, *The Diaries of Sir Alexander Cadogan*, op. cit., 259.
33. Conrad Black, *Franklin Delano Roosevelt: Champion of Freedom* (London, 2003), 540.
34. All quotations in the following paragraph are from: Winston S. Churchill, *The Second World War, Vol 3, The Grand Alliance* (London, 1950), 290–2.
35. Ibid., 321.
36. Andrew Roberts, *Churchill: Walking with Destiny* (London, 2018), 655–6.
37. Zhores A. Medvedev and Roy A. Medvedev, *The Unknown Stalin* (London, 2006).
38. Roberts, *Walking with Destiny*, op. cit., 660.
39. Ibid., 660.
40. Winston S. Churchill, Broadcast on the Soviet–German War, London, 22 June 1941.
41. Martin Gilbert, *Churchill: A Life* (London, 2000), 703.
42. David Reynolds and Vladimir Pechatnov, *The Kremlin Letters: Stalin's Wartime Correspondence with Churchill and Roosevelt* (New Haven, CT, 2018), 26–7.
43. Ibid., 28–30.
44. John Erickson, *Stalin's War with Germany, Vol I, The Road to Stalingrad* (London, 2000) and *Stalin's War with Germany, Vol II, The Road to Berlin* (London, 1999).

45. H. V. Morton, *Atlantic Meeting*, with foreword by David Owen (London, 2016).

46. Harry L. Hopkins, 'Memorandum by Mr Harry L. Hopkins, Personal Representative of President Roosevelt', *Foreign Relations of the United States Diplomatic Papers, 1941, General, The Soviet Union, Volume I* (31 July 1941), Office of the Historian.

47. Reynolds and Pechatnov, *The Kremlin Letters*, op. cit.

48. William Attenborough, *Diagnosing Churchill: Bipolar or 'Prey to Nerves'?* (Jefferson, NC, 2019), 178–9.

49. Reynolds and Pechatnov, *The Kremlin Letters*, op. cit., 11.

50. Laurence Rees, *World War II: Behind Closed Doors: Stalin, The Nazis and The West* (London, 2008).

51. Reynolds and Pechatnov, *The Kremlin Letters*, op. cit., 41.

52. Roberts, *Walking with Destiny*, op. cit., 752.

53. Ibid., 754–5.

54. Ibid., 805.

55. Reynolds and Pechatnov, *The Kremlin Letters*, op. cit., 429.

56. Ibid., 843.

57. Martin Gilbert, *Winston S. Churchill, Vol VII, Road to Victory 1941–1945* (London, 1988), 995.

58. Roberts, *Churchill*, op cit., 729.

59. Ed Vulliamy and Helena Smith, 'Athens 1944: Britain's Dirty Secret', *The Guardian* (2014), accessed online 3 August 2021.

60. Francois de La Rochefoucauld, *Maxims*, trans by Stuart D. Warner and Stephane Douard (South Bend, IN, 2001), 4.

61. Churchill used this phrase in a letter to Violet Bonham Carter. The daughter of British prime minister Herbert

Asquith, Bonham Carter was a lifelong friend and confidante of Churchill's.

62. David Owen, *In Sickness and In Power: Illness in Heads of Government, Military and Business Leaders since 1900* (London, 2016), 40–51.

63. Field Marshal Lord Alanbrooke, *War Diaries 1939–1945*, eds Alex Danchev and Dan Todman (London, 2002), 679.

64. Charles E. Bohlen, *The Transformation of American Foreign Policy* (New York, 1969), 44.

65. Arthur M. Schlesinger Jr, 'Foreword', in *My Dear Mr Stalin: The Complete Correspondence between Franklin D. Roosevelt and Joseph V. Stalin*, ed Susan Butler (New Haven, CT, 2005).

66. Ibid.

67. Ibid., xv, 29.

68. Roy Jenkins, *Franklin Delano Roosevelt* (London, 2005), 165–6.

69. Hansard, HC vol 408, col 1291 (27/2/1945).

70. Ibid., col 1269.

71. Ibid., col 1275.

72. Ibid., col 1276.

73. Ibid., col 1280.

74. Ibid., col 1284.

75. Ibid.

76. Ibid., col 1294.

77. National Archives CAB 65/51/26, Confidential Annex to WM (45) 26.

78. National Archives CAB 65/52/1, Confidential Annex to WM (45) 39.

79. Hansard, HC vol 446, cols 557–8–86 (23/1/1948).

80. Winston S. Churchill, 'The Sinews of Peace ("Iron Curtain Speech")', Westminster College, Fulton, Missouri, 5 March 1946.
81. Ibid.
82. Ibid.
83. Ibid.
84. Ibid.
85. Ibid.
86. Ibid.
87. Ibid.
88. Ibid.
89. Winston S. Churchill, 'United States of Europe' speech, University of Zurich, 19 September 1946.
90. A. Roberts, *Walking with Destiny*, op. cit., 927.
91. Gill Bennett, 'Challenging Communism', *Six Moments of Crisis Inside British Foreign Policy* (Oxford, 2013).
92. Ibid., 30, quoting from 'Documents on British Policy Overseas No. 57'.
93. Hansard, HC vol 478, cols 469–470 (26/7/1950).
94. Max Hastings, *The Korean War* (London, 1987), 393–4.
95. Gilbert, *Churchill: A Life*, op. cit., 915,
96. Roberts, *Walking with Destiny*, op. cit., 942.
97. Ibid., 945.
98. Ibid.
99. Hansard, HC vol 537 col 1893 (1/3/1955).
100. Ibid., col 1895.
101. Ibid., col 1895–6.
102. Ibid., col 1897.
103. Ibid., col 1905.
104. 'Rear-Admiral John Hervey – Obituary', *The Telegraph* (2016), accessed online 3 August 2021.

6 Face-Off in Europe

1.   'George Kennan's "Long Telegram"', 22 February 1946, History and Public Policy Program Digital Archive, National Archives and Records Administration, Department of State Records (Record Group 59), Central Decimal File, 1945–1949.

2.   R. Crosby Kemper III, 'Introduction: The Rhetoric of Civilisation', *Winston Churchill: Resolution, Defiance, Magnanimity, Goodwill* (Columbia, MO, 1996), 26.

3.   Chris Cook, Polina Ivanova, and Laura Pitel, 'Ships going dark: Russia's grain smuggling in the Black Sea', *The Financial Times* (29 June 2022).

4.   Harry S. Truman, 'Special Message to the Congress on Greece and Turkey: The Truman Doctrine' (21 March 1947), The Truman Library.

5.   George C. Marshall, 'The Marshall Plan Speech' (5 June 1947), The George C. Marshall Foundation.

6.   Charles L. Mee, Jr, *The Marshall Plan: The Launching of the Pax Americana* (New York, 1984), 103–4.

7.   Ibid., 262.

8.   Austria, Belgium, Denmark, France, Greece, Iceland, Ireland, Italy, Luxembourg, the Netherlands, Norway, Portugal, Sweden, Switzerland, Turkey, and the UK.

9.   Tony Judt, *Postwar: A History of Europe since 1945* (London, 2017), 90.

10. Richard West, *Tito and the Rise and Fall of Yugoslavia* (London, 1994), 230.

11. John Rodden, 'The Tragedy of "June 17": East Germany's "Workers' Uprising" at Sixty', *Global Society*, 51 (2014), 169–74.

12. 'Working Notes from the Session of the CPSU CC

Presidium on 31 October 1956', 31 October 1956, History and Public Policy Program Digital Archive, compiled by V. N. Malin. Translated for CWIHP by Mark Kramer.

13.   'The North Atlantic Treaty', *NATO* (1949).

14.   'The Sources of Soviet Conduct', or 'X Article', was published in *Foreign Affairs* in July 1947. Though signed pseudonymously by 'X', it was well known at the time that the author was George Kennan, who had been chargé at the US embassy in Moscow. The article was an expansion on his widely circulated State Department cable of 22 February 1946 called 'The Long Telegram' and became famous for setting forth the doctrine of containment.

15.   David Owen, *In Sickness and In Power: Illness in Heads of Government, Military and Business Leaders since 1900* (London, 2016), chapter 4.

16.   Kennedy's secretary, Evelyn Lincoln, found the paper on the floor of Air Force One and squirreled it away with other notes. Kennedy often used the quotation in campaign speeches and attributed it to Abraham Lincoln.

17.   W. R. Smyser, *Kennedy and the Berlin Wall: A Hell of a Lot Better than a War* (Lanham, MD, 2009).

18.   This was Khrushchev's expression, meaning 'why not stir up trouble?' and was said to Rodion Malinovsky, the Russian defence minister, in April 1962. John Lewis Gaddis, *The Cold War: A New History* (London, 2005), 75–8.

19.   Adlai Stevenson, UN Security Council Address on Soviet Missiles in Cuba, 25 October 1962.

20.   Aleksandr Fursenko and Timothy Naftali, *One Hell of*

a Gamble: The Secret History of the Cuban Missile Crisis (London, 1997), 240–3.

21. 'Document 70. Letter from Chairman Krushchev to President Kennedy', *Office of the Historian* (1962), accessed online 3 August 2021.

22. John F. Kennedy, Address to the Nation on the Nuclear Test Ban Treaty, 26 July 1963.

23. Thomas Crump, *Brezhnev and the Decline of the Soviet Union* (London, 2014).

24. Zhores A. Medvedev, *Andropov* (Oxford, 1983), 104.

25. What became known as the Brezhnev Doctrine was first articulated by Brezhnev at a meeting of the Warsaw Pact in Czechoslovakia on 3 August 1968. It was formally presented as an official document known as 'Sovereignty and the International Obligations of Socialist Countries' published by *Pravda* in September 1968.

26. Judt, *Postwar*, op. cit., 497.

27. Egon Bahr, 'Wandel durch Annäherung [Change through Rapprochement]' speech, the Evangelical Academy in Tutzing, 15 July 1963.

28. Gill Bennett, 'Challenging the KGB Operation Foot, September 1971' in *Six Moments of Crisis Inside British Foreign Policy* (Oxford, 2013).

29. Archie Brown, *The Rise and Fall of Communism* (London, 2010), 463.

30. V. M. Zubok, *A Failed Empire: The Soviet Union in the Cold War from Stalin to Gorbachev* (Chapel Hill, NC, 2009), 311.

31. David C. Gompert, Hans Binnendijk, and Bonny Lin, 'The Soviet Decision Not to Invade Poland, 1981',

Blinders, Blunders, and Wars: What America and China Can Learn (Santa Monica, CA, 2014), 139–148.

32. Crump, *Brezhnev and the Decline of the Soviet Union*, op. cit., 191.

33. Ibid., 190.

34. Ibid., 192.

35. Timothy Nunan, *Humanitarian Invasion: Global Development in Cold War Afghanistan* (Cambridge, 2018).

36. Crump, *Brezhnev and the Decline of the Soviet Union*, op. cit., 194–5.

37. Rodric Braithwaite, *Afgantsy: The Russians in Afghanistan 1979–89* (London, 2012).

38. *Common Security. A Programme for Disarmament, Report of the Independent Commission on Disarmament and Security Issues* (London, 1982).

7 Russia on the Road to Reform

1. Zhores A. Medvedev, *Andropov* (Oxford, 1983), 64, 108–9.

2. William Taubman, *Gorbachev: His Life and Times* (London, 2017), 141.

3. Ibid., 138.

4. Ibid., 139–40.

5. Christian Schmidt-Häuer, *Gorbachev: The Path to Power* (London, 1986), 88.

6. Archie Brown, *The Rise and Fall of Communism* (London, 2010), 482

7. Ibid.

8. Christopher M. Andrew and Vasili Mitrokhin, *The Mitrokhin Archive II: The KGB and the World* (Allen

Lane, 2005), 450–1. Also referred to in Christopher Andrew, *The Secret World: A History of Intelligence* (London, 2018), 105, 130.

9. Ibid.

10. Brown, *The Rise and Fall*, op. cit., 408–9.

11. Ibid., 105.

12. Martha Brill Olcott, 'Yuri Andropov and the "National Question"', *Soviet Studies*, 37/1 (1985), 112.

13. Ben Fowkes, 'The National Question in the Soviet Union under Leonid Brezhnev: Policy and Response', eds Edwin Bacon and Mark Sandle, *Brezhnev Reconsidered* (London, 2002), 68, 81–3.

14. Brill Olcott, 'Yuri Andropov and the "National Question"', op. cit., 112.

15. Brian Whitemore, 'Andropov's Ghost' (9 February 2009), Radio Free Europe Radio Liberty.

16. Taubman, *Gorbachev*, op. cit., 150.

17. Ibid., 153.

18. 'TV Interview for BBC ("I like Mr Gorbachev. We can do business together")', *Speeches, Interviews & Other Statements* (17 December 1984), Margaret Thatcher Foundation.

19. Michael Evans, 'Soviet Union was Ready to Scramble 100 Nuclear Bombers in 1983, Files Reveal', *The Times* (2020), accessed online 3 August 2021.

20. Archie Brown, 'Did Gorbachev as General Secretary Become a Social Democrat?', *Europe-Asia Studies, Special Issue: Perestroika: A Reassessment*, 65/2 (2013), 200.

21. Taubman, *Gorbachev*, op. cit., 194.

22. Ibid., 195.

23. David Owen, *Human Rights* (London, 1978), 70.

24. Ronald Reagan, *The Reagan Diaries* (London, 2007), 332.

25. John-Thor Dahlburg, *Soviet Leader Mikhail Gorbachev: 'Nice Smile' With 'Teeth of Iron'* (28 November 1987), AP News.

26. 'Joint Soviet-United States Statement on the Summit Meeting in Geneva' (21 November 1985), Ronald Reagan Presidential Library & Museum.

27. Taubman, *Gorbachev*, op. cit., 274.

28. Ibid., 298.

29. Andrew, *The Secret World*, op. cit., 696.

30. Taubman, *Gorbachev*, op. cit., 295.

31. Ronald Reagan, *An American Life: The Autobiography* (New York, 1990), 675.

32. Robert M. Gates, *Duty* (London, 2014), 336.

33. Helene Cooper, Eric Schmitt, and David E. Sanger, 'Debating Exit from Afghanistan, Biden Rejected Generals' Views', *The New York Times* (2021), 5.

34. Mikhail Gorbachev's address to the 43rd United Nations General Assembly Session (7 December 1988).

35. Ibid.

36. Ibid.

37. 'The Curtain Rises: Eastern Europe, 1989: EPILOGUE: 10 Years, 10 Months, 10 Weeks and 10 Days: With breathtaking speed, the East Bloc has been transformed. But the struggle is not over', *Los Angeles Times* (1989), accessed online 3 August 2021.

38. Gorbachev speaking in German in East Berlin on 7 October 1989. 'Gefahren warten nur auf jene, die nicht auf das Leben reagieren' can also be translated as 'Dangers await only those who do not react to life.' '2

Oct: Gorbachev in East Berlin' (25 March 2009), BBC
News.

39. David Childs, *The Fall of the GDR: Germany's Road to
Unity* (Harlow, 2001), 87.

40. Prime Minister's Office, 10 Downing Street and The Rt
Hon Boris Johnson MP, 'PM Call with Secretary General
of NATO: 22 March 2021', GOV.UK (2021).

41. Percy Cradock, *In Pursuit of British Interests: Reflections
On Foreign Policy Under Margaret Thatcher and John
Major* (London, 1997), 110–11.

42. Ibid., 113.

43. '1989: Malta Summit Ends Cold War', On This Day
1950–2005 (n.d.), BBC News.

44. Alexander Galkin and Anatoly Chernyaev, eds, *Mikhail
Gorbachev i germanskii vopros* (Moscow, 2006), 454–66.

45. Patrick Salmon, Keith Hamilton, and Stephen Twigge,
eds, 'Documents on British Policy Overseas, series III,
volume VII: German Unification, 1989–1990', *Whitehall
Histories* (Oxford; New York, 2010), 411–17.

46. Taubman, *Gorbachev*, op. cit., 433.

47. Ibid., 442.

48. Ibid., 456.

49. Paul Hendrickson, 'Yeltsin's Smashing Day', *The
Washington Post* (1989), accessed online 3 August 2021.

50. Taubman, *Gorbachev*, op. cit., page 512.

51. Cradock, *In Pursuit of British Interests*, op. cit., 118–19.

52. Bryan Brumley, 'Shevardnadze Resigns, Blames Soviet
Reactionaries' (20 December 1990), AP News.

53. Frank Elbe, 'The Diplomatic Path to Germany Unity',
Bulletin of the German Historical Institute, 46 (2010),
33–46. Elbe was Genscher's chief of staff at the time.

54. Taubman, *Gorbachev*, op. cit., 547.

55. Mary Elise Sarotte, 'A Broken Promise? What the West Really Told Moscow About NATO Expansion', *Foreign Affairs*, 93/5 (2014), 91–2, 94–5.

56. 'Ambassador Rodric Braithwaite Diary, 5 March 1991', *National Security Archive*, accessed online 3 August 2021.

57. Cradock, *In Pursuit of British Interests*, op. cit., 120.

58. Ibid.

59. Taubman, *Gorbachev*, op. cit., 621.

60. Ibid., 622–3.

61. John Major, 'Mr Major's Press Conference in Moscow – 1 September 1991', John Major Archive (1991), accessed online 3 August 2021.

8 Yeltsin: A Free Spirit

1. Sharyl Cross, 'Russia and NATO Toward the Twenty-first Century: Conflicts and Peacekeeping in Bosnia-Herzegovina and Kosovo', *The Journal of Slavic Military Studies*, 15/2 (2002), 1–58.

2. Warren Zimmerman, *Origins of a Catastrophe: Yugoslavia and Its Destroyers – America's Last Ambassador Tells What Happened and Why* (New York, 1999).

3. David Owen, ed, *Bosnia–Herzegovina: The Vance/Owen Peace Plan* (Liverpool, 2013), 180–1.

4. David Owen, *Balkan Odyssey* (London, 1995), 162.

5. Christopher Andrew, *The Secret World: A History of Intelligence* (London, 2018), 711–15.

6. Ibid., 714.

7. Ivo H. Daalder and Michael E. O'Hanlon, *Winning Ugly: NATO's War to Save Kosovo* (Washington, DC, 2000), 167–75.

8. Ibid., 209.

9. Wesley K. Clark, *Waging Modern War: Bosnia, Kosovo, and the Future of Combat* (New York, 2001), 389.

10. Ibid., 398.

11. Ibid., 395.

12. Clark, *Waging Modern War*, op. cit., 377.

13. Major General William L. Nash, US commanding general of the multinational force in Bosnia, makes this point in his chapter 'NATO, Bosnia, and the Future', in Susan Eisenhower, ed, *NATO at Fifty: Perspectives on the Future of the Transatlantic Alliance* (Washington, DC, 1999).

14. 'US Troops Rescue Russians from Kosovo Albanians', Reuters (1999); see also 'Sniper Wounds Russian Peacekeeper in Kosovo', Reuters (1999).

15. Cross, 'Russia and NATO Toward the Twenty-first Century', op. cit.

16. Constantine C. Menges, *China: The Gathering Threat* (Nashville, TN, 2005), 276.

17. Thomas L. Friedman, 'Foreign Affairs; Now a Word From X', *The New York Times* (1998), accessed online 3 August 2021.

18. Peter Conradi, *Who Lost Russia? How the World Entered a New Cold War* (London, 2017), 47.

19. George F. Kennan, 'America and the Russian Future' (April 1951), *Foreign Affairs*.

20. Karen Dawisha, *Putin's Kleptocracy: Who Owns Russia?* (New York, 2014); Catherine Belton, *Putin's People: How the KGB Took Back Russia and then Took on the West* (London, 2020).

21. Dawisha, *Putin's Kleptocracy*, op. cit., 18.

22. Leon Aron, *Boris Yeltsin: A Revolutionary Life* (New York, 2000), 590.

23. David Owen, *In Sickness and In Power: Illness in Heads of Government, Military and Business Leaders since 1900* (London, 2016), 117–18.

24. Andrei Zolotov, Jr, 'President Draws Criticism From All Political Camps' (10 August 1999), *The Moscow Times*.

25. Steve Rosenberg, 'The Man who Helped Make ex-KGB Officer Vladimir Putin a President', BBC News (2019), accessed online 3 August 2021.

9 Putin's Russia

1. Karen Dawisha, *Putin's Kleptocracy: Who Owns Russia?* (New York, 2014), 42–3.

2. Ibid., 43.

3. Vladimir Putin, with Nataliya Gevorkyan, Natalya Timakova, and Andrei Kolesnikov, *First Person: An Astonishingly Frank Self-Portrait by Russia's President Vladimir Putin* (New York, 1999).

4. Mark Galeotti, *We Need to Talk about Putin: How the West Gets Him Wrong* (London, 2019), 34–5.

5. Antony Beevor, *Russia: Revolution and Civil War 1917–1921* (London, 2022).

6. Matthew Dal Santo, 'Putin's Plan to Restore the Romanovs (Part 2)', *The Interpreter* (2016), accessed online 3 August 2021.

7. Galeotti, *We Need to Talk about Putin*, op. cit., 17.

8. Ibid., 60.

9. Ibid.

10. Peter Conradi, *Who Lost Russia? How the World Entered a New Cold War* (London, 2017), 126.

11. Catherine Belton, *Putin's People: How the KGB Took Back Russia and then Took on the West* (London, 2020), 227.

12. Ibid.

13. Ibid., 233.

14. Ibid.

15. Stenogram of Putin's press conference (23 June 2003), *Kremlin*.

16. Lord David Alliance, a close friend of mine, also had a 10 per cent stake in OEMK.

17. Ray Leonard, 'Khodorkovsky, Yukos, and Putin: The Achievement of Khodorkovsky, Why It Was Destroyed, and the Consequences', *Problems of Post-Communism*, 63/2 (2016), 121–6.

18. Galeotti, *We Need to Talk about Putin*, op. cit., 15.

19. 'Transcript: Bush, Putin News Conference', CNN (2001), accessed online 3 August 2021.

20. Constantine C. Menges, *China: The Gathering Threat* (Nashville, TN, 2005), 451.

21. 'About NRC', NATO–Russia Council (n.d.), accessed online 3 August 2021.

22. 'Speech at a Meeting of the NATO–Russia Council', President of Russia (2002), accessed online 3 August 2021.

23. 'About NRC', NATO–Russia Council (n.d.), accessed online 3 August 2021.

24. Strobe Talbott, 'Chapter 9', *The Russian Hand: A Memoir of Presidential Diplomacy* (New York, 2002).

25. George Kennan, 'A Fateful Error', *The New York Times* (1997), accessed online 3 August 2021.

26. Talbott, *The Russian Hand*, op. cit., 232.

27. Edward Glover and Sir Roderic Lyne, 'The Long Telegram', *InsideOut*, 58 (2021), 15–17.

28. Ibid., 17.

29. Ibid., 16.

30. Ibid.

31. Ibid.

32. Ibid.

33. Ibid.

34. Ibid., 17.

35. Ibid.

36. Ibid.

37. George Friedman, 'Russia's Search for Strategic Depth', *Geopolitical Futures* (2020), accessed online 3 August 2021.

38. President Putin, 'State of the Nation Address to Parliament', 25 April 2005.

39. Andrew S. Weiss, 'Five Myths about Vladimir Putin', *The Washington Post* (2012).

40. Sam Jones, 'Ukrainian billionaire Dmitry Firtash: "Putin will go further. What will Europe do then?" *Financial Times* (29 July 2022).

41. 'Speech at Meeting with German Political, Parliamentary and Civic Leaders', President of Russia (2008), accessed online 3 August 2021.

42. 'The Foreign Policy Concept of the Russian Federation', Permanent Mission of the Russian Federation to the European Union (2008), accessed online 3 August 2021.

43. 'Independent International Fact-Finding Mission on the Conflict in Georgia' (2009), accessed online 3 August 2021.

44. 'Remarks by the President in Address to the Nation

on Libya', The White House, President Barack Obama (2011), accessed online 3 August 2021.

45. Jeffrey Goldberg, 'The Obama Doctrine' (April 2016), *The Atlantic*.

46. 'Medvedev Rejects Putin "Crusade" Remark over Libya', BBC News (2011), accessed online 3 August 2021.

47. Steven Lee Myers, *The New Tsar: The Rise and Reign of Vladimir Putin* (London, 2015), 403.

48. Ibid., 403.

49. David Owen, *The UK's In-Out Referendum: EU Foreign and Defence Policy Reform* (London, 2015).

50. The Budapest Memorandum on Security Assurances refers to three identical political agreements signed at the OSCE conference in Hungary on 5 December 1994 to provide security assurances by its signatories, the Russian Federation, the US, and the UK, to the accession of Belarus, Kazakhstan, and Ukraine to the Treaty on the Non-Proliferation of Nuclear Weapons.

51. Guy Chazan, 'How War in Ukraine Convinced Germany to Rebuild its Army', *Financial Times* (2022), accessed online 23 May 2022.

52. Ibid.

53. David Owen, *Europe Restructured: The Eurozone Crisis and its Aftermath* (London, 2012).

54. 'Address by President of the Russian Federation', President of Russia (2014), accessed online 3 August 2021.

55. The full text of Lord Owen's speech to the Moscow State Institute of International Relations on 16 November 2017 is available on Lord Owen's website:

www.lorddavidowen.co.uk/category/international/other-international/.

56. President Obama speaking at the end of a Nuclear Security Summit in The Hague, 24–25 March 2014.

57. Sir Robert Owen (chair), 'Report into the Death of Alexander Litvinenko', *The Litvinenko Inquiry* (2016). See also Luke Harding, *A Very Expensive Poison: The Definitive Story of the Murder of Litvinenko and Russia's War with the West* (London, 2016).

58. Owen, 'Report into the Death of Alexander Litvinenko', op. cit.

59. Ibid.

60. Ibid., chapter 12, para 9.215, 244.

61. Lord Mark Sedwill, 'It's Time for Global Britain to Roar: With Brexit Done and Joe Biden in the White House, a Rousing Call to Arms', *Daily Mail* (2021), accessed online 3 August 2021.

62. 'UK Exposes Russian Cyber Attacks', GOV.UK (2018), accessed online 3 August 2021.

63. 'UK Condemns Russian Intelligence Services over Vaccine Cyber Attacks', GOV.UK (2020), accessed online 3 August 2021.

64. 'Russia: UK and US Expose Global Campaign of Malign Activity by Russian Intelligence Services', GOV.UK (2021), accessed online 3 August 2021.

65. 'Government Response to the Intelligence Committee of Parliament Report: "Russia"' (2020).

66. Special Counsel Robert S. Mueller, III, 'Report on the Investigation into Russian Interference in the 2016 Presidential Election', vol I (2019).

67. Ibid.

68. 'Foreign Threats to the 2020 US Federal Elections', National Intelligence Council (2021).

69. Ibid.

70. Tony Blair, speaking at a press conference as reported in *The Times*. Lucy Fisher, 'I'm deeply sorry but I did the right thing and stand by my decision', *The Times* (2016), accessed online 1 Sept. 2021.

71. Sherard Cowper-Coles, *Cables from Kabul: The Inside Story of the West's Afghanistan Campaign* (London, 2011), 262.

72. Serhii Plokhy, *The Gates of Europe: A History of Ukraine* (London, 2016), 298–9.

73. Ibid., 317.

74. Niall Ferguson, 'Henry Kissinger at 99: How to Avoid Another War', *The Sunday Times Magazine* (12 June 2022), 34.

10 Britain, Russia, and the Wider World

1. 'Global Britain in a Competitive Age', *The Integrated Review of Security, Defence, Development and Foreign Policy* (2021).

2. 'Putin's Next Move: Russia's President Menaces His People and Neighbours', *The Economist* (2021), 7.

3. 'Global Britain in a Competitive Age', op. cit.

4. David Charter, 'Kissinger Warns of "Colossal Danger" to World from a US–China Cold War', *The Times* (2021), accessed online 3 August 2021.

5. David Owen, *In Sickness and In Power: Illness in Heads of Government, Military and Business Leaders since 1900* (London, 2016). Also *Hubris: The Road to Donald Trump, Power, Populism, Narcissism* (London, 2018).

6.   Plato, *Euthyphro/Apology/Crito/Phaedo/Phaedrus*, translated by H. N. Fowler (Cambridge, MA, 1914). The Ancient Greek original has been added in italics by the author of this book, 238a.

7.   Aristotle, *Art of Rhetoric*, translated by J. H. Freese, (Cambridge, MA, 1926), 1378b.

8.   Ian Kershaw, *Hitler 1889–1936: Hubris* (London, 1998); Ian Kershaw, *Hitler 1936–1945: Nemesis* (London, 2000).

9.   Edward Glover and Sir Roderic Lyne, 'The Long Telegram', *InsideOut*, 58 (2021), 17.

10.   Chris Smyth, 'Kate Bingham Says Britain Is Put at Risk by Civil Service Groupthink', *The Times* (23 November 2021).

11.   Matthew Campbell, 'A Message from Putin', *Sunday Times Magazine* (2020), 22–9.

12.   'G7 Foreign and Development Ministers' Meeting: Communiqué, London, 5 May 2021', GOV.UK (2021), accessed online 24 August 2021.

13.   Ibid.

14.   Mark Galeotti, *We Need to Talk about Putin: How the West Gets Him Wrong* (London, 2019), 100.

15.   Ibid., 100–1.

16.   '75th session of the UN General Assembly', President of Russia (2020), accessed online 3 August 2021.

17.   Ibid.

18.   'MH17 Disaster: Dutch Take Russia to European Rights Court' (2020), BBC News, accessed online 24 August 2021.

19.   'Russian Foreign Ministry Says Only The Hague to Blame For Collapse of Consultations Over MH17' (2020), Sputnik News, accessed online 24 August 2021.

20. This was the guiding philosophy of Deng Xiaoping's foreign policy, adopting the advice of Sun Tzu, China's ancient master strategist: 'Appear weak when you are strong, and strong when you are weak.' It served for over three decades until President Xi sounded its death knell by saying in 2017 to a congress in Beijing that 'it is time for us to take centre stage in the world'.

21. Yang Jiechi, China's most senior foreign policy official, speaking at high-level Chinese–US talks in Anchorage on 19 March 2021 attended by Secretary of State Blinken. 'US and China Trade Angry Words at High-Level Alaska Talks' (2021), BBC News, accessed online 24 August 2021.

22. Boris Johnson, 'Ukraine Needs Time and Cash. We Must Give It Both – and Prove to Putin the West Is Not Fickle', *The Sunday Times* (19 June 2022).

23. David Ludlow and David Owen, *British Foreign Policy After Brexit* (Hull, 2017), 82–3.

24. Patrick Wintour, 'UK Aid Cut Seen as Unforced Error in "Year of British Leadership"', *The Guardian* (2021), accessed online 3 August 2021.

25. Andrew Monaghan, *The New Politics of Russia: Interpreting Change* (Manchester, 2016), 9.

26. 'The EU and Russia: Before and Beyond the Crisis in Ukraine', European Union Committee, parliament.uk (n.d.), accessed online 3 August 2021.

27. Anne Applebaum, *Red Famine: Stalin's War on Ukraine* (London, 2018).

28. Anne Applebaum, *The Twilight of Democracy: The Failure of Politics and the Parting of Friends* (London, 2020).

29. G. John Ikenberry, *A World Safe for Democracy: Liberal*

Internationalism and the Crises of Global Order (London, 2020), 14.

30. Ibid.
31. Ibid., 275
32. Ibid., 276.
33. Ibid., 310–11.

Index